P9-DDP-943

Social Work With Immigrants and Refugees

ABOUT THE EDITORS

Fernando Chang-Muy, JD, is the Thomas O'Boyle Lecturer in Law at the University of Pennsylvania School of Law, where he teaches refugee law and policy. He also lectures on immigration and social work, and on organizational effectiveness, at the Graduate School of Social Policy and Practice, Executive Education Program, with a focus on strategic planning, board governance, and resource development.

Drawing upon his experience in law, refugee camp administration, and philanthropy, Fernando also provides independent consulting, coaching, and training to government agencies, local and national philanthropic institutions, social service agencies, and cultural organizations. His specific areas of expertise that help to strengthen the effectiveness of organizations include: strategic planning, board governance, resource development (with a focus on individual donor campaigns), human resource development, and meeting and process facilitation. Recent clients include the United Nations—UNAIDS, the Commonwealth of Pennsylvania Department of Aging, and the City of Philadelphia's Law as well as Health departments. He has also served as director of the local site of Hispanics in Philanthropy, a $50 million nationwide philanthropic collaborative increasing the net amount of dollars flowing to Latino nonprofits.

He is a former program officer at the Philadelphia Foundation, and past coordinator of the Emma Lazarus Collaborative, a funding collaborative that, through matching grants from the Open Society Institute, supported nonprofit organizations providing service and advocacy for immigrants and refugees. He has also served as start-up founding director of the Liberty Center for Survivors of Torture, a federally funded project that provides services and advocacy for survivors of torture. He is a former cochair of the Philadelphia Bar Association's International Human Rights Committee; and a former assistant dean and Equal Opportunity Officer of the College at Swarthmore College, where he also taught International Human Rights.

From 1988 to 1993, he served as legal officer with two United Nations (UN) agencies: the Office of the UN High Commissioner for Refugees (UNHCR) and the World Health Organization (WHO), serving as the human rights officer for its Global Program on AIDS. Before joining the UN, he was a staff attorney at Community Legal Services in Philadelphia where he served as director of the Southeast Asian Refugee Project, managing the provision of free legal aid to low-income people in Philadelphia.

He is a graduate of Loyola (BA), Georgetown (MA), Antioch (JD), and Harvard Law School's Negotiation Program. Awards include 1982–1983 Reginald Heber Smith Fellowship (Reggie) awarded by Congress through Howard University to law school graduates committed to civil rights; the 1990 21st Century Trust Fellowship from the United Kingdom; the 2001 Dr. Martin Luther King, Jr., Social Justice Award from the Rutgers University School of Law; the 2002 Michael Greenberg GALLOP award for leadership, activism, and legal advocacy; the 2007 La Justicia Award from the Hispanic Bar Association of Pennsylvania; and the 2007 Delaware Valley's Most Influential Latinos from El Concilio and the Multicultural Affairs Congress. In July 2008, Philadelphia Mayor Michael Nutter appointed him to the Board of the Philadelphia Human Relations Commission.

Elaine P. Congress, DSW, is professor and associate dean at Fordham University Graduate School of Social Service. She is on the International Federation of Social Workers (IFSW) United Nations team and is a member of the executive committee of the NGO Committee on Migration and the planning committee of the NGO Committee on the United Nations International Decade of the World's Indigenous Peoples. In addition she serves as the North American representative on the IFSW Permanent Committee on Ethical Issues.

Dr. Congress is a past president of the New York City chapter of NASW and currently a member of the national NASW board of directors. She has been appointed and serves on the NASW Presidential Diversity Initiative Committee on Immigration. In New York City, Dr. Congress is co-Principal Investigator on a New York Community Trust–funded immigrant project that involves all the New York City schools of social work, as well as the New York City Administration for Children's Services (ACS).

Dr. Congress has many publications on cultural diversity and ethics in social work. She is the author of five books including two editions of *Multicultural Perspectives in Working With Families,* published by Springer Publishing Company; *Social Work Values and Ethics,* published both in English and Korean by Wadsworth Publishing Company; and *Teaching Social Work Values and Ethics: A Curriculum Resource,* published by the Council on Social Work Education (CSWE). She has been the editor of a special issue on cultural diversity for the journal, *Crisis Intervention and Time Limited Treatment.*

Dr. Congress has authored many journal articles and book chapters on cultural diversity, immigrants, social work ethics, and education. Recently her publications have focused on comparative ethics with journal articles that compared the NASW Code of Ethics to social work codes in Australia and Korea. Other articles have looked at social work practice with immigrant families in health care settings and group work with immigrant children in urban schools. She has been on the editorial boards of the *Journal of Immigrant and Refugee Studies* as well as the *Journal of Social Work Values and Ethics, Journal of Multicultural Social Work, Journal of Social Work Education, Families in Society,* and *Social Work.*

When Dr. Congress began in the social work field, she first worked with immigrants as a direct practitioner, as a supervisor, and as an administrator in a community mental health clinic in Brooklyn. There she worked with Latino immigrants from Mexico, the Caribbean, and Central and South America. Her experience with diverse Latino clients led her to develop the culturagram that helps practitioners individualize families from diverse cultural backgrounds.

Dr. Congress has a Bachelor in Arts (BA) magna cum laude from Brown University with high honors in American Civilization where she was named an Elisha Benjamin Andrews scholar. She also has a Masters in Arts in Teaching (MAT) from Yale University and a Masters in Arts (MA) in Psychology from the New School for Social Research. In the social work field she received a Masters in Science in Social Work (MSSW) from Columbia University, and a Doctor in Social Welfare (DSW) from City University of New York.

Social Work With Immigrants and Refugees

Legal Issues, Clinical Skills and Advocacy

FERNANDO CHANG-MUY, JD
ELAINE P. CONGRESS, DSW
EDITORS

SPRINGER PUBLISHING COMPANY
NEW YORK

Springer Publishing Company, LLC
11 West 42nd Street
New York, NY 10036
www.springerpub.com

Acquisitions Editor: Jennifer Perillo
Production Editor: Julia Rosen
Cover design: Mimi Flow
Composition: Apex CoVantage

10 11/ 5 4 3 2

Library of Congress Cataloging-in-Publication Data

Social work with immigrants and refugees : legal issues, clinical skills, and advocacy / Fernando Chang-Muy, Elaine P. Congress, editors.
p. cm.
Includes bibliographical references and index.
ISBN 978-0-8261-3335-9 (alk. paper)
1. United States—Emigration and immigration. 2. Immigrants—United States—Social conditions. 3. Social work with immigrants—United States. 4. Social service—United States. 5. Crime—United States. 6. Women immigrants—United States—Social conditions. 7. Children of immigrants—Education—Law and legislation—United States. I. Chang-Muy, Fernando. II. Congress, Elaine Piller.
JV6465.S63 2008
362.87'530973—dc22 2008033651

Printed in the United States of America by Bang Printing.

Dedication

Para mis padres que inmigraron sin ningún apoyo; para Len e Isabel que me ofrecen todo el apoyo.

—*Fernando Chang-Muy*

For my grandfather who at 17 emigrated from Germany to begin a new life in the Vereinigten Staaten von Amerika.

For all immigrants who have overcome many challenges and have contributed so much to our country.

—*Elaine Congress*

Contents

Contributors

Tanya Broder, JD, is the public benefits policy director in the Oakland, CA office of the National Immigration Law Center. Ms. Broder focuses primarily on analyzing the ways in which federal, state, and local governments have been implementing the welfare and immigration laws passed in 1996. She writes articles and policy analyses, provides technical assistance, co-counsels litigation, and presents trainings to legal and social service providers, legislative staff, and community-based organizations. Before joining NILC in 1996 she worked as a policy analyst for the Northern California Coalition for Immigrant Rights and as a staff attorney for the Legal Aid Society of Alameda County in Oakland. Ms. Broder holds a juris doctor from Yale Law School.

Patricia Brownell, PhD, LMSW, is associate professor at the Fordham University Graduate School of Social Service (GSSS). She joined the Fordham faculty in 1995 after 26 years of service with the New York City Human Resources Administration. Dr. Brownell has been active in the fields of domestic violence, aging, public welfare, and forensic social work for over 30 years. She is a John A. Hartford Foundation Faculty Scholar, serves as United Nations representative for the International Network for the Prevention of Elder Abuse (INPEA) and is president of the National Association of Social Workers—New York City Chapter. Recent publications include a coedited book, *Elder Abuse and Mistreatment: Policy, Practice and Research* (2006) with M. Joanna Mellor.

Alina Das is a supervising attorney and teaching fellow with the Immigrant Rights Clinic at New York University School of Law. She works with clinic students to defend the rights of immigrants facing deportation and detention and to provide support for community organizations' immigrant rights campaigns. Prior to joining the Immigrant Rights Clinic, Ms. Das was a Soros Justice Fellow and staff attorney at the New York State Defenders Association Immigrant Defense Project, where she engaged in litigation and advocacy on issues involving the immigration consequences of criminal charges and convictions. Prior to joining the Immigrant Defense Project, Ms. Das clerked for the Honorable Kermit V. Lipez of the United States Court of Appeals for the First Circuit. Ms. Das is a graduate of Harvard University, New York University Wagner Graduate School of Public Service, and New York University School of Law.

Robin Creswick Fenley, LCSW, has worked in diverse fields of aging for over 20 years, including skilled nursing facilities, adult day care, in-patient psychiatry, home care, elder abuse, and government. A doctoral candidate and adjunct instructor at Fordham University, Ms. Fenley has developed training curricula on the continuum of long-term care issues and presents nationally on these topics.

Betty Garcia, PhD, LCSW, is a professor in the Department of Social Work Education at California State University, Fresno. She received her Masters in Social Work at San Diego State University School of Social Work and obtained a PhD in Social Psychology at Boston University. Dr. Garcia has more than 20 years of practice experience in mental health settings, including prison and community-based clinics, doing group work, individual treatment, and sexual abuse evaluation and treatment with children. Dr. Garcia's primary teaching is in theory of practice with individuals, couples, groups, and families as well as public mental health. She has developed certificate programs in cultural competency and interprofessional collaboration.

Dr. Garcia has sat on several CSWE Commissions, the NASW National Board of Directors, and the *Affilia* corporate board. She has chaired the NASW National Committee on Racism and Ethnic Diversity (NCORED).

Carmen Ortiz Hendricks, DSW, ACSW, joined Yeshiva University Wurzweiler School of Social Work as associate dean and professor in 2005 after being on the faculty of the Hunter College School of Social Work of the City University of New York since 1980.

Dr. Hendricks is the lead author with Jeanne Finch and Cheryl Franks of *Learning to Teach—Teaching to Learn: A Guide to Social Work Field Education* by the Council on Social Work Press (2005). She is coeditor of *Intersecting Child Welfare, Substance Abuse and Family Violence: Culturally Competent Approaches* with Rowena Fong and R. McRoy (2006, CSWE Press). Her latest publication for CSWE Press is *Women of Color as Social Work Educators: Strengths and Survival,* by H. Vakalahi, S. Starks, and C. Ortiz Hendricks (2007).

As a member of NASW's National Committee on Racial and Ethnic Diversity, Dr. Hendricks was a major contributor to the development of NASW's Standards for Cultural Competence in the Social Work Practice. She also served as president of the New York City Chapter of NASW 1996–1998, and was honored with the Chapter Service Award in 2001. Dr. Hendricks is a founding member of the New York City NASW chapter's Latino Social Work Task Force (2001–present).

Marielena Hincapié, JD, is director of programs and staff attorney at the Los Angeles office of the National Immigration Law Center (NILC). As NILC's director of programs, Ms. Hincapié manages the employment, public benefits, and immigration work of the organization; and she specializes in protecting and advancing the rights of immigrant workers. Ms. Hincapié has dedicated her legal career to protecting and advancing the rights of immigrant workers, particularly those who are undocumented. She writes articles and policy analyses, provides technical assistance, and presents training to legal and social service providers, labor unions, and community-based organizations. Her work also focuses on using legal tools to help support community and labor organizing efforts, as well as to help build and strengthen community coalitions to improve working conditions for all low-wage workers. Before joining NILC, she worked for the Legal Aid Society of San Francisco's Employment Law Center, where she founded the center's Immigrant Workers' Rights Project. Ms. Hincapié holds a juris doctor degree from Northeastern University School of Law.

Denise Michultka is a clinical psychologist with 15 years of experience in providing forensic and therapeutic services to survivors of torture and war trauma. She has written articles in the area of anxiety disorders related to war trauma and torture and testified as an expert witness nationally in cases involving trauma related to war and torture experiences.

Dr. Michultka is currently director at the Liberty Center for Survivors of Torture, a nonprofit center specializing in the treatment of survivors of torture and in training legal, medical, and social service professionals on cultural awareness and issues involved in refugee mental health.

Victoria Neilson is the legal director of Immigration Equality, a national organization fighting for equal immigration rights for the lesbian, gay, bisexual, transgender, and HIV-positive community. Immigration Equality works to end discriminatory immigration policies while providing legal advice and representation to LGBT and HIV-positive immigrants and asylum seekers.

Len Rieser is codirector of the Education Law Center (ELC), a statewide advocacy organization with offices in Philadelphia and Pittsburgh. ELC focuses on problems of quality and equity in Pennsylvania's public education system, especially for poor children, children of color, children with disabilities, and culturally and linguistically diverse children. Mr. Rieser has been at the Law Center since 1982; before that, he was an attorney with the Civil Rights Division, U.S. Department of Justice. He graduated from the University of Chicago Law School in 1976.

Jennifer Rose, JD, is the gender equity specialist under the Office of the Chancellor at the University of Hawaii at Manoa. She is responsible for providing training and advocacy for students, staff, and faculty with respect to sexual harassment, sexual assault, and stalking on campus. Ms. Rose was formerly a director at the Domestic Violence Clearinghouse and Legal Hotline in Hawaii.

Ms. Rose has worked on violence against women issues in Hawaii for the last 10 years, particularly in building bridges between the domestic violence and immigrants rights communities. She is an adjunct professor at the University of Hawaii William S. Richardson School of Law, where she teaches the Family Law Clinic.

Ms. Rose is currently assisting the Family Violence Prevention Fund in a technical assistance project building the capacity of the United States Territories to address domestic and sexual violence and human trafficking. Ms. Rose sits on the advisory boards of the National Network to End Violence Against Immigrant Women and the National Asian Pacific Islander Institute on Domestic Violence. She received her Juris Doctor from UCLA School of Law in 1994 and has been an advocate in the Violence Against Women movement for the last 17 years.

Jasmeet Kaur Sidhu serves as Senior Counsel at Alliance for Justice (AFJ). Jasmeet works with many immigrant rights groups to provide training, technical assistance, and guidance on advocacy issues through AFJ's Nonprofit Immigrant Advocacy Initiative. Prior to joining AFJ, Jasmeet was an associate, most recently in the litigation department at Williams Mullen in Richmond, Virginia, and previously at Kirkpatrick and Lockhart, Preston Gates Ellis LLP in New York City. While working as an associate, Jasmeet performed various pro bono legal services in conjunction with the Hispanic Chamber of Commerce in Richmond, Virginia, and also represented pro bono clients seeking asylum as a volunteer attorney for Human Rights First in New York.

Jasmeet graduated from the University of North Carolina at Chapel Hill School of Law in 2002. Prior to attending law school, Jasmeet was a staff assistant at Amnesty International's Washington, D.C. office, where she was actively involved in various international campaigns and legislative programs. She earned her BA at Duke University and her JD at the University of North Carolina at Chapel Hill.

Sarah Blair Smith, MSW, has a BA in Art History from Wellesley College (1974) and an MAT in Elementary Education from Monmouth University (1997). She received her MSW from the University of Pennsylvania in 2008. While at Penn, her area of concentration was health care and her field placements were in the neonatal intensive care unit at The Children's Hospital of Philadelphia and the obstetrics/gynecology service at the Hospital of the University of Pennsylvania (HUP). Sarah was a social worker on the cardiac floor at HUP during the summer of 2007 and currently is a social worker with the Heart Failure/Heart Transplant Team at HUP.

Rachel B. Tiven is the executive director of Immigration Equality, a national organization fighting for equal immigration rights for the lesbian, gay, bisexual, transgender, and HIV-positive community. Immigration Equality works to end discriminatory immigration policies while providing legal advice and representation to LGBT and HIV-positive immigrants and asylum-seekers.

Sujata Warrier is the director of the New York City Program of the New York State Office for the Prevention of Domestic Violence. She trains and provides technical assistance to professionals in various systems such as health care, law enforcement, criminal and civil justice, and human and social services on the issue of domestic violence. Additionally, she provides assistance on legislative and policy issues on battered immigrant women for the state.

She continues to work in Manavi, a pioneering South Asian women's organization in New Jersey. She also serves on other boards and groups: the Rape Crisis Center of Columbia University, the Asian Pacific Islander Institute on Domestic Violence, and the National Network to End Violence Against Immigrant Women. She is also a faculty on the 10-state National Health Initiative of the Family Violence Prevention Fund as well as faculty at the National Judicial Institute.

Foreword

This comprehensive book, edited by Dr. Elaine Congress and Mr. Fernando Chang-Muy, is a significant addition to the social work literature on services to immigrants and refugees. The volume is distinguished by its emphasis on the broad range of social work activity with newcomer populations, the influence of the legal system on the reception of immigrants, their eligibility and restrictions to federal, state and local services, and the significance of advocacy in practice with newcomers.

The integration of legal issues and advocacy in discussions of health, mental health, education, employment, special populations, cultural competence and practice "theory" provides breadth, depth and cohesion to the volume. The content clearly reflects the book's title, "*Social Work with Immigrants and Refugees: Legal Issues, Clinical Skills and Advocacy.*" The book is also notable for its application of knowledge to practice which is reflected by excellent case material and relevant questions that examine the connection between cases and concepts. The editors and contributors who have expertise in the field of immigration are lawyers, social workers, clinical practitioners, administrators and academics. Therefore, a multi-discipline analysis of immigration laws and policies, services to immigrants and refugees, and views on the nature of the immigration experience are presented.

The discussion of the legal grounds for entering the United States, the grounds for exclusion and deportation, paths to citizenship and laws that take into account special circumstances of juvenile immigrants and immigrant women who experience violence provides essential knowledge for practice. Plans for assistance that entail collaboration with immigration attorneys and service organizations connect the legal issues with the practice situations. Collaborative efforts on an asylum petition or gathering information for proof of abuse that could ultimately result in a change of an individual's immigration status to legal permanent resident are examples. Analysis of the laws also enables social workers to better understand how the legal structure influences policies and procedures that encourage or discourage immigrants' social and economic integration into the community-at-large. Since the legal and policy landscape is broadened in each of the chapters, the reader can further assess the degree of inclusion or exclusion that immigrants encounter.

The United States' ambivalence toward immigration is reflected in historic swings between inclusion and exclusion of newcomers. The emerging themes in this volume on barriers to services for immigrants, the erosion of rights and civil liberties (particularly for undocumented individuals) and the anti-immigrant sentiments portray the growing restrictions surrounding immigration and the shift toward exclusion. The sections on advocacy, however, provide knowledge of the skills and strategies for policy changes that address the extensive type problems noted above. Advocacy that entails work on behalf of immigrant individuals, their families and community is also informative for current problems of family separation due to the possible deportation of a parent, employment exploitation, housing violations or discrimination against an immigrant community. The presentations on immigrants' rights and eligibility for federal programs also dovetail with discussions on advocacy as worker familiarity with the former is necessary for effective advocacy practice.

This timely publication is a compendium of current social work practice with immigrant and refugee populations. Within the context of clinical work, legal issues that influence the lives of newcomers are highlighted. The book is a major contribution to social workers and their clients as it addresses advocacy on behalf of immigrants and refugees during a social, economic and political period that restricts immigrants' rights and service access. It is informative for a wide readership of practitioners, students and faculty in graduate social work programs and law schools. It also serves as a reference for service organizations and a text for both in-service programs and courses on social work practice with immigrant and refugee populations.

Dr. Diane Drachman
Associate Professor, University of Connecticut School of Social Work

Foreword

Social workers play a critical role in strengthening American families. They are at the forefront of battles to find employment and housing for their clients and education for children. Social workers also help people navigate the complex laws and regulations of programs such as social security, taxes, public school registration, health care, and even applications for drivers and marriage licenses.

The face of America is changing, but the American dream is not. Social workers need to understand that immigrant communities strive for the same goals as all other Americans, but bring with them unique experiences and challenges. This text will help social workers ensure they maintain the highest professional standards by raising awareness of both the strengths and challenges of the immigrant community.

Although the needs of the immigrant community are very similar to those of native-born citizens, there are a number of specific challenges immigrants face. First, it is important to understand the background on migration and the current immigrant legalization process. We have a system that does not effectively achieve family unification and the integration of immigrant families into American life. This results in a number of social and psychological challenges for first and second generation families as they struggle to make it in America. These challenges are addressed in the first two chapters of the text.

Chapter Eight provides an overview of employment issues confronting newcomers. This is a complicated issue as many immigrants need help navigating their employment and legal status. Immigrants also represent a vastly diverse group of workers—ranging from low-skilled laborers who sometimes hold two or three jobs, to high-level technology and healthcare professionals. Each contributes to our economy in a necessary way, but often face different struggles.

Another facet are newcomers who may have criminal records. Chapter Seven provides an overview to social workers on the specialized field where criminal and immigration laws intersect.

Many undocumented immigrants and refugees often face a host of mental and physical wounds as a result of their terrifying journeys into the United States: the daily fear of raids, detection and deportation; abuses and lack of protection in the workplace, as well as experiences ranging from physical injuries from low-wage jobs to sexual assault. The chapters on health and mental health issues will raise awareness of these and other issues faced by immigrant populations.

Many immigrants often arrive with their families—or begin to build families once they arrive. However, within a family unit there can be a blend of immigration status, which impacts access to education, health care, employment, and a host of issues. Part Three of this volume on family issues—which includes separate chapters on children and access to education, women, the elderly, and lesbian and gay newcomers—sheds light on these challenges.

Finally, the text ends by shifting from individual services to focus on systemic change. As former Executive Director of the National Immigration Forum, an immigration advocacy organization, and now as Executive Director of America's Voice, another advocacy organization, I cannot overstate the importance of empowering clients and collaborating with other local, state and national non profits to advocate for fair and just treatment of immigrants. The final chapter in this volume seeks to educate social workers on the importance of not only providing direct clinical service, but also engaging in a variety of activities, ranging from education to lobbying, in an effort to produce policy changes that will have a beneficial effect on immigrant families and the communities in which they settle.

I applaud social work students, professors, and social workers who seek to serve and empower the immigrant community. This text is a great tool toward raising awareness of the many issues immigrants face, and helping them find solutions. But most of all, I applaud the immigrants in our country, from the beginning of the forming of the colonies to the present, who have shaped the strong fabric of our nation.

Frank Sharry
Executive Director
America's Voice

Acknowledgment

We would like to thank the students from both our universities who helped us in the development of the book. They include social work students Kate M. Abramson, Brandis Anderson, Brianna L. Almaguer, Raj Bhandari, Sara R. Folks, Kimberly M. Najito, Anastasia Shown, Kathleen A. Sweeney, Amanda W. Tuffli, Katherine Walker, John M. Wenger, and Namhee Yun from the University of Pennsylvania. We would also like to acknowledge the contribution of Maya Tsekenis (MSW, Fordham University, 2008) who helped with research for the book and Fordham undergraduate Matt Macri who helped with the reference lists. We would also like to thank Julia Rosen, Production Editor.

And of course this book would never have been published if not for Jennifer Perillo, senior acquisitions editor at Springer. In fact, this book was born because of Jennifer's inquisitive and creative thinking: Fernando Chang-Muy, one of the coeditors, was interviewed by a social work journal on immigration issues. Jennifer, always learning, reading, and researching, called him and asked if he would be interested in writing a book on social work and immigration. In addition, Jennifer (who is also a connector and matchmaker) knew Dr. Elaine Congress, who had previously published *Multicultural Perspectives in Working With Families* with Springer Publishing Company. Jennifer brought Fernando and Elaine together to coedit *Social Work With Immigrants and Refugees.* From the very beginning Jennifer realized that successful social work practice with immigrants must involve understanding of the legal context. Therefore major acknowledgment goes to Jennifer, without whom this book would not be possible. Jennifer's work on this book, however, did not stop with developing the idea for this coedited book and bringing the authors together to work on the project. Through every stage of the book she has continued to be insightful, intelligent, dedicated, and very committed to helping us move toward completion of the book, which we hope serves to demonstrate the inextricable connection between legal and social work practice with immigrants.

Introduction

FERNANDO CHANG-MUY AND ELAINE CONGRESS

This text tries to answer a question that began over 300 years ago when Europeans first arrived in this country: how to welcome the stranger! It could be argued that Native Americans may have been the first social workers: They assessed the newcomers' strengths (the Native Americans supported the Pilgrims' strong work ethic, which helped in their survival); identified their weaknesses (Native Americans provided guidance to the newcomers on where and how to farm, since they did not know the landscape); and empowered the newcomers to integrate (the Native Americans' support eventually helped the immigrants unite and evolve into what later became the United States of America).

Three hundred years later, in the late nineteenth century, as newcomers kept arriving in the United States, Jane Addams continued the process of welcoming the strangers. Addams, considered one of the founders of the modern social work field, established settlement houses, which today might be considered a multiservice, direct-service agency. Settlement houses were created with the express purpose of providing for the basic needs of low-income people, the majority of whom were immigrants.

Addams's settlement house, Hull House, was located in Chicago's west side, which was home to many recent European immigrants. This community of central, southern, and eastern Europeans, like those who came before them, had many strengths as well as needs, which Hull House tried to address. Among the projects that the members of the Hull House started were the Immigrants' Protective League (IPL), which provided direct services as well as advocated for systemic change in the treatment of immigrants. The IPL provided direct services by trying to help immigrants adjust to living in America. Activities included establishing waiting rooms at railroad stations, where multilingual men and women helped recent arrivals find their relatives or friends. The IPL expanded from direct-service strategies to systems-change strategies when it carried out investigations into organizations such as employment agencies and loan companies, which claimed they were providing services for immigrants but were instead exploiting the newcomers. This text in essence gives homage to immigrants. Their arrival in part resulted in the establishment of settlement houses, which later became social service agencies and subsequently founded the entire field of social work. Teachers, students, and practitioners of social work have jobs, thanks to immigrants!

In this context of welcoming the stranger—from the Pilgrims' landing, through the establishment of the settlement houses, and on to this very day—this text continues to explore how we assist newcomers. In a systematic way, we try to raise awareness of the strengths and challenges facing today's newcomers, so as to make service providers and the organizations they work in more effective in serving and advocating on behalf of the immigrant community.

Both authors are of immigrant background, which began their interest in immigration issues.

Fernando reports that when his parents arrived in the United States in the 1960s in southern Florida, there was no formal social service agency to give them the lay of the land—at least none that they were aware of. The Chicago settlement houses did not make it to Miami! Or if they did, they certainly did not make themselves culturally accessible by hiring bilingual, bicultural staff or posting culturally appropriate signage and social marketing. He, as a minor child, ended up serving as the interpreter, the translator, and the social worker for his family—much as many immigrant children still act as cultural brokers for their parents today.

Elaine remembers that her paternal grandfather immigrated to the United States when he was 17. When he arrived he did not have any work or family here and only limited education, as he had left school at the age of 12 to be apprenticed to a blacksmith on a farm in Germany. The resourcefulness and hard work of immigrants never ceases to amaze her as she thinks of how he, as a teenager, traveled across the Atlantic on his own, arrived in the United States without knowing a word of English, finally found a laborer's job on the railroad, learned English by going to school at night, and later raised six children, the youngest of whom, her father, he was able to send to college.

So in the spirit of ensuring that the immigrants continue to utilize their strengths—as workers, as parents, as families, as creators and adopters of the culture, as buyers and sellers and contributors to the economy—and to support social workers and their agencies to ensure that their services are appropriate and accessible, we offer this text. While the demographics of the immigrant communities have changed over time (from Europeans in the 1800s to Latin Americans, Asians, and Africans today), what has *not* changed are the strengths and assets that the newcomer communities bring, and the challenges they face. This text is as relevant now as it could have been 100 years ago, and as it surely will be 100 years in the future. This book is particularly important now, as immigrants—especially those who are undocumented—are essentially under siege in a post-9/11 antiterrorist framework.

THE ORGANIZATION AND CONTENTS OF THIS BOOK

Part I of the text, "Overview," reminds us of the immigrant roots of the United States. The book first explores the changing demographics of immigrant newcomers in chapter 1. The text then turns to legal classifications of immigrants. Chapter 2 deconstructs legal terms that social workers need to be familiar with in order to provide effective services and be able to collaborate with and navigate the legal system. This chapter seeks to help social workers better understand the legal meaning of terms such as *nonimmigrant, immigrant, green-card holder,* and *citizen.*

Part II of the text, "Immigration and Social Work Practice," begins by exploring theories of cultural competency (chapter 3) and social work practice (chapter 4). These chapters will help readers reflect on their service provision strategies (i.e., asset-based, family-oriented, or a hybrid of various models). The hope is that these chapters will help readers articulate and/or recognize their own theoretical and/or personal biases, and also present readers with a variety of methods to utilize in working with newcomers.

The text then turns to specific societal issues and challenges that newcomers face, and the legal and other remedies that social workers can use to assist them. Specifically, we turn to the intersection of immigration and health (chapter 5), mental health (chapter 6), criminal justice issues (chapter 7), and employment (chapter 8). Issues of particular interest to immigrant communities, such as the exploitation of immigrant workers (and appropriate legal remedies); immigrant access to health services and public benefits; the triple mental health trauma many refugees and asylees face; and the issue of newcomers as victims of crime as well as the immigration consequences of criminal conviction will be discussed.

Part III, "Children and Family Issues," deals with family groups, which, although inherently strong, are made vulnerable because of their immigrant status in the United States. In chapter 9, we explore challenges immigrant families face such as access to public schools and language issues faced by the children. Chapter 10 explores the particular challenges faced by immigrant women who, by virtue of being alone in this country and dependent on their spouses, may be especially vulnerable to crimes such as domestic violence or trafficking. Chapter 11 describes issues of family separation faced by U.S. citizens who are separated from their LBGT partners, due to discriminatory immigration laws. Finally, chapter 12 addresses the issues of isolation and access to services faced by elderly immigrants, as well as legal issues faced by the elderly in trying to naturalize.

The text ends by picking up where Hull House and the Immigrant Protective League in Chicago began. As mentioned earlier, not only was Jane Addams's settlement house a place that provided direct services, but it also served as a place that sought to influence legislation on a diverse spectrum of laws. In collaboration with the settlement house network, individual social workers and social service agencies, before such terminology became common, succeeded at the federal level in advocating for legislation in immigration law, child labor law, women's suffrage, unemployment compensation, workers' compensation, and other issues of the Progressive agenda during the first two decades of the twentieth century.

Continuing in that spirit, Part IV of this text—"Immigration Policy"—ends by urging practitioners to expand their strategies and advocate not only for individual clients (at the micro level), but as well to advocate for change at the organizational/agency level (mezzo level) and at the federal, state, and local levels (macro level). Chapter 13 looks at the various federal programs available (or not) to immigrant communities, and discusses ways in which those programs might make necessary services even more accessible. The final chapter urges practitioners to advocate for fair, just, and equal treatment of immigrants—either working with clients, through their agencies, or as individuals.

SPECIAL FEATURES OF THIS TEXT

In order to make this text especially useful for students, instructors, and practitioners, we have included some special features throughout the text. At the end of most chapters, hypothetical case studies (often based on the authors' own experiences working with immigrants in social service agencies) and discussion questions will assist students in applying theory to practice. These case studies should make clear to students the multiple issues involved in working with immigrants. Also included at the end of most chapters are additional resources—Web sites, books, articles, and other sources of further information about immigration issues.

The appendixes in the book include sample affidavits that will serve as templates for practitioners as they advocate for their newcomer clients. For example, sample affidavits for asylum are included.

Finally, for instructors, sample syllabi and PowerPoints will help in facilitating class discussion. These materials are available to those who adopt the text. For more information, visit the book's Web site at http://www.springerpub.com/prod.aspx?prod_id=33355.

We hope that after reading this book, students, faculty, and practitioners will come away with a sense of the assets that newcomers bring, as well as an understanding of the challenges they face and roadmaps to help them navigate around those barriers, so that ultimately both old and newcomer communities can work together to make this land of immigrants even stronger than ever.

Fernando Chang-Muy
Elaine Congress

PART I

Overview

1

Introduction: Legal and Social Work Issues With Immigrants

ELAINE CONGRESS

Immigration is not only a current U.S. phenomenon. Since the beginning of recorded history human beings have frequently migrated in search of food, lodging, freedom, and security. The United Nations (2006) estimates that in 2005, there were approximately 191 million international migrants in the world. Although some view migrants as financially dependent, migrants contribute annually an estimated U.S. $2 trillion to the economies of the countries in which they live (Grange, 2006).

Over the last 60 years the United Nations has developed a number of human rights treaties that support the rights of migrants, beginning with the Universal Declaration of Human Rights (adopted in 1948) and including the Convention on the Elimination of All Forms of Racial Discrimination (adopted in 1965), the International Covenant on Economic, Social and Cultural Rights (1966), the International Covenant on Civil and Political Rights (1966), the Convention on the Elimination of All Forms of Discrimination Against Women (1979), the Convention Against Torture and Other Cruel, Inhuman or Degrading Treatment or Punishment (1984), and the Convention on the Rights of the Child (1989). Another UN convention, the International Convention on the Protection of the Rights of All Migrant Workers and Members of Their Families (1990), also specifically relates to the human rights of migrants.

The International Federation of Social Workers (IFSW), which consists of professional social work associations in 84 countries and which represents 500,000 social workers, also has an International Policy on Migration (2005) that promotes the human rights of migrants and their families. The policy clearly states that immigrants should have the same rights as citizens:

> IFSW believes that social workers should support the abolition of legal measures which restrict migrants' rights or establish reduced standards of rights, freedoms, and responsibilities, compared with those enjoyed by citizens of the host nation. (International Federation of Social Workers, 2005, p. 3)

The National Association of Social Workers (NASW) has also addressed the needs of immigrants:

> NASW supports immigration and refugee policies that uphold and support equity and human rights, while protecting national security. The social work profession recognizes that the challenge of competing claims is formidable; however, immigration policies must promote social justice and avoid racism and discrimination or profiling on the basis of race, religion, country of origin, gender, or other grounds. NASW has a special interest in the impact of refugee and immigration policies on families and children and supports policies that encourage family reunification and ensures that children do not grow up unduly disadvantaged by the immigration status of their parents. (National Association of Social Workers, 2006)

Given the great diversity and myriad needs of the growing immigrant population, it is essential that social workers understand the legal, political, as well as psychological and social issues surrounding immigration. Although migration is an international phenomenon, the focus of this book will be immigration in the United States, specifically laws, policies, and practice issues relevant to professional work with immigrants in the United States. Social workers, regardless of their setting, increasingly work with immigrants and their families.

This chapter will begin with a snapshot of current immigration patterns and a profile of the U.S. immigrant population. It will then discuss the impetus behind immigration. Next, a brief history of immigration patterns will be discussed, leading up to present-day policies and sentiments. Finally, the implications for social work practice will be examined.

CURRENT TRENDS IN IMMIGRATION

This book will primarily discuss the issues and concerns of immigrants in the United States. Yet it is important to note that immigration is a global issue; while the United States has the largest immigrant population (38,355,000 immigrants living in the United States in 2005), other countries such as Germany (10,144,000), Ukraine (6,833,000), and France (6,471,000) are also home to millions of migrants. Several countries in the Middle East, such as the United Arab Emirates (71.4%) and Kuwait (62.1%), report that over half of their populations are immigrants (United Nations Department of Economic and Social Affairs, 2006).

Immigrants in the United States

According to the U.S. Census (2003), 11.7% of the current population is foreign-born, while 30% of these immigrants are naturalized citizens (Passel, Capps, & Fix, 2004). The actual number of foreign-born people living in the United States is 33,500,000, and over a third (11,206,000) of them have entered since 1990 (U.S. Census, 2003).

Immigrants by State

According to the Department of Homeland Security, the top six states in terms of immigrant populations are: California, New York, Florida, Texas, New Jersey, and Illinois. Not surprisingly, large urban areas are host to large numbers of immigrants. In New York City, for example, 35.9% of the population is foreign born (New York City Office of City Planning, Population Division, 2004).

Table 1.1 shows the metropolitan areas with the highest numbers of legal permanent residents.

While there are many immigrants in large urban areas, there has also been an increase in immigrants in urban, suburban, and rural areas throughout the United States. For example, in diverse communities such as Denver, Colorado, 23% of the population is Hispanic, while a large number of Hmong immigrants live in St. Paul, Minnesota (American Community Survey, 2006).

Table 1.2 shows the flow of legal immigrants by state, 1998–2007. Note that nearly all states show an increase during that time period.

Table 1.1

PERSONS OBTAINING LEGAL PERMANENT RESIDENT STATUS BY CORE-BASED STATISTICAL AREA (CBSA) OF RESIDENCE: FISCAL YEARS 1998–2007 (RANKED BY 2007 LPR FLOW)

GEOGRAPHIC AREA	1998	1999	2000	2001	2002	2003	2004	2005	2006	2007
New York-Northern New Jersey-Long Island, Pennsylvania, NY-NJ-PA	120,975	120,533	132,382	157,419	154,420	117,484	138,577	172,844	224,439	175,753
Los Angeles-Long Beach-Santa Ana, CA	74,422	71,420	92,773	121,860	133,404	79,588	110,824	98,241	120,881	95,413
Miami-Fort Lauderdale-Pompano Beach, FL	43,992	43,124	67,835	74,037	62,509	36,594	49,816	79,558	98,918	78,172
Washington-Arlington-Alexandria-Rockville, DC-VA-MD-WV	25,557	24,643	29,995	39,546	38,253	29,643	32,275	37,146	54,549	40,698
Chicago-Naperville-Joliet, IL-IN-WI	31,627	35,099	34,199	45,916	44,652	30,555	43,846	49,015	49,748	39,504
San Francisco-Oakland-Fremont, CA	27,723	23,032	32,233	39,313	36,344	26,228	37,232	33,876	38,348	35,652
Houston-Sugar Land-Baytown, TX	13,801	15,897	19,079	27,901	29,680	16,133	34,996	34,788	31,557	26,850
Boston-Cambridge-Quincy, MA-NH	11,407	11,441	19,260	23,748	25,533	16,555	22,712	27,135	28,469	24,679
Dallas-Fort Worth-Arlington, TX	12,911	13,795	19,642	24,655	23,836	15,553	25,235	28,961	26,639	23,272
Atlanta-Sandy Springs-Marietta, GA	7,612	7,253	11,660	15,436	16,600	8,506	12,970	25,347	25,270	22,056
San Jose-Sunnyvale-Santa Clara, CA	13,163	11,374	19,085	29,354	28,067	13,420	21,210	19,557	18,258	19,255

Philadelphia-Camden-Wilmington, PA-NJ-DE-MD	9,982	10,302	13,841	16,154	14,734	11,285	14,699	22,675	20,754	18,455
San Diego-Carlsbad-San Marcos, CA	9,827	10,680	15,009	22,211	22,365	12,781	20,031	19,299	17,271	18,296
Seattle-Tacoma-Bellevue, WA	10,488	8,268	11,953	15,660	17,211	12,647	13,826	18,940	17,095	16,862
Riverside-San Bernardino-Ontario, CA	9,584	9,592	13,189	18,362	19,705	10,711	17,473	15,523	19,467	16,779
Orlando-Kissimmee, FL	3,770	3,409	7,281	7,235	5,726	4,109	6,018	10,428	17,409	14,618
Detroit-Warren-Livonia, MI	9,830	9,635	11,559	14,681	14,282	9,181	12,665	15,862	14,040	12,875
Phoenix-Mesa-Scottsdale, AZ	3,266	4,714	7,620	11,836	12,553	7,464	12,678	13,394	15,219	11,943
Minneapolis-St. Paul-Bloomington, MN-WI	5,700	4,969	7,016	9,203	11,416	7,113	10,139	12,921	15,828	11,879
Tampa-St. Petersburg-Clearwater, FL	4,145	3,497	6,276	8,507	8,501	4,064	7,238	11,841	13,543	10,730
Las Vegas-Paradise, NV	3,970	6,435	5,371	7,507	7,530	4,966	7,010	7,826	12,705	10,373
Sacramento-Arden-Arcade-Roseville-Woodland, CA	4,997	4,963	7,969	11,868	10,983	6,574	9,132	12,368	12,767	9,764
Denver-Aurora, CO	4,181	4,510	5,239	8,018	8,031	7,068	7,311	7,807	8,401	7,384
Baltimore-Towson, MD	3,921	3,876	4,523	5,610	6,612	4,974	5,852	6,959	8,621	6,898
Portland-Vancouver-Beaverton, OR-WA	4,747	3,964	6,838	8,915	10,683	6,007	7,338	8,924	8,201	6,885

(continued)

Table 1.1

PERSONS OBTAINING LEGAL PERMANENT RESIDENT STATUS BY CORE-BASED STATISTICAL AREA (CBSA) OF RESIDENCE: FISCAL YEARS 1998–2007 (RANKED BY 2007 LPR FLOW) ***(continued)***

GEOGRAPHIC AREA	1998	1999	2000	2001	2002	2003	2004	2005	2006	2007
Honolulu, HI	4,205	3,276	4,719	4,843	4,202	3,733	4,909	4,956	5,728	5,507
Bridgeport-Stamford-Norwalk, CT	3,076	3,126	4,268	4,681	4,198	3,038	4,737	6,192	7,662	5,154
Columbus, OH	1,642	1,222	1,946	3,958	3,562	3,179	3,703	5,037	5,568	4,768
Austin-Round Rock, TX	2,089	2,416	3,120	4,458	5,601	3,425	4,273	5,415	4,973	4,551
Providence-New Bedford-Fall River, RI-MA	2,509	2,549	3,250	3,657	3,998	3,094	4,637	4,976	5,936	4,426
Nashville-Davidson—Murfreesboro—Franklin, TN	1,196	1,068	2,144	2,502	2,433	1,511	2,415	3,997	4,939	4,227
San Antonio, TX	2,657	2,736	2,958	3,942	4,929	3,322	3,680	4,582	4,345	4,142
Fresno, CA	4,111	3,136	4,311	4,148	5,211	3,562	4,873	3,969	4,772	4,124
Charlotte-Gastonia-Concord-Rock Hill, NC-SC	1,535	1,291	2,214	3,188	3,198	2,309	2,744	4,312	4,851	4,103
El Paso, TX	3,358	3,556	4,109	6,297	4,057	2,490	4,157	3,736	4,295	4,004
Hartford-West Hartford-East Hartford, CT	2,540	2,605	3,712	3,942	3,730	2,868	4,080	4,730	5,498	3,901
Oxnard-Thousand Oaks-Ventura, CA	3,118	3,242	3,863	5,241	4,870	2,967	4,520	3,621	4,093	3,818
Jacksonville, FL	1,075	1,271	2,388	2,645	3,462	1,812	2,841	4,464	3,877	3,657

Saint Louis, MO-IL	2,006	2,481	3,352	4,933	5,600	3,618	4,197	5,830	3,793	3,618
Stockton, CA	1,890	2,263	2,790	3,235	2,877	2,161	3,448	3,327	4,299	3,551
Raleigh-Cary, NC	1,389	1,165	1,810	3,006	2,487	1,935	2,621	3,634	3,910	3,435
Kansas City, MO-KS	1,813	1,979	2,829	3,052	3,519	3,122	3,492	3,640	3,552	3,146
Cleveland-Elyria-Mentor, OH	2,506	2,449	3,156	4,146	4,306	2,612	3,214	4,547	3,773	3,135
Cincinnati-Middletown, OH-KY-IN	1,305	1,100	1,521	2,737	2,549	1,784	2,424	3,163	3,384	3,096
Virginia Beach-Norfolk-Newport News, VA-NC	1,347	1,594	1,886	2,064	1,988	1,755	2,161	2,673	2,917	3,054
Salt Lake City, UT	2,148	2,233	2,292	3,332	3,342	1,914	2,703	3,254	3,566	3,052
Worcester, MA	1,316	1,165	1,710	2,384	2,911	1,857	2,845	3,615	3,678	2,962
Bakersfield, CA	1,983	1,946	2,589	2,609	3,465	2,515	3,191	2,668	3,176	2,896
Cape Coral-Fort Myers, FL	657	505	935	1,267	1,107	664	1,315	2,107	3,218	2,884
Naples-Marco Island, FL	778	962	1,497	1,698	1,554	935	1,408	2,136	3,413	2,864
Other CBSAs	113,982	114,132	156,046	191,207	192,457	131,514	179,549	216,414	223,039	190,072
Other metropolitan areas	95,823	95,564	131,333	163,104	164,360	111,912	153,807	186,218	190,022	161,917
Other micropolitan areas	18,159	18,568	24,713	28,103	28,097	19,602	25,742	30,196	33,017	28,155
Non-CBSA	15,260	12,771	13,635	14,754	14,088	10,629	12,628	14,004	15,450	13,197
Unknown	117	123	125	24	25	14	15	23	27	26
Total	**653,206**	**644,787**	**841,002**	**1,058,902**	**1,059,356**	**703,542**	**957,883**	**1,122,257**	**1,266,129**	**1,052,415**

From *Yearbook of Immigration Statistics: 2007*, by United States Department of Homeland Security, 2007, Washington, DC: U.S. Department of Homeland Security, Office of Immigration Statistics. Retrieved April 20, 2008, from http://www.dhs.gov/xlibrary/assets/statistics/yearbook/2007/table05.xls

Table 1.2

PERSONS OBTAINING LEGAL PERMANENT RESIDENT STATUS BY STATE OF RESIDENCE: FISCAL YEARS 1998–2007

STATE OF RESIDENCE	1998	1999	2000	2001	2002	2003	2004	2005	2006	2007
California	169,923	160,924	216,447	281,469	289,422	175,579	253,858	232,014	264,667	228,941
New York	96,452	96,764	105,521	113,698	114,531	89,538	103,151	136,815	180,157	136,739
Florida	59,756	57,216	94,474	104,148	90,460	52,770	76,178	122,915	155,986	126,277
Texas	44,285	49,294	63,391	85,905	88,142	53,412	92,440	95,951	89,027	77,278
New Jersey	35,044	34,008	39,778	59,587	57,478	40,699	50,699	56,176	65,931	55,834
Illinois	33,122	36,895	36,052	48,087	47,095	32,413	46,896	52,415	52,452	41,971
Massachusetts	15,844	15,125	23,302	28,847	31,498	20,127	28,067	34,232	35,558	30,555
Virginia	15,650	15,111	19,985	26,767	25,319	19,726	22,104	27,095	38,483	29,682
Georgia	10,424	9,377	14,707	19,370	20,496	10,794	16,681	31,527	32,202	27,353
Maryland	15,523	15,543	17,565	21,919	23,677	17,770	20,549	22,868	30,199	24,255
Pennsylvania	11,912	13,465	17,970	21,328	19,428	14,606	18,813	28,902	25,950	22,811
Washington	16,886	13,003	18,245	22,977	25,631	17,935	19,758	26,480	23,803	22,657
Michigan	13,914	13,614	16,655	21,386	21,724	13,515	18,851	23,591	20,907	18,727
Arizona	6,177	8,651	11,935	16,197	17,588	10,955	19,507	18,986	21,529	17,528
North Carolina	6,403	5,774	9,193	13,861	12,868	9,451	11,036	16,710	18,987	15,469
Ohio	7,684	6,832	9,201	14,653	13,827	9,787	12,072	16,892	16,585	14,078
Minnesota	6,959	5,932	8,554	11,091	13,477	8,406	12,097	15,449	18,249	13,814
Connecticut	7,760	7,861	11,263	12,089	11,213	8,274	12,335	15,334	18,697	12,932
Nevada	6,093	8,268	7,757	9,459	9,447	6,336	8,798	9,823	14,713	12,308
Colorado	6,497	6,965	8,167	12,451	12,027	10,661	11,255	11,975	12,713	11,039
Tennessee	2,796	2,575	4,837	6,234	5,674	3,367	5,844	8,960	10,037	8,942
Oregon	5,895	5,217	8,479	9,560	12,083	6,946	8,540	9,623	9,188	7,905
Wisconsin	3,718	3,038	5,034	8,442	6,486	4,357	5,580	7,907	8,339	7,381
Hawaii	5,458	4,292	6,047	6,282	5,478	4,899	6,405	6,480	7,499	7,236
Indiana	3,970	3,546	4,105	5,980	6,838	5,241	6,262	6,913	8,122	6,639
Missouri	3,576	4,157	5,988	7,574	8,585	6,160	7,050	8,742	6,852	6,459
Other[a]	6,243	6,470	5,732	6,677	5,965	5,605	7,112	5,996	7,175	5,402

Utah	3,352	3,547	3,667	5,218	4,871	3,159	4,346	5,082	5,749	5,168
South Carolina	2,119	1,770	2,253	2,862	2,952	1,942	2,672	5,028	5,291	4,788
Kentucky	2,012	1,528	2,902	4,525	4,667	3,038	3,820	5,265	5,504	4,340
Oklahoma	2,272	2,367	4,550	3,471	4,215	2,385	3,578	4,702	4,590	4,269
Kansas	3,179	3,251	4,554	4,018	4,500	3,804	4,139	4,512	4,277	4,141
Louisiana	2,179	2,034	2,981	3,751	3,176	2,214	3,095	3,776	2,693	3,475
Alabama	1,604	1,271	1,894	2,246	2,562	1,689	2,247	4,200	4,277	3,393
Rhode Island	1,973	2,043	2,513	2,802	3,048	2,492	3,740	3,852	4,778	3,354
New Mexico	2,193	2,439	3,951	5,186	3,374	2,336	3,076	3,513	3,805	3,112
Iowa	1,655	1,771	3,035	5,014	5,570	3,419	4,067	4,535	4,085	3,103
Nebraska	1,267	1,437	2,201	3,839	3,655	2,827	3,002	2,996	3,795	3,066
Arkansas	913	937	1,594	2,561	2,531	1,903	2,288	2,698	2,924	2,722
District of Columbia	2,372	2,130	2,528	3,034	2,719	2,491	2,148	2,457	3,775	2,541
New Hampshire	1,009	999	1,992	2,578	2,995	1,868	2,280	3,298	2,987	2,272
Delaware	1,060	1,024	1,563	1,847	1,856	1,487	1,705	2,991	2,263	2,085
Idaho	1,500	1,904	1,914	2,285	2,229	1,686	2,299	2,768	2,377	2,044
Alaska	1,007	1,055	1,364	1,389	1,557	1,188	1,261	1,524	1,554	1,617
Mississippi	695	696	1,074	1,338	1,145	729	1,312	1,829	1,480	1,593
Maine	708	558	1,123	1,185	1,265	992	1,322	1,907	1,717	1,488
Vermont	511	494	802	950	1,003	550	814	1,042	894	791
West Virginia	375	392	569	736	635	483	634	847	763	721
South Dakota	354	351	445	668	899	487	747	881	1,013	668
Montana	298	306	488	484	419	453	452	589	505	575
North Dakota	472	312	414	556	770	331	591	864	649	496
Wyoming	159	251	247	306	278	253	304	321	376	380
Unknown	4	3	–	15	8	7	6	9	1	1
Total	**653,206**	**644,787**	**841,002**	**1,058,902**	**1,059,356**	**703,542**	**957,883**	**1,122,257**	**1,266,129**	**1,052,415**

Note: – Represents zero.
[a]Includes U.S. dependencies and armed forces posts.
From *Yearbook of Immigration Statistics: 2007,* by United States Department of Homeland Security, 2007, Washington, DC: U.S. Department of Homeland Security, Office of Immigration Statistics. Retrieved April 20, 2008, from http://www.dhs.gov/xlibrary/assets/statistics/yearbook/2007/table04.xls

Immigrants by Legal Status

The majority of immigrants living in the United States are classified as legal permanent residents—that is, people who are authorized to live here permanently. Table 1.3 shows legal permanent residents by their region and country of origin.

Much of the current political controversy has arisen about undocumented immigrants—that is, those who are living in the United States illegally. Although the number of undocumented people cannot be accurately measured, based on the U.S. Census Bureau, Current Population Survey (2003) it is estimated that in 2004 as many as one-third of the foreign-born population (10,300,000) were undocumented (Wassem, 2007). Most of these immigrants (80%) were from Mexico and other Latin American countries (Wassem, 2007).

Table 1.4 shows the undocumented population by country of birth.

Demographics of Immigrant Population

Table 1.5 shows the average age, gender, marital status, and occupation of legal permanent residents to the United States. Broadly speaking, the majority were over age 21; married; and (for those whose employment status is known, and who are employed outside the home) employed in managerial, professional, and related capacities.

A common misconception is that many undocumented immigrants are male, unemployed, and single. In 2003, an overwhelming majority of undocumented men (more than 90%) worked—a rate higher than that for U.S. citizens or legal immigrants (Passel, Capps, & Fix, 2004). Also over 40% of undocumented adults are women, and the majority (54%) of undocumented men live in married couples or other families (Passel, 2005). Fewer than half of undocumented men are single and unattached.

REASONS FOR MIGRATION

Migration does not always mean travel from one country to another. Many migrants are intranational migrants and migrate within their own countries, often from a rural to an urban area. This is particularly true for countries in Africa where many have multiple cultural and linguistic identities because of forced migration brought about by climate change and civil war (Amkpa, 2008).

Table 1.3

PERSONS OBTAINING LEGAL PERMANENT RESIDENT STATUS BY REGION AND COUNTRY OF BIRTH: FISCAL YEARS 1998–2007

REGION AND COUNTRY OF BIRTH	1998	1999	2000	2001	2002	2003	2004	2005	2006	2007
REGION										
Asia	219,371	198,918	264,413	348,256	340,494	243,918	334,540	400,098	422,284	383,508
North America	252,503	270,719	338,959	405,638	402,949	249,968	342,468	345,561	414,075	339,355
Europe	90,572	92,314	130,996	174,411	173,524	100,434	133,181	176,516	164,244	120,821
South America	45,281	41,444	55,823	68,484	74,151	55,028	72,060	103,135	137,986	106,525
Africa	40,585	36,578	44,534	53,731	60,101	48,642	66,422	85,098	117,422	94,711
Oceania	3,922	3,658	5,105	6,071	5,515	4,351	5,985	6,546	7,384	6,101
Unknown	972	1,156	1,172	2,311	2,622	1,201	3,227	5,303	2,734	1,394
Total	**653,206**	**644,787**	**841,002**	**1,058,902**	**1,059,356**	**703,542**	**957,883**	**1,122,257**	**1,266,129**	**1,052,415**
COUNTRY										
Mexico	131,353	147,402	173,493	205,560	218,822	115,585	175,411	161,445	173,749	148,640
China, People's Republic	36,854	32,159	45,585	56,267	61,082	40,568	55,494	69,933	87,307	76,655
Philippines	34,416	30,943	42,343	52,919	51,040	45,250	57,846	60,746	74,606	72,596
India	36,414	30,157	41,903	70,032	70,823	50,228	70,151	84,680	61,369	65,353
Colombia	11,801	9,928	14,427	16,627	18,758	14,720	18,846	25,566	43,144	33,187
Haiti	13,434	16,514	22,337	27,031	20,213	12,293	14,191	14,524	22,226	30,405
Cuba	17,304	14,019	18,960	27,453	28,182	9,262	20,488	36,261	45,614	29,104
Vietnam	17,635	20,335	26,553	35,419	33,563	22,087	31,524	32,784	30,691	28,691
Dominican Republic	20,355	17,811	17,465	21,195	22,515	26,159	30,506	27,503	38,068	28,024
Korea	14,222	12,795	15,721	20,532	20,724	12,382	19,766	26,562	24,386	22,405
El Salvador	14,577	14,581	22,543	31,089	31,060	28,231	29,807	21,359	31,782	21,127

Table 1.3

PERSONS OBTAINING LEGAL PERMANENT RESIDENT STATUS BY REGION AND COUNTRY OF BIRTH: FISCAL YEARS 1998–2007 *(continued)*

REGION AND COUNTRY OF BIRTH	1998	1999	2000	2001	2002	2003	2004	2005	2006	2007
Jamaica	15,123	14,693	15,949	15,322	14,835	13,347	14,430	18,345	24,976	19,375
Guatemala	7,747	7,294	9,942	13,496	16,178	14,386	18,920	16,818	24,133	17,908
Peru	10,141	8,414	9,579	11,062	11,918	9,409	11,794	15,676	21,718	17,699
Canada	10,130	8,782	16,057	21,752	19,352	11,350	15,569	21,878	18,207	15,495
United Kingdom	8,976	7,647	13,273	18,278	16,297	9,527	14,915	19,800	17,207	14,545
Brazil	4,380	3,887	6,943	9,448	9,439	6,331	10,556	16,662	17,903	14,295
Pakistan	13,083	13,485	14,504	16,393	13,694	9,415	12,086	14,926	17,418	13,492
Ethiopia	4,199	4,262	4,053	5,092	7,565	6,635	8,286	10,571	16,152	12,786
Nigeria	7,730	6,742	7,831	8,253	8,105	7,872	9,374	10,597	13,459	12,448
Ecuador	6,843	8,882	7,651	9,665	10,561	7,066	8,626	11,608	17,489	12,248
Bangladesh	8,616	6,038	7,204	7,152	5,483	4,616	8,061	11,487	14,644	12,074
Ukraine	7,444	10,102	15,511	20,914	21,190	11,633	14,156	22,745	17,140	11,001
Venezuela	3,129	2,498	4,693	5,170	5,228	4,018	6,220	10,645	11,341	10,692
Iran	7,873	7,176	8,487	10,425	12,960	7,230	10,434	13,887	13,947	10,460
Poland	8,451	8,773	10,090	11,769	12,711	10,510	14,326	15,351	17,051	10,355
Russia	11,517	12,321	16,940	20,313	20,771	13,935	17,410	18,055	13,159	9,426
Egypt	4,826	4,421	4,450	5,159	4,852	3,348	5,522	7,905	10,500	9,267
Taiwan	7,094	6,700	9,019	12,120	9,775	6,917	9,005	9,196	8,086	8,990
Thailand	3,090	2,366	3,753	4,245	4,144	3,126	4,318	5,505	11,749	8,751
Honduras	6,456	4,793	5,917	6,571	6,435	4,645	5,508	7,012	8,177	7,646
Ghana	4,455	3,707	4,339	4,023	4,248	4,410	5,337	6,491	9,367	7,610
Germany	5,440	5,166	7,565	9,790	8,888	5,064	7,099	9,264	8,436	7,582
Kenya	1,693	1,407	2,197	2,501	3,199	3,209	5,335	5,347	8,779	7,030
Trinidad and Tobago	4,845	4,259	6,635	6,618	5,738	4,138	5,384	6,568	8,854	6,829

Japan	5,128	4,202	7,049	9,578	8,248	5,971	7,697	8,768	8,265	6,748
Somalia	2,623	1,690	2,393	3,007	4,535	2,444	3,929	5,829	9,462	6,251
Romania	5,104	5,678	6,863	6,628	4,887	3,655	4,571	7,103	7,137	5,802
Albania	4,220	3,695	4,755	4,358	3,765	3,362	3,840	5,947	7,914	5,737
Guyana	3,960	3,290	5,719	8,279	9,938	6,809	6,351	9,317	9,552	5,726
Argentina	1,503	1,387	2,317	3,297	3,661	3,129	4,805	7,081	7,327	5,645
Soviet Union (former)	6,323	5,022	3,263	2,707	2,403	1,072	929	2,899	6,229	5,090
Uzbekistan	600	1,221	1,631	2,031	2,317	1,445	1,995	2,887	4,015	4,665
Morocco	2,402	2,970	3,614	4,958	3,387	3,137	4,128	4,411	4,949	4,513
Israel	1,982	1,847	2,783	3,744	3,826	2,741	4,160	5,755	5,943	4,496
Turkey	2,676	2,215	2,606	3,215	3,375	3,029	3,835	4,614	4,941	4,425
Armenia	1,144	1,250	1,253	1,762	1,800	1,287	1,833	2,591	6,317	4,351
Lebanon	3,283	3,033	3,662	4,579	3,935	2,956	3,818	4,282	4,083	4,267
Cambodia	1,436	1,394	2,138	2,462	2,800	2,263	3,553	4,022	5,773	4,246
Liberia	1,611	1,351	1,570	2,273	2,869	1,766	2,757	4,880	6,887	4,102
Bulgaria	3,731	4,171	4,917	4,400	3,608	3,825	4,253	5,635	4,828	3,981
Jordan	3,244	3,269	3,900	4,572	3,964	2,927	3,431	3,748	4,038	3,917
Iraq	2,217	3,360	5,087	4,965	5,174	2,450	3,494	4,077	4,337	3,765
Indonesia	1,017	1,186	1,767	2,525	2,418	1,805	2,419	3,924	4,868	3,716
Nicaragua	3,511	13,327	20,947	19,634	10,659	4,094	4,009	3,305	4,145	3,716
Serbia and Montenegro[a]	2,399	1,886	2,742	6,203	10,387	2,994	3,331	5,202	5,891	3,586
Hong Kong	5,272	4,910	5,407	8,300	6,075	3,574	3,951	3,705	3,256	3,527
Nepal	476	453	616	945	1,137	2,095	2,878	3,158	3,733	3,472
France	2,342	2,196	3,442	4,569	3,797	2,375	3,595	4,399	4,258	3,423
Cameroon	690	824	860	791	984	927	1,309	1,458	2,919	3,392
Burma	1,370	1,200	1,201	1,373	1,356	1,193	1,379	2,095	4,562	3,130
South Africa	1,897	1,577	2,824	4,090	3,861	2,210	3,370	4,536	3,201	2,988
Sudan	1,158	1,346	1,531	1,650	2,921	1,883	3,211	5,231	5,504	2,930
Bolivia	1,509	1,444	1,761	1,819	1,664	1,376	1,768	2,197	4,025	2,590

(continued)

Table 1.3

PERSONS OBTAINING LEGAL PERMANENT RESIDENT STATUS BY REGION AND COUNTRY OF BIRTH: FISCAL YEARS 1998 TO 2007 *(continued)*

REGION AND COUNTRY OF BIRTH	1998	1999	2000	2001	2002	2003	2004	2005	2006	2007
Laos	1,606	846	1,358	1,398	1,245	896	1,147	1,242	2,892	2,575
Italy	1,817	1,512	2,448	3,096	2,578	1,644	2,346	3,066	3,215	2,569
Costa Rica	1,199	883	1,310	1,733	1,591	1,246	1,755	2,278	3,109	2,540
Australia	1,139	1,103	2,044	2,811	2,557	1,836	2,604	3,193	3,249	2,518
Yemen	1,857	1,160	1,789	1,607	1,227	1,382	1,760	3,366	4,308	2,396
Syria	2,835	2,048	2,367	3,350	2,557	1,938	2,256	2,831	2,918	2,385
Belarus	978	1,320	2,170	2,901	2,923	1,858	2,255	3,503	3,086	2,328
Chile	1,228	1,085	1,700	1,921	1,839	1,310	1,810	2,404	2,774	2,274
Malaysia	1,010	991	1,551	2,439	2,124	1,200	1,987	2,632	2,281	2,149
Cape Verde	812	902	1,079	868	871	745	1,015	1,225	1,780	2,048
Sierra Leone	952	970	1,585	1,878	2,246	1,492	1,596	2,731	3,572	1,999
Panama	1,637	1,640	1,829	1,867	1,680	1,164	1,417	1,815	2,418	1,916
Sri Lanka	1,084	899	1,118	1,505	1,529	1,246	1,431	1,894	2,191	1,831
Afghanistan	830	877	1,011	1,202	1,759	1,252	2,137	4,749	3,417	1,753
Fiji	1,717	1,599	1,483	1,452	1,208	1,095	1,593	1,422	2,115	1,637
Kazakhstan	539	723	1,493	2,310	2,315	1,740	1,906	2,223	2,073	1,604
Spain	1,040	869	1,254	1,711	1,361	917	1,339	1,888	1,971	1,578
Bosnia-Herzegovina	4,209	5,412	11,525	23,594	25,329	6,155	10,552	14,074	3,789	1,569
Togo	246	254	386	487	935	1,187	2,041	1,523	1,720	1,565
Georgia	295	310	493	786	886	735	964	1,389	2,003	1,554
Ireland	944	804	1,296	1,505	1,398	983	1,531	2,088	1,906	1,503
Uruguay	367	267	426	541	536	469	787	1,154	1,664	1,418
Unknown	972	1,156	1,172	2,311	2,622	1,201	3,227	5,303	2,734	1,394
Netherlands	914	773	1,337	1,679	1,549	981	1,303	1,815	1,651	1,368

Lithuania	1,191	1,147	1,349	1,732	1,786	2,266	2,480	2,417	1,885	1,361
Moldova	562	753	1,251	2,068	2,103	1,151	1,507	3,506	3,036	1,356
Hungary	806	694	1,023	1,263	1,274	1,021	1,272	1,567	1,704	1,266
Macedonia	785	569	790	921	821	653	775	1,070	1,317	1,227
Cote d'Ivoire	364	303	439	596	629	483	666	930	2,067	1,193
Saudi Arabia	703	759	1,063	1,178	1,014	735	906	1,210	1,542	1,171
Azerbaijan	504	738	1,036	1,152	1,164	746	969	1,523	2,371	1,166
Sweden	818	821	1,264	1,682	1,376	963	1,270	1,517	1,376	1,145
Congo, Democratic Republic	155	87	123	145	178	110	155	260	738	1,129
Uganda	355	250	418	457	575	455	721	858	1,372	1,122
Guinea	46	5	3	11	16	29	347	495	1,110	1,088
Eritrea	641	325	382	540	560	556	675	796	1,593	1,081
Belize	494	572	757	936	966	588	871	876	1,252	1,073
Zimbabwe	186	184	322	475	484	358	628	923	1,049	1,057
New Zealand	625	522	964	1,205	1,117	877	1,131	1,293	1,100	1,047
Algeria	804	789	906	875	1,030	759	805	1,115	1,300	1,036
Senegal	372	368	554	663	530	522	769	913	1,367	1,024
Portugal	1,529	1,058	1,343	1,609	1,313	808	1,069	1,125	1,409	1,019
Kuwait	747	801	1,015	1,258	1,056	707	1,091	1,152	1,230	1,017
Singapore	388	355	668	1,100	1,033	582	966	1,204	997	985
Congo, Republic	118	190	189	311	677	513	670	1,064	1,600	972
Saint Lucia	509	529	599	674	583	488	616	832	1,212	928
Czechoslovakia (former)	342	318	665	863	897	543	673	784	1,442	927
Greece	855	719	950	1,155	1,009	651	769	1,070	1,124	882
Tanzania	339	313	480	476	577	554	747	829	949	832
Gambia	226	183	231	390	343	263	422	581	897	826
Slovak Republic	491	492	549	809	725	674	800	965	1,111	763

(continued)

Table 1.3

PERSONS OBTAINING LEGAL PERMANENT RESIDENT STATUS BY REGION AND COUNTRY OF BIRTH: FISCAL YEARS 1998–2007 *(continued)*

REGION AND COUNTRY OF BIRTH	1998	1999	2000	2001	2002	2003	2004	2005	2006	2007
United Arab Emirates	329	310	435	460	472	380	586	812	1,006	758
Grenada	655	661	655	645	634	481	609	840	1,068	751
Bahamas	602	398	766	924	808	423	586	698	847	738
Switzerland	825	647	1,029	1,298	1,004	632	855	1,092	983	705
Barbados	725	715	777	895	813	516	630	846	959	689
Mauritania	78	24	88	117	124	131	170	275	720	651
Belgium	419	426	670	814	769	455	638	859	716	638
Kyrgyzstan	111	189	388	582	473	356	439	656	785	597
Zambia	212	143	211	295	308	280	359	499	672	576
Latvia	369	444	548	711	683	458	605	768	892	568
Saint Vincent and the Grenadines	413	442	497	559	480	322	400	625	756	567
Paraguay	275	216	338	401	356	207	328	516	719	545
Mongolia	26	41	46	102	135	153	229	323	497	530
Denmark	454	367	537	706	609	405	566	718	699	517
Austria	290	230	405	522	483	295	402	532	524	485
Croatia	547	580	1,058	2,853	3,798	1,153	1,511	1,780	945	482
Tonga	229	281	349	327	331	238	327	309	437	438
Dominica	283	40	95	93	148	204	132	198	471	428
Finland	314	307	377	497	426	241	388	574	542	426
Tunisia	200	150	307	438	540	353	457	495	510	417
Antigua-Barbuda	297	454	429	461	380	301	414	440	570	415

Mali	83	72	109	119	105	124	163	277	408	412
Estonia	128	142	239	348	343	235	322	438	423	368
Rwanda	52	97	73	148	217	109	163	276	502	357
Saint Kitts-Nevis	404	463	500	463	342	310	299	342	458	347
Norway	296	307	459	547	431	320	405	423	481	343
Samoa	146	91	184	165	157	178	203	173	283	290
Czech Republic	144	145	244	307	267	267	457	476	344	287
Benin	47	59	62	75	137	76	185	193	275	258
Burundi	51	16	28	79	120	74	100	186	320	257
Burkina Faso	14	17	48	68	64	60	103	128	221	238
Turkmenistan	44	65	97	94	93	84	117	148	248	217
Angola	66	57	87	94	92	59	107	188	272	199
Suriname	143	141	256	245	247	180	166	300	314	197
Libya	165	156	180	223	158	140	185	223	271	186
Macau	276	294	270	340	284	244	192	133	189	178
Tajikistan	66	104	156	187	181	137	167	207	239	172
United States	30	29	35	63	64	32	57	183	333	171
Qatar	60	78	97	125	108	72	125	174	226	138
Cyprus	119	106	160	216	158	123	143	196	180	137
Bahrain	52	70	106	118	85	59	116	140	148	133
Malawi	39	41	61	70	56	62	83	131	131	123
Bermuda	62	63	71	98	108	92	100	116	160	108
Oman	25	40	51	55	61	76	122	101	155	103
Niger	282	12	30	1,330	1,263	808	62	126	116	97
Gabon	21	4	18	32	41	40	50	66	85	95
Iceland	111	79	129	134	93	97	105	135	145	95
Netherlands Antilles	61	35	53	114	97	59	72	116	100	93
Mauritius	37	38	54	84	83	57	65	99	108	88
Slovenia	57	58	76	142	140	64	88	114	115	87

(continued)

Table 1.3

PERSONS OBTAINING LEGAL PERMANENT RESIDENT STATUS BY REGION AND COUNTRY OF BIRTH: FISCAL YEARS 1998–2007 *(continued)*

REGION AND COUNTRY OF BIRTH	1998	1999	2000	2001	2002	2003	2004	2005	2006	2007
Mozambique	39	31	41	48	54	36	59	54	78	81
Chad	8	24	23	44	47	8	23	31	73	74
Montserrat	65	80	70	61	42	36	33	50	90	66
Namibia	24	13	30	54	46	40	40	63	56	57
Aruba	23	14	25	29	32	27	31	42	51	55
Madagascar	42	26	33	61	43	40	54	60	72	53
Malta	58	43	54	57	44	37	57	74	70	53
Bhutan	6	4	D	5	14	15	17	30	78	52
Central African Republic	6	3	4	11	13	6	17	24	51	52
Botswana	12	5	13	24	30	27	34	54	53	49
Marshall Islands	6	3	3	D	26	26	48	32	53	48
British Virgin Islands	55	76	67	70	43	43	35	41	47	40
Cayman Islands	28	18	31	23	24	35	38	37	65	40
All other countries	22	33	46	49	61	35	43	65	53	40
Luxembourg	21	11	26	34	32	16	13	35	28	39
Guadeloupe	30	54	51	84	38	35	59	48	53	38
Brunei	19	16	16	27	28	20	22	49	25	32
Papua New Guinea	10	14	21	26	26	34	19	44	30	31
Turks and Caicos Islands	46	27	46	33	31	26	28	34	52	31

French Polynesia	14	9	13	16	12	14	13	19	37	27
Anguilla	26	20	25	55	20	26	22	35	32	25
Guinea-Bissau	165	134	204	273	289	176	5	26	25	25
Djibouti	15	6	14	22	30	16	37	50	34	23
Martinique	20	23	20	22	19	14	26	37	30	23
Lesotho	4	5	9	6	13	5	14	12	18	14
Swaziland	8	8	12	18	12	23	15	16	11	13
American Samoa	4	11	7	28	26	16	12	15	28	11
Palau	6	D	3	3	10	8	6	8	8	11
Kiribati	4	–	3	–	4	4	D	4	8	10
Solomon Islands	5	D	7	7	7	5	6	3	5	10
French Guiana	D	5	13	8	6	4	3	8	15	9
Maldives	D	–	D	9	9	15	7	6	D	9
Micronesia, Federated States	4	D	5	9	D	4	5	6	12	7
Seychelles	4	10	18	18	20	16	25	16	15	7
Monaco	6	5	12	9	17	3	7	7	4	6
Equatorial Guinea	7	D	5	3	8	D	13	10	13	4
U.S. Virgin Islands	D	5	3	6	9	4	13	8	7	3
Total	**653,206**	**644,787**	**841,002**	**1,058,902**	**1,059,356**	**703,542**	**957,883**	**1,122,257**	**1,266,129**	**1,052,415**

Note: D = Data withheld to limit disclosure. – Represents zero.
[a]Yugoslavia (unknown republic) prior to February 7, 2003.
From *Yearbook of Immigration Statistics: 2007,* by United States Department of Homeland Security, 2007, Washington, DC: U.S. Department of Homeland Security, Office of Immigration Statistics. Retrieved April 20, 2008, from http://www.dhs.gov/xlibrary/assets/statistics/yearbook/2007/table03d.xls

Table 1.4

COUNTRY OF BIRTH OF THE UNAUTHORIZED IMMIGRANT POPULATION: JANUARY 2006 AND 2000

COUNTRY OF BIRTH	ESTIMATED POPULATION IN JANUARY 2006	ESTIMATED POPULATION IN JANUARY 2000	PERCENT OF TOTAL 2006	PERCENT OF TOTAL 2000	PERCENT CHANCE 2000 TO 2006	AVERAGE ANNUAL CHANGE 2000 TO 2006
All countries	11,550,000	8,460,000	100	100	37	515,000
Mexico	6,570,000	4,680,000	57	55	40	315,000
El Salvador	510,000	430,000	4	5	19	13,333
Guatemala	430,000	290,000	4	3	48	23,333
Phillippines	280,000	200,000	2	2	40	13,333
Honduras	280,000	160,000	2	2	75	20,000
India	270,000	120,000	2	1	125	25,000
Korea	250,000	180,000	2	2	39	11,667
Brazil	210,000	100,000	2	1	110	18,333
China	190,000	190,000	2	2	–	–
Vietnam	160,000	160,000	1	2	–	–
Other countries	2,410,000	1,950,000	21	23	24	76,697

Note: – Figure rounds to 0.0. Detail may not sum to totals because of rounding.
From *Estimates of the Unauthorized Immigrant Population Residing in the United States: January 2006,* by M. Hoefer, N. Rytina, & C. Campbell, 2007. Retrieved April 20, 2008, from http://www.dhs.gov/xlibrary/assets/statistics/publications/ill_pe_2006.pdf

Unfortunately there are an increasing number of forced sexual and economic migrants, those who do not willingly decide to immigrate but often become victims of modern-day slavery. It is estimated that approximately 600,000 to 800,000 people are trafficked across international borders each year. Trafficking also occurs internally, with victims moved within a single country. The U.S. government estimates 14,500 to 17,500 people are trafficked to the United States each year (National Conference on State Legislatures, 2007).

Migration is not a one-way street and an increasing number of migrants frequently return to their country of origin. The concept of *transnationalism,* first used to describe multinational companies, was widened in the 1990s to refer to individuals and groups who move across boundaries but remain financially and socially connected to their countries of origin. As described by Schiller, Basch, and Blanc-Szanton (1992), transnationalism is a process by which people establish and maintain sociocultural connections across geopolitical borders. The speed of air travel

Table 1.5

PERSONS OBTAINING LEGAL PERMANENT RESIDENT STATUS BY GENDER, AGE, MARITAL STATUS, AND OCCUPATION: FISCAL YEAR 2007

CHARACTERISTIC	TOTAL	MALE	GENDER FEMALE	UNKNOWN
AGE				
Total	1,052,415	471,377	581,031	7
Under 1 year	10,209	4,058	6,151	–
1 to 4 years	29,110	13,931	15,179	–
5 to 9 years	50,705	26,007	24,697	1
10 to 14 years	68,184	35,066	33,116	2
15 to 19 years	91,166	46,239	44,926	1
20 to 24 years	101,099	42,848	58,250	1
25 to 29 years	121,014	48,750	72,264	–
30 to 34 years	136,508	62,383	74,125	–
35 to 39 years	113,790	53,351	60,439	–
40 to 44 years	85,853	38,337	47,515	1
45 to 49 years	63,673	27,467	36,205	1
50 to 54 years	50,044	20,784	29,260	–
55 to 59 years	40,266	15,721	24,545	–
60 to 64 years	32,284	12,465	19,819	–
65 to 74 years	43,367	17,733	25,634	–
75 years and over	15,137	6,233	8,904	–
Unknown	6	4	2	–
BROAD AGE GROUPS				
Total	1,052,415	471,377	581,031	7
Under 16 years	174,899	87,731	87,164	4
16 to 20 years	97,042	48,229	48,813	–
21 years and over	780,468	335,413	445,052	3
Unknown	6	4	2	–
MARITAL STATUS				
Total	1,052,415	471,377	581,031	7
Single	387,252	200,264	186,984	4
Married	610,134	258,710	351,424	–
Widowed	28,011	3,307	24,704	–
Divorced/separated	22,307	6,899	15,408	–
Unknown	4,711	2,197	2,511	3
OCCUPATION				
Total	1,052,415	471,377	581,031	7
Management, professional, and related occupations	106,763	65,319	41,444	–
Service occupations	53,218	29,222	23,996	–

(continued)

Table 1.5

PERSONS OBTAINING LEGAL PERMANENT RESIDENT STATUS BY GENDER, AGE, MARITAL STATUS, AND OCCUPATION: FISCAL YEAR 2007 *(continued)*

CHARACTERISTIC	TOTAL	MALE	FEMALE	UNKNOWN
Sales and office occupations	40,732	18,221	22,511	–
Farming, fishing, and forestry occupations	15,152	12,062	3,090	–
Construction, extraction, maintenance, and repair occupations	9,340	9,125	215	–
Production, transportation, and material moving occupations	45,529	33,502	12,027	–
Military	72	52	20	–
No occupation/not working outside home	507,200	177,759	329,437	4
Homemakers	146,284	3,739	142,545	–
Students or children	272,537	136,043	136,490	4
Retirees	9,300	4,201	5,099	–
Unemployed	79,079	33,776	45,303	–
Unknown	274,409	126,115	148,291	3

Note: – Represents zero.
From *Yearbook of Immigration Statistics: 2007,* by United States Department of Homeland Security, 2007, Washington, DC: U.S. Department of Homeland Security, Office of Immigration Statistics. Retrieved April 20, 2008, from http://www.dhs.gov/xlibrary/assets/statistics/yearbook/2007/table08.xls

as well as technological advances such as e-mail and cell phones have augmented the development of transnationalism. It has been suggested that women more than men frequently travel back to their homelands as transnational migrants (Alicea, 1997).

While a growing number of migrants are transnational in that they maintain strong ties with their countries of origin and frequently return to their home countries, their status is not without risks, especially for those who might want to stay in the United States. Often an undocumented person who returns home may face the risk of being unable to reenter his or her home country. There are others who can never geographically return home, as for example political refugees who can never return home again, which may contribute to their stress as immigrants.

In addition to forced migration due to economic reasons, there are also persons who seek refuge in another country because of fear of persecution on account of their race, religion, nationality, social group, or political opinion. Not only economic migrants, but also refugees, asylees, and women trafficked for work or sex are equally vulnerable in the receiving country. Table 1.6 shows the recent numbers of refugees who have arrived in the United States, by country of origin.

The Push-Pull Theory of Immigration

As discussed above, there are many theories as to why people migrate to another country. The push-pull theory first articulated by Lee (1966) proposes that migrants are often "pushed" from their country of origin by economic hardship, or by political and social oppression, and "pulled" to the country of destination by hopes of better economic opportunities and political and religious freedom. It has been suggested that push factors are most important in achieving refugee status, while pull factors best explain immigrants leaving their country of origin. In reality migrants have come to the United States because of both push and pull factors.

Push and pull factors that contribute to migration can be considered on three levels: the *macro,* the *mezzo,* and the *micro.* The macro refers to the political, economic, geographic, and social factors that affect immigrants both in their country of origin and their country of destination. Mezzo refers to the social and community relationships of both those who migrate and those who stay behind; while micro refers to the personal characteristics and freedom to leave of those who choose to migrate.

Since the beginning, macro forces have continually affected the course of migration and the current impact of globalization has increased migration around the world. Very few people use only products that are grown or manufactured locally. We see a continual trend whereby those in developing countries because of increasing poverty are often forced to migrate to more developed countries. In recent years, those who live in the poorest countries have been made even poorer by climate change. Climate change has brought extreme drought, flooding, and natural disasters that have made agriculture no longer viable. This loss of resource

Table 1.6

REFUGEE ARRIVALS BY REGION AND COUNTRY OF ORIGIN: FISCAL YEARS 1997–2006

REGION AND COUNTRY OF ORIGIN	1997	1998	1999	2000	2001	2002	2003	2004	2005	2006
REGION										
Africa	6,069	6,665	13,048	17,624	19,070	2,550	10,719	29,110	20,746	18,185
Asia	11,771	13,669	14,041	13,622	15,356	6,885	5,862	10,896	14,977	9,245
Europe	48,450	54,260	55,877	37,664	31,526	15,406	11,269	9,254	11,316	10,456
North America	2,986	1,587	D	3,233	2,968	1,924	305	2,998	6,368	3,145
Oceania	–	–	–	–	–	–	–	–	–	–
South America	–	–	D	–	5	8	149	579	331	119
Total	**69,276**	**76,181**	**85,076**	**72,143**	**68,925**	**26,773**	**28,304**	**52,837**	**53,738**	**41,150**
COUNTRY										
Afghanistan	–	88	365	1,709	2,930	1,683	1,453	959	902	651
Algeria	–	–	12	57	31	–	4	D	D	D
Angola	–	–	–	D	34	16	21	20	21	13
Armenia	NA	NA	35	20	27	30	63	88	86	87
Azerbaijan	NA	NA	210	259	449	114	406	407	299	77
Belarus	NA	NA	1,008	1,050	971	680	702	659	445	350
Bosnia-Herzegovina	21,357	30,906	22,699	19,033	14,593	3,461	525	244	61	16
Burma	182	186	295	637	543	128	203	1,056	1,447	1,612
Burundi	33	24	223	165	109	62	16	276	214	466
Cambodia	–	–	–	–	23	4	7	3	9	9
Cameroon	19	15	9	7	5	6	6	D	6	29
Central African Republic	–	–	D	–	D	–	D	24	–	23
Chad	45	41	22	D	D	D	D	4	–	4
China, People's Republic	–	–	D	D	12	9	9	3	13	21
Colombia	–	–	–	–	–	8	149	577	323	115

Congo, Democratic Republic	45	52	42	1,354	260	107	251	569	424	405
Congo, Republic	–	–	27	11	6	5	41	73	43	66
Cote d'Ivoire	–	D	5	–	D	3	4	–	5	23
Croatia	–	–	1,660	2,995	1,020	109	144	92	39	D
Cuba	2,911	1,587	2,018	3,184	2,944	1,919	305	2,980	6,360	3,143
Djibouti	16	15	8	–	12	D	D	6	–	–
Equatorial Guinea	–	–	–	12	–	–	D	–	25	11
Eritrea	7	9	32	94	109	13	23	128	327	538
Estonia	NA	NA	71	81	57	38	28	27	17	7
Ethiopia	197	152	1,873	1,347	1,429	330	1,702	2,689	1,663	1,271
Gambia	16	50	13	13	5	–	9	3	–	6
Georgia	–	–	50	30	49	14	53	33	11	4
Haiti	75	–	91	49	24	5	–	17	8	–
Indonesia	–	D	26	14	5	18	17	5	6	10
Iran	1,305	1,699	1,750	5,145	6,590	1,540	2,471	1,786	1,856	2,792
Iraq	2,679	1,407	1,955	3,158	2,473	471	298	66	198	202
Kazakhstan	NA	NA	412	284	291	222	118	312	80	124
Kenya	–	13	D	11	13	24	3	–	D	5
Kuwait	–	–	–	13	–	6	–	14	–	–
Kyrgyzstan	NA	NA	140	147	116	69	46	100	38	15
Laos	939	–	19	64	22	18	13	6,005	8,517	830
Latvia	NA	NA	167	103	125	57	49	52	25	21
Liberia	231	1,494	2,495	2,620	3,429	559	2,957	7,140	4,289	2,402
Lithuania	NA	NA	20	16	40	D	21	13	9	–
Macedonia	–	–	3	D	D	4	13	–	–	D
Mauritania	–	–	D	–	202	6	–	–	3	88
Moldova	NA	NA	1,035	1,056	1,168	1,022	616	1,711	1,016	721
Nigeria	7	312	625	50	85	28	57	34	11	15
Pakistan	–	–	–	6	3	–	18	11	9	20

(continued)

Table 1.6

REFUGEE ARRIVALS BY REGION AND COUNTRY OF ORIGIN: FISCAL YEARS 1997–2006 ***(continued)***

REGION AND COUNTRY OF ORIGIN	1997	1998	1999	2000	2001	2002	2003	2004	2005	2006
Russia	NA	NA	4,386	3,723	4,454	2,105	1,394	1,446	5,982	6,003
Rwanda	100	86	153	345	94	47	47	176	183	112
Serbia and Montenegro[a]	3	–	14,280	524	153	1,860	1,839	151	40	11
Sierra Leone	57	176	675	1,128	2,004	176	1,378	1,086	829	439
Somalia	4,974	2,951	4,320	6,026	4,951	237	1,994	13,331	10,405	10,357
Soviet Union (former)	27,072	23,349	194	282	133	–	–	–	–	–
Sudan	277	1,252	2,393	3,833	5,959	897	2,139	3,500	2,205	1,848
Syria	–	–	D	18	8	4	3	–	7	27
Tajikistan	NA	NA	9	24	9	4	13	D	6	4
Togo	30	15	93	511	280	16	47	35	72	18
Tunisia	–	3	–	D	10	–	–	–	–	–
Turkmenistan	NA	NA	16	D	7	D	4	7	D	D
Uganda	9	D	12	18	12	D	D	8	10	20
Ukraine	NA	NA	8,649	7,334	7,172	5,216	5,065	3,482	2,889	2,483
Uzbekistan	NA	NA	818	693	681	394	166	426	271	527
Vietnam	6,660	10,288	9,622	2,841	2,730	2,988	1,354	974	2,009	3,039
Yemen	–	–	D	D	–	–	D	8	D	11
Zimbabwe	–	–	–	–	6	–	–	D	D	13
All other countries	30	7	33	38	52	35	32	15	19	40
Total	**69,276**	**76,181**	**85,076**	**72,143**	**68,925**	**26,773**	**28,304**	**52,837**	**53,738**	**41,150**

Note: D = Data withheld to limit disclosure. – Represents zero. NA = Not available. This table excludes Amerasian immigrants.

[a]Yugoslavia (unknown republic) prior to February 7, 2003.

From *Yearbook of Immigration Statistics: 2006,* by United States Department of Homeland Security, 2007, Washington, DC: U.S. Department of Homeland Security, Office of Immigration Statistics. Retrieved April 20, 2008, from http://www.dhs.gov/xlibrary/assets/statistics/yearbook/2006/table14D.xls

has led to forced migration within the victims' countries from rural to urban areas and ultimately in many cases to the United States, Canada, Australia, and European countries (Congress, 2007). Political unrest and violence have also led many to leave their own lands and sometimes has resulted in migrants' ability to gain refugee status. (See Chapter 2 for more information about the law regarding refugee status.)

On a mezzo level the nature of relationships in the country of origin and destination often contributes to migration. Those who have very strong ties to community and family in the country of origin are less likely to immigrate as compared to those for whom the ties are more tenuous. Within a large family it is interesting to note who becomes an immigrant and who chooses to remain behind. In terms of mezzo pull factors, *chain migration* occurs when more and more immigrants are attracted to locations in which relatives and friends have migrated previously (Faist, 1997).

Finally, micro factors contribute to decisions and ability to migrate. Older people may be less likely to migrate because of stronger ties in the country of origin and anxiety about learning a new language and culture (Potocky-Tripodi, 2002). Those with a higher education in the country of origin may believe that there are more job opportunities in a destination country than in their homeland. Those who are extremely poor may remain dependent upon receiving funds from richer relatives who have already migrated before they are able to leave. Micro personality factors have also been linked to immigrant decisions to migrate. Those who are not risk takers or are more present oriented (Fischer, Martin, & Straubhaar, 1997) are seen as less likely to immigrate.

The push and pull theory with a three-level approach is helpful in understanding the multiple factors that contribute to immigrants' decision to migrate. In social work practice with immigrants, however, we are often so focused on helping immigrants cope with their current situation that we do not sufficiently look at the immigrants' issues before migration or the transit to this country. Drachman (1992) suggests a three-part approach to social work practice with immigrant families. First, it is important to understand immigrants in their countries of origin. What factors, political, economic, social, relationship, and personal, contributed to their decisions to immigrate? What was the situation like in their home countries? Once here do they frequently go back to their countries of origin? Do they in fact live in two countries? Do they want to return? Can they ever go home again? Many refugees as well as some immigrants who have escaped political, religious, and social oppression can never return. The chapters in this volume on cultural competency and mental health will address some of these issues.

The second stage involves transit. For some, transit may involve a long plane ride, for others (especially those who have entered without documents from our southern borders), it may entail a dangerous desert or water crossing. Social workers who work with immigrants need to understand the personal immigration history of their clients in order to best help them.

The chapters on legal classification of immigrants (chapter 2), as well as the chapters on physical health (chapter 5) and mental health (chapter 6), will also address these topics.

HISTORY OF IMMIGRATION IN THE UNITED STATES

Often referred to as a country of immigrants, the United States has changed policy toward immigrants throughout its existence depending on economic and social trends. The racial or ethnic makeup of the immigrants, and the countries from which the majority of immigrants came, have changed throughout our history; initially immigrants were White western Europeans with the exception of forced migrants from Africa, while in recent years the greatest numbers of immigrants have come from Asia, the Caribbean, South and Central America, and Mexico.

Table 1.7 shows the number of legal permanent residents arriving in the United States from 1820 through 2007. Many of the ebbs and flows in immigration will be explained in the following section.

For its first hundred years the United States was most receptive to immigrants because of the need to foster its economic and social growth, and also because its citizens believed that this country could provide a refuge for those fleeing from oppression around the world. In sharp contradiction to the U.S. self-image of providing sanctuary to those seeking freedom, during the same period, large numbers of forced migrants were brought from Africa to the United States as slaves.

Despite this initial, positive environment toward immigration, concern grew that immigrants contributed to crime and poverty. This concern led to the first restrictive Immigration Act of 1882, which excluded the admission of convicts, paupers, and those viewed as mentally defective. Proponents of the act felt that these populations would be unemployed and thus dependent upon public funds for financial support. That same year, an act that limited immigration based on national origin was passed:

Table 1.7

PERSONS OBTAINING LEGAL PERMANENT RESIDENT STATUS: FISCAL YEARS 1820 TO 2007

YEAR	NUMBER	YEAR	NUMBER	YEAR	NUMBER	YEAR	NUMBER
1820	8,385	1870	387,203	1920	430,001	1970	373,326
1821	9,127	1871	321,350	1921	805,228	1971	370,478
1822	6,911	1872	404,806	1922	309,556	1972	384,685
1823	6,354	1873	459,803	1923	522,919	1973	398,515
1824	7,912	1874	313,339	1924	706,896	1974	393,919
1825	10,199	1875	227,498	1925	294,314	1975	385,378
1826	10,837	1876	169,986	1926	304,488	1976[9]	499,093
1827	18,875	1877	141,857	1927	335,175	1977	458,755
1828	27,382	1878	138,469	1928	307,255	1978	589,810
1829	22,520	1879	177,826	1929	279,678	1979	394,244
1830	23,322	1880	457,257	1930	241,700	1980	524,295
1831	22,633	1881	669,431	1931	97,139	1981	595,014
1832	60,482	1882	788,992	1932	35,576	1982	533,624
1833	58,640	1883	603,322	1933	23,068	1983	550,052
1834	65,365	1884	518,592	1934	29,470	1984	541,811
1835	45,374	1885	395,346	1935	34,956	1985	568,149
1836	76,242	1886	334,203	1936	36,329	1986	600,027
1837	79,340	1887	490,109	1937	50,244	1987	599,889
1838	38,914	1888	546,889	1938	67,895	1988	641,346
1839	68,069	1889	444,427	1939	82,998	1989	1,090,172
1840	84,066	1890	455,302	1940	70,756	1990	1,535,872
1841	80,289	1891	560,319	1941	51,776	1991	1,826,595
1842	104,565	1892	579,663	1942	28,781	1992	973,445
1843	52,496	1893	439,730	1943	23,725	1993	903,916
1844	78,615	1894	285,631	1944	28,551	1994	803,993
1845	114,371	1895	258,536	1945	38,119	1995	720,177
1846	154,416	1896	343,267	1946	108,721	1996	915,560
1847	234,968	1897	230,832	1947	147,292	1997	797,847
1848	226,527	1898	229,299	1948	170,570	1998	653,206
1849	297,024	1899	311,715	1949	188,317	1999	644,787
1850	369,980	1900	448,572	1950	249,187	2000	841,002
1851	379,466	1901	487,918	1951	205,717	2001	1,058,902
1852	371,603	1902	648,743	1952	265,520	2002	1,059,356
1853	368,645	1903	857,046	1953	170,434	2003	703,542
1854	427,833	1904	812,870	1954	208,177	2004	957,883
1855	200,877	1905	1,026,499	1955	237,790	2005	1,122,257
1856	200,436	1906	1,100,735	1956	321,625	2006	1,266,129
1857	251,306	1907	1,285,349	1957	326,867	2007	1,052,415
1858	123,126	1908	782,870	1958	253,265		
1859	121,282	1909	751,786	1959	260,686		
1860	153,640	1910	1,041,570	1960	265,398		
1861	91,918	1911	878,587	1961	271,344		
1862	91,985	1912	838,172	1962	283,763		

(continued)

Table 1.7

PERSONS OBTAINING LEGAL PERMANENT RESIDENT STATUS: FISCAL YEARS 1820 TO 2007 *(continued)*

YEAR	NUMBER	YEAR	NUMBER	YEAR	NUMBER	YEAR	NUMBER
1863	176,282	1913	1,197,892	1963	306,260		
1864	193,418	1914	1,218,480	1964	292,248		
1865	248,120	1915	326,700	1965	296,697		
1866	318,568	1916	298,826	1966	323,040		
1867	315,722	1917	295,403	1967	361,972		
1868	138,840	1918	110,618	1968	454,448		
1869	352,768	1919	141,132	1969	358,579		

[a]Includes the 15 months from July 1, 1975, to September 30, 1976, because the end date of fiscal years was changed from June 30 to September 30.
From *Yearbook of Immigration Statistics: 2007,* by United States Department of Homeland Security, 2008, Washington, DC: U.S. Department of Homeland Security, Office of Immigration Statistics. Retrieved April 20, 2008, from http://www.dhs.gov/xlibrary/assets/statistics/yearbook/2007/table02.xls

the Chinese Exclusion Act of 1882. This act stopped immigration from China and barred Chinese from becoming American citizens; it was finally repealed in 1943. It demonstrates how attitudes changed toward Chinese immigrants based on U.S. political and economic factors. In the mid-1800s Chinese were actively recruited to the United States for work, but when an economic recession occurred in the 1880s, it was deemed necessary to exclude them. Then in 1943, when the United States needed China as a political ally during World War II, Chinese were again accepted.

The laws of the 1880s introduced three major new elements into our immigration policies (Potocky-Tripodi, 2002): (a) restrictions based on personal characteristics, (b) restrictions based on national origin, and (c) protection of American labor. These three elements shaped future U.S. policies on immigrants (Potocky-Tripodi, 2002).

During the late 1800s and early 1900s, immigrants first from northern and western Europe and then from southern and eastern Europe continued to stream into the United States to provide for the increased labor needs that accompanied expanding industrialization and urbanization. Simultaneously the sentiment grew that immigrants were more likely to be poor, criminal, or taking jobs from U.S.-born workers. This anti-immigrant attitude culminated in the Immigration Act of 1917, which excluded illiterates (who were more likely to be from southern or eastern Europe), and further restricted admission of Asian immigrants.

As a strengthening of U.S. anti-immigration policies, the Immigration Act of 1924 restricted European immigration to 150,000 a year and established a national origins quota system based on the 1890 census. Since most immigrants from southern and eastern Europe did not arrive until after 1890, this provision was similar to the 1917 Immigration Act that excluded illiterates in that it favored admission for those from northern and western Europe. An interesting note especially in light of current immigration concerns is that immigrants from the western hemisphere were exempt from these quotas in an attempt to keep good relationships with our southern neighbors and also ensure an available cheap workforce.

Legislation in 1948 (Displaced Persons Act), in 1953 (Refugee Relief Act), and in 1957 (Refugee Escapee Act) was passed to provide for those who were displaced by the war or who were escapees from communist regimes. The Immigration and Nationality Act of 1952 sought to unite existing laws. There was a modified quota system that still favored northern and western Europeans, who were thought to more easily be assimilated into American society (Potocky-Tripodi, 2002). Within the quota system preference was given to those with higher education and skills, as well as to those who had relatives in the United States. In summary, the first 200 years of our country's history demonstrated a change from an initial open immigration policy to a more restrictive policy that seemed related to ebbs and flows in the economic, social, and political world.

The Immigration and Nationality Act, as amended in 1965, marks the beginning of contemporary immigration legislation. It abolished the national quota system, thus eliminating race, national origin, or ethnicity as a basis for immigration status. An admissions preference system based on family relationships and employment was established. This act led to the increase of immigrants from Asia and Latin America, rather than from Europe. Admission and resettlement of refugees, many of whom had fled from war-torn southeast Asia, was furthered by the Refugee Act of 1980.

A concern over the increase of undocumented immigrants led to the passage of the Immigration Reform and Control Act of 1986 (IRCA). Its three major provisions dealt with undocumented immigrants: (a) increased fines to those who hired illegal immigrants, (b) increased border control, and (c) amnesty granted to those who had lived continuously in the United States since 1982. The latter led to the legalization of almost 3 million immigrants (Potocky-Tripodi, 2002).

The Immigration Act of 1990 focused on legal immigration and increased total annual immigration by 40%. It revised family preference and employment skills preferences and added a new diversity category to increase admissions from countries from which there had been few admissions since 1965 (Europeans). A growing concern that even legal immigrants might be using public benefits led to the Personal Responsibility and Work Opportunity Reconciliation Act of 1996. This act barred legal immigrants from receiving public benefits. Concern about benefits use also led to the Illegal Immigration Reform and Immigrant Responsibility Act (1996) that increased restrictions on undocumented immigrants, with the exceptions that those who have been affected by domestic violence could apply for benefits and that nonprofits were exempted from asking immigrant status in order to determine benefit eligibility.

Coupled with the growing anti-immigrant sentiment there has been an increasing fear of terrorism that did not begin with, but has heightened since, the terrorist attacks of September 11, 2001. The Antiterrorism and Effective Death Penalty Act of 1994 (AEDPA), for example, expedited procedures for removing alien terrorists and excluding them from entering the United States.

In the last five years there has been an increasing anti-immigrant sentiment across the United States. On the federal level, a 2005 bill, the Border Protection Anti-Terrorism and Illegal Immigration Control Act, would have made it illegal to assist undocumented immigrants. It passed the House of Representatives, but fortunately not the Senate. This bill would have placed social workers in a difficult situation, as the NASW Code of Ethics forbids discrimination based on ethnicity or national origin. In 2008 the NASW board of directors voted that discrimination based on immigration status would also be added to our Code of Ethics.

Much of the anti-immigrant sentiment has taken the form of suggested state legislation, and in the first half of 2007 over 1,400 bills were filed in the state legislatures on immigrant issues (National Conference on State Legislatures, 2007), many of them proposing restrictive policies. A continual concern, however, especially when there are an increasing number of proposed discriminatory laws against immigrants, is the appropriate role for social workers when their ethical principles collide with state or federal laws.

IMPLICATIONS FOR SOCIAL WORK PRACTICE AND EDUCATION

This book is written to help social workers better understand the challenging and ever-changing policy and practice issues surrounding work with immigrants. From the beginning of the profession's existence, social workers have worked with immigrants. A major focus of recent professional work has been the development of culturally competent practice (which is discussed at length in chapter 4).

The NASW Code of Ethics defines the focus of professional practice with immigrants in sections on culturally competent practice. Immigration status was also recently added as a category of people for whom social workers should oppose discrimination.

Social work educators have also tried to prepare students to work with an increasing number of immigrant clients. The Council on Social Work Education (CSWE) Educational Policy and Accreditation Standards (2008) speak to the importance of the infusion of culturally competent content as well as preparing students for practice in the global world. Many schools have developed specializations and special courses on immigrant practice and provided field placements for practice experiences with different immigrant groups.

A major goal of social work education has been to educate students about the values and ethics on which the profession is based. In recent years the need to educate social work students not only on social work values and ethics, but also on human rights, has received increasing attention (Congress, 2006). Social work students need to understand immigrant issues through a human rights lens.

The UN International Convention on the Protection of the Rights of All Migrant Workers and Their Families (1990) relates especially to protecting the human rights of immigrants, and an understanding of this convention often provides an important place to begin with the understanding of immigrant issues in the United States. This UN document promotes that documented and undocumented migrants and their families should be granted the same human rights as all citizens of the country.

The International Convention on the Protection of the Rights of All Migrant Workers and their Families is an important document for several reasons. First, since almost all migrants are involved in unrecorded or "off the books" employment, the document in effect covers almost all immigrants. Another positive feature of the convention is that it includes the families of migrants, that is, women who might not be working or children who were too young to work, thus extending the scope of the coverage to additional immigrants who are not working. As this is a UN International Convention and the United States has chosen not to sign on to this treatise, it is not legally binding in the United States. Yet it provides an important step and sets standards for nations in acknowledging the human rights of migrants around the world, and it provides an important background policy document for teaching social work students about immigrant needs and issues.

ADDITIONAL RESOURCES

Constitutional Rights Foundation. History on Immigration: http://www.crf-usa.org/immigration/immigration_history.htm
Department of Homeland Security: http://www.dhs.gov/ximgtn/
IFSW International Policy on Migrants: http://www.ifsw.org/en/p38000213.html
IFSW International Policy on Refugees: http://www.ifsw.org/en/p38000216.html
NASW Immigration Policy Tool Kit: http://www.socialworkers.org/diversity/ImmigrationToolkit.pdfResouce on Immigrants
National Immigration Forum: www.immigrationforum.org
U.S. Citizenship and Immigration Services: www.uscis.gov

REFERENCES

Alicea, M. (1997). "A chambered Nautilus": The contradictory nature of Puerto Rican women's role in the social construction of a transnational community. *Gender and Society, 11*(5), 597–626.

American Community Survey. (2006). Data Profile Highlights: Colorado. Retrieved February 24, 2008, from http://factfinder.census.gov/servlet/ACSSAFFFacts?_event=Search&geo_id=&_geoContext=&_street=&_county=&_cityTown=&_state=04000US08&_zip=&_lang=en&_sse=on&pctxt=fph&pgsl=010

Amkpa, A. (2008, February 11). Ghana Overview: Region, institutions, people, culture, contemporary issues. Immigrant Project Symposium, Shomberg Center, New York.

Congress, E. (2006, November 13). Panel presentation, Red Light Children Film Forum. Fordham University, New York.

Congress, E. (2007, September 6). The impact of climate change on migrants: Current issues and future challenges. Department of Public Information/Non-Governmental Organizations Conference, United Nations, New York.

Council on Social Work Education (2008). Educational Policy and Accreditation Standards, Retrieved August 12, 2008, from http://www.cswe.org/NR/rdonlyres/2A81732E-1776-4175-AC42-65974E96BE66/0/2008EducationalPolicyandAccreditationStandards.pdf

Drachman, D. (1992). A stage of migration framework for service to immigrant populations. *Social Work, 37*, 68–72.

Faist, T. (1997). The crucial meso-level. In T. Hammar, G. Brochmann, K. Tamas, & T. Faist (Eds.), *International migration, immobility and development: Multidisciplinary perspectives* (pp. 187–218). New York: Berg.

Fischer, P., Martin, R., & Straubhaar, T. (1997). Should I stay or should I go? In T. Hammar, G. Brochmann, K. Tamas, & T. Faist (Eds.), *International migration, immobility and development: Multidisciplinary perspectives* (pp. 49–90). New York: Berg.

Grange, M. (2006). *Strengthening protection of migrant workers and their families with international human rights treaties.* Geneva: International Catholic Migration Commission.

International Federation of Social Workers. (2005). *International policy on migration.* Berne, Switzerland: Author.

Lee, E. (1966). A theory of migration. *Demography, 3,* 47–57.

National Association of Social Workers. (2006). *Social Work Speaks: NASW Policy Statements, 2006–2009.* Washington, DC: NASW Press.

National Conference on State Legislatures. (2007). 2007 Enacted state legislation related to immigrants and immigration. Retrieved March 2, 2008, from http://www.ncsl.org/programs/immig/2007Immigration831.htm

New York City Office of City Planning, Population Division. (2004). *The newest New Yorkers 2000.* New York: NYC-DCP #04–09.

Passel, Jeffrey S. (2005). *Unauthorized migrants: Numbers and characteristics.* Washington, DC: Pew Hispanic Center. Retrieved from http://pewhispanic.org/files/reports/46.pdf

Passel, J., Capps, R., & Fix, M. (2004). *Undocumented immigrants: Facts and figures.* Washington, DC: The Urban Institute.

Potocky-Tripodi, M. (2002). *Best practices for social work with refugees and immigrants.* New York: Columbia University Press.

Schiller, N. G., Basch, L., & Blanc-Szanton, C. (1992). *Towards a transnational perspective on migration: Race, class, ethnicity and nationalism reconsidered.* New York: New York Academy of Sciences.

United Nations Department of Economic and Social Affairs. (2006). *Countries with the largest percentage of population from international migration.* Retrieved March 2, 2008, from http://www.un.org/esa/population/publications/2006Migration_Chart/Migration2006.pdf

United States Census. (2003). *Foreign born population of the United States: March 2002.* Retrieved March 9, 2008, from http://www.census.gov/prod/2003pubs/p20–539.pdf

Wassem, R. (2007). Unauthorized aliens in the United States: Estimates since 1986. CRS Report for Congress. Retrieved July 21, 2008, from http://fpc.state.gov/documents/organization/39561.pdf

2

Legal Classifications of Immigrants

FERNANDO CHANG-MUY

Given the evolving demographics of the United States, and the movement of people across borders, nonprofit organizations and social workers must ensure that programs and services respond so as to meet the needs of diverse clients. Effective organizations and their staff provide direct clinical services in health, mental health, employment, and education fields. In addition to their ability to provide such services, however, social workers should also have a working knowledge of the immigration issues that their clients may face. Legal issues regarding immigration may serve as barriers to care by adding mental and physical health stressors and thus impeding resolution of other core issues.

This chapter will describe ways that persons can enter the United States for a short term, legal methods that newcomers can use to enter and stay in the United States for a long term, grounds to exclude persons from entering the United States, grounds for deportation, and finally, paths to citizenship. The purpose of this chapter is to increase the knowledge of service providers by providing a framework of legal immigration concerns. This comprehensive understanding of a client's strengths and challenges, as well as legal and other barriers, will allow the provider to develop, in partnership with the client, a comprehensive action plan to move forward. The ultimate desired outcome is consumers who are engaged participants in their own lives and those of their communities.

When confronted with a newcomer client, social workers should ascertain *how* the person entered the United States, and what immigration status the person holds *now,* as a way to determine a legal remedy. If there are questions regarding a client's legal standing, social workers may want to refer to a private attorney or nonprofit agency that specializes in immigration issues. This chapter is designed to give social workers a basic working knowledge of the law so they can make appropriate referrals with sufficient facts to assist the immigration specialist if one is needed.

SHORT-TERM ENTRANCE TO THE UNITED STATES

U.S. immigration law sets out a variety of ways in which newcomers can enter the country legally. This section will deal with *short-term* methods of entry. Typically, nonimmigrants (to be called "newcomers" in this chapter) who enter the United States for a short term might do so for humanitarian reasons, tourism, education, or short-term employment.

In order to enter the United States, all nonimmigrant newcomers must have a passport and most will also require a visa. Just as in order to enter a room, one needs a door and a key, a passport (issued by the country of origin) is analogous to the door, and a visa (issued by the U.S. Embassy or consulate in the country of origin) is the key permitting newcomers to enter the room (in this context, the United States). While many newcomers need a visa, the Visa Waiver Program (VWP) allows citizens of specific countries to travel to the United States for tourism or business for up to 90 days *without* having to obtain a visa. In turn, and as a reciprocal agreement, U.S. citizens do not have to apply for a visa to enter those countries. All countries participating in the Visa Waiver Program are regarded as developed countries (e.g., most European countries).

A visa allows newcomers to travel to the United States as far as the port of entry (airport or land border crossing). Beyond that, immigration matters are the responsibility of the U.S. Department of Homeland Security (DHS). The U.S. Immigration officials working for the DHS, Immigration and Customs Enforcement (ICE) branch, have the authority to permit newcomers to enter the United States. Officers from ICE decide how long newcomers can stay for any particular visit.

The following sections refer to U.S. immigration law, which provides definitions for "aliens" who enter as nonimmigrants, that is, for a short term. These definitions are found in section 101 (a) 15 of the Immigration and Nationality Act. For most of the scenarios described below, newcomers are given an Arrival/Departure Card (a white card) that is stapled to their passport upon entry. Social workers will want to look at this white card to ascertain when the individual entered and until when they are allowed to remain. Note, too, that in many cases the client's family members may also be eligible to remain in the United States. Thus the social worker may be providing services not just to the *principal* newcomer, but possibly to a spouse or child who is in the United States accompanying the individual.

Entering for Humanitarian Reasons

Of special interest to social workers are the nonimmigrant or short-term visas given to persons who may have entered legally and whose visas expired, or who entered without visas. They are now undocumented or "illegal," but for the reasons described below, are given permission by the government to remain.

One category is that of witnesses or informants. If the government feels that a newcomer is in possession of critical reliable information concerning a criminal organization or enterprise; and is willing to supply or has supplied such information to federal or state court; and their presence in the United States is essential to the success of an authorized criminal investigation or the successful prosecution of an individual involved in the criminal organization or enterprise, that person is allowed to remain in the United States to testify. In such cases the newcomer's passport may be stamped with the letter S, which is a designation as to the kind of visa he or she obtained in order to enter legally. (The lay terminology is S as in "snitch.") The person's spouse, married and unmarried sons and daughters, and parents may also be eligible to come into the United States to join the person providing the testimony (8 U.S.C. § 101(a)(15)(S)).

In this situation, the government may turn to a social service agency to provide assistance or counseling in areas such as mental health, physical health, and/or employment. In these situations, it is crucial that social workers understand the reason the person is in the United States and what the family's visa status might be so as to provide appropriate counseling and referrals.

Another reason persons, especially women, may be allowed to remain in the United States is because they are, or have been, victims of trafficking. If a person is physically present in the United States, American Samoa, or the Commonwealth of the Northern Mariana Islands, or at a port of entry, on account of such trafficking, and has complied with any reasonable request for assistance in a federal, state, or local prosecution of these acts, the person is allowed to remain. Persons who are victims of trafficking may be given a special document, or may have their passports stamped with a letter T (if they have a passport). This is a designation that they have been classified as victims of trafficking and are allowed to remain in the United States legally (8 U.S.C. § 101(a)(15)(T)).

Finally, there may be newcomers in the United States who have suffered substantial physical or mental abuse as a result of having been a victim of *criminal* activity. Examples of such activity include:

> Rape; torture; trafficking; incest; domestic violence; sexual assault; abusive sexual contact; prostitution; sexual exploitation; female genital mutilation; being held hostage; peonage; involuntary servitude; slave trade; kidnapping; abduction; unlawful criminal restraint; false imprisonment; blackmail; extortion; manslaughter; murder; felonious assault; witness tampering; obstruction of justice; perjury; or attempt, conspiracy, or solicitation to commit any of the above mentioned crimes. (8 U.S.C. § 101(a)(15)(U)(iii))

If the newcomer has been or is being helpful to a federal, state, or local law enforcement official investigating or prosecuting a criminal act, the person may be allowed to remain in the United States. Persons who are considered "victims of certain criminal activity" may be given a special document, or may have their passports stamped with a letter U (if they have a passport). This is a designation that they have been classified as victims of criminal activity and are allowed to remain in the United States legally.

Entering for Tourism

As mentioned above, another major reason newcomers may enter the United States is to engage in tourism "for business or temporarily for pleasure." Sometimes, newcomers enter legally as tourists, but then do not leave when required and become undocumented or illegal. When newcomers enter temporarily as visitors for business or pleasure, their passport may be stamped with the letter B, which is a designation as to the kind of visa they obtained in order to enter legally (8 U.S.C. § 101(a)(15)(B)).

Entering to Study

Another major reason why newcomers enter the United States is to study. There are several subcategories or visa types for which individuals may apply in order to enter the United States to study for a short term.

Newcomers may enter the United States as students to study "at an established college, university, seminary, conservatory, academic high school, elementary school, or other academic institution or in a language training program in the United States" (8 U.S.C. § 101(a)(15)(F)(i)). When newcomers enter temporarily as students, in their passport may be stamped the letter F, which is a designation as to the kind of visa they obtained in order to enter legally.

Newcomers may also enter the United States as "exchange scholars" to work as students, scholars, trainees, teachers, professors, research assistants, and/or specialists. They may also enter the United States as a recognized leader in a field of specialized knowledge or skill, for the purpose of teaching, instructing or lecturing, studying, observing, conducting research, consulting, demonstrating special skills, or receiving training (8 U.S.C. § 101(a)(15)(J)). When newcomers enter temporarily as exchange scholars, their passport may be stamped with the letter J, which is a designation as to the kind of visa they obtained in order to enter legally.

Another method of entering the country to study is coming to the United States to pursue a full course of study at an established vocational or other recognized nonacademic institution. When newcomers enter for this purpose, their passport may be stamped with the letter M, which is a designation as to the kind of visa they obtained in order to enter legally (8 U.S.C. § 101(a)(15)(M)(i)).

Entering to Work

Social workers in a nonprofit setting may be providing services to newcomers who entered the United States legally to work. Many newcomers enter the United States to work in health settings (typically as nurses) or as agricultural workers, or as skilled and unskilled workers in other fields. Most of these types of visas also allow the *family* of the principal worker to enter the United States as well. With the agricultural workers who enter seasonally, social workers may be approached for help with health, education, or employment discrimination issues, all of which are more fully described in subsequent chapters. When newcomers enter temporarily to work, in their passport may be stamped the letter H, which is a designation as to the kind of visa they obtained in order to enter legally.

Another category that the U.S. government uses to designate a newcomer who enters to work is an intracompany transferee. Large corporations who move their employees back and forth use this designation to obtain permission for their non-U.S. workers to enter the country. Spouses and children may also accompany the principal intracompany worker. Although large companies may have human resource departments that help their employees with social service needs, the employees or the spouses may need the help of a social service agency for issues related to health, mental health, employment, or education. When newcomers enter temporarily to work as intracompany transferees, in their passport may be stamped the letter L, which is a designation as to the kind of visa they obtained in order to enter legally (8 U.S.C. § 101(a)(15)(L)).

There are also newcomers who enter the United States because they have shown "extraordinary" abilities in the sciences, arts, education, business, or motion picture and television productions (8 U.S.C. § 101(a)(15)(O)(i)). When newcomers enter temporarily to work because of their reputation as extraordinary workers, their passport may be stamped with the letter O, which is a designation as to the kind of visa they obtained in order to enter legally.

If a newcomer enters the United States to specifically perform as an artist or entertainer, individually or as part of a group, or is an integral part of the performance of such a group, in their passport may be stamped the letter P, which is a designation as to the kind of visa they obtained in order to enter legally (8 U.S.C. § 101(a)(15)(P)(ii)(I)).

Finally, given the diminishing numbers of U.S. citizens entering religious communities, many U.S. faith-based institutions are turning to other countries to bring in religious workers. When newcomers enter temporarily to work in a religious institution as religious workers, in their passport may be stamped the letter R, which is a designation as to the kind of visa they obtained in order to enter legally.

Entering as a Foreign Government Official

Washington, D.C., is home to many embassies of other governments. In addition, other nations establish consulates that provide services to their nationals in a number of states across the United States—Texas, New York, California, and Pennsylvania, to name a few. The visas that foreign government officials might use to enter the United States are diplomatic visas, designated with the letter A or G. The government allows the "attendant, servant, or personal employee" of the principal diplomat to enter the United States. In their passport may be stamped the letter A-3 or G-5, which is a designation that they have been classified as the employee of the principal diplomat. Although it may be rare for the diplomat to enter a social service agency, it may be possible for the attendant or servant to seek help from a social worker and, hence, it is important to know this legal classification so as to make the appropriate referral because these employees may be victims of abuse at the hands of their employers.

REMAINING IN THE UNITED STATES PERMANENTLY

In addition to entering the United States as a nonimmigrant for a short term in the various categories described above, individuals may enter as immigrants and be able to live permanently in the United States. If they choose, they never have to return to their country of origin. Just as nonimmigrant visas are for individuals who want to enter temporarily, immigrant visas are for people who intend to live in the United States permanently. Terms such as *obtaining a green card* or *lawful permanent residence* are synonymous with obtaining an immigrant visa.

Although there are a number of methods by which newcomers can enter or remain in the United States legally and permanently, this section will cover the main avenues for lawful permanent residence that are relevant to social work practice, that is, obtaining residence by:

1. Family Sponsorship
2. Employment Sponsorship
3. Refuge/Asylum
4. Violence Against Women
5. Special Juvenile Status
6. Cancellation of Removal
7. Diversity Visa Program

Each of these will be examined in the following sections.

Family Sponsorship

A newcomer who wishes to become a lawful permanent resident of the United States may do so if there is a close relative who can act as a sponsor. As part of a comprehensive intake with newcomers, social workers may want to assess if a client has an immediate family member, both for immigration reasons as well as for family support (though not all family members may be a source of social or immigration support). Chapter 4 discusses the Family Systems approach to social work. This framework of working with the entire family may also prove useful from an immigration law perspective.

U.S. immigration law only recognizes certain types of relationships for purposes of obtaining lawful permanent residence. Only a U.S. citizen or permanent resident mother/father, brother/sister, husband/wife, or child over 21 can sponsor a foreigner. Procedurally, the U.S. citizen or permanent resident needs to file the appropriate documentation and prove that he/she has enough income or assets to support the person who wishes to immigrate. By ascertaining whether the client has an immediate relative as described above, the social worker can make a more efficient referral to an immigration nonprofit provider or private attorney, as a way to help the client remain in the United States.

The relative sponsor and the intending immigrant must successfully complete certain steps in the immigration process in order to come to the United States. Some of the key steps include:

1 Filing Immigration Form I-130, Petition for Alien Relative.
2 Demonstrating adequate income or assets to support the intending immigrant, and accepting legal responsibility for financially supporting their family member, by completing and signing a document called an Affidavit of Support Immigration Form I-134. For low-income families, this may prove an obstacle in helping newcomers obtain permanent residence through family sponsorship.

Even if income status is not an obstacle in obtaining permanent residence, there may still be a backlog in obtaining an immigrant visa (or green card). Section 201 of the Immigration and Nationality Act (INA) sets a limit of 226,000 family-sponsored visa numbers per year. Because of this limit, immigrants who apply for a visa number may not get one immediately after their immigrant visa petition is approved. In some cases, several years can pass between the time the USCIS approves the immigrant visa petition and the State Department assigns an immigrant visa number. Thus, immigrants from some countries have to “wait in line” (in their country of origin) in order to be admitted.

Because U.S. law also limits the number of immigrant visas available by country, immigrants from countries with a high demand for U.S. immigrant visas (such as Mexico, India, China, and the Philippines) may have to wait even longer—sometimes for decades—for visas to become available.

Based on Anglo-American definitions of family (i.e., the nuclear family), U.S. immigration law only recognizes these categories: spouse, parents, and children. So for example, an uncle cannot sponsor a niece, and a grandparent cannot sponsor a grandchild. In other words, immigration preferences are based on the closeness of the family relationship. People who want to become immigrants based on family relationship are divided into preference categories, based on the closeness of the relationship, and if their immigrant visa petition is approved, they must wait for an immigrant visa number to become available. There are a limited number of visas allowed in each preference category each year.

An exception exists for immediate relatives of U.S. citizens, which includes parents, spouses, and unmarried children under the age of 21. These petitioners do not have to wait for an immigrant visa number to become available once their immigrant visa petition is approved. An immigrant visa number will be immediately available for immediate relatives of U.S. citizens. This is referred to as *unlimited family-based immigration.*

The annual limits, based on preference, are as follows:

1. First preference: Unmarried sons and daughters of citizens: 23,400 plus any numbers not required for fourth preference.
2. Second preference: Spouses and children, and unmarried sons and daughters of permanent residents: 114,200, plus the number (if any) by which the worldwide family preference level exceeds 226,000, and any unused first preference numbers:
    a. Spouses and children: 77% of the overall second preference limitation, of which 75% are exempt from the per-country limit;
    b. Unmarried sons and daughters (21 years of age or older): 23% of the overall second preference limitation.
3. Third preference: Married sons and daughters of citizens: 23,400, plus any numbers not required by first and second preferences.
4. Fourth preference: Brothers and sisters of adult citizens: 65,000, plus any numbers not required by first three preferences.

Table 2.1

U.S. DEPARTMENT OF STATE VISA BULLETIN (MAY 2008) FAMILY VISAS

FAMILY	ALL CHARGEABILITY AREAS EXCEPT THOSE LISTED	CHINA-MAIN LAND BORN	INDIA	MEXICO	PHILIPPINES
1	March 8, 2002	March 8, 2002	March 8, 2002	July 8, 1992	March 15, 1993
2A	June 8, 2003	June 8, 2003	June 8, 2003	May 1, 2002	June 8, 2003
2B	June 1, 1999	June 1, 1999	June 1, 1999	April 1, 1992	February 15, 1997
3rd	June 8, 2000	June 8, 2000	June 8, 2000	July 22, 1992	April 1, 1991
4th	August 8, 1997	January 15, 1997	January 1, 1997	December15, 1994	March 8, 1986

From "Statutory Numbers," by U.S. Department of State, 2008, *Visa Bulletin, 118*(8). Retrieved from http://travel.state.gov/visa/frvi/bulletin/bulletin_4205.html

Table 2.1 lists the cut-off date for family sponsorships as of May 2008. For example, if a U.S. citizen filed an immigration application to sponsor his or her foreign sibling (fourth preference) in, say, July 1997 (prior to the cut-off date listed, August 8, 1997), that foreign sibling would finally receive a visa in May 2008, the month of this bulletin. (The bulletin is updated monthly.) If the sibling is from China, India, Mexico, or the Philippines, the waiting period would be even longer (see last row going across).

Employment Sponsorship

In addition to entering and remaining in the United States permanently based on family sponsorship as described above, newcomers can enter and remain permanently if there is an employer willing to sponsor them. Section 201 of the INA provides a yearly limit of 140,000 employment-based immigrant visas which, like the family visas, are divided into five preference categories.

First: Priority workers: Persons of extraordinary ability in the sciences, arts, education, business, or athletics

Second: Professionals holding advanced degrees, or persons of exceptional ability in the arts, sciences, or business

Third: Skilled workers, professionals holding baccalaureate degrees, and other workers

Fourth: Amerasians, widow(er)s, battered spouses or children of U.S. citizens, or other special immigrant juveniles

Fifth: Employment creation investors

Table 2.2 lists the cut-off date for employment-based applications as of May 2008.

Depending on the preference category, part of the sponsorship through an employer process may first require a certification from the

Table 2.2

U.S. DEPARTMENT OF STATE VISA BULLETIN (MAY 2008) EMPLOYMENT VISAS

EMPLOYMENT BASED	ALL CHARGEABILITY AREAS EXCEPT THOSE LISTED	CHINA-MAIN LAND BORN	INDIA	MEXICO	PHILIPPINES
1st	C[a]	C	C	C	C
2nd	C	January 1, 2004	January 1, 2004	C	C
3rd	March 1, 2006	March 22, 2003	November 1, 2001	July 1, 2002	March 1, 2006
Other Workers	January 1, 2003	January 1, 2003	January 1, 2003	January 1, 2003	January 1, 2003
4th	C	C	C	C	C
Certain Religious Workers	C	C	C	C	C
5th	C	C	C	C	C
Targeted Employment Areas/ Regional Centers	C	C	C	C	C

[a]C=current, that is, numbers are available for all qualified applicants.
From "Statutory Numbers," by U.S. Department of State, 2008, *Visa Bulletin, 118*(8). Retrieved from http://travel.state.gov/visa/frvi/bulletin/bulletin_4205.html

U.S. Department of Labor (DOL) certifying among other factors, that there is a need for workers in a particular sector and afterwards, after the certification from the Department of Labor is obtained, filing a petition with United States Citizenship and Immigration Services in the Department of Homeland Security (USCIS).

Again, in the context of obtaining a comprehensive history of the newcomer client so as to be able to resolve challenges and refer appropriately, social workers may want to inquire about educational background and particular skills. If clients have no family member to sponsor them as a way of obtaining permanent residence, it may be that the client has a particular skill that is needed in the region or area where the client lives. The social worker may then act as a bridge or link between the needs of the employer and the skills of the employee/client/newcomer.

Refuge/Asylum

The social worker's role in providing support to newcomers is perhaps most relevant in applications for asylum. More than 100 nations have signed a UN treaty binding the signatory to provide refuge to persons who meet the definition of refugee: the 1951 Convention and the 1967 Protocol Relating to the Status of Refugees. The United States signed the treaty in 1967 and incorporated the principles of the treaty into domestic law through congressional enactment of the 1980 U.S. Refugee Act.

Under the Refugee Act, a refugee is a person who has fled his or her country of origin because of past persecution or because of a well-founded fear of persecution on account of race, religion, nationality, political opinion, or a membership in a particular social group. If the person is not in the United States, he or she may apply overseas to *enter already recognized* as a refugee. If the person is already within the United States, for example, having entered as a visitor, or a student, or even entered with or without documents, he or she may apply for asylum. Regardless of the location, applicants must prove a "well founded fear, of persecution on account of race, religion, nationality, political opinion, or a membership in a particular social group" (8 U.S.C. § 101(a)(42)).

For newcomers entering the United States who are already recognized as refugees, the social worker's role is relevant in providing, perhaps above all, mental health counseling. As will be described in chapter 5, some newcomers, but especially those entering as refugees, have suffered three traumas: in the country of origin, in flight, and now in the host country due to factors such as language, customs, and alienation.

For newcomers who are applying for asylum in the United States, the social worker's role can be helpful to support the client in obtaining legal assistance in filing the case, and later, in helping both the client and attorney in supporting the application through affidavits. The social worker can help in drafting an affidavit to submit to the government, helping the client prove the first part of the refugee test: that the applicant is indeed afraid and that the social worker is proving therapy to alleviate the fear of past (and future) persecution if deported to the country of origin. In addition, the social worker may also be helpful in assisting with research on human rights abuses to support the second part of the definition: persecution as substantiated through reported human rights violations. (See the appendixes at the back of this volume for actual affidavits.)

Violence Against Women Act (VAWA)

Just as a social worker's role is important in an application for asylum, so is that role equally important in supporting newcomer women who are survivors of violence. Before the Violence Against Women Act, which was passed in 1994, U.S. citizen and permanent resident husbands could hold newcomer women in virtual slavery, dangling the sponsorship application for a lawful residence as a carrot, forcing the women to endure abuse.

Through the immigration provisions of the Violence Against Women Act, newcomer women who are married to lawful permanent residents or U.S. citizens can self-petition without needing the support of the abusive sponsor/husband. (Unmarried children under the age of 21 who have not filed their own self-petition may be included in petitions as *derivative beneficiaries.*) This provision allows immigrant women to safely flee domestic violence and even prosecute their abusers (8 U.S.C. § 204(a)(1)).

In addition, the law now also extends immigration relief to immigrant victims of sexual assault, human trafficking, and other violent crimes who agree to cooperate in criminal investigations or prosecutions. A key goal of VAWA's immigration protections is to cut off the ability of abusers, traffickers, and perpetrators of sexual assault to blackmail their victims with threats of deportation, and thereby avoid prosecution. VAWA allows immigrant victims to obtain immigration relief without their abusers' cooperation or knowledge.

As with asylum petitions, social workers can assist women who have been victims in proving abuse by helping their clients put together the evidence required to prove a case of abuse, which will ultimately result in lawful permanent residence. Social workers can assist by helping to provide proof of abuse, through affidavits and other documents, by:

- Submitting affidavits from others that the marriage was ended within the past two years for reasons connected to domestic violence
- Getting copies of the Protection From Abuse Order
- Obtaining hospital records, if any, of medical treatment because of the abuse
- Obtaining police records to show that the police had been called
- Submitting an affidavit that the social worker is providing counseling

Not only can social workers help spouses, but other newcomers may be helped as described below:

- *A parent* may self-petition if the parent of a child who has been abused by a U.S. citizen or lawful permanent resident spouse. Children (under 21 years of age and unmarried), including those who may not have been abused, may be included on the petition as derivative beneficiaries, if they have not filed their own self-petition.
- *Children* may self-petition if they are battered children (under 21 years of age and unmarried) who have been abused by a U.S. citizen or lawful permanent resident parent.

As with spousal abuse, the social worker's role can be twofold: providing paralegal services by helping abused immigrants obtain documents to prove their abuse so as to obtain lawful permanent residence, as well as offering counseling related to the trauma and violence they have endured.

Special Juvenile Immigrant Status (SJIS) Act

Immigrant children who are county dependents because they are victims of abuse, neglect, or abandonment are among the most vulnerable people in the United States. But in many cases, the children through their advocates can obtain a critical legal benefit that will help the children gain control in their lives and successfully transition to adulthood.

Newcomer children who have experienced abuse suffer the same emotional and physical problems as abused U.S. citizen children—and often more. Added to the other issues facing them, newcomer youth without documentation will not be able to work legally or qualify for in-state tuition at college, and they face the constant threat of deportation. In addition, the counties caring for the children will not qualify for federal foster care matching funds if the children remain undocumented. Federal immigration law, however, provides that dependent newcomer children in government placement can apply for lawful permanent residency as "special immigrant juveniles" (8 U.S.C. § 1101(a)(27)(J); 8 C.F.R. § 204.11(c)).

A social worker's role, especially when working with children and youth, is crucial in raising awareness of this benefit both to clients as well as to government agencies and other nonprofit providers. If the children have counsel or county caseworkers, they too can help to complete and submit the necessary paperwork to help the child obtain lawful permanent residence.

As mentioned above, abused newcomer children who are *not* county dependents may still be eligible for immigration benefits. A newcomer who was battered or abused by a U.S. citizen or permanent resident parent or spouse may be able to apply for permanent residence under the Violence Against Women Act immigration provisions discussed earlier. In this case the child (or spouse) does not have to have been taken in by the county or made a court dependent. However, the abuser must have been a permanent resident or U.S. citizen.

The social worker's role can be to assist in the completion of the application for this immigration status, which will result in lawful permanent residence. The child must complete USCIS forms, obtain a special medical exam, and provide fingerprints, a photograph, and proof of age. The application must include an order from a family or dependency court of that state that the child is eligible for long-term foster care due to abuse, neglect, or abandonment. Although there is a fee for the application process, a process to obtain a fee waiver is often available.

The Department of Homeland Security, U.S. Citizenship and Immigration Service (formerly the Immigration and Naturalization Service or INS) will grant the applicant employment authorization (if relevant to the youth) as soon as the application is filed, and schedule a date for the Special Immigrant Juvenile Status interview. Generally, USCIS will decide the case at the time of the SIJS interview. While the child is a juvenile court dependent it is important to apply for SIJS because the process may take from 6 to 18 months after submitting the application to get an SIJS interview. If the child is released before the interview takes place, the current USCIS policy is to deny the case.

Cancellation of Removal

Presently, persons under deportation proceedings may achieve permanent residence through a process called "Cancellation of Removal." In order to obtain this remedy or relief, applicants must show that they (a) have been continuously present in the United States for a minimum of 10 years, (b) are persons of good moral character, and (c) that their deportation would result in "exceptional and extremely unusual hardship" to their parents, spouses, and children who are U.S. citizens or permanent residents.

A social worker's role can be to help the applicant obtain legal representation, and to help put together the evidence needed to prove these criteria described above. For example, social workers can help gather materials to prove the "continuous presence" requirement: bills, letters, and affidavits from neighbors, teachers, or even social workers themselves.

The social worker, however, can be most helpful in supporting proof of the third criteria, hardship. The standard of hardship can be proven by affidavits attesting that the applicant's deportation will result in "exceptional and extremely unusual hardship" to their qualifying relatives: parents, spouse, and children who are U.S. citizens or permanent residents. Depending on the facts, this criterion may be difficult to prove. For example, if a client has a U.S.-born autistic child, the social worker can help to prove that it would cause exceptional and extremely unusual hardship to the U.S. child if the mother were deported. The social worker's role in attesting to the mother's unique role in caring for the child would strengthen the application. (See appendix for a sample cancellation affidavit.)

Diversity Visa Program

The Congressionally mandated Diversity Immigrant Visa Program (DV) makes available 50,000 permanent resident visas annually, drawn from random selection among all entries, to persons who meet strict eligibility requirements from countries with low rates of immigration to the United States. Just as the chances of winning a state lottery are minimal, so are the chances of winning an immigration visa lottery.

Nevertheless, for those clients who have few remedies to obtain lawful permanent residence as described above (no opportunity for obtaining residency based on a family or employment sponsorship; no refugee claim, no abuse, the client is not a juvenile, no hardship for cancellation), then social workers can present this as a very remote option to clients, as a way to residency. The process involves submitting an application *electronically* at www.dvlottery.state.gov. Paper entries are no longer accepted. Applicants can submit their forms themselves or they have a representative such as a lawyer submit the application on their behalf.

The DV lottery is designed to increase the diversity of the overall pool of immigrants coming to the United States. Countries that are proportionately overrepresented in the immigrant population are excluded. Countries that have sent more than 50,000 immigrants to the United States in the past five years are included. Therefore, as of 2008, individuals from the following countries cannot apply:

- Canada
- China—mainland China (nationals of Hong Kong, Macau, and Taiwan *are* included)
- Colombia
- Dominican Republic
- El Salvador
- Haiti
- India
- Jamaica
- Mexico
- Pakistan
- Philippines
- Russia
- South Korea
- United Kingdom (natives of Northern Ireland and Hong Kong are eligible, but natives of Anguilla, Bermuda, British Virgin Islands, Cayman Islands, Falkland Islands, Gibraltar, Montserrat, Pitcairn, St. Helena, and the Turks and Calicos Islands are not eligible)
- Vietnam

EXCLUSION FROM ENTERING THE UNITED STATES

The next major area of immigration law involves excluding persons from entering. All governments have reasons for excluding foreign nationals from entering their borders. Most governments, including the United States, base their decisions for not admitting foreigners on health, economic, or criminal reasons.

Section 212 of the Immigration Act states that aliens will not be admitted into the United States for any of the following reasons:

1 Health-related grounds
2 Criminal and related grounds
3 Security and related grounds
4 Public charge
5 Labor certification
6 Illegal entrants and immigration violators
7 Documentation requirements
8 Ineligible for citizenship
9 Aliens previously removed
10 Miscellaneous (polygamists; abductors; other crimes)

Of particular relevance to social workers are those grounds related to health and criminal status. Clients may approach a social service agency not necessarily for themselves, but for a relative who wishes to enter as a nonimmigrant or as an immigrant, under any of the methods described in the preceding sections of this chapter. However, they may not be admitted if any of the grounds in the list above applies.

As described in more detail in chapter 11, a newcomer who has a communicable disease of public health significance, including HIV, will not be admitted. However, a waiver exists for this rule and a social worker's role in helping the newcomer obtain a waiver is crucial.

The criteria for obtaining a waiver includes proving first that the newcomer is either an asylee or refugee or has a lawful permanent resident anchor (husbands or wives of U.S. citizens or lawful permanent residents; unmarried sons and daughters of U.S. citizens or lawful permanent residents; or parents of U.S. citizens or lawful permanent residents).

Second, the applicant for the waiver must also prove that if the individual is admitted to the United States, there will be:

1 Minimal danger to the public health
2 Minimal possibility of the spread of HIV
3 No cost to a government agency without that agency's prior consent

The social worker's role in submitting an affidavit in support of the individual's request for admission is crucial.

DEPORTATION AFTER ENTERING THE UNITED STATES

The next major section of the U.S. Immigration Act deals with deporting persons who are already in the United States. As with the grounds for excluding individuals from their territory, all governments also have reasons for deporting foreign nationals from their countries. Most governments, including the United States, base their reasons for deporting almost along the same lines as the reasons for not admitting persons. Again, the reasons are typically based on health, criminal, or economic grounds.

The U.S. Immigration Act section 237 states that the following classes of aliens are deportable from the United States:

1 Inadmissible at time of entry or of adjustment of status or violates status: Any alien who at the time of entry or adjustment of status was within one or more of the classes of aliens inadmissible by the law existing at such time is deportable.
2 Criminal offenses:
   a Crimes of moral turpitude
   b Multiple criminal convictions
   c Aggravated felony
   d Controlled substances
   e Certain firearm offenses
   f Crimes of domestic violence, stalking, or violation of protection order, crimes against children
3 Failure to register and falsification of documents
4 Security and related grounds
5 Public charge
6 Unlawful voters. Any alien who has voted in violation of any federal, state, or local provision, statute, ordinance, or regulation is deportable.

Unlike the grounds of exclusion where it may be a relative of a newcomer who approaches a social service agency for help in bringing over the individual, in this case, it may actually be the deportable individual who is the client of the social worker at an agency.

In addition to presenting with issues related to health, mental health, and so forth, the client may also have an immigration issue and may be deportable based on any one of the reasons stated above. Again, in order to make an informed and effective referral, the social worker needs to understand the context of the immigration laws dealing with deportation.

Noteworthy is the first ground of deportation, which makes reference to all the grounds of exclusion, as becoming the first ground of deportation. For example, if the person was not HIV positive upon entering, but is now HIV positive, this is a ground for removal, since all of the reasons to exclude become reasons to deport.

Another relevant ground for deportation is one related to criminal grounds. A social worker's client may be an immigrant or a U.S. citizen who is abused by her husband. If he is not a U.S. citizen, and the victim has a protection order, the alien is deportable. These issues will be discussed in greater detail in subsequent chapters.

PATHS TO CITIZENSHIP

The final portions of the U.S. Immigration Act of relevance to social workers deal with how immigrants can become citizens. The United States, unlike other countries, grants citizenship under three circumstances:

1. Citizenship by parentage
2. Citizenship by birth on U.S. soil
3. Citizenship by application

Many countries do have laws and customs passing on citizenship by blood: for example, if your parents are German, you are German at birth. Similarly, U.S. immigration laws follow the principle of *jus sanguine.* Other countries (though not all) also pass on citizenship if the individual is born on their soil. Similarly, U.S. immigration laws follow the principle of *jus solis.*

However, unlike other countries (such as Germany and Mexico until very recently), U.S. immigration law provides a third path and also allows citizenship by *application,* even if the applicant had neither a U.S. father or mother, was not born on U.S. soil, and was born abroad. For example, a newcomer arrives in the United States as a student (see section I. above, entering as a short-term nonimmigrant student). The person then becomes a lawful permanent resident based on a marriage to a U.S. citizen or lawful permanent resident, or based on sponsorship by an employer (see the previous section "Employment Sponsorship"). In these cases, after a three- to five-year period of being a lawful permanent resident, the individual can apply for naturalization—hence citizenship by application (8 U.S.C. § 301).

Applicants for citizenship, however, must comply with U.S. citizenship laws, which include:

- Being at least 18 years old
- Being a permanent resident of the United States
- Having lawful permanent residency for 3 to 5 years
- During the last 5 years, being inside the United States for 30 months or more (exceptions apply)
- Having the ability to read, write, and speak basic English
- Having the ability to pass the civics test
- Being a person of good moral character

For clients who have English as their second language, passing the test of reading, writing, and speaking basic English may be a problem. This is especially true for elderly newcomers, who may have been residents for a long period of time, but for a number of reasons, are not able to speak English. For elderly persons who are already residents, however, if they are over the age of 65 and have resided in the United States as permanent residents for at least 20 years, they have different requirements for history and government knowledge: they may also be tested in the language of their choice because they are exempt from the English literacy requirements (8 U.S.C. § 312). (Chapter 12 deals with more issues concerning elderly immigrants.)

Social workers may want to urge their lawful permanent clients to seriously consider applying for U.S. citizenship since benefits include:

- The right to vote
- Faster family sponsorship
- Public benefits/entitlements
- Educational grants and scholarships
- Travel issues
- Nondeportation if convicted of a crime

CASE STUDIES

The following case studies illustrate the types of situations that social workers may encounter in working with immigrant clients and their families. Knowledge of immigration law as discussed in this chapter may be helpful in discussing options with these clients. You are invited to answer the questions following each case.

Case Study 1

A profoundly mentally disabled 65-year-old man from Jamaica comes to the United States on a visitor's visa. His arrival departure card has expired. He is being cared for here by his brother, a U.S. citizen, who would like to have him stay here so as to continue to provide the needed care and family support.

This man has no close family in Jamaica. He was brought here after a string of paid caretakers were found to have been neglecting and abusing him. His brother, who is committed to providing care for him in the United States, says there is no institution in Jamaica with which he is familiar that can provide care for the newcomer. The newcomer's physical health is fine at this time; yet he needs constant attention like a young child. (He is unmarried and childless, and his parents are deceased.)

1 What social work issues are raised by this case?
2 What legal issues (both immigration and nonimmigration) are raised by this case?
3 Are there any legal remedies for this client?
4 What can a social worker do on a micro (direct) level to help this client?
5 What issues, if any, as to the nonprofit (mezzo or organizational development) are raised by this case?
6 What advocacy (macro) issues are raised by this case?

Case Study 2

Your clients, a married couple, are missionaries in Ukraine. They are both children of U.S. citizens; the husband was born in Poland and the wife in the Philippines, but both acquired U.S. citizenship at birth. They are expecting a baby next month, and it will be born in Ukraine. Will the child have U.S. citizenship? Why or why not?

1 What social work issues are raised by this case?
2 What legal issues are raised by this case?

Case Study 3

An undocumented woman marries a U.S. citizen and is admitted to the United States as an immediate relative. One year later, they have a child. Six months later, the U.S. citizen husband walks out and refuses to help her in any further immigration proceedings.

1 What social work issues are raised by this vignette?
2 What legal issues are raised by this vignette?
3 Are there any legal remedies for this client?
4 What mezzo (organizational development issues) are raised by this vignette?
5 What advocacy (macro) issues are raised by this vignette?
6 What happens to the undocumented spouse?
7 What happens if this couple should legally divorce after 20 months? How will this affect the woman's immigration status?
8 What if the U.S. citizen spouse dies after 20 months?

ADDITIONAL RESOURCES

The Center for Human Rights and Constitutional Law: http://www.centerforhumanrights.org. The Center offers a Manual for Special Immigrant Juveniles: http://immigrantchildren.org/documents/Final_Manual.doc

Destination USA, "What Is a Visa?": http://www.unitedstatesvisas.gov/whatis/index.html

Foreign Born.com, Visas and Immigration Area: http://www.foreignborn.com/visas_imm/start_here/1start_here.htm

Immigrant Legal Resource Center: http://www.ilrc.org/sijs.php

National Network for Immigrant and Refugee Rights: www.nnirr.org

National Immigration Law Center: www.nilc.org

U.S. Citizenship and Immigration Services: www.uscis.gov

U.S. Department of State, Diversity Visa Program: http://travel.state.gov/visa/immigrants/types/types_1322.html

Visa Law Immigration Information, The ABCs of Immigration: www.visalaw.com/abcs.html

REFERENCES

All of the following references are to the U.S. Immigration Act, 8 U.S. Code.

8 U.S.C. 1101 (a) (15) Non-Immigrants Definitions

8 U.S.C. 1154 Immigrant processing

8 U.S.C. 1101 (a) (42) Refugee definition
U.S.C. § 1101(a)(27)(J), Special Immigrant Juvenile
8 USC 101 (2) (42) Violence Against Women Act
8 U.S.C. 1182 Inadmissible aliens
8 U.S.C. 1227 Deportable aliens
8 U.S.C. 1401 Citizenship

RESOURCES

For Nonimmigrant Visa Classifications: http://www.uscis.gov/portal/site/uscis/menuitem.5af9bb95919f35e66f614176543f6d1a/?vgnextoid=e6c08875d714d010VgnVCM10000048f3d6a1RCRD&vgnextchannel=ca408875d714d010VgnVCM10000048f3d6a1

For Immigrant Visa Classifications: http://travel.state.gov/visa/immigrants/types/types_1326.html

U.S. Department of State Visa Bulletin: http://travel.state.gov/visa/frvi/bulletin/bulletin_1360.html

U.S. Immigration and Nationality Act, 8 USC: www.uscis.gov

For Immigrant Children: Center for Human Rights and Constitutional Law: http://immigrantchildren.org/SIJS/

For AIDS waiver: National Immigration Project: http://www.nationalimmigrationproject.org/HIV/2004HIVManual/2004hivmanual/page7.html

PART II

Immigration and Social Work Practice

3

Culturally Competent Social Work Practice With Immigrant Populations

CARMEN ORTIZ HENDRICKS

Culturally competent social work practice (CCSWP) is an ethical responsibility for all social workers (National Association of Social Workers, 1999, 2001, 2007), and an absolute necessity when working with immigrant populations. Social workers need to understand the full spectrum of issues faced by immigrants before they leave their country of origin; what they experience immigrating; and what they face upon arrival in the United States (Drachman, 1992; Drachman & Ryan, 1991). Immigration imposes a sociocultural, economic, and psychological toll on people that does not go away completely over time.

Cultural competence requires a holistic approach that combines biological, psychological, social, and internal spiritual elements in services, allowing for the opportunity to address other major problems clients may have such as depression, low self-esteem, and family problems. Culturally competent practice includes, but is not limited to, knowledge of a range of cultures, histories, worldviews, values, and beliefs; understanding of communication patterns and appropriate interviewing techniques; strengths and differences among and within diverse racial/ethnic groups; cultural expectations and help-seeking behaviors; and the integration of traditional, indigenous, spiritual practices that attend to the spiritual needs of families and children of color (Webb, 2001).

The social work focus on "person-in-environment" takes on new meaning when working with immigrant populations. Social workers need to be skilled practitioners to work with diverse clients traumatized by poverty, discrimination, exploitation, war, famine, violence, genocide, and a range of physical and emotional problems related to leaving their homeland for a strange and all too often hostile environment. Social workers may recognize trauma in the lives of their diverse immigrant clients, but they need help to incorporate this knowledge into effective practice interventions.

Special attention needs to be directed towards particular immigrant groups in U.S. society that are likely to require a range of human services because of differences in: (a) addressing health and mental health issues; (b) customs, traditions, beliefs and values; (c) family structures, child-rearing practices, and gender roles; (d) language and literacy; and (e) political ideology and oppressive experiences.

This chapter looks at some culturally sensitive and competent ways to serve immigrant clients by examining what is meant by cultural competence in social work practice, and how this applies to work with immigrant populations. It will examine the institutional arrangements that contribute to ongoing racism and xenophobia, and the kinds of responses needed to help integrate immigrants into the fabric of American society. There will be an attempt to classify culturally competent interventions and treatment plans that are effective with individuals and families from diverse communities. Social workers also need to take leadership in developing culturally competent organizations that advocate for policies, procedures, and practices designed to ensure access to culturally competent services for all in need.

IMMIGRATION PATTERNS IN THE UNITED STATES

Immigration patterns dramatically shift and change in the United States. Throughout the 1800s and the early part of the twentieth century, charity workers primarily worked with White European immigrants who were diverse in terms of ethnicity, religion, social class, and political ideology. Much has been written about this earlier immigration and how it shaped people's lives, beginning with long sea voyages to crowded urban ghettos to unfair labor practices and the discrimination and exploitation that immigrants faced. Immigration reached a peak at the turn of the twentieth century with the mass immigrations from southern and central Europe—Italy, Ireland, Germany, and Poland, most of whom were Catholics and Jews. Social workers served these populations in the settlement houses of large urban settings while beginning to forge an identity as a new profession.

Throughout U.S. history, immigrants have faced both positive and negative attitudes toward immigration. Positive attitudes include: immigrants enrich the U.S. culture; immigrants can be socialized to be good Americans; and immigrants contribute to the U.S. economy by taking jobs that most Americans do not want to hold. Negative attitudes include: immigrants take jobs away from Americans; immigrants are a drain on the U.S. economy; immigrants contaminate American culture and threaten American values; and immigrants bring new political points of view that weaken democratic ideals. America's ambivalence toward immigrants continues today. Since September 11, 2001, a strongly negative attitude and punitive approach to immigration has become the norm as the United States confronts terrorism and maintains homeland security. However, this ambivalence has not stemmed the flow of immigration.

According to the Pew Research Center, "If current trends continue, the population of the United States will rise to 438 million in 2050, from 296 million in 2005, and 82% of the increase will be due to immigrants arriving from 2005 to 2050 and their U.S.-born descendants" (Pew Hispanic Center, 2008).

The report further states that the Latino/Hispanic population, already the largest and fastest-growing minority group in the United States, will triple in size to 29% of the U.S. population in 2050 (compared to 14% in 2005). In fact, by 2050, the non-Hispanic White population will become the minority or 47% of the U.S. population. This is one reason why much of the immigration debate in America today seems to focus primarily on one major immigration stream—Mexican legal and undocumented immigrants.

Huntington recently wrote (2004) that the "single most immediate and most serious challenge to America's traditional identity comes from the immense and continuing immigration from Latin America, especially Mexico." Huntington believes that the United States is an Anglo-Protestant nation, and this tradition is being threatened by Hispanics who are trying to make the nation "into two people, two cultures, and two languages." Anti-immigration sentiment like this often overlooks the positive contributions that immigrants make to the United States, or the fact that immigrants provide "new energy, new tastes, and new strivers who want to lunge into the future" (Brooks, 2004).

The sheer numbers of immigrants entering this country, and the debates surrounding them, clearly underscore the important role that social workers can play in meeting the needs of immigrant individuals, families, and communities who are not always welcomed members of U.S. society.

DEFINING CULTURALLY COMPETENT SOCIAL WORK PRACTICE

In providing human services today regardless of the geographic region in which they work, social workers will meet diverse immigrant clients. Broad categories of people—Asian, Hispanic/Latino, eastern European, people from the former Soviet Republic, Africans, and Indians—include large numbers of heterogeneous groups with different ethnic, racial, linguistic, historical, political, cultural, and religious identities and experiences. Most social workers may not know (for example) where Mali is nor appreciate its cultural traditions, but do know how to deal with loss and trauma in its many forms. Sooner or later clients from many parts of the world will walk into a social service agency, and social workers need to be ready to meet these clients and their myriad needs.

The social work profession has been very concerned about defining and preparing practitioners to engage in culturally competent practice. A number of documents in professional social work organizations address the issue of culturally competent practice. The NASW Code of Ethics includes a provision on Cultural Competence and Social Diversity (1.05) that focuses on culture as a strength in the lives of people. "Social workers should understand culture and its function in human behavior and society, recognizing the strengths that exist in all cultures" (NASW, 1999, p. 9). Social workers are also advised to "have a knowledge base of their clients' cultures and be able to demonstrate competence in the provision of services that are sensitive to clients' cultures and to differences among people and cultural groups" and to "obtain education about and seek to understand the nature of social diversity and oppression with respect to race, ethnicity, national origin, color, sex, sexual orientation, age, marital status, political belief, religion, and mental or physical disability" (NASW, 1999, p. 9).

The NASW Standards for Cultural Competence in Practice spell out in more detail different areas in which individual social workers, as well as agencies, can engage in culturally competent practice. The following 10 standards are included (NASW, 2001):

1. ethics and values
2. self-awareness
3. cross-cultural knowledge
4. cross-cultural skills
5. service delivery
6. empowerment and advocacy
7. diverse workplace
8. professional education
9. language diversity
10. cross-cultural leadership

Learning to be culturally competent practitioners is not only important for professional social workers, but also needs to be incorporated into the education of future social workers. To accomplish this goal, the Council on Social Work Education (CSWE) has incorporated provisions on cultural competency into their Educational Policy and Accreditation Standards (2001) that mandate the integration of curriculum "content that promotes understanding, affirmation, and respect for persons from diverse backgrounds," as well as the provision of social services that are "culturally relevant" and that prepare students for "recognizing diversity within and between groups" (p. 9).

"Cultural competence requires hard work, commitment, and experience. It entails more than speaking the language of the client or gaining specialized knowledge about a particular cultural group. Cultural competence means understanding the value of culture as perceived by clients, and appreciating how culture guides behavior and gives meaning to life. Culture shapes and influences individual health and mental health beliefs, family practices, human behavior, and even the outcomes of interventions" (Ortiz Hendricks & Fong, 2006, p. 136). Culture "affects everything we think and do from how we treat our aging relatives, to when and how we recognize a child's transition into adulthood, to what we do when we feel sick" (Center for Cross-Cultural Health, 1997, p. x). "Cultural competence... implies a heightened consciousness of how clients experience their uniqueness and deal with their differences and similarities within a larger social context" (NASW, 2001, p. 8). The *Standards for Cultural Competence in Social Work Practice* define cultural competence as "the process by which individuals and systems respond respectfully and effectively to people of all cultures, languages, classes, races, ethnic backgrounds, religions, and other diversity factors in a manner that recognizes, affirms, and values the worth of individuals, families, and communities and protects and preserves the dignity of each" (Center for Cross-Cultural Health, 1997, p. 11).

Fundamentally, cultural competence is the ability and the will to respond to the needs of clients arising from their culture, and the worker's and client's ability to use their culture as a resource, strength, or tool to meet common human needs. Culturally competent social work practice involves a range of professional knowledge, skills and values that address the complex cultures emerging in a society from the interplay of power and privilege associated with race and ethnicity, gender and sexual orientation, religion and spirituality, social class and status, age and abilities" (NASW, 2007). The emphasis in this definition is on power, privilege, and oppression of people based on characteristics they cannot control to a large extent.

To truly help immigrant clients, social workers need to understand power and how it is constructed and used to oppress people. Social workers then have to work to change the conditions that continue to oppress immigrants. In the NASW *Code of Ethics* (1999), social workers have an ethical responsibility to the broader society, which includes social and political action (6.04) in the form of expanding choice and opportunity for all people; promoting respect for diversity; and preventing and eliminating domination, exploitation, and discrimination. Therefore, understanding of and sensitivity to clients' cultures is insufficient without translating this understanding and sensitivity into social action.

CULTURAL COMPETENCY IN AGENCY PRACTICE

Furthermore, social agencies have tended to put the onus of responsibility on social workers to be culturally competent. According to Lum (1999), "[T]he worker achieves cultural competence after developing cultural awareness, mastering knowledge and skills, and implementing an inductive learning methodology" (p. 175). But cultural competence is both a personal and organizational quest. It requires organizational awareness and sensitivity. Agencies spend thousands of dollars yearly training workers to become more culturally aware and sensitive; providing them with knowledge of different client groups; educating them about the impact of cultural differences on help-seeking behaviors; and encouraging them to adapt intervention strategies for different populations and needs. However, attention to the worker's individual growth in knowledge and skills is insufficient without simultaneously paying attention to the agency context within which workers serve clients (Fong & Gibbs, 1995; Nybell & Gray, 2004).

Cultural Competency in Child Welfare

One of the most challenging and controversial issue facing immigrants is the child welfare system with its disproportionate representation of racial/ethnic minority children and families in the system. "Over-representation of adolescents of color in the juvenile justice system result from decisions made very early on regarding the need to remove children from their homes; decisions that are based in some large part on the family's color or race" (Walker, Spohn, & DeLone, 2000, p. 6).

Immigrant families face numerous challenges when they come into contact with the public child welfare system. Language barriers, the stress of immigration, sociocultural dislocation, and discriminatory U.S. policies toward immigrants contribute to the likelihood that immigrant families are more vulnerable and therefore more likely to enter the child welfare system. Child abuse and neglect may be the result of failed systems of care that further traumatize parents and children of color who are at greatest risk. When parents cannot find adequate help for their own or their children's problems, they are at a loss as to where they can turn to for help and often lack understanding of the kind of help they will receive (Webb, 2001).

Cultural Competency in Health Care

There are tremendous disparities around who gets quality health and human services in the United States. Immigrant clients may be overrepresented in criminal justice, juvenile delinquency services, and public welfare programs, but they are also underutilizing health and mental health care services (Fong, McRoy, & Ortiz Hendricks, 2006). Poverty may be the principal underlying reason in these disparities. Social workers should keep in mind several factors that impinge on immigrants' effective use of health services: (a) length of stay in the United States; (b) size of the family; (c) emotional and financial support of family; (d) documented or undocumented status; (e) minimum wage or less than minimum wage jobs; (f) financially supporting family members in the country of origin; (g) youth of the population; (h) single-parent households; (i) lack of marketable skills; (j) residence in inner-city neighborhoods with substandard housing, inadequate schools, and inadequate services; and (j) limited English-speaking proficiency. Racism and discrimination further oppress immigrants in the United States, and put all immigrant groups at risk.

RECOMMENDATIONS FOR SUCCESSFUL CCSWP WITH IMMIGRANT POPULATIONS

Culturally Competent Organizations

Social workers need to feel competent and effective in carrying out very complex roles and functions with regards to services to immigrants. In order to do this they require the support and guidance of culturally competent organizations. These organizations need to enact a two-prong strategy: (a) continued recruitment and retention of diverse workers who can understand the language and culture of diverse clients; and (b) ongoing preparation of all staff as culturally and linguistically effective practitioners.

Cultural competence begins with administrative support and encouragement, quality supervision and oversight, strong peer relationships, and manageable caseloads. It also requires well-educated, well-trained, and experienced social workers who can effectively deal with increasingly diverse and troubled immigrant individuals and families.

- Agencies need to help workers keep abreast of new policies and procedures, and changing state and federal laws.
- Agencies need to train staff to adopt new strategies for dealing with such issues as mental illness, addiction, AIDS, or incarceration. Workers need to be prepared to identify and intervene in these problems and make proper referrals for treatment when indicated, and they have to do this in culturally competent ways that strengthen immigrant communities.
- Agencies need to outreach and establish connections with immigrant communities, as well as coalitions, councils, or other collaborative boards, to examine the issues confronting immigrants and problem-solve ways to reduce them.
- They need to build public and private agency partnerships that can address the range of service needs that immigrants present with, and find additional resources to support immigrants especially as they transition to new ways of life.

- Agencies need to provide ongoing and well-crafted training opportunities for all levels of staff. Social workers need and want training in cultural awareness and sensitivity, especially in light of observed incidents of staff bias toward immigrant populations. Sometimes social workers can make decisions based on race or ethnicity or the socioeconomic background of clients, but if the worker is an immigrant this bias may be an occupational hazard that affects the specific merits of a case. More extensive training that focuses on cultural, sociological, and psychological factors of the immigrant experience for specific immigrant populations is necessary to address such difficult and complex issues as racial or class bias.

Many of these suggestions indicate that human service professionals already know what is needed to help immigrants succeed in the United States and to reduce discrimination and oppression. What is needed is the combination of power and resources to implement these recommendations.

Research

There is not enough known about successful interventions with immigrant communities. Research is needed to enhance treatment options and to appreciate best practice interventions and outcomes, and to determine which approaches are more successful with which immigrant populations. Research is particularly needed on resiliency to determine the factors that keep immigrants intact and healthy. Research also needs to unpack large ethnic groupings by analyzing subgroup or intergroup relationships. For example, there are few studies that examine the disproportionate numbers of Central American or Southeast Asian immigrants in child maltreatment reports or their relationship to other groups.

Advocacy

Immigrant families and children, and especially immigrants of color, are traumatized by multiple factors in the environment that stress and deplete their health and mental health in this country. Social arrangements and social policies maintain immigrant families in ghettoized communities plagued by violence. The only way to change these social arrangements is to examine the child welfare, social welfare, health, and mental health care systems while simultaneously working to remedy the problems that bring immigrant families and children into the system in the first place. Poverty, violence, substance abuse, and mental health problems are among the factors fueling the growth of child maltreatment, and as a result, protecting children and reducing the level of trauma that they are exposed to requires more than mere child protective services or foster care placements (McRoy & Vick, 2001).

Dramatic social changes and broad responses are needed in many areas including education, public welfare, child welfare, juvenile justice, criminal justice, substance abuse, physical health, and mental health programs that often interact with the very same families but do not collaborate in their care or treatment. Creating safe environments, including adequate housing, nutrition, and health care, is a prerequisite to achieving a notable downward trend in all forms of maltreatment.

It is not hard to understand how immigrants, particularly single individuals or families, struggling financially with little education and job skills, with little social support and often enormous social isolation, and with extensive lifelong histories of trauma, might be at greater risk of depression and health problems. Culturally competent social workers are central figures in the promotion of the health and well-being of countless immigrant populations, now and into the future.

CASE STUDIES

The following cases illustrate life experiences commonly encountered by immigrants. You are invited to discuss the following questions about each vignette.

1 What social work issues are raised by this vignette?
2 What legal issues are raised by this vignette?
3 What aspects of the experience suggest a crisis, and why? How would you prioritize the immigrant's needs?
4 What cultural aspects impact the situation? How would a culturally competent practitioner address the issue? How might a lack of cultural awareness on the part of the practitioner impact the situation?
5 What strengths might the immigrant derive from his or her culture in this vignette?

6 What, if anything, could be done on an organizational (mezzo) level to help in this case? What could or should be done on the policy (macro) level?

Case Study 1: Mamadou and Moussa

Mamadou and Moussa were two immigrants from Mali who came to the United States with a dream of a better life for their children—one forging a path for his fellow countrymen, and the other, his cousin, navigating a classic immigrant route behind the wheel of a taxi.

Their long road to New York began 20 years ago, when Moussa, a member of the Sinonke tribe, arrived from the Malian capital of Bamako. He was one of the very first to come here from his arid, landlocked nation on the fringes of the Sahara Desert.

Moussa helped his family back home by sending them money whenever he could. Soon more members of his tribe followed, and in keeping with their cultural traditions, Moussa opened his doors and helped them get established. These Malian immigrants lived together and shared everything; anyone from the same Sinonke tribe had a guarantee of a home in New York City. Soon, the Bronx neighborhood of Highbridge was home to a large Malian community.

A few years ago, Moussa helped establish a mosque in the Bronx. The mosque also had a school to help new arrivals learn to speak, read, and write English. Moussa enjoyed giving advice to his countrymen about how to survive in the United States and how to adjust to this society. His vision was for his community to contribute positively and constructively in the United States.

That vision was shattered when a fast-moving fire gutted the four-story apartment building where the men lived with their families, killing five sons of one and the wife and four children of the other. The entire community shared in their terrible loss.

This true and tragic immigrant story reported by Williams and Fernandez in *The New York Times* (2006) brought great attention to the Malian community in the Bronx.

Case Study 2: Mr. S

Mr. S, a Bangladeshi immigrant, was upset that his 13-year-old daughter was failing in school. He found her diary and although he could not read English well, he could tell that it had something to do with boys and possibly sex too. Furious, he told his daughter he was going to talk to her teacher. Panicked, the daughter told her friend, who encouraged her to claim that her father was abusing her. Her friend told a teacher, and the family's three children were immediately removed from the home and placed in a non-Muslim, non-Bangladeshi home. The youngest child, age three, could not speak English. She refused to eat or wash in the foster care home. The father was encouraged by his court-appointed attorney to sign an admission of guilt to end the case quickly, although the father did not understand the document or its ramifications (Coalition for Asian American Children and Families, 2001, p. 12).

Case Study 3: Mr. Y

Mr. Y is a 49-year-old Chinese male with end-stage renal disease who is receiving hemodialysis. He was born and raised in mainland China. He paid a fee of $35,000 to come into the United States via illegal means six years ago. He has not yet paid off the smuggling fee. As a result of the treatment schedule, Mr. Y has difficulty finding and keeping a job with flexible hours. As his financial situation worsens, Mr. Y is also forced to relocate from place to place, depending on the kindness of strangers.

Mr. Y spent most of his adult life in the Fujian province in eastern China. He grew up in a poor farming family and community. His parents died a few years ago and he has no siblings. Mr. Y married his wife from his village and they have three children. Mr. Y feels he came from a disadvantaged family and married the only person who would have him. He described his wife as angry, depressed, and highly critical and argumentative. She ran the household and him. He worked hard on the farm, and did not like to socialize much. Mr. Y appears to have learned to be silent and tolerant of not having his needs met.

Because of poverty, the villagers looked down on his family and they were very isolated. As he grew older, Mr. Y also felt ashamed of his poverty. He could not see any hope of a better future for himself or his children even if he worked his fingers to the bone on the farm for the rest of his life. He noticed that many young people took the risk of losing their lives by paying large sums of money with high interest rates in order to be smuggled into a foreign country. Illegal immigration to Mr. Y is not a moral, ethical or even a safety issue. It is a means of survival and of upward mobility. He borrowed money and made plans to come to America. He firmly believed that this was the beginning of a golden opportunity for him to earn money, respect, and a different life for himself and his children.

Mr. Y took a 58-day boat ride from the Fujian province before reaching the shores of the United States. His primary goal upon arriving in the United States was to earn as much money as possible to pay back the smugglers and send money home. He worked very hard, day and night. He agonized over his inability to speak and understand English. He remained close to his Chinatown enclave. He missed his family and his country. He forced himself to work even harder and to regularly send money home to his family. His living arrangements and his jobs were very unstable, unsafe, and substandard. Sometimes Mr. Y had to live with more than 10 people in one basement and worried about them stealing his money or what little food he had. He frequently did not have enough money for food and lived on just a bun for a day. Eventually Mr. Y became ill and was admitted to the hospital. Mr. Y's frustration increased because he could not work and the dream of a better future for his family seemed to be falling apart. He appeared restless, anxious, and angry over his destitute circumstances. When the social worker first met Mr. Y, he desperately requested help with finding a job and a cheaper apartment. He was also becoming noncompliant with his medical treatment.

ADDITIONAL RESOURCES

Administration on Aging, *Achieving Cultural Competence* (guidebook): http://www.aoa.gov/prof/adddiv/cultural/cc-guidebook.pdf

Center for Human Diversity: www.centerforhumandiversity.org

The Commonwealth Fund, *Taking Cultural Competency From Theory to Action*: http://www.commonwealthfund.org/publications/publications_show.htm?doc_id=414097

National Association of Social Workers, *Standards for Cultural Competence*: http://www.socialworkers.org/practice/standards/NASWCulturalStandards.pdf

National Association of Social Workers, *Immigration Policy Toolkit:* http://www.socialworkers.org/diversity/ImmigrationToolkit.pdf

The National Center for Cultural Competence, Georgetown University Center for Child and Human Development: http://www11.georgetown.edu/research/gucchd/nccc/

REFERENCES

Brooks, D. (2004, February 24). The Americano Dream. Op-Ed Column, *New York Times.*

Center for Cross-Cultural Health. (1997). *Caring across cultures: The providers' guide to cross-cultural health care.* St. Paul, MN: Author.

Council on Social Work Education. (2001). *Educational policy and accreditation standards (EPAS).* Alexandria, VA: Author.

The Coalition for Asian American Children and Families (CAACF). (2001). *Crossing the divide: Asian American families and the child welfare system.* Retrieved August 12, 2008, from www.cacf.org

Drachman, D. (1992). A stage-of-migration framework for service to immigrant populations. *Social Work, 37*(1), 68–72.

Drachman, D., & Ryan, A. S. (1991). Immigrants and refugees. In A. Gitterman (Ed.), *Handbook of social work practice with vulnerable populations* (pp. 618–646). New York: Columbia University Press.

Fong, L. G. W., & Gibbs, J. T. (1995). Facilitating service to multicultural communities in a dominant culture setting: An organizational perspective. *Administration in Social Work, 19*(2), 1–24.

Fong, R., McRoy, R., & Ortiz Hendricks, C. (Eds.). (2006). *Intersecting child welfare, substance abuse, and family violence: Culturally competent approaches.* Washington, DC: Council on Social Work Education.

Huntington, S. (2004). The Hispanic challenge. *Foreign Policy.* Retrieved February 23, 2004, from http://www.foreignpolicy.com/story/cms

Lum, D. (1999). *Cultural competent practice: A framework for growth and action.* Belmont, CA: Brooks Cole.

McRoy, R., & Vick, J. (2001). Intersecting child welfare, substance abuse and domestic violence. In R. Fong, R. McRoy, & C. Ortiz Hendricks (Eds.), *Intersecting child welfare, substance abuse and family violence: Culturally competent approaches* (pp. 1–34). Alexandria, VA: Council on Social Work Education.

National Association of Social Workers. (1999). Code of ethics. Washington, DC: NASW Press.

National Association of Social Workers. (2001). *Standards for culturally competent social work practice.* Washington, DC: NASW Press.

National Association of Social Workers. (2007). Indicators for the Achievement of the NASW Standards for Cultural Competent Practice. Retrieved July 20, 2008, from http://www.socialworkers.org/practice/standards/NASWCulturalStandardsIndicators2006.pdf

Nybell, L. M., & Gray, S. S. (2004). Race, place, space: Meanings of cultural competence in three child welfare agencies. *Social Work, 49*(1), 17–26.

Ortiz Hendricks, C., & Fong, R. (2006). Ethnic sensitive practice with children and families. In N. B. Webb (Ed.), *Working with traumatized youth in child welfare* (pp. 135–154). New York: Guilford Press.

Pew Hispanic Center. (2008). Retrieved July 20, 2008, from http://www.nhcsl.com/newsletters/february2008/

Sun, An-Pyng. (2000). Helping substance-abusing mothers in the child welfare system: Turning crisis into opportunity. *Families in Society, 81*(2), 142–151.

Walker, S., Spohn, C., & DeLone, M. (2000). *Color of justice, race, ethnicity and crime in America* (2nd ed.). Belmont, CA: Wadsworth Publishing Company.

Webb, N. (2001). *Culturally diverse parent-child and family relationships: A guide for social workers and other practitioners.* New York: Columbia University Press.

Williams, T., & Fernandez, M. (2007). Horrific fire unites cultures in rituals of belief. *The New York Times,* March 10, 2007, Retrieved July 20, 2008, from http://www.lexisnexis.com/us/lnacademic/results/docview/docview.do?docLinkInd=true&risb=21_T439159918&format=GNBFI&sort=RELEVANCE&startDocNo=1&resultsUrlKey=29_T4349159921&cisb=22_T4349159920&treeMax=true&treeWidth=0&csi=6742&docNo=20

4 Theory and Social Work Practice With Immigrant Populations

BETTY GARCIA

Social work practice with immigrant populations poses many complicated challenges due to the multiple issues associated with the immigrant experience, ranging from personal adjustment issues to regional and federal policy initiatives. The increased visibility and growth of immigrant populations in the United States has captured the public's attention as it has in previous waves of immigration in American history (particularly in the early twentieth century, the 1920s, and the 1940s). The national debate on immigration has featured a climate of antagonism toward immigrants and unyielding efforts to restrict the participation of undocumented immigrants in the American economy. Although there is some question regarding the actual number of undocumented workers in the United States—whether 12 million or twice that amount—we can expect that social workers involved in service delivery to immigrants will encounter undocumented individuals and thus will have to deal with many complex issues.

The heightened national attention on the exponential growth of immigrant populations has been framed in the media to emphasize "foreign presence within U.S. borders" with minimal attention to the contribution of immigrant workers to the U.S. economy and American life. Rumbaut (2005, p. 14) proposes that current immigration represents "a dialectical consequence of the expansion of the nation to its post–World War II position of culture global hegemony" and as the United States has become more "involved in the world, the world has become more deeply involved in America." He goes on to suggest that the sociopolitical challenges associated with enhanced pluralization cannot be reduced to "simply internal matters" (p. 17). This perspective is illustrated by an inclination by many to label all undocumented immigrants as "illegal" rather than distinguish and recognize the productive economic role that many immigrants have in American society. Because of the increased international focus on immigration, social workers have an even greater responsibility to engage in critical thinking about immigration and exercise incisiveness in their engagement with immigrants and assessment of their needs.

Successful practice with immigrants is guided by concepts and theories that enhance perception of their presenting concerns, and provide a basis for precise assessment that lead to relevant interventions to enhance their functioning and expand their resources. This chapter will address theoretical and conceptual resources for practice with immigrant populations with the intention of identifying conceptual frameworks and ideas that can serve as guides to assist in the development of practice orientations and skills that meet the multifaceted needs of immigrants and their communities.

Attention to immigrant issues and human rights issues is a social work concern in that "social workers see the impact of immigrant and refugee polices in their everyday practice . . . and often find that their ability for effective practice "is constrained by immigration policies. . . . [particularly] . . . policies that limit family visitation and . . . reunification" (National Association of Social Workers [NASW], 2006, p. 8). Moreover, NASW proposes that policies are needed to provide "relief to long-term resident undocumented families" and to support amnesty and citizenship paths for those who have responsibly dealt with their immigration status (NASW, 2006, p. 8). For these reasons, NASW advocates for an end to human rights violations, provision of fair and humane immigration laws and practices, a well as foreign policies that alleviate the conditions that lead individuals to emigrate from their countries. The last chapter of this text will address the role of macro advocacy in social work practice.

The first part of this chapter will discuss assumptions about the role of theory as well as implications for skills and interventions. It will also address concepts that, although distinct from theories in their scope and function, are invaluable in their capacity to provide a basis for systemic implementation of practice skills. A central question is, "What theory, used in what way, in relation to what life experiences?" I propose that the complexity and nature of practice with immigrants requires practitioner knowledge of the larger societal debates and perspectives as well as individual, family, and community needs of immigrant populations.

The second part of this chapter will discuss theories and concepts that can frame practice with immigrants, beginning with themes and issues currently being discussed in the sociopolitical context and the American sensibility about how to respond to immigrant presence. Finally, the chapter will conclude with a summary of various perspectives of social work theory, from empowerment to family systems, and how these various perspectives can inform aspects of the immigrant experience and address the needs of immigrants and their communities.

THE ROLE OF THEORY AND CONCEPTS IN GUIDING PRACTICE

Theory of practice curriculum introduces both *theories* and *concepts* as frameworks to guide practice. In principle, theories are distinguished by their capacity to provide accuracy in describing discrete phenomena, their predictive value (Hawkings, 1998) and by their ability to represent a "set of statements about the relationships between facts and/or concepts" (Pozzuto, 2007, p. 71). Concepts, on the other hand, although more limited, signify dynamics and/or factors associated with a category; that is, they identify the uniqueness and relationship between particular entities. Although not expected to describe reality, theories are expected to "make sense of what would otherwise be inscrutable or unmeaning... findings" (Kaplan, 1964, p. 302) and facilitate a "particular way of seeing and acting" (Pozzuto, 2007, p. 79).

Pozzuto's thoughtful discussion on types of theories similarly points out dissimilar functions of two general categories of social work theories: *technical-rational* theories and *generative* theories. Drawing from Kondrat's (1992) work, he proposes that technical-rational theory is intended for explanation whereas generative theory "is intended for understanding" (p. 69), for the purpose of creating better lives, meeting basic human needs, and changing social structures. The postmodern conception of theory, as discussed by Pozzuto and demonstrated by Dean (2001), brings attention to how different theories lead to distinct, myriad lens that interpret experience from diverse value assumptions that lead to explicit intervention approaches (i.e., techniques and strategies) and attends to the value assumptions underlying various theoretical frames. Theoretical frames with underlying values that are inclusive, seek complexity, recognize resources within individuals, and articulate real-world barriers as well as transactional dynamics have been selected for discussion in this chapter.

Societal and Legal Contexts

The scope of practice with immigrants requires the use of theories and concepts that assist in the development of accuracy in perceiving immigrants from *their* point of view and process skills that promote active listening and attunement, which undergird engagement with immigrant populations. This requires suspension of one's own biases and beliefs, comprehension of viable theories and concepts, and the ability to draw on theories for the purpose of enhancing observation, recognizing the world of the immigrant, and engaging in a way that creates the foundation for successful professional intervention.

The increasingly punitive reactions and intense political debates that currently frame the context of practice with immigrants are such that denial of these contextual environmental realities by helping professionals can potentially compromise the ethical qualities that distinguish professional practice. Any discussion on the role of theory in social work practice with immigrants would be remiss if it were not to consider the following environmental factors in the person-environment, transactional perspective that guides social work formulations and interventions.

The early twenty-first century has witnessed the intensified use of raids, legal initiatives, and anti-immigrant sentiments and motives unlike any seen in U.S. history since the early twentieth century (Montgomery, 2007). The legislative and regional reactions to reduce undocumented presence affects employers, landowners, and documented and undocumented immigrants alike in ways that threaten to undermine local economies, and threaten community life in neighborhoods across the country. Efforts to eliminate nondocumented immigrant presence in the United States oscillate to such a degree that they are akin to moving targets in their focus; however, certain broad intentions maintain center attention in legislative initiatives and regional responses. At the federal level, current broad policy themes include increased border security, harsher employer/landlord penalties, increased severity in citizenship paths, enhanced community surveillance programs, and a modified guest worker program. Methods suggested to address each of these are described below.

Increased Border Security

- Fund a fortified southern border fence that would include virtual features
- Increase the size of the southern border patrol force by almost double and, potentially, hire private contractors (i.e., mercenaries) as part of the patrol force
- Train more enforcement personnel, including local police
- Detain more undocumented immigrants caught at the border
- Penalize landowners for border tunnels on their properties where immigrant passage has occurred

Harsher Employer/Landlord Penalties

- Raise fines for employers who hire undocumented workers (e.g., "reckless" hiring of undocumented workers leading to $50,000 fines); making the hiring of undocumented workers a felony rather than a misdemeanor charge; defining offenses as criminal rather than civil
- Require federally funded employers to implement an employment verification system, and to dismiss workers whose social security numbers do not match social security records within 90 days
- Impose fines on landlords who rent to undocumented residents
- Require registration for a rental permit

Increased Severity in Citizenship/Residency Pathways

- Establishment of a three-tier system for immigrants to secure citizenship status that would require, for some, application for immigration in their home country
- Require a $370 replacement card for legal permanent residents (i.e., green card holders) who were issued their documentation between 1979 and 1989 and do not have expiration dates
- Increase citizenship fees to $1,000

Enhanced Surveillance Initiatives

- Require law enforcement to investigate the citizenship status of individuals arrested for a felony or a DUI
- Issue tickets (e.g., $500) to drivers who cannot speak adequate English with police officers
- Conduct informal investigations on immigrants who commit misdemeanors
- Increase barriers to securing state identification documents

Modified Guest Worker Program

- Streamline an inefficacious agricultural guest worker program
- Create conditions (via an ambiguous legal status for nondocumented workers) that promote a marginalized underclass comprised of nondocumented and legal residents in American society

Although it may be tempting to limit one's analysis of the origins of the hostile and exclusionary reactions of some American policy makers to American economic factors, there is much international evidence to support the role of international factors, such as a general undermining of worker's rights around the world (Lee, 2006).

Experiences of Immigrants

The experiences of immigrants and their families are filled with examples of personal, social, economic, and political issues that require coping, adjustment, and adaptation. These events can be experienced as traumatic and/or may exacerbate past traumas. The proposed policies described above give practitioners a sense of the currently hostile sociopolitical climate that immigrants encounter once they arrive in the United States. Recognition and acknowledgment of trends in the environment such as politics, economics, and demographics, are basic to a transactional approach in practice. Elements of immigrants' experiences that are essential to explore in assessment for the purpose of formulation and focus of interventions include:[1]

1. The process of immigration: Was the move voluntary or involuntary? Anticipated or not anticipated? What were the points of transit on the way to the United States? Who was left behind, what separations occurred with family members? What is the status of immigration documentation?
2. Social power changes and coping: Have there been socioeconomic, educational, occupational adjustments? Shifts in new employment or unemployment status? Shifts in family decision making due to structural family changes? What are the effects of language and literacy fluency in the new country? Is the immigrant facing workplace-related stressors? If so, what types of stressors (e.g., supervisory, interpersonal, xenophobic, immigration authorities)?

3. Economic and housing resources: What are the immigrant's debt commitments and assets? What is the status of housing (e.g., quality), transportation, access to communication technology?
4. Physical and psychological health status: Are the immigrant's basic needs for food and shelter being met? Can the immigrant utilize and/or access professional health providers and/or cultural healers? Are there any antecedent health conditions prior to immigration, during the immigration process (e.g., loss of health, limb)? What is the immigrant's current health status?
5. Family system and social networks: What are the family constellations, structures, communication patterns, multigenerational experiences, and coping abilities? What social support systems, if any, is the family involved with (e.g., extended family, friends, religious, community, political, recreational)? To what degree is the individual or family isolated and/or active with social contacts?
6. Cultural: Profile and qualities of individuals' social identity? In what ways and to what degree is the individual identified with his or her traditional culture, with the new American culture, and/or with other cultures (e.g., religious, people with disabilities, gender orientation)?

Assessment issues to address in practice with immigrants will vary depending on service delivery mission, as will the scope of practice, and an all-inclusive review of significant concerns is beyond the focus of this chapter. Other chapters will address in more detail topics such as health (chapter 5), mental health (chapter 6), employment (chapter 8), and other issues that immigrants face. However, the list presented above may be useful to the practitioner in acknowledging the range of multilevel and multisystemic concerns in the lives of immigrants that theoretical approaches and concepts are in principle invoked in the helping relationship and in advocacy efforts.

CONCEPTUAL AND THEORETICAL RESOURCES FOR PRACTICE WITH IMMIGRANT POPULATIONS

The contextual and experiential issues noted above highlight the importance of informed practice with immigrants that is multisystemic (i.e., micro, mezzo, macro) and is based on theoretical orientations that facilitate direct service based on strong clinical process skills and promote macro level interventions. Frey and Dupper's (2005) discussion on the need for a "broader clinical approach" in the twenty-first century due to the presentation of increasingly complex problems articulates a key theory of practice considerations with immigrants. Practice has never been more compelled to require knowledge, values, and skills that include clinical interventions and "multilevel interventions that target both personal issues and social justice concerns" (p. 34). Moreover, there is an increase in the social work practice literature that addresses the need for theoretical approaches that take into account power differentials, empowerment, and critical thinking as provided (for example) by feminist, postmodernist, and oppression theories and concepts. This growing literature in social work is direly needed for the multifaceted and trying situations faced by practitioners serving this population.

Strong clinical skills that build trust and rapport, and demonstrate cultural and linguistic competency, are particularly needed with immigrants who all too often experience adversarial encounters within their new host country. At the same time, macro level interventions, learned from work with individuals and families and based upon strong clinical skills, are also needed for engagement and macro advocacy efforts and/or program and policy development. Practitioners must necessarily demonstrate clinical skill in engaging individuals and families, regardless of the level of intervention. The many social work skills that have a vital role in practice with this group cannot all be addressed here. However, the following brief descriptions of different approaches will identify theoretical orientations and concepts that are vital in grounding practice that is curious, inclusive, and collaborative.

Unequivocally, effective practice with immigrants embodies a biopsychosocial, spiritual, cultural perspective within a person environment interaction, and a transactional framework for the purpose of addressing the numerous levels of adaptation (e.g., personal, familial, economic, political) evoked by the immigration process. The biopsychosocial concept focuses our attention on contributions of *health status, behavioral* (thoughts, feelings, actions), *familial, social* network, and societal factors in the lives of immigrants. The *spiritual* and *cultural* aspects focus our attention on immigrants' beliefs, values, and practices that bring meaning to their lives whether they are religious, nonmaterial, or civic in nature. Cultural competence will be addressed more fully later.

The person-environment interaction, transactional approach (Woods & Hollis, 2000) emphasizes evaluating the "goodness of fit" between needs and environmental resources to meet those needs. Discounting or omitting critical assessment information can lead to lost opportunities to join the client in reflection of significant events and exploration of individual choice and environmental resources as promoted in a transactional approach. The bio-psychosocial, cultural, spiritual transactional foundations of social work practice promote looking clearly at strengths, needs, and vulnerabilities of the individual and in the physical and social environment for the purpose of assessment and intervention.

While national sentiment currently is inclined to understand immigrants' behavior by exclusively focusing on *their* behavior as the unit of analysis, the person-environment focus suggests factoring in macro level factors (such as poverty and federal policies, for example) to more fully understand the experiences of immigrants. Overreliance on factors related to individual behavior risks blaming the victim, which could result in social workers colluding with a largely unresponsive and unreceptive environment. Likewise, overreliance on environmental factors risks disempowering the individual by not recognizing and/or minimizing choices and decisions exercised by individuals themselves. The art of social work practice in this case requires holding several perspectives, individual and environmental, in mind and holding an either/and perspective, rather than either/or approaches.

Acknowledgment of the multifaceted dimensions of human experience is supported by the strengths perspective (Saleebey, 2006) and empowerment approach (Gutierrez, Parsons, & Cox, 1998; Rose, 2000) in that these frameworks promote exploration of psychosocial resources identified by immigrants themselves, from their own subject viewpoint. The following will present several theoretical perspectives and associated questions relevant to practice with immigrants.

EMPOWERMENT THEORY

Empowerment theory is quintessentially a social work approach in that it promotes social justice and advocacy, addresses the role of social power, normalizes difference, and occurs on personal, interpersonal, and political levels that encompass power relations (Gutierrez & Lewis, 1999; Payne, 2005). As an advocacy-oriented approach, empowerment concepts promote critical thinking, examination of knowledge construction, and the development of "resources, strategies and competencies to attain personal and collective goals" (Lee, 2001). By taking into account social justice and highlighting the inequity in socioeconomic structures and their effects on individuals, this approach opens up previously unrecognized alternatives and reduces the isolation and marginalization (Rose, 1990) so acutely experienced by immigrant populations. The social justice, problem solving, and historical perspectives provided in empowerment concepts address issues related to class, ethnicity, and gender (Lee, 2001). Thus, although driven by social and political factors, the empowerment approach is a psychologically transformative experience that strengthens connections.

While social practices that are co-constructed, mutual, collaborative, and inclusive are key components of empowerment work, an important challenge that remains is the preparation of practitioners who can develop working relationships where meaning making is produced by all participants and where all perspectives are legitimized (Rose, 2000). As a theory that highlights the relational aspects of practice and advocacy as a means to open new options for individuals, empowerment provides a framework within which immigrants are identified for services, then engaged in service delivery and advocacy efforts that affect their communities.

Empowerment Perspective: Implications for Practice

- Engagement skills: Without making assumptions about the immigrant's social identity and level of acculturation, what engagement skills are needed to attune to the individual and connect for the purpose of empowerment work?
- Personal: What needs to be known about the individual's worldview and his or her hopes in order to join him or her and move toward greater empowerment?
- Interpersonal: In relation to the individual's cultural worldview, who or what are important "others," whose participation would facilitate empowerment?
- Political: What is the individual's understanding and meaning making of the emigration and resettlement in America? What type of activities or discussions would be useful to facilitate the individual's framing (if not done already) of the sociopolitical factors that have a role in his or her life experiences? How can his or her efforts for advocacy be supported?

CULTURAL COMPETENCE

Practice with immigrant populations by definition occurs in diverse settings with diverse populations and requires skill in providing effective services in a context of difference. The factors noted above on the context of the immigrant experience and immigrant life course events illuminate the importance of practitioner competence in working with different ethnic cultures. This competence must include a wide range of skills that span from direct, face-to-face practice to organizational, programmatic policies that embody appreciation of diversity and demonstrate leadership in service delivery with diverse populations.

Cross-culturally competent direct service skills must draw from several conceptual frameworks and display a capacity for bringing knowledge of different cultures to one's practice. However, all this must be balanced with ethics, awareness of one's personal biases, and critical thinking about limitations in professional knowledge (Dean, 2001; Laird, 1998; Walker & Staton, 2000). Foremost, practitioners must manage ambiguity in the initial stages of contact with diverse individuals, focus on engagement skills, and bring some knowledge of the immigrant's historical and cultural context to bear. However, as Sue (1998) points out, this "knowledge" must be treated as hypothetical until the individual (immigrant) informs us of his or her uniqueness.

There are specific models and approaches that are valuable for their distinctive conceptual contributions. Cross, Bazron, Dennis, and Issacs (1989) provide a continuum-based model that includes doing harm at one end, various points of competence achievement in the middle, and, most importantly, as an anchor at the competence end of the continuum, the model emphasizes the vitally significant role of organizational proficiency and competency. A major contribution of the Cross et al. model is the reminder that individuals alone cannot maintain culturally competent practice in organizational settings; commitment to difference must be demonstrated at the organizational level.

NASW (2007) recently published the Indicators for the Achievement of the Standards for Cultural Competence in Social Work Practice, which were produced by the NASW National Committee on Ethnic and Racial Diversity (NCORED). The development of the indicators advances the previously published Cultural Competence Standards by operationalizing the standards and further expanding awareness of domains of the standards that address practitioner awareness and skills, service delivery, advocacy, workforce concerns, professional education, language diversity, and leadership. Also, the National Center for Cultural Competence at Georgetown University offers materials and tools to assist in self-assessment of professionals and organizations and strategies for improving competency. Both of these sources are cited in Additional Resources at the end of this chapter.

For more information on cultural competence, see chapter 3.

Cultural Competence and Proficiency: Implications for Practice

- Engagement: Practitioners need to ask themselves,
  - What do I need to do to have credibility as a helping professional in the eyes of the immigrant and his or her family?
  - In relation to an immigrant's culture, what would be useful to know in order to start a conversation with him or her, or the family? How do I say hello in a way that communicates presence?
- Culturally Competent Self-Awareness
  - What cultural baggage do I bring to my encounters with immigrants from cultures that are unfamiliar to me (e.g., negative stereotypes)?
  - What messages did I grow up with, in my family and my neighborhood, about difference?
  - How clear am I about my social and cultural identity in relation to values, beliefs, and practices that I share with groups that I identify with (e.g., how did I get my name)?
- Sustaining culturally competent interventions with immigrants, their families, and communities:
  - What do I need to take initiative in exploring diversity considerations in supervision (e.g., structure, probes, responsive supervisor)?
  - How do I use supervision to balance the knowledge I bring to my practice with the process skills that promote learning about the immigrants themselves?
- Organizational Proficiency
  - What message does my organization (at all levels) convey regarding cultural competence? Is it something that staff is encouraged to explore; is it something that the organization states in its mission and purpose?
  - What supports do I need to pursue culturally competent practice in my organizational setting?

STRENGTH-BASED PRACTICE

The strengths perspective (Saleeby, 2002) promotes attention to the assets and resources embodied by all individuals, particularly in expression and manifestation of resilience, wisdom, and knowledge. As an empowerment-based perspective, a strengths approach intends to "discover and expand resources" (p. 9). It is distinguished by a focus on the significance of relational skills and partnership, is inclusive, and supports experiences that facilitate regeneration and wholeness (Rose, 2000; Saleeby, 2002). Practice from a strengths perspective demonstrates validation and recognition of individual uniqueness, capacity of individuals to overcome hurtful life events, and significance of belonging to a community as a measure of individual wholeness (Saleeby, 2002). Outcomes will show a noticeable expansion of resources to meet the needs of individuals and their families, and a greater sense of well-being and life satisfaction based on possession of hope for the present and the future.

Strengths Perspective: Implications for Practice

Exploratory questions to guide recognition of strengths identified by Saleeby (2002) focus on survival, support, high points in individuals' lives, hoped-for possibilities, and esteem. Such areas of inquiry would potentially open up the following with immigrants:

- What decisions and adaptations were made in response to stressors regarding the departure from the country of origin, during the immigration transition, and in the resettlement process?
- What inner strength and supports were used by the immigrants and their families as a means to persevere in their decisions, and to protect themselves?
- Who has been there to support the individual (within the family, friendships, community groups, religious communities, and other organizations) in the transition, immigration, and resettlement? How were these resources found (e.g., the person found them, or were they given)? What requests have been made for support that were not responded to?
- What have been some exceptionally positive parts of the individual's and the family's lives in the past that perhaps represent something they would like to reestablish in their lives in their

new home? What individuals or organizations have helped them achieve their hopes?
- What kinds of events and activities in the immigrant's life signify contentment and well-being?

Information about an immigrant's successes in overcoming challenges is informative in identifying long-term goals related to "flourishing and growth" and different from short-term survival goals regarding resettlement priorities, such as housing, food, employment, and/or legal issues. Finding out about what the immigrant had to cope with will also reveal a measure of what and how much strength and support the individual and family has. The individual's image of "a good life" will convey meaningful values that may be cultural or spiritual in nature or may identify the very purpose of the immigration. Most significant is the view of cultural identifications and practices as strengths and resources, rather than deficits.

ECOSYSTEMS THEORY

Systems theory (Von Bertalanffy, 1968) and *ecological theory* combine in a theoretical formulation, *ecosystems theory* (Germain & Gitterman, 1996), that highlights the interdependent and adaptive aspects of behavior. Payne's (2005) summary of systems theory points out the importance of understanding behavior in the context of systems (e.g., family, peer support, culture, Immigration and Customs Enforcement/ICE) with which individuals interact. Moreover, Payne discusses various features of systems functioning, such as boundaries and open and closed interactions and entropy that assist us in comprehending individual and family behavior. Ecological theory illuminates the significant role of goodness of fit between system needs (e.g., food, housing, validation, social support, safety, integration into one's community) and environmental resources and adaptive coping that is required for optimal functioning by all size systems such as immigrants and their families and communities.

Systems and Ecological Theory: Implications for Practice

- What systems are the immigrant and his or her family part of (e.g., social network, extended family, spiritual, religious, civic, cultural) that are essential to know about in order to view their behavior in context?

- What adaptive, coping responses have the immigrant and his or her family demonstrated, to what situations, under what conditions? How can the worker assist in applying these adaptive responses to other challenges or settings (e.g., reframe, invoke internalized or external cultural resources to enhance coping with stressful or overwhelming situations)?
- How can the worker collaboratively support the immigrant and family in utilizing and applying creative and imaginative alternatives to problem solving (e.g., promoting equifinality, that is, identifying many alternative ways to achieve a proposed goal)?

FAMILY SYSTEMS THEORY

As a theory of family systems, Bowen Family theory focuses our attention on multigenerational issues, differentiation of family members, family emotional field, triangulation, emotional cutoff, and societal emotional process (Kerr & Bowen, 1988). Bowenian theory is invaluable for its focus on multigenerational issues, patterns, and themes and the use of the genogram as a vehicle for the exploration of multigenerational family experiences and responses to those experiences. As such it directs our attention to the powerful role of family history, self-image, coping, and interaction in influencing an individual immigrant's development of complexity.

From a larger system perspective, the concept of triangulation suggests evaluation of the potentially powerful role of organizations. For example, the system could be seen as consisting of the government (e.g., U.S. Immigration and Customs Enforcement as one point of the triangle, advocacy groups as another part of the triangle, and of course, immigrant families themselves as the third part). Also, "Bowen recognized . . . class and ethnic prejudice as examples of toxic social emotional processes" and the importance of high levels of differentiation to cope with these "destructive social influences" (Nichols & Schwartz, 2007, p. 85).

A culturally competent application of family systems theory recognizes the uniqueness of traditional cultures and the intersections between acculturation and traditional values. This suggests it would be extremely important to explore and understand the meaning of family behaviors in the cultural context of each family, and utilize family systems theory to develop hypotheses to be matched with the family's realities.

Family Systems Theory: Implications for Practice

- Who is defined as family (relatives, neighbors, friends, religious community members)?
- What is the family experience in the emigration and resettlement? Were family members left behind? If so, what adjustments did this mean for the family?
- What theoretical biases might the practitioner bring regarding boundary issues? What kinds of questions should be raised before making assumptions regarding parentification of minors (e.g., the effect on the minor) that could interfere with seeing the family function in its wholeness?
- What life cycle *and* life course events has the family experienced in the immigration process and how has the family coped with these experiences?

OPPRESSION CONCEPTS

Oppression concepts enhance practice knowledge and skills in that they represent frameworks that explore the role of social power in the lives of immigrants, their families, and their communities. Social power is essential to understand because it endows unearned privilege and can cast social groups as targets of negative stereotypes. *Critical thinking* concepts complement analysis of social power and its effects in personal life (e.g., the public is personal) in their emphasis on analyzing underlying value assumptions of propositions and also by bringing clarity to situations through an examination of diverse perspectives (Gambrill, 2005). Oppression concepts thus contribute an understanding of how low social power and lack of societal validation for certain individuals illuminates ways that populations can be marginalized, invalidated, and deemed invisible. Rose (2000) proposes that oppression is foremost a relational dynamic that is perpetrated at the societal institutional level. However, it is carried out and maintained via the interactional, day-to-day activities between individuals. For example, a practitioner can maintain oppression via roles that are ascribed by virtue of institutional contexts.

Bulhan[2] (1987) developed indicators that are insightful in understanding the impact of oppression in the lives of individuals. This formulation of oppression focused on the role of liberty as the freedom to make choices, and oppression as the absence of liberty, introduces stressors relative to captivity. The liberty-based choices compromised by oppression are:

- *Space:* Physical and economic—the freedom and resources to go where one wants, and the quality of those choices. This has implications for understanding the effects of colonization, slavery, and segregation.
- *Time:* Although we assume all individuals have choices regarding how they use their 24 hours per day, we must ask, "How much time is yours?" and factor in time demands introduced by responsibilities and roles (e.g., single parent, worker, slave).
- *Energy:* Are individuals' lives characterized by living to work or working to live? How is an individual's energy expended, on what tasks, determined by whom? Who is benefiting from the use of one's time?
- *Access to information:* The digital divide has become legend in the twenty-first century as a measure of marginalization and underclass status. To what degree is there equal distribution of access to information via press, technology, social sources? Inquiry is directed thus: "Who defines the rules of information access, societal norms, and values promulgated via media?" and "What is the basis of regulation governing information access?"
- *Mobility:* This regards one's freedom to go where, when, and with whom one chooses and is directly related to the factors identified above. The experience of documented and undocumented immigrants alike with Immigration and Customs Enforcement (ICE) workplace raids seeking undocumented immigrants with criminal histories and intensified surveillance (e.g., review of documentation if there is due cause to suspect nondocumentation) has prompted a diminished sense of safety in immigrant and traditional communities resulting in fear of public visibility.

Bulhan (1987) proposed a constrained-strained theory of oppression that identified three key dynamics:

1 Constraint: The objective social conditions that impose limits on privileges and rights. These include barriers, social and institutional in origin, that create, maintain, and justify inequities of the rights and privileges of individuals, such as immigrants.

2 Strain: The subjective world of perceptions, feelings, and meanings. Strain refers to the experience of undermined and/or depleted psychological resources and results in distortion or diminishment of perceptual and attitudinal capacities. Individual and familial variations in abilities to adapt to the strain can result in various types of vulnerabilities.
3 Threshold of tolerance: The presence of cultural norms and laws, extralegal and legal sanctions that regulate and control diversity and difference.

Oppression Concepts: Implications for Practice

- In what ways have the immigrant and his or her family experienced constraints? Under what conditions, and in what context? Who were the participants? What were the outcomes? How have the individual and family coped and adapted to constraints related to their documented or undocumented status?
- How does the immigrant manage and interpret his or her life experience arising from negative stereotypes and/or constraints? Who does the immigrant blame (himself or herself, the family, their culture)? Does he or she hold perspectives that may contribute to their challenges (e.g., possibly behavioral, legal, societal, or religious beliefs)?
- How can the worker explore the implications of power differentials in interactions with the immigrant and as a focus of supervisory feedback?

PRACTITIONER SELF-AWARENESS

Concepts that aid professional self-awareness represent a cornerstone of practice knowledge with immigrant populations. The loaded and potentially highly charged context of practice with immigrants requires heightened awareness of countertransferential issues that can arise *both* in relation to the individual experience (Goldstein, 2001) and intergroup experience as Bowen's (1978) societal projection concept shed light on. Interpersonal countertransference concepts remind practitioners to be mindful of how vulnerabilities and needs may be exacerbated due to the timing of the contact or how working with a particular person may arouse feelings from the practitioner's own past. Bowen's concept highlighted how social groups can impose unwanted qualities onto other social groups, thus suggesting a role that the professional's social identity (i.e., group identifications) can have in response to immigrant qualities, real or imagined.

Practitioner Self-Awareness: Implications for Practice

- What awareness does the worker bring in relation to culturally based countertransference and societal projection? What motivation and commitment does the worker have to explore these issues (e.g., same ethnicity workers of different class backgrounds and/or acculturation levels)?
- How will the worker manage his or her comfort and discomfort levels in practice (i.e., explore the triggers), particularly in relation to differences in affect conveyed in communication (i.e., differences in communication styles)?

CONCLUSION

National and regional responses to the presence of immigrants is characterized by several themes. Significant consideration has been given to the creation of a guest worker program, various strategies for providing options to secure citizenship status, shoring up a border patrol, and building of a border fence. At times where national legislation has not clarified policy toward immigrants, regional alternatives have gushed forth. These regional alternatives and national debates are the context of social work practice and have impact on social workers' perspectives. Theory and concepts guide practice, in principle, to enhance and promote effective interventions.

America has seemingly lost perspective on its origins as a land of immigrants; instead, federal, state, and local policies (both proposed and enacted) are attempting to manage the presence of immigrants in increasingly hostile and punitive ways. These conditions challenge social workers to creatively and critically utilize theories and concepts in line with the ethical and professional mandate that promotes social justice and recognizes the self-determination and dignity of all individuals, families, and communities. Theories that promote an understanding of the sociopolitical context of immigrant populations, as well as linguistic and cultural competencies, are essential for effective social work practice.

CASE STUDIES

The following case studies illustrate life experiences commonly encountered by immigrants. You are invited to discuss the following questions about each case.

1. What social work issues are raised by this vignette?
2. What legal issues are raised by this vignette?
3. What additional key information would help you understand the identified concerns?
4. What is the role and function of the social worker working with the client and/or family in this vignette?
5. What short-term interventions and resources do you think would be helpful in this situation? Long-term interventions and resources?
6. Which theory (or theories) of social work practice discussed in this chapter provide the best framework for analyzing or responding to the situation described in the vignette?
7. What, if anything, could be done on an organizational (mezzo) level to help in this case? What could or should be done on the policy (macro) level?

Case Study 1: Stripped Status

A 25-year-old woman from South America travels to the United States alone on a student visa for graduate study in biology at a college in the Northeast. While in college, she starts dating a young man, 27, from southern California. She is absorbed in her studies and has little social contact except for her relationship with her boyfriend.

At the end of their studies they marry and move to southern California, a location which is far from his family, and where she does not have any established friendships or social contacts. Upon arrival in southern California she immediately applies for permanent residency. However, before her application is approved, her husband dies in a swimming accident. The U.S. Immigration "widow penalty" policy requires that her application be denied, because she is no longer married to a U.S. citizen.

Case Study 2: Pickup for Detention

Gabriela, 8, and Roberto, 10, the youngest of four siblings with immigrant parents, ride the bus every morning for an eight-mile drive to school.

Their parents are farm workers who live in a California Central Valley neighborhood and work in different fields depending on the season. One morning, the bus is stopped by the California Highway Patrol. Officials board the bus and take Gabriela and Roberto into custody. The children are driven to a detention center administered by U.S. Immigration and Customs Enforcement. At the detention facility they are informed that their parents were apprehended and are being detained for deportation. Gabriela and Roberto will be held in detention until deportation along with their parents.

Case Study 3: Citizenship Application

After a year in detention, the Ramos family (Rosalie, 37; Ricardo, 39; and two daughters, ages 7 and 11) are released after one of Ricardo's sisters, a U.S. citizen, files for their permanent residency due to the failing health of Ricardo's brother. Ricardo's brother is a U.S. citizen, whose health is deteriorating due to diabetes and commencement of dialysis. Ricardo's health status in general is good, except for the loss of his foot, which occurred during his immigration three years ago. While relieved to be out of detention, the family must now deal with the family health issues and adjustment issues as they reintegrate into their community life.

Case Study 4: Raids in the Neighborhood

Alicia is a single parent who lives with her 16-year-old daughter and 17-year-old son in a small rural community on the East Coast. Both her children are well on their way to completing high school and hope to enter college. Alicia's parents were immigrant farm workers, as was she until the age of 12. Born in the United States, a high school graduate, and employed as a store clerk, she is strongly influenced by the traditional Latino culture practiced by her parents.

Recent raids by the ICE agency in her community have sought out undocumented immigrants with criminal backgrounds. In the last month a large farming employer was raided by ICE agents, who arrested approximately 1,350 individuals and from that group, identified 234 who were undocumented and had criminal histories. This raid was one of several that has terrified the community because of the risk of arrest for residents who appear to be undocumented, even though they are documented or legal citizens. Alicia, like many of her neighbors, only leaves the house when she has to (i.e., for work) and has arranged for food delivery at her home by an individual who provides that service at an exorbitant cost.

NOTES

1. Assessment content modified from Melendez (2006).
2. I understand that Dr. Bulhan developed these concepts in conjunction with Chet Pierce, MD.

ADDITIONAL RESOURCES

National Association of Social Workers, Indicators for the Achievement of the Standards for Cultural Competence in Social Work Practice: http://www.socialworkers.org/practice/standards/NASWCulturalStandardsIndicators2006.pdf

National Center for Cultural Competence at Georgetown University: http://www11.georgetown.edu/research/gucchd/nccc/index.html

Social Work Today (offers numerous articles about practice with immigrants): www.socialworktoday.com

REFERENCES

Bowen, M. (1978). *Family therapy in clinical practice.* New York: Jason Aronson.

Bulhan, H. (1987). The constrained-strained theory: A general theory of deviance. *BHM Review 1.* Boston: Basic Health Management, Inc.

Cross, T., Bazron, B., Dennis, K., & Issacs, M. (1989). *Towards a culturally competent system of care* (Vol. 1). Washington, DC: CASSP Technical Assistance Center, Georgetown University Child Development Center.

Dean, R. (2001). The myth of cross-cultural competency. *Families in Society, 82*(6), 623–630.

Frey, A., & Dupper, D. (2005). A broader conceptual approach to clinical practice for the 21st century. *Children & Schools, 27*(1), 33–44.

Gambrill, E. (2005). *Critical thinking in clinical practice* (2nd ed.). New York: Wiley.

Germain, C., & Gitterman, A. (1996). *The life model of social work practice: Advanced theory and practice.* New York: Columbia University Press.

Goldstein, E. (2001). *Object relations theory and self psychology in social work practice.* New York: The Free Press.

Gutierrez, L., & Lewis, E. (1999). *Empowering women of color.* New York: Columbia University Press.

Gutierrez, L., Parsons, R., & Cox, E. (1998). *Empowerment in social work practice.* Pacific Grove, CA: Brooks/Cole.

Hawkings, S. (1998). *A brief history of time.* New York: Bantam Books.

Kaplan, A. (1964). *The conduct of inquiry.* New York: Chandler Publishing Company.

Kerr, M., & Bowen, M. (1988). *Family evaluation: An approach based on Bowen theory.* New York: W.W. Norton & Company.

Kondrat, M. D. (1992). Reclaiming the practical: Formal and substantive rationality in social work. *Social Service Review, 66*(2), 237–255.

Laird, J. (1998). Theorizing culture: Narrative ideas and practice principles. In M. McGoldrick (Ed.), *Revisioning family therapy: Race, culture and gender in clinical practice* (pp. 20–36). New York: Guilford Press.

Lee, J. (2001). *The empowerment approach to social work practice: Building the beloved community* (2nd ed.). New York: Columbia University Press.

Lee, T. (2006, April 17). A new domestic and global strategy. *The Nation*, 20–22.

Melendez, M. (2006). *Assessing psychosocial stressors and supports of immigrant families.* Course handout. Boston: Simmons College, School of Social Work.

Montgomery, D. (2007, August 19). Immigration anger seems to usher in era of xenophobia. *Fresno Bee* (Fresno, CA), pp. A1, A22.

National Association of Social Workers. (2006). *Immigration policy toolkit. President's Initiative, weaving the fabrics of diversity, 2006–2008.* Washington, DC: Author.

National Association of Social Workers. (2007). *Indicators for the achievement of the NASW standards for cultural competence in social work practice.* Washington, DC: Author.

Nichols, M., & Schwartz, R. (2007). *The essentials of family therapy.* Boston: Pearson/Allyn & Bacon.

Payne, M. (2005). *Modern social work theory* (3rd ed.). Chicago, IL: Lyceum Books.

Pozzuto, R. (2007). Understanding theory, practicing social work. In S. Witkin & D. Saleebey (Eds.), *Social work dialogues.* Alexandria, VA: Council on Social Work Education.

Rose, S. (1990). Advocacy/empowerment: An approach to clinical practice for social work. *Journal of Sociology & Social Welfare, 17*(2), 41–51.

Rose, S. (2000). Reflections on empowerment-based practice. *Social Work, 45*(5), 403–412.

Rumbaut, R. (2005). The melting pot and the pot: Assimilation and variety in American life. In P. Kivisto (Ed.), *Incorporating diversity: Rethinking assimilation in a multicultural era* (pp. 154–173). Boulder, CO: Paradigm.

Saleeby, D. (2002). *The strengths perspective in social work practice* (3rd ed.). Boston: Pearson/Allyn & Bacon.

Sue, S. (1998). In search of cultural competence in psychotherapy and counseling. *American Psychologist, 53*(4), 440–448.

Von Bertalanffy, L. (1968). *General systems theory: Foundations, development, applications.* New York: George Braziller.

Walker, R., & Staton, M. (2000). Multiculturalism in social work ethics. *The Journal of Social Work Education, 36*(3), 449–462.

Woods, M. E., & Hollis, F. (2000). *Casework: A psychosocial therapy* (5th ed.). New York: McGraw-Hill.

5 Social Work and Physical Health Issues of Immigrants

SARAH BLAIR SMITH

This chapter will deal with major health care issues that social workers need to know in working with immigrants. It will provide an introduction to the many complex, interconnected issues that social workers and their immigrant clients face as they navigate the United States health care system in an attempt to obtain quality health care.

In 2005, 5.6% of the population (16.8 million people) were legal permanent residents (LPRs) and 3.5% (10.5 million people) were estimated to be undocumented (Hoefer, Rytina, & Campbell, 2006). In other words, over 27 million people living in this country are immigrants who, depending upon when they arrived and their socioeconomic status, may have limited or no access to health insurance and limited access to health care. Furthermore, one-fifth of low-wage workers in the United States are immigrants and nearly half of all working immigrants, both documented and undocumented, earn less than twice the minimum wage. Immigrants often face medical conditions due to the interconnected issues of their employment, low socioeconomic status, lack of funds to buy health insurance or pay for health care, and lack of government and private sector policies, which do not protect the immigrant worker (AFL-CIO, 2005; Broder, 2007; Goldman, Smith, & Sood, 2006; Montoya, 2005).

As is discussed in chapter 8, immigrants are disproportionately represented in low-wage jobs in farming, fishing, forestry, maintenance, meat packing and poultry industries, manufacturing, construction, landscaping, the service industries, and garment industry sweatshops. Within these sectors, undocumented immigrants are more likely to work in the less skilled and more hazardous jobs. They face long days of hard physical labor that can cause or contribute to health problems such as musculoskeletal or repetitive motion injuries. Unsafe work conditions can lead to exposure to chemicals (in pesticides and chemical-based cleaning supplies), organic dust, allergens, and toxic gases, which can result in skin rashes, respiratory disease, and, in the long run, cancer (AFL-CIO, 2005; Lashuay et al., 2002; Pransky et al., 2002; Ruttenberg & Lazo, 2004; Schenker, 2007; Villarejo, 2003). The following two examples provide a glimpse of the myriad problems faced by immigrants as they try to support themselves and their families in this country. It is to be hoped that these examples will raise awareness about the role of the social worker in these situations.

In 2002, the Asian Immigrant Women Workers Clinic in Oakland, California, examined the health of women who attended their clinic and worked in California sewing factories, and the clinic found that 99% had diagnosed work-related injuries including back, neck, or shoulder strains or sprains causing pain severe enough to interfere with their daily activities. About one-third had not seen a doctor for their injuries. Almost all of the women (97%) were eligible to file for workman's compensation but either were not aware of the program or were afraid to file for fear of what their employer would do to them if they did (Lashuay et al., 2002).

The AFL-CIO (2005) conducted a study of Hispanics working in the construction industry and found that in 2000, although they made up less than 16% of the construction workforce, they suffered 23.5% of the fatal injuries. They also found that one of the major contributing factors to the fatalities was the lack of safety training in the workers' language. After trainings were conducted in Spanish, the workers reported using safe work practices, such as harnesses when working above the ground and protective equipment such as goggles. These trainings reduced the number of injuries and deaths (AFL-CIO, 2005; Ruttenberg & Lazo, 2004).

Against this backdrop of low wages, dangerous employment, lack of insurance, and lack of status, this chapter will examine policies that support health care services for documented, undocumented, and mixed-status families; barriers to health care; the healthy migrant phenomenon and acculturation; and health issues faced by specific immigrant groups such as detainees, workers, seniors, women, and children.

Finally, the chapter will look at some of the implications for social work practice that arise from these issues and provide discussion questions and several case studies.

FEDERAL LEGISLATION AFFECTING IMMIGRANT HEALTH CARE

A number of federal laws provide protections to all persons and help to make services accessible. For example, Title VI of the Civil Rights Act of 1964 prohibits organizations that receive federal funds from discriminating against individuals on the basis of race, creed, color, or national origin. The federal Office of Civil Rights and the courts have determined that discrimination on the basis of national origin includes failing to provide accommodation for individuals who do not speak or read English. Organizations receiving federal funds must provide oral and written language assistance to limited English proficient (LEP) individuals in a timely manner and at no cost to the individual if the language difference will adversely affect medical care or the provision of social services (Frates & Saint-Germain, 2004). Translator and interpreter services make it possible for patients who do not speak English to communicate with their health care providers.

In 1986, Congress passed the Consolidated Omnibus Budget Reconciliation Act of 1986, which included the Emergency Medical Treatment and Labor Act (EMTALA). This law ensures emergency medical care for all people who enter the emergency department of a hospital, including undocumented immigrants, regardless of their ability to pay. Hospital emergency departments must screen and stabilize all patients and cannot reject uninsured patients or transfer them to charity or county hospitals without first stabilizing them. This law makes it possible for immigrants to receive emergency treatment even if they do not have insurance or the financial resources to pay for their health care (Staiti, Hurley, & Katz, 2006).

The Personal Responsibility and Work Opportunity Reconciliation Act of 1996 (PRWORA) bars immigrants other than refugees and asylees from enrolling in Medicaid and State Children's Health Insurance Program (SCHIP) for the first five years of residency if they entered the United States on or after August 22, 1996. However, after five years, qualified immigrants can apply for Medicaid and SCHIP if they meet eligibility requirements (Broder, 2007). Unfortunately, not all immigrants are qualified. Section 1011 of the Medicare Modernization Act of 2003 authorized the disbursement of funds to hospitals and other facilities that provide emergency health care to undocumented immigrants. Originally, the facilities were required to ask immigrants their status at the time of treatment and give that information to the government in order to be reimbursed. A revision allows the data to be obtained indirectly. Unfortunately, there is still confusion about the law, and immigrants fear that if they seek care they will be discovered and deported. The fear of this law has acted as a barrier to undocumented immigrants who need emergency health care (Staiti et al., 2006). Entitlement to public benefits based on legal status is explored in more detail in chapter 13.

HEALTH CARE AVAILABLE FOR IMMIGRANTS

In addition to broad legislation discussed previously, an additional patchwork of federal laws enacted over the past two decades have made it very confusing to understand the type of health services available to immigrants of differing legal status. It is imperative that social workers have a good understanding of eligibility so that they can effectively assist their clients, especially those who do not understand English, the U.S. health care system, or U.S. laws.

PRWORA includes exceptions for certain types of services that are not affected by immigrant status. All immigrants, regardless of status, have "access to public health programs providing immunizations and/or treatment of communicable disease symptoms (whether or not those symptoms are caused by such a disease)" (Broder, 2007, p. 3). EMTALA provides emergency medical treatment for all immigrants, regardless of status or ability to pay; and PRWORA continues to allow all immigrants, regardless of status, to be eligible for Emergency Medicaid if they would be eligible for their own state's Medicaid program (Broder, 2007). Emergency Medicaid provides time-limited coverage for a medical emergency that is defined as "any severe medical condition (including labor and delivery) for which the absence of immediate medical attention could place an individual's health in serious jeopardy, seriously impair bodily functions, or result in serious dysfunction of any bodily organ or part" (Fremstad & Cox, 2004, p. 14). Once the coverage expires, it is up to the treating physician, health clinic, or hospital to reapply if the situation is still life threatening.

Documented Immigrants

As discussed in Chapter 2, documented immigrants are those who hold proper documentation (passport and visa). This category includes refugees, asylees, and lawful permanent residents. Refugees and asylees are exempt from the five-year ban and are eligible for Medicaid and SCHIP benefits for the first 18 months they are in the United States as long as they meet income requirements. After that, they must reapply in order to continue their coverage. Other qualified immigrants are eligible for Medicaid and SCHIP benefits five years after entry into the United States as long as they meet eligibility requirements (Broder, 2007).

During the first five years that documented immigrants are in this country, it is often a challenge for them to access health care. By 2004, however, in response to the PRWORA limitations, 21 states had chosen to use state funds to provide some form of replacement Medicaid and SCHIP health insurance to low-income immigrants regardless of their date of entry into the United States and, sometimes, regardless of their immigrant status as long as they meet income eligibility requirements. Unfortunately, state-funded programs are tied to state revenues and can be cut back or discontinued if revenues decrease (Aiker & Urrutia, 2004). Other options are safety net providers such as public and private hospitals, community health clinics, and nonprofit clinics (Broder, 2007; Staiti et al., 2006). In some states, documented immigrants may be eligible for breast and gynecologic cancer screenings and treatment. Because the access is dependent on the city, county, and state in which the individual resides, social workers must be aware of the laws governing access to health care and the health resources available in their geographic region.

Undocumented Immigrants

As noted above, undocumented immigrants are ineligible for almost all federal programs except Emergency Medicaid, hospital emergency department care, immunizations, and testing and treatment of symptoms of communicable diseases. In addition, they may be eligible for city, county, and state public health clinics depending upon local laws as well as nonprofit neighborhood clinics staffed by volunteers (Broder, 2007; Staiti et al., 2006).

Mixed-Status Families

The definition of a mixed-status family is a family in which at least one parent is a noncitizen and at least one child is a citizen (Capps, Kenney, & Fix, 2003). In 2002, 72% of the children who had noncitizen parents were citizens. The citizen children in mixed-status families are entitled to the same public insurance benefits as all citizen children who are eligible based on income, yet one in five of these children remained uninsured in 2002. This rate is 74% higher than children of citizen parents. The lack of insurance is due to language barriers or lack of awareness of the child's eligibility for Medicaid or SCHIP. Sometimes, though, it is due to fear of the application process if a parent is undocumented (Capps, Kenney, & Fix, 2003).

Waiver of Excludability

A key legal immigration issue affecting newcomers is the provision in the Immigration Act that excludes persons from entering the country if they have a "contagious disease of public health significance" (U.S. Citizenship and Immigration Services [USCIS], 2008, January 28). Such diseases now include chancroid, gonorrhea, granuloma inguinale, HIV, infectious leprosy, lymphogranuloma, venerium, infectious syphilis, and active tuberculosis (USCIS, 1991, May 31). These medical conditions, which can serve to exclude persons from entering the country, however, can be waived by applying for a Waiver of Excludability.

Having established reasons to exclude persons from entering the United States, the immigration law, however, does provide for a process to request a waiver so as to allow the person admission to the United States. Applicants use Immigration Form I-601, Application for Waiver of Ground of Inadmissibility (USCIS, 2008, February 28). This is where social workers and providers can have an important impact on keeping families together. In order to gain admission, the form requires the applicant to prove his or her entry will cause:

1 Minimal danger to the public health
2 Minimal possibility of the spread of HIV
3 No cost to a government agency without that agency's prior consent

In filing this waiver with the government, a social worker's affidavit, attesting as to how he or she will provide counseling to the individual should the individual be admitted, may help in persuading the government to allow the person to enter the country.

BARRIERS TO HEALTH CARE FOR IMMIGRANTS

Despite some laws that provide health care protection to immigrants, regardless of legal status, immigrants nevertheless face barriers that limit their access to health care. Obviously, immigrant status is a barrier to health care if the immigrant is undocumented or has not lived in this country for five years. Other barriers also exist that prevent or deter immigrants from receiving health care. These challenges include fear, lack of money or health insurance, language barriers, cultural issues, lack of knowledge of the U.S. health care system, and lack of facilities and transportation.

Fear

Fear can play a major role in the decision not to seek health care. Immigrants unfamiliar with health care providers might be fearful of the experience or might fear the news of a serious diagnosis (Garcés, Scarinci, & Harrison, 2006). Many undocumented immigrants fear they will be discovered, reported to the Department of Homeland Security (DHS), and deported if they apply for public health insurance for a citizen child. Although public assistance offices may only require documentation of citizenship of the person who will be covered, not the parent applying for the child or others living in the same household, the fear still exists (Broder, 2007; Derose, Escarce, & Lurie, 2007). Immigrants fearing discovery might provide inaccurate, incomplete, or no contact information or no medical history when seeing a health care provider. Lack of complete or accurate medical information can result in a delay or mistake in diagnosis and treatment (Staiti et al., 2006).

Documented immigrants, who are eligible for Medicaid and other public benefits after the first five years of residence, may be fearful that use of these benefits will cause them to be classified as a public charge, which may be grounds for deportation. According to the U.S. Citizenship and Immigration Services, use of Medicaid, SCHIP, WIC, food stamps, immunizations, prenatal care, testing and treatment of communicable diseases, emergency medical assistance, and other noncash benefits does *not* constitute a public charge, but the fear still exists and limits access to care (DHS, 1999; Derose et al., 2007). Social workers who are aware of local, state, and federal regulations regarding immigrant eligibility for specific programs can alleviate some of these fears and encourage use of the benefits.

Lack of Money and Health Insurance

Studies have shown that almost half of all working immigrants, particularly the undocumented, earn less than twice the minimum wage and live in poverty. In addition, only 26% of documented workers have access to health insurance through their employer (AFL-CIO, 2005; Broder, 2007; Goldman et al., 2006; Montoya, 2005). PWORA bans most immigrant access to public health insurance for the first five years of residence in the United States. A Kaiser Family Foundation report (Aiker & Urrutia, 2004) indicates that in 2002, while only 15% of native citizens did not have health insurance, between 42% and 51% of noncitizens did not. Without health insurance, many families will be less likely to receive preventive care and will not seek necessary medical care until it becomes an emergency. In addition, when they do seek care, they will have difficulty paying because of their low income (Aiker & Urrutia, 2004). Lack of insurance and low socioeconomic status are effective barriers to access to health care for the immigrant population.

Language Barriers

The inability of patient and provider to communicate in the same language can be an almost insurmountable barrier to access to and quality of patient health care. According to Brach, Fraser, and Paez (2005), more than 10 million people living in the United States either do not speak English at all or speak it poorly. Immigrants who do not speak English or do not have a health care provider who speaks their language are less likely to seek health care. They are also less likely to receive good quality care when they do seek it (Brach et al., 2005). The provision of nondiscrimination based on national origin, by agencies that receive federal funds, may result in the provision of oral and written language assistance (interpreters and translators) to those who do not speak, understand, or read English well, as is mandated by Title VI of the Civil Rights Act of 1964; and it does reduce the barrier somewhat. However, neither the law nor its regulations specifically details exactly what the services must be (Frates & Saint-Germaine, 2004). The four-prong test as laid out in the law is broad enough to possibly still result in barriers to service.

Social workers and health care providers must consider a number of issues when attempting to address the language barrier. The best option for the immigrant needing health care is that the provider, that is, the nurse, the doctor, the social worker, be him/herself bilingual or bicultural. If the provider agency has not hired such culturally competent direct service workers, a second option is for the agency to use certified medical interpreters who are present on site and have been trained in medical terminology, ethics, and the importance of confidentiality. Often these interpreters are also capable of understanding and explaining cultural aspects of the interaction that might impact care (International Medical Interpreters Association [IMIA], 2007). Unfortunately, just as there may not be sufficient nurses, doctors, and/or social workers who can communicate *directly* with the English language learner, similarly, there is a need for trained and certified medical interpreters. In addition, many health care workers (including nurses, social workers, and physicians) have not received training in how to use interpreters. If on-site interpreters are not available, another option might be trained telephonic interpreters who are accessed using telephones with two receivers. This type of 24-hour service is particularly helpful if one needs an interpreter who speaks a less common language or dialect.

Still other options are trained bilingual staff and ad hoc interpreters, including family members and friends. Confidentiality becomes an issue with family and friends because Health Insurance Portability and Accountability Act (HIPAA) regulations prohibit health care workers from discussing a patient's care with anyone else without their consent. It is important not to use anyone under the age of 18 to interpret in a medical setting unless the patient refuses a trained interpreter or there are no other options. Using a child as an interpreter may result in the child being exposed to parental medical issues that should be kept confidential. Another problem may occur when children are kept out of school to interpret for parents who must see health care providers.

Communication barriers often result in poor quality communication between the patient and the health care provider that can lead to misdiagnosis or a threat to the patient's life if, for example, the directions for patient care or medicine dosages are misunderstood. In addition, patients might not seek care until they are critically ill because they are afraid of being misunderstood (Staiti et al., 2006). Social workers can and should be vigilant in advocating for increased translator and interpreter services at their agency or medical setting, not just for the convenience of the patient, but for their safety and improved health. Many large metropolitan hospitals have arranged for electronic or staff interpretation, but with the multiplicity of languages and limited resources skilled interpretation is not always available.

Cultural Issues

Gregg and Saha (2006) define culture as a "set of behaviors and guidelines that individuals use to understand the world and how to live in it" (p. 543). As discussed in chapter 1, today's immigrants come to the United States from all over the world and they bring with them their own cultures, including religion, language, behaviors, and family, community, and societal structures. This cultural component is a benefit to the immigrants because it provides a familiar structure to their lives and also a connection to their past. It can also be a barrier, though, when it conflicts with U.S. culture. This is particularly true in the area of health care, when cultural barriers create a "cultural distance" between an immigrant's culture and the health care provider's Western culture (Gregg & Saha, 2006, p. 542). Cultural competency and cultural sensitivity by the health care provider can bridge the distance. Cultural competency and sensitivity refer to one's ability to be aware of the fact that there are cultural differences and to be sensitive to and respectful of those differences. When working with an immigrant patient, it is important to ask about that person's culture and try to understand how it will impact the care that the immigrant wants, needs, and ultimately receives. It is also important not to generalize or develop stereotypes based on one immigrant's cultural beliefs (Congress, 2004).

Although chapter 3 explores the issue of cultural competency in more depth, it is important to note that most native-born residents of Western countries believe that most illnesses are caused by something physical (e.g., bacteria, viruses, poor nutrition, old age) that can be treated with such things as antibiotics or surgical procedures. Some immigrants, however, depending on country of origin, might attribute the cause to spiritual or religious factors or being out of balance with nature (Congress & Lyons, 1992; Ma, 1999; Murguía, Peterson, & Zea, 2003). Prior to emigrating to the United States, many immigrants have had little or no exposure to Western medicine, so they might hesitate to seek treatment for a physical ailment from a Western health care provider. Instead, they might use herbal remedies, acupuncture, spiritual folk healers, folk remedies, reflexology, massage, chiropractic, or homeopathy (Congress & Lyons, 1992; Dhooper, 2003; Ma, 1999; Murguía et al., 2003; Shpilko, 2006). If an immigrant does go to a Western physician, he might not disclose that he is also using a traditional remedy due to the belief (real or perceived) that the physician will not understand. If a physician has an understanding of some of the culture-bound syndromes of Central Americans, for example, and respectfully asks the patient about the use of traditional treatments, the patient might be willing to share the information that he is using a folk remedy. This knowledge will allow the physician to discuss the traditional treatment and its potential side effects or complications if used with Western medicine (Murguía et al., 2003).

In addition, some Asian cultures believe in the interconnectedness of the mind, body, and spirit; and they treat all three systems if a patient is ailing. If an Asian patient seeks care from a Western physician, and is given a prescription for some pills but nothing for his mind or spirit, he might disregard the prescription. If, however, the Western physician takes the time to ask his patient about his traditional beliefs about the interconnectedness of the mind, body, and spirit, he might prescribe medicine for the body, and also recommend acupuncture and meditation to heal the mind and spirit (Dhooper, 2003).

Culturally competent health care providers (and in their absence, interpreters) who understand and respect the value of traditional and alternative health care treatments are an essential component of Western facilities that treat immigrants. Social workers who can advocate for their patients and be part of an organization's development and implementation of ongoing programs to address cultural competency should also be an integral part of these organizations. Not only should social workers advocate on behalf of their clients (micro advocacy), so too should social workers advocate *within* the workplace to ensure that systems are in place to make services available *(mezzo* advocacy). This text will end with an exploration of systemic or *macro* advocacy aimed at changing city, state, or federal policies—another important function, particularly in the context of examining health care policies.

Cultural competence also extends to the physician's bedside manner when providing a diagnosis. For example, Shpilko (2006) points out that in Russia a cancer diagnosis is not discussed with the patient in the hospital. Rather, the diagnosis is discussed with family members who then choose a time and place to inform the patient when he can be surrounded by supportive family and friends. If the physician tells the patient, it could be seen as a sign of disrespect for the family's traditional values. But if the physician tells the family and not the patient, he is violating the patient's right to privacy, which is guaranteed in HIPAA. In other cultures, the challenge is to find the locus of power, sometimes the husband, sometimes the elderly grandfather or grandmother, as the target of the communication. There is no easy solution to this dilemma, but it is one that health care providers might face, should be aware of, and will need to navigate when they care for immigrants.

The cultural issue also involves the idea of self-care. Immigrants uncomfortable with Western medicines sometimes choose to diagnose and medicate themselves and their families using medicines from their country of origin. Shpilko (2006) describes elderly Russian immigrants and Dyck (2006) describes Sikh women who used medications brought from their countries of origin because they were familiar with the drugs and their use. Unfortunately, sometimes these drugs can be dangerous to the user's health because they are past expiration or because they might interact with drugs prescribed by U.S. physicians who are unaware the immigrant is taking another drug. Western physicians must know enough to ask about other medications being used but they must also develop a good rapport with their patients so the patients will answer honestly.

Confusing U.S. Health Care System

Trying to navigate the U.S. health care system is confusing and intimidating even if one speaks English and has a basic understanding of preventive health care, how to schedule and keep appointments, the reasons for diagnostic tests, and the meaning of all the terminology and restrictions that are part of U.S. health insurance. Imagine what it would be like to be a newly arrived immigrant who does not speak or understand English, has had little exposure to Western medicine or health care facilities, and has limited resources to pay for medical care. It is no wonder that so few immigrants seek care unless they are desperately ill. The complexity of the U.S. health care system is a very successful barrier to immigrant health care.

Research also shows that immigrants often do not have a primary care provider, do not visit doctors, and do not get preventive care (Fremstad & Cox, 2004). Those with limited resources rarely spend money on a doctor's visit when they do not feel sick. Unfortunately, all people need periodic physicals to make sure they are healthy and, if not, to identify a medical condition, such as diabetes, in the early stages while it can be controlled with diet, not when it has advanced to the stage that it requires insulin injections. Infants and children also need well-child visits, to monitor their growth and development and to receive all their immunizations on time.

Another barrier to immigrant health care is the confusion about who is and is not eligible for various federal programs, a confusion that was compounded by PRWORA (Derose et al., 2007). Eligibility requirements for immigrant health care get even more confusing when one considers state-funded and run Medicaid and SCHIP programs that are open to documented immigrants and sometimes even to undocumented immigrants. The available services, however, vary by state and year. The language barrier makes the situation even more confusing (Derose et al., 2007; Fremstad & Cox, 2004). In addition, even many immigrants who are eligible for federal or state programs do not enroll in state Medicaid and SCHIP programs based on the unfounded fear of being declared a public charge (Aiker & Urrutia, 2004; Fremstad & Cox, 2004).

Immigrants are not the only ones who are confused about these health care programs. Program employees are also confused about what questions they can ask regarding immigrant status and social security numbers (SSN). Applicants (but only applicants) for Medicaid or SCHIP are required to provide their SSNs; state employees who are working with the immigrant may ask nonapplicant family members to give their SSNs but federal rules allow immigrants not to specify the immigrant status or the SSN. Immigrants are not required to list the country of birth or country of origin, even if those questions are on an application. In addition, no one is required to provide his SSN if he is seeking emergency Medicaid (Tumlin, 2007).

Lack of Facilities and Transportation

Lack of nearby facilities, too few primary care providers and specialists willing to take uninsured immigrants, and lack of transportation are also barriers that hinder immigrant access to health care (Fremstad & Cox, 2004). Over the years, communities with large numbers of immigrants have developed safety net health care providers for the immigrant population. Communities who are just starting to experience an influx of immigrants are struggling to develop health care options for them and may not have adequate resources to address immigrant health care needs (Staiti et al., 2006). Transportation can also be a barrier to health care both in urban and rural settings. Sometimes public transportation is available but the immigrant lacks the money to pay for it while other times there is no transportation or it can take several buses to get there. Zuroweste (2007) states that only 44% of migrant farm workers own a car. In rural settings, lack of a car can make it as difficult to access health care as lack of a token in the city.

IMMIGRANT HEALTH ISSUES

Due in part to the issues listed above (fear, lack of culturally competent providers, and confusing federal, state, and local laws), Goldman and colleagues (2006) report on data from the 2000 Los Angeles Family and Neighborhood Survey (LAFANS), Los Angeles County, California, which show that approximately one-quarter of the foreign-born in Los Angeles County never had a medical checkup and one in nine had never visited a doctor. The numbers are even worse for the undocumented: 42% had not visited a doctor within the past year and only 11% had been hospitalized (Goldman et al., 2006). Although these figures include Asians, Central Americans, and Africans, it is important for health care providers not to lump these groups together as aggregates and assume that they share a common culture. It is necessary to look at the subpopulations and individuals that comprise the ethnic group (Congress, 2004; Mui, Kang, Kang, & Domanski, 2007; Pang, Jordan-Marsh, Silverstein, & Cody, 2003). Cultural differences and responses to the changed dynamics of family relationships and life in the United States will vary not just because of the culture of the country of origin but also because of individual differences. In addition, the role of and the expectations for men, women, children, and seniors will vary by and within their culture and their family structure.

Healthy Migrant Phenomenon and Acculturation

The "Healthy Migrant Phenomenon" has been described by Fennelly (2006) as the idea that, when individuals migrate from their country of origin to the United States, they arrive in a healthier state than native-born residents. Although they have higher rates of some infectious diseases, Fennelly (2006) reports that they generally receive better ratings in the areas of health risk factors, chronic conditions, and mortality. Schenker (2007) describes a similar concept, which he calls the "Healthy

Immigrant Hypothesis," when he talks about immigrant Latinas who have better than expected birth outcomes when they first arrive in the United States.

The concept of acculturation, or the "paradox of assimilation," states that immigrant health care declines the longer the immigrant lives in the United States because, over time, immigrants will gradually adopt the culture of the United States, including the language, norms, and values. Along with the norms and values, the immigrants adopt less healthy eating habits and less healthy lifestyle choices, such as high-risk sexual behavior, cigarette smoking, and substance abuse (Derose et al., 2007; Fennelly, 2006; Schenker, 2007). Leaving behind supportive family and social networks in their home country also contributes to the deterioration in health. In addition, settling in a new country and culture is stressful and can contribute to health problems (Fennelly, 2006). Acculturation has been linked to increases in preterm, low birth weight babies, adolescent risk behaviors, anxiety and depression, and general mortality The longer immigrants are in this country, the more closely their rates of health risks, chronic conditions (such as obesity, diabetes, and cancer), and mortality approach that of native-born citizens and the more health care they need but are often unable to get (Fennelly, 2006; Schenker, 2007).

Medical Issues of Immigration Detainees

In 2007, approximately 27,000 immigrant detainees were being held in federal penitentiaries, prisons, local jails, and service processing centers that are overseen by DHS's Bureau of Immigration and Customs Enforcement (ICE). Because they are not considered to be prisoners, they are not entitled to legal channels of appeal (Dow, 2007). ICE is responsible for establishing detention standards for medical care, hunger strikes, and suicide prevention and intervention as well as detention standards for environmental health and safety. ICE must also make sure that the management of each facility housing detainees maintains those standards (DHS, 2006).

According to Tumlin (2007), recent reports document detainee difficulties obtaining medical care, which sometimes resulted in long-term health problems or death. Some examples include failure to provide medication to detainees and failure to respond to requests for medical care in a timely manner. The DHS Office of Inspector General (OIG) examined compliance with the detention standards at five facilities used by ICE to house detainees and issued a report in December 2006 that confirmed Tumlin's examples. The OIG found that 21% of detainees did not receive the required initial medical screening (or the screening was not documented), 23% did not receive required physical exams (or the exams were not documented), 40% of all nonemergency medical requests were not responded to within the specified timeframe, 62% of the time the staff did not follow all the monitoring guidelines for detainees on hunger strikes, and 13% of the time the staff did not record 15-minute security checks for detainees on suicide watch (DHS, 2006). Every violation that the OIG reported could, and sometimes did, hurt the detainees and adversely affect their health.

Work-Related Medical Issues

Approximately 81% of immigrant families have at least one full-time worker, but that worker is much more likely to be employed in a low-wage job than a native citizen is (Aiker & Urrutia, 2004). Agriculture, fishing, forestry maintenance, meat packing, manufacturing, construction, service and hospitality industries, day labor, and garment industry sweatshops are the industries that hire the largest numbers of immigrants and they are also some of the industries with high rates of injury (AFL-CIO, 2005; Kugel, 2007; Lashuay et al., 2002; Montoya, 2005; Pransky et al., 2002; Schenker, 2007; Villarejo, 2003).

Immigrant workers in these industries suffer musculoskeletal injuries that can be isolated or cumulative over time. These injuries occur from improperly lifting or carrying heavy objects or from performing too much stoop labor. Workers can develop carpal tunnel syndrome from repetitive hand and arm motions used in their jobs (Zuroweste, 2007).

They can also develop environmental injuries from exposure to chemicals. The arms and hands of farm workers who pick produce can develop skin irritation due to exposure to pesticides sprayed on the plants. With continued exposure over a long period of time, the irritation can turn into dermatologic disease.

Farm workers and maintenance workers can develop respiratory problems from breathing in the airborne pesticides or cleaning chemicals that, with long-term exposure, can turn into chronic respiratory disease. Long-term exposure to some chemicals can even cause cancer or neurologic disease (AFL-CIO, 2005; Schenker, 2007; Villarejo, 2003).

The AFL-CIO (2005) reports that immigrants are not as likely as native citizens to complain about hazardous job conditions or to stay home from work after an injury for fear of losing their jobs. Unfortunately, if workers return to work before the injury has healed sufficiently, it can become more severe and inhibit the worker's ability to do the same job any more (AFL-CIO, 2005). Many workers do not stay home after being injured because they lack health insurance and cannot afford to miss work and pay for a doctor visit. Without insurance or money, the injured immigrant worker has little hope of receiving care. In addition, over 50% of foreign-born workers surveyed in one study did not know about workman's compensation (AFL-CIO, 2005; Zuroweste, 2007).

It is estimated that there are over 25 million migrant workers employed in agriculture, construction, meat packing/poultry industries, and the seasonal service industry and that over 53% are undocumented. Migrant worker health is adversely affected by the migratory lifestyle, since it is more difficult to access care when workers are unfamiliar with local resources in their temporary homes (Kugel, 2007; Zuroweste, 2007). Zuroweste (2007) reports that migrant workers have a higher rate of diabetes than nonmigrant workers and that babies born to migrant working women have a high rate of congenital abnormalities. In addition, tuberculosis (TB) rates are 30%–50% higher in the migrant population than in the general population.

In 1984, the Migrant Clinicians Network (MCN) was founded as a tracking and referral program for migrant workers. The network clinicians work in state and local health departments, federally funded mobile/community health centers, and federally qualified health centers that are located in areas with high numbers of migrant workers. The clinics provide basic health care; screenings for TB, mammograms, and Pap smears; follow-up care for chronic conditions such as diabetes and hypertension; and prenatal care. They also provide screening, diagnosis, and treatment for breast, cervical, and colon cancer. Participating clinicians provide education about the importance of preventive care, screenings, and prenatal care. When a migrant worker patient is getting ready to move, his clinician makes sure the patient knows the location of the next clinic, and, with patient approval, transfers his medical records to the new clinic. Continuity of care is particularly important in the management of chronic conditions and communicable diseases such as tuberculosis. In addition, the MCN has developed specific networks to track and provide continuity of care for diabetes, specific cancers, and TB (Kugel, 2007).

SPECIAL POPULATIONS

Female, child, and elderly immigrants face special health challenges; this section will examine in more detail some of the challenges facing these vulnerable immigrant populations.

Health Care for Senior Immigrants

Elderly immigrants are the most underserved seniors in the health care system because of language and cultural barriers (Mui et al., 2007). Many elderly immigrants do not speak English well, if at all, making it difficult to describe symptoms and understand physician recommendations. It becomes even more difficult if the provider does not understand the patient's culture. In addition, Mui and colleagues (2007) report that elderly Asians who do not speak English often choose not to get health care in order to save face by not having to admit that they do not speak English or understand what is being said. Social workers should consider the idea of saving face when working with LEP individuals, particularly seniors.

Cultural differences may also affect the way immigrant seniors adjust to the aging process and cope with chronic illness. As noted previously, many immigrants prefer traditional medicines and health care and this preference is particularly true of seniors. Unfortunately, seniors also tend to have more chronic illnesses that require regular monitoring and care. Avoidance of the U.S. health care system may also cause these elderly immigrants to become seriously ill (Mui et al., 2007; Pang et al., 2003).

Often the seniors emigrate to the United States to join adult children who are already settled here. In their country of origin, these seniors were the caregivers and the children sought their advice. Here, however, the role is reversed, and seniors who may not speak English or understand how to navigate U.S. society and the health care system are dependent upon their children for their care. The dependence may cause stress that can aggravate existing health conditions and/or cause immigrant seniors to neglect health care so they do not have to ask for help (Fitzpatrick & Freed, 2000). The relationship becomes particularly difficult if the children have further redefined the traditional role because of acculturation to the United States (Pang et al., 2003). Chapter 12 examines issues of elderly immigrants in more detail.

Health Care for Immigrant Women

The LAFANS data from 2000 show that 20% of undocumented women had never received a checkup (four times the rate for native-born women) and 7% had never seen a physician. The percents would be even more distressing if pregnancies (with their hospital deliveries) were not factored in. While these numbers are for Los Angeles County, California, not the entire United States, it is still possible to deduce that some of the barriers discussed earlier play a role in the low numbers of immigrant women who get checkups just as they do for most immigrants. With women's health issues, however, the literature indicates that culture, language, lack of a usual source of care, and access to health insurance are four of the most formidable barriers.

In Western medicine, one focus of women's health care is on breast and gynecologic cancer screenings. Studies have shown that female immigrants are much less likely than female citizens to have Pap smears and mammograms (De Alba, Hubbell, McMullin, Sweningson, & Saitz, 2005). According to Matin and LeBaron (2004), often the reason is due to religious and cultural beliefs. Muslims place a high value on modesty, bodily privacy, and premarital virginity, which conflicts with Western standards of health care, with their focus on gynecologic exams and Pap smears by the age of 21. The conflict creates tension between the patient and the physician, who is seen as being insensitive to Muslim cultural and religious beliefs. Results of another study indicate that Latinas also tend to be modest and, as a result, often avoid breast and gynecologic cancer screenings (Garcés et al., 2006). It is crucial for the health and well-being of all immigrant women for health care professionals to develop a sensitivity to and respect for the cultures and religious beliefs of their immigrant patients while still finding a way to provide quality medical care and screenings.

Immigrant women also face barriers accessing health care when they are pregnant. All immigrants, regardless of status, are eligible for Emergency Medicaid for labor and delivery. They are not necessarily eligible, however, for prenatal care, even though studies have shown that lack of prenatal care can increase poor pregnancy outcomes such as prematurity and possible resulting long-term disabilities (American Academy of Pediatrics, 1997). Eventually, the Centers for Medicare and Medicaid Services amended the SCHIP regulations to allow states to use SCHIP funds to provide prenatal care to pregnant women, regardless of immigrant status. As of April 2006, 7 states allowed enrollment for prenatal care and another 18 states provided state-funded coverage (KFF, 2006). Even in Western culture, women's health issues are still sensitive topics because they concern private parts of the body. Addressing women's health issues becomes even more difficult for immigrant women whose cultural and religious beliefs stress modesty and virginity. This is yet another reason why culturally competent health care and social service practitioners are sorely needed, particularly when dealing with immigrant communities.

Health Care for Immigrant Children

In 1997, the American Academy of Pediatrics stated that, "Every child within the geographic boundaries of the United States, regardless of that child's 'status,' should have full access to all social, educational, and health services that exist at the local, state, and federal levels for the care and benefit of children" (American Academy of Pediatrics, 1997, p. 153). The United States still has a long way to go to implement these recommendations. According to a report on young immigrant children issued by the Urban Institute (Capps, Fix, Ost, Reardon-Anderson, & Passel, 2004), immigrant children under 6 make up 22% (5.1 million) of the 6 and under population of the United States; 93% of those children are citizens living in mixed-status families; over 50% live in low-income families; and they are more than twice as likely to be uninsured as children of native citizens (22% vs. 11%).

Because many immigrant children do not have regular health care providers or receive regular well-baby/child visits, they may not have received appropriate immunizations and may have undiagnosed health problems including parasitic and infectious diseases and vaccine-preventable diseases (American Academy of Pediatrics, 1997). The usual barriers to access to health care (fear, language, culture, income, and insurance), also apply to children, many of whom are eligible for Medicaid or SCHIP coverage based on family income and child citizenship status. Unfortunately, it will take significant culturally appropriate outreach efforts in the community to increase enrollment in these programs. Once the children have insurance, it will take more outreach to get them, and their families, into the habit of accessing preventive health care and seeking treatment for easy-to-treat conditions before they become critical (Lessard & Ku, 2003).

IMPLICATIONS FOR SOCIAL WORK PRACTICE

Social workers who work with immigrants must be particularly cognizant of the NASW Code of Ethics (1999) section on Values (Service, Social Justice, Dignity and Worth of the Person, Importance of Human Relationships, Integrity, and Competence) and the Ethical Principles that derive from them. Social workers must use those values as a foundation and guide in their practice with this population. Many individuals in this population are vulnerable because of the barriers they face living in the United States and some are particularly vulnerable because of their undocumented status. The barriers of immigrant status, language, income and health insurance status, and culture impact every aspect of an immigrant's life. When those barriers adversely affect access to health care the negative impact is even greater, for the status of one's health affects every other facet of one's life including school, work, family relationships, and community relationships. Social workers in the field of health care must actively address the issues of language, culture, and income/health insurance status as well as legal status when working with immigrants.

Social workers, by their training, have the unique ability to assist the immigrant in all aspects of his life, from helping him connect with community resources to attempting to find insurance coverage, to acting as an advocate for him within the health care system. One of the first goals a health care social worker should work toward is establishing trust with the immigrant client. Trust can lead to a working relationship between the immigrant and the social worker where the immigrant feels safe telling his story and describing his cultural and religious beliefs so that the worker will be able to help the client identify his needs and clarify how those needs interconnect with the health care system. The social worker can then act as a bridge or cultural mediator between the immigrant and the health care provider in an effort to ensure that both the immigrant's health care and cultural needs are met (Carr, 2006; Congress, 2004). If the immigrant establishes a degree of comfort with the health care provider, it is more likely that he or she will continue to participate in and be compliant with a plan of care.

Social workers must develop a broad knowledge base of the resources in their clients' geographic region as well as federal and state laws regarding access to those resources and immigrant status. While it is impossible for one person to be an expert in everything, it is important to develop relationships with experts in topics such as immigrant or employment law, so there is someone to ask when questions arise. It is crucial to know what services the local public and nonprofit welfare and social service agencies offer as well as the barriers to those services. This knowledge will make it easier to help the immigrant client. It is also crucial to develop a working list of physicians, pharmacists, clinics, and hospitals that are willing to see immigrants with limited financial resources, whose staff is culturally competent and sensitive to the needs of immigrants, and who have trained bilingual staff, interpreters, and translators to communicate effectively.

Social workers must make an ongoing commitment to education, their own and others in the health care field. They need to address the question of their own cultural competence and, as they work with individual patients, strive to learn more of that person's cultural and religious beliefs. In addition, they need to educate those with whom they work about the cultural and religious beliefs of the patients they are seeing and the social issues faced by the patient and the population, which might impact patients' ability to be compliant with and actively participate in their care (Congress, 2004; Fennelly, 2006). Social workers can and do play a major role in helping immigrants access and use appropriate medical care. They can also advocate for a health care system that would be available to all based on medical need rather than immigration status.

CASE STUDIES

The following case studies illustrate the types of health issues that social workers may encounter in working with immigrant clients and their families. You are invited to discuss the questions following each case.

Case Study 1: Pedro

Pedro is an undocumented migrant farm worker from Mexico. He has a wife, Jovita, and three children, ages 3, 5, and 7. The 3-year-old and 5-year-old were born in the United States, but the 7-year-old and Jovita were born in Mexico. Spanish is their native language and none speaks English except the 7-year-old. They are currently working in Florida, picking blueberries, but the crop is almost done so they are getting ready to move to South Carolina where the blueberries are almost ready for picking. They share a house with one other family and three single men. All have been working together—the men in the fields and the women packing the blueberries. Two of the single men have cars and provide rides for the rest as needed. They plan on moving to the next picking location together.

Pedro has been coughing a lot lately, has been tired, and for the past two weeks has been waking up with night sweats. Jovita finally has convinced him to go to the local health center and has found a friend willing to drive him there. The local health center clinicians belong to the Migrant Clinician's Network. After examining him, the clinician does a skin test and gets the friend to bring him back in two days to read it. At the second visit, the clinician diagnoses Pedro with an active case of tuberculosis (TB). Pedro will need to be hospitalized for a short time and then will need to continue taking a combination of daily medicines for months. After a few weeks he will be able to return to work as long as he continues taking his medicines. The clinician also convinces the friend to bring Jovita and the three children in for testing as well. The youngest child is diagnosed with an active case and the older two children and Jovita have the latent form of TB. The youngest child will be hospitalized for a few weeks while the two older children and Jovita can be treated with daily medicine at home. They will need to take the medicines for between nine months and a year. Jovita can continue working but Pedro will not be able to return to work for about a month.

Pedro and Jovita are depending on the friend for a ride to the next job in South Carolina. The job in Florida is over and they can no longer stay in their temporary housing there. By the time the child is diagnosed, all the workers except the friend have moved on to South Carolina. The friend needs to leave as well in order to keep working. The clinician refers the family to the social worker at the clinic and to the hospital social worker. A referral is also made to the Migrant Clinician's Network near the South Carolina farms where the migrants are moving.

1. What social work issues are raised by this vignette?
2. What legal issues are involved because the workers are undocumented?

3 What can the social worker do to help this family in the short run and long term?
4 What can the social worker and the clinician do about the other workers and family members who were exposed to TB and have moved on?

Case Study 2: Maria

A young woman named Maria has recently emigrated from Cuba and was able to bring her medical records with her. She moved to Columbus, Ohio, because she had a cousin there. Neither she nor her cousin speaks English. Maria has had gynecologic issues for several years and needs to continue being followed for the condition. Her cousin takes her to the local health clinic, where some of the staff are bilingual and she can communicate easily with them. Unfortunately, the clinician must refer Maria to a specialist. Maria is uncomfortable with the idea but knows she needs to go to the appointment. Workers at the clinic assure her that, on the day of the appointment, they will have a trained interpreter from the clinic available to go with her. Unfortunately, on the day of the appointment, Maria arrives at the clinic and finds out that the interpreter is sick and cannot go. It took months to get this appointment and, if it is cancelled, Maria will need to wait several more months for a new appointment. Both she and the clinician agree that she cannot wait for a new appointment so the clinic offers to have the bilingual social worker take her.

Maria and the social worker meet with the specialist and Maria gives him all her medical records. The specialist, who does not speak or read Spanish, looks at the records and says he cannot do anything with them. First of all, they are in Spanish and he does not read Spanish. Second of all, he has no way of verifying if they are real medical records because he cannot speak with the physician in Cuba whose office they came from. He tells the patient that he must ignore that the records exist and start diagnosing her from the beginning. She has been on a particular medication for this condition but he refuses to continue prescribing it until he has done a complete workup.

1 What social work issues are raised by this case?
2 What legal issues are raised by this case?
3 What can the social worker do to help Maria?

4 What, if anything, could be done on an organizational (mezzo) level to help in this case? What could or should be done on the policy (macro) level?

Case Study 3: Phuong

Phuong is a documented immigrant from Vietnam, who arrived in the United States in March, 2005. She is slowly learning English, but is not comfortable speaking it and still has difficulty understanding it. Phuong has a full-time job working in a factory. She assembles tiny parts so she needs good eyesight. Her employer does not provide health insurance. Her income is less than two times the federal poverty level and she has a 10-year-old son who lives with her. She and her son live in Philadelphia and have been able to live on what she earns. She reports that she has always been in good health so she has not visited a doctor since she arrived in this country.

Lately Phuong has been feeling very tired and has started losing weight. She always seems to be thirsty now and has to urinate often. In addition, her vision is now blurry, which makes it hard to do her job. She talks to a friend at the factory who tells her about a local health clinic where some of the staff speak Vietnamese. She takes a day off from work and gets to the clinic early to wait in line to see a clinician. Phuong brings her son with her, because she is scared to go alone and afraid that there will be no one there that day who speaks Vietnamese. After waiting three hours, Phuong sees the doctor, who does not speak Vietnamese, but who brings in one of the desk clerks to interpret. Phuong knows the desk clerk, who lives in the neighborhood, and she does not want the clerk to know her personal business. Phuong has her son tell the doctor and the clerk she wants her son, not the clerk, to be her interpreter. The doctor tells Phuong, with her son translating, that he thinks she has diabetes but that she will need to have some lab work done to verify that. She will need a fasting four-hour glucose tolerance test that must be started when the lab opens in the morning and she will need to stay at the lab for the entire time. Phuong will need to miss another day of work and her son will need to miss another day of school in order for her to take the test. The doctor stresses how important it is that Phuong take the test as soon as possible for confirmation of the doctor's diagnosis. While waiting for the test, the doctor gives Phuong a special diet to follow, but the diet does not list any Vietnamese foods. Phuong is not used to eating

American food so she says she cannot eat the foods on the diet. The doctor refers her to the clinic social worker.

1 What social work issues are raised by this case?
2 What legal issues are raised by this case?
3 What would you, as Phuong's social worker, do to help Phuong and her son?
4 What, if anything, could be done on an organizational (mezzo) level to help in this case? What could or should be done on the policy (macro) level?

ADDITIONAL RESOURCES

General Web Sites

Center on Budget and Policy Priorities: www.cbpp.org

The Henry J. Kaiser Family Foundation: http://www.kff.org/

Kaiser Commission on Medicaid and the Uninsured (information on immigrant access to and utilization of health insurance and health care): http://www.kff/org/kcmu

National Council of La Raza: www.nclr.org

National Immigration Law Center: http://www.nilc.org/

The Pew Hispanic Center (fact sheets and reports on immigration issues concerning Hispanics): http://pewhispanic.org/

Urban Institute (sections on health and health care, immigrants, families, children, and race): http://www.urbaninstitute.org/

The Urban Institute, *The Health and Well-being of Young Children of Immigrants* (a very comprehensive look at the lives of young immigrant children): http://www.urban.org/uploadedPDF/311139_ChildrenImmigrants.pdf

U.S. Citizenship and Immigration Services (especially sections on laws and regulations and humanitarian benefits): http://www.uscis.gov/portal/site/uscis

Web Sites Concerning Medical Interpreting

AMA Office Guide to Communicating with Limited English Proficient Patients: http://www.ama-assn.org/ama1/pub/upload/mm/433/lep_booklet.pdf

International Medical Interpreters Association (home page): http://www.mmia.org/

Medical Interpreting Standards of Practice: http://www.mmia.org/standards/standards.asp

Other Resources

Aroian, K. J. (2005). Equity, effectiveness, and efficiency in health care for immigrants and minorities: the essential triad for improving health outcomes. *Journal of Cultural Diversity, 12*(3), 99–106.

Choi, H. (2001). Cultural marginality: A concept analysis with implications for immigrant adolescents. *Issues in Comprehensive Pediatric Nursing, 24*(3), 193–206.

Congress, E. P. (2004). Cultural and ethical issues in working with culturally diverse patients and their families: The use of the Culturagram to promote cultural competent practice in health care settings [Electronic version]. *Social Work in Health Care,*

39(3/4), 249–262. Provides a good tool for the social worker who will be working with culturally diverse populations—helps give a visual picture of the patient/client.

Cosman, Madeleine Pelner. (2005). Illegal aliens and American medicine. *Journal of American Physicians & Surgeons, 10*(1), 6–10.

de Alba, I., Hubbell, F. A., McMullin, J. M., Sweningson, J. M., & Saitz, R. (2005). Impact of U.S. citizenship status on cancer screening among immigrant women. *Journal of General Internal Medicine, 20*(3), 290–296.

Dyck, I. (2006). Travelling tales and migratory meanings: South Asian migrant women talk of place, health and healing. *Social & Cultural Geography, 7*(1), 1–18.

Ghazal Read, J., & Emerson, M. O. (2005). Racial context, black immigration and the U.S. black/white health disparity. *Social Forces, 84*(1), 181–199.

Goldman, D. P., Smith, J. P., & Sood, N. (2006). Immigrants and the cost of medical care. *Health Affairs, 25*(6), 1700–1711.

Kemp, C., & Rasbridge, L. A. (2004). *Refugee and immigrant health: A handbook for health professionals.* New York: Cambridge University Press.

Kullgren, J. T. (2003). Restrictions on undocumented immigrants' access to health services: The public health implications of welfare reform. *American Journal of Public Health, 93*(10), 1630–1633.

Lai, K. (2005). Managing the drug regimens of immigrants from other cultures. *American Journal of Health—System Pharmacy, 62*(2), 205–210.

Lasser, K. E., Himmelstein, D. U., & Woolhandler, S. (2006). Access to care, health status, and health disparities in the United States and Canada: Results of a cross-national population-based survey. *American Journal of Public Health, 96*(7), 1300–1307.

Marks, L., & Warboys, M. (Eds.). (1997). *Migrants, minorities, and health: Historical and contemporary studies.* London: Routledge.

Migration and health: a complex relation. (2006, September 23). *Lancet, 368*(9541), 1039.

Pransky, G., Moshenberg, D., Benjamin, K., Portillo, S., Thackrey, J. L., & Hill-Fotouhi, C. (2002). Occupational risks and injuries in non-agricultural immigrant Latino workers. *American Journal of Industrial Medicine, 42*(2), 117–123.

Rashidi, A., & Rajaram, S. S. (2001). Culture care conflicts among Asian-Islamic immigrant women in U.S. hospitals. *Holistic Nursing Practice, 16*(1), 55–64.

Villarejo, D. (2003). The health of U.S. hired farm workers. *Annual Review of Public Health, 24*(1), 175.

Weitzman, M., & DuPleiss, H. M. (1997). Health care for children of immigrant families. *Pediatrics, 100*(1), 153–156.

White, K. (1998). Cultural sensitivity needed to protect girls at risk of mutilation. *Journal of Women's Health, 7*(7), 793–795.

REFERENCES

AFL-CIO. (2005, August). *Summary: Immigrant workers at risk: The urgent need for improved workplace safety and health policies and programs.* Washington, DC. Retrieved January 25, 2008, from http://hesa.etui-rehs.org/uk/newsevents/files/immigrant_risk.pdf

Aiker, J. C., & Urrutia, M. (2004). *Immigrants and health coverage: A primer.* (Publication #7088). Washington, DC: Henry J. Kaiser Family Foundation, the Kaiser

Commission on Medicaid and the Uninsured. Retrieved January 25, 2008 from www.kff.org/uninsured/upload/Immigrants-and-Health-Coverage-A-Primer.pdf

American Academy of Pediatrics, Committee on Community Health Services. (1997). Health care for children of immigrant families. [Electronic version] *Pediatrics, 100*(1), 153–156.

Brach, C., Fraser, I., & Paez, K. (2005). Crossing the language chasm: An in-depth analysis of what language-assistance programs look like in practice. [Electronic version] *Health Affairs, 24*(2), 424–434.

Broder, T. (2007). *Overview of immigrant eligibility for federal programs.* Washington, DC: National Immigration Law Center. Retrieved January 25, 2008, from http://www.nilc.org/immspbs/special/pb_issues_overview_2007–10.pdf

Capps, R., Fix, M., Ost, J., Reardon-Anderson, J., & Passel, J. S. (2004). *The health and well-being of young children of immigrants.* Washington, DC: Urban Institute. Retrieved January 25, 2008, from http://www.urban.org/uploadedPDF/311139_ChildrenImmigrants.pdf

Capps, R., Kenney, G., & Fix, M. (2003). *Health insurance coverage of children in mixed-status immigrant families.* (Snapshots of America's Families, III, No. 12). Washington, DC: Urban Institute. Retrieved March 23, 2008, from http://www.urban.org/publications/310886.html

Carr, D. D. (2006). Implications for case management. [Electronic version] *Lippincott's Case Management, 11*(4), 195–204.

Congress, E. P. (2004). Cultural and ethical issues in working with culturally diverse patients and their families: The use of the Culturagram to promote cultural competent practice in health care settings [Electronic version]. *Social Work in Health Care, 39*(3/4), 249–262.

Congress, E. P., & Lyons, B. P. (1992). Cultural differences in health benefits: Implications for social work practice in health care settings. *Social Work in Health Care, 17*(3), 81–96.

De Alba, I., Hubbell, F. A., McMullin, J. M., Sweningson, J. M., & Saitz, R. (2005). Impact of U.S. citizenship status on cancer screening among immigrant women. [Electronic version] *Journal of General Internal Medicine, 20*(3), 290–296.

Derose, K. P., Escarce, J. J., & Lurie, N. (2007). Immigrants and health care: Source of vulnerability. [Electronic version] *Health Affairs, 26*(5), 1258–1268.

Dhooper, S. S. (2003). Health care needs of foreign-born Asian Americans: An overview. [Electronic version] *Health & Social Work, 28*(1), 63–73.

Dow, M. (2007). Designed to punish: Immigrant detention and deportation. [Electronic version] *Social Research, 74*(2), 533–546.

Dyck, I. (2006). Travelling tales and migratory meanings: South Asian migrant women talk of place, health, and healing. [Electronic version] *Social and Cultural Geography, 7*(1), 1–18.

Fennelly, K. (2006). Listening to the experts: Provider recommendations on the health needs of immigrants and refugees. [Electronic version] *Journal of Cultural Diversity, 13*(4), 190–201.

Fitzpatrick, T. R., & Freed, A. O. (2000). Older Russian immigrants to the U.S.A.: Their utilization of health services. [Electronic version] *International Social Work, 43*(3), 305–323.

Frates, J., & Saint-Germain, M. (2004). Introduction: Health and human service delivery to limited English proficient and immigrant communities: Policy, management, and educational issues. [Electronic version] *International Journal of Public Administration, 27*(1/2), 1–13.

Fremstad, S., & Cox, L. (2004). *Covering new Americans: A review of federal and state policies related to immigrants' eligibility and access to publicly funded health insurance.* Washington, DC: Henry J. Kaiser Family Foundation, the Kaiser Commission on Medicaid and the Uninsured. Retrieved January 25, 2008, from http://www.kff.org/medicaid/7214.cfm

Garcés, I. C., Scarinci, I. C., & Harrison, L. (2006). An examination of sociocultural factors associated with health and health care seeking among Latina immigrants. [Electronic version] *Journal of Immigrant Health, 8*(4), 377–385.

Goldman, D. P., Smith, J. P., & Sood, N. (2006). Immigrants and the cost of medical care. [Electronic version] *Health Affairs, 25*(6), 1700–1711.

Gregg, J., & Saha, S. (2006). Losing culture on the way to competence: The use and misuse of culture in medical education. [Electronic version] *Academic Medicine, 81*(6), 542–547.

Henry J. Kaiser Family Foundation. The Kaiser Commission on Medicaid and the Uninsured. (2006,). *Medicaid and SCHIP eligibility for immigrants.* Washington, DC. Retrieved January 25, 2008, from www.kff.org.medicaid/upload/7492.pdf

Hoefer, M., Rytina, N., & Campbell, C. (2006, August). *Estimates of the unauthorized immigrant population residing in the United States: January 2005.* Washington, DC: Office of Immigration Statistics, Policy Directorate, U.S. Department of Homeland Security. Retrieved March 23, 2008, from http://www.dhs.gov/xlibrary/assets/statistics/publications/ILL_PE_2005.pdf

International Medical Interpreters Association. (2007). *Medical interpreting standards of practice.* Boston, MA. Retrieved January 25, 2008, from http://www.mmia.org/standards/standards.asp

Kugel, C. (2007, February). *MCN health network: A tracking and referral program for mobile underserved patients.* PowerPoint presentation presented at the 16th Annual Global Health Education Consortium Conference, Santo Domingo, Dominican Republic. Retrieved February 23, 2008, from http://www.globalhealth-ec.org/GHEC/Events/Conf07/PConf/Presentations/A2_Kugel_Candace.ppt

Lashuay, N., Burgel, B. J., Harrison, R., Israel, L., Chan, J., Cusic, C., et al. (2002, January). *"We spend our days working in pain": A report on workplace injuries in the garment industry.* Oakland, CA: Asian Immigrant Women Advocates. Retrieved January 25, 2008, from http://aiwa.org/workingreport.pdf

Lessard, G., & Ku, L. (2003). Gaps in coverage for children in immigrant families. [Electronic version] *The Future of Children, 13*(1), 101–115.

Ma, G. X. (1999). Between two worlds: The use of traditional and western health services by Chinese immigrants. [Electronic version] *Journal of Community Health, 24*(6), 421–437.

Matin, M., & LeBaron, S. (2004). Attitudes toward cervical cancer screening among Muslim women: A pilot study. [Electronic version] *Women & Health, 39*(3), 63–77.

Montoya, I. D. (2005). Health services considerations amongst immigrant populations. [Electronic version] *Journal of Immigrant & Refugee Services, 3*(3/4), 15–27.

Mui, A. C., Kang, S., Kang, D., & Domanski, M. D. (2007). English language proficiency and health-related quality of life among Chinese and Korean immigrant elders. [Electronic version] *Health and Social Work, 32*(2), 119–127.

Murguía, A., Peterson, R. A., & Zea, M. C. (2003). Use and implications of ethnomedical health approaches among Central American immigrants. [Electronic version]. *Health & Social Work, 28*(1), 43–51.

National Association of Social Workers. (1999). *Code of Ethics,* rev. 1999. Washington, DC: Author. Retrieved September 23, 2007, from http://www.socialworkers.org/pubs/code/code.asp?print= 1

Pang, E. C., Jordan-Marsh, M., Silverstein, M., & Cody, M. (2003). Health-seeking behaviors of elderly Chinese Americans: Shifts in Expectations. [Electronic version] *The Gerontologist, 43*(6), 864–874.

Pransky, G., Moshenberg, D., Benjamin, K., Portillo, S., Thackrey, J. L., & Hill-Fotouhi, C. (2002). Occupational risks and injuries in non-agricultural immigrant Latino workers. [Electronic version] *American Journal of Industrial Medicine, 42*(2), 117–123.

Ruttenberg, R., & Lazo, M. (2004). *Spanish-speaking construction workers discuss their safety needs and experiences.* (Residential Construction Training Program Evaluation Report). Silver Spring, MD: Center to Protect Workers' Rights. Retrieved January 25, 2008, from http://www.cpwr.com/pdfs/pubs/research_pubs/

Schenker, M. (2007, February). *Healthcare challenges of global migrants: Farmworker health.* PowerPoint presentation presented at the 16th Annual Global Health Education Consortium Conference, Santo Domingo, Dominican Republic. Retrieved February 23, 2008, from http://www.globalhealth-ec.org/GHEC/Events/Conf07/PConf/Presentations/A1_Schenker.ppt

Shpilko, I. (2006). Russian-American health care: Bridging the communication gap between physicians and patients. [Electronic version] *Patient Education and Counseling, 64*(1–3), 331–341.

Staiti, A. B., Hurley, R. E., & Katz, A. (2006). *Stretching the safety net to serve undocumented immigrants: Community responses to health needs* (Issue Brief No. 104). Washington, DC: Center for Studying Health System Change. Retrieved January 25, 2008, from http://www.hschange.com/CONTENT/818/818.pdf

Tumlin, K. (2007). Immigration detention centers under the microscope: Recent reports reveal widespread violations of the national detention standards. *Immigrants Rights Update, 21*(6). Retrieved March 28, 2008, from http://www.nilc.org/immlawpolicy/arrestdet/ad090.htm

U.S. Citizenship and Immigration Services (1991, May 31). Section 34.2. *Definitions of communicable disease of public health significance.* Retrieved April 11, 2008, from http://www.uscis.gov/propub/ProPubVAP.jsp?dockey=e1659c9dabe6255b7df61da07cd60e5d

U.S. Citizenship and Immigration Services. (2008, January 28). *Immigration and nationality act.* Chapter 2—Qualifications for admission of aliens; travel control of citizens and aliens: Act 212—General classes of aliens ineligible to receive visas and ineligible for admission; waivers of inadmissibility. Retrieved April 11, 2008 from http://www.uscis.gov/propub/ProPubVAP.jsp?dockey=cb90c19a50729fb47fb0686648558dbe

U.S. Citizenship and Immigration Services. (2008, February 28). Form I-601: Instructions for application of waiver of grounds for inadmissibility. Retrieved April 11, 2008, from http://www.uscis.gov/files/form/I-601instr.pdf

U.S. Department of Homeland Security. (1999, May 25). *Fact sheet: Public charge.* Retrieved February 25, 2008, from U.S. Citizenship and Immigration Services Government Portal Online via http://www.uscis.gov/files/pressrelease/public_cfs.pdf

U.S. Department of Homeland Security, Office of Inspector General. (2006, December). *Treatment of immigration detainees housed at immigration and customs enforcement facilities.* Retrieved February 24, 2008, from http://www.dhs.gov/xoig/assets/mgmtrpts/OIG_07–01_Dec06.pdf

Villarejo, D. (2003). The health of U.S. hired farm workers. [Electronic version] *Annual Review of Public Health, 24,* 175–193.

Zuroweste, E. (2007, February). *Health care challenges of global migrants: US migrant farmworkers and other mobile populations.* PowerPoint presentation presented at the 16th Annual Global Health Education Consortium Conference, Santo Domingo, Dominican Republic. Retrieved February 23, 2008, from http://www.globalhealth-ec.org/GHEC/Events/Conf07/PConf/Presentations/A1_Zuroweste_Ed.ppt

6 Mental Health Issues in New Immigrant Communities

DENISE MICHULTKA

As the numbers and complexities of the newcomer population increase, so will the necessity for social work and mental health professionals to discover and create the methods and means for addressing the myriad of mental health concerns that these individuals may experience. Outreach and prevention services that are specific to a particular cultural or high-risk group, including community-based interventions, are essential. Culturally and linguistically appropriate therapeutic services and models will increase the effectiveness and efficaciousness of mental health treatment. Further opportunities to explore multiculturalism in an applied area such as immigrant mental health can lead to new understanding and exploration of general issues in psychology and social work including resilience, trauma, and human diversity.

This chapter will explore the definition of *mental health* in its various culturally conscripted significances, with special emphasis on the topic of strength-based perspectives and resiliency in the immigrant population. Further attention will be given to the aspects of immigrant experiences that are unique, such as the triple trauma paradigm and other trauma-based pathologies. Next, the chapter will cover the complexities of psychosocial assessment with new immigrants as well as the determination of appropriate levels of intervention including specialized treatment options. Finally, the chapter will conclude with suggestions for specialized considerations for therapy with newcomers, with a focus on working with immigrant children and families.

CULTURAL DEFINITIONS OF MENTAL HEALTH

All cultures define, prioritize, and create methods to measure the mental health of their communities with specific value-laden structures. In many cultures, life itself is defined as a series of challenges that an individual must endure to arrive well prepared for the next realm of existence. For other cultures it is the family's well-being (both past and present) that defines status, happiness, and success. For still others, adequate life status equals balance, either in a spiritual or biophysical system. In any case, most new immigrants will have a different and potentially conflicting view of their mental health diagnosis, prognosis, and desired treatment than their mental health practitioner. These differences, if unexplored, ignored, or confronted in a conflictual win/lose showdown, will certainly render any treatment offered less effective, if not completely inutile or dangerous (if it interacts with conflicting traditional methods of healing).

In the area of personal or psychological symptoms, the practitioner must understand the individual's personal belief about the etiology and prognosis of their symptoms. People who believe that their symptoms are the consequence of an external force (a curse, a social characteristic, their birth order, or animal guide) will be unmotivated to participate in a mental health intervention based solely on talking about their feelings. A client who believes in predetermination may question a therapy that looks at changing how they make life decisions. A client who follows the edict that personality is decided by signs, views, or birth order will find an intervention focused on "changing" personality type confusing at best, laughable at worst.

Further, many cultures hold unique beliefs to explain the body-brain or somatic-emotional relationship. Some traditions stress the primacy of the physical and explain and treat emotional symptoms as secondary to a biological imbalance or the negligence of correct diet, herbs, and so forth. Others focus on the effects of external factors (fear, bad winds, evil eye) on the biological systems and ignore emotionality completely. Some explanations (including the U.S.-based behavioral medicine) target emotions and explore how emotional states affect biological systems in both negative and positive ways. Clearly, the client's belief about the body/brain/emotion triad is critical in finding an intervention that will meet their personal criterion for effectiveness.

There may be spiritual, meaning-based explanations for symptoms that must be uncovered and addressed for the mental health treatment to be effective. For example, child soldiers who were forced to violate and kill their elders may explain their symptoms as a punishment from their ancestors for breaking a societal taboo. Treatment may have to include a ceremonial cleansing or forgiveness from elders in the community, to be complete, in a case such as this.

Practitioner's Definitions of Mental Health

In exploring the client's beliefs, it is also imperative for the mental health practitioner to question, and in some cases, decide to put aside his or her own belief assumptions and expertise in mental health to join with the client in a therapeutic manner (Sachs, 1987). This may be a true definition of a culturally competent mental health provider: one who can, in a neutral manner, balance his or her own definitions, beliefs, and methodologies while respecting and working through the systems propagated by their client.

The inability to create a feeling of collaboration, mutual respect, and understanding will leave a new immigrant client and mental health practitioner at odds and make positive intervention impossible. Psychotherapists in particular need to understand and validate their immigrant client's individual/cultural conceptualization of the symptom or problem. They must also recognize their own value-laden judgments as to the functioning and lifestyles of their immigrant clients (Kleinman & Good, 1985).

U.S.-based mental health providers are frequently criticized by immigrant clients for their focus on feeling good or having happiness as a life's goal (a concept very foreign to most other cultures, even in other industrialized nations). The isolation of individual well-being to the possible detriment of the family or cultural unit is also frequently a source of conflict between immigrant clients and mental health providers. In collective cultures, counseling based on the idea that personal growth or achievement is the desired goal will be frowned upon.

One of the most common sources of tension between immigrant clients and their mental health practitioners is the structure and parameters of the therapeutic relationship itself. In most developing nations, educated people such as mental health professionals are sought out because of their perceived wisdom and knowledge. The expectation is generally that a learned person will listen to your concern and then utilize their expertise to guide you. The reflective (ask, not guide) nonstructured methodologies of counseling or therapy as practiced in the United States may be unpopular, confusing, and frustrating to new immigrant clients who may feel especially pressured to "fix" or cure their symptoms rapidly. They may perceive the professional's neutral reflective feedback as an insult. Even the professional environment (large metal desk, bright lights, closed door), may mimic an interrogation session rather than a consultation about healing. In these situations, the client may experience trauma triggers that increase anxiety and distress, making the therapeutic invention null.

RESILIENCY IN IMMIGRANT POPULATIONS

The idea of resiliency as a general concept describes the ability of a person or a people to withstand a physical, emotional, or social crisis, and respond to such circumstances with a return to a general sense of self-power (positive self-efficacy and a feeling of personal control), supportive and mutually benefiting relationships, and the ability and desire to accept current challenges and to gain mastery over new skills within a reasonable amount of time. It may be that the behavioral factors (what the outside world sees and describes as "adjustment") are based on a cognitive ability to process the events of the "transition" in a meaningful and rule-guided manner (which is to say, the ability of the individual or group to integrate the experience into a working schema or definition that creates some level of comfort rather than distress).

The inability to create such an understanding and the resulting feelings of incompetence, fear of reexperiencing the crisis, lack of confidence in the community and/or governing institutions, and lack of motivation/capacity to complete the tasks required in daily life posttransition are the basic symptoms and syndromes related to trauma.

Resiliency (or the lack thereof) is based on a multileveled response that can neither be easily predicted/defined, nor computed within any individual. Clearly, vulnerability and strengths are found in both the internal and external resources and environments of those involved (Silove, Tarn, Bowles & Reid, 1991). A mix of genetics, temperament, development, and cognitive, spiritual, and physical characteristics as influenced by a political, economic, social, or religious reality, all determine postcrisis functioning in the case of new immigrants (Westermeyer, 1989).

For example, a highly intelligent, middle-class attorney, with rigid expectations of himself, may have a more difficult challenge in second-language acquisition after immigration than a migrant worker with less academic preparation, less concern about embarrassment, lower expectations, and a higher level of exposure to the host community. Even the age and developmental stage of the individual upon immigration may determine adjustment (Guarnaccia and Lopez, 1998), with younger, less established people demonstrating higher levels of resiliency after a cultural transition than their elders.

Resiliency may also be influenced by family and community factors. Close, unified, low-conflict families or community units with a collective goal and understanding of immigration as a process may share resources, offer emotional buffering, and provide meaning to the difficult immigration transition that will enhance both the individual's and group's ability to adjust. The role of the individual within the family or community, or the role of the immigrant community within the larger society, may also foster a sense of belonging, obligation/responsibility, and structure that lessens the disruption of immigration.

The voluntary or forced nature of immigration may also be a defining factor in resiliency. Sadly, few immigrants select to leave their home, family, status, professions, and safety for an adventure. War, oppression, severe economic hardship, and natural disaster are more often the impetus for immigration. Not only do these factors affect the immigrant's feelings of personal control, but the very nature of the immigration experience—which may include a lack of planning, separation from family, vulnerability in travel, history of trauma, lack of economic resources, and so forth, may also negatively impact resiliency.

Culture is a major determinate of most aspects of perception, coping skills, and success in the immigrant experience. Cultural expectations define timelines for transitions, factors that create life satisfaction and success, appropriateness of mobility, relationship to the natural world, and role of history and ancestry. Culture may determine the decision making as well as the prioritization of family, spirituality/religion, work, recreation, and education in the life of a person and a people. The fit between the host culture and culture of origin is one factor in posttransition functionality for individuals. Cultures that are similar, or have defined roles within the structure of the other, allow for less challenging transitions.

In the face of crisis, or symptom presentation, many new immigrant communities may utilize traditional methods of creating health and positive adjustments. These interventions may be individual or collective. These practices may include community-wide ceremonies, storytelling, or social support for new immigrants. Some interventions may address the physical level (massage, sweating, etc.), the biochemical system (herbs, teas), and/or emotional functioning (ceremony, journaling, dreaming, etc.). In addition, new immigrants may share practical resources, such as housing, money lending, job connections, and cultural education. Obviously such paths to resiliency only serve an individual that has chosen them and should not be initiated by a social service practitioner.

What is critical for a social service professional is to recognize and affirm healthy and positive functioning in new immigrants and to credit and encourage the use of those methods, ideas, institutions, and individuals that are supporting resiliency naturally.

PHASES OF IMMIGRANT ADJUSTMENT

The transition from one country to another involves a great many challenging tasks, including securing legal status, language acquisition, stable employment, safe housing, social integration, and family reunification. A new immigrant and new immigrant community will complete these tasks on a chronological schedule unique to themselves and their experiences. However, there are stages of adjustment (not unlike the stages of processing grief) that one can expect in normal integration. Each phase also brings with it various needs from social service providers. Table 6.1 describes the phases, and the accompanying needs of each.

IMMIGRANTS AND TRAUMA

A major mental health vulnerability in the new immigrant population is, often, the variety of traumatic experiences that have forced these individuals into the role of refugee, asylum seeker, or exile. It has been demonstrated that voluntary economic immigrants have differential levels of psychological symptoms than do those with forced immigration scenarios (Escobar, Hoyos Nervi, & Gara, 2000). Even higher levels of mortality within first generation immigration have been documented in those with refugee status as opposed to self-selected immigrants (Jablensky et al., 1994).

Table 6.1

PHASES OF IMMIGRANT ADJUSTMENT

STAGES OF ACCULTURATION & POSSIBLE SERVICE IMPLICATIONS		
PHYSICAL EVENTS	**PSYCHO-SOCIAL EXPERIENCE**	**SERVICE IMPLICATIONS**
	ARRIVAL	
• Reunited with family • Located in new home • Children enrolled in school • Initial medical screening • Case manager assigned from resettlement agency • Referred for ESL, employment and other services • Paperwork, red tape, other print-based requirements	• High expectations • Relief • Grateful to be safe • Hopeful for future and/or • Feeling over-whelmed • Confusion • Disorientation • Mixed emotions and/or • Numbed out/state of shock and/or • Resentment • Anger	• Excited to be studying • Grateful for help and support • Pleased to be in a community • Excited to get to know an American • Sense of purpose and schedule • Fearful/nervous about learning new language, or • Unfocused • Nonrelated or unconnected, or • Resentful • Restless • Impatient
	REALITY	
• Culture shock • Negative experiences • Losses realized • Intergenerational conflict in families • Values and faith conflicts across cultures • Conflict within refugee communities • Realization that many obstacles must be overcome to have the life they dream of	• Culture shock • Awareness of challenges and difficulties • Disappointment and anger • Feeling over-whelmed • Fear, sense of abandonment • Preoccupation with losses • Frustration • Memories of traumatic events • Resent and anger	• Difficulty concentrating • Detachment • Short-term memory loss • Doesn't complete or forgets assignments • Flashbacks • Fatigue • Falling asleep in class • Startle response/ hypervigilance • Lateness or frequent absence • Somatic complaints (headache, stomachache, etc.)
	NEGOTIATION (OR MARGINALIZATION SEE BELOW)	
• Begin to understand and accept new environment	• Begins to accept losses • Healing from trauma	• Dedication to classroom learning • Complete assignments

(continued)

Table 6.1

PHASES OF IMMIGRANT ADJUSTMENT *(continued)*

STAGES OF ACCULTURATION & POSSIBLE SERVICE IMPLICATIONS		
PHYSICAL EVENTS	**PSYCHO-SOCIAL EXPERIENCE**	**SERVICE IMPLICATIONS**
• Takes action to move ahead • Developing English capacity • Stability and structure in daily living • Affiliation with ethnic group • Rebuilding support systems • Defining new roles and identity	• Commitment to succeed • Growing sense of self-determination and control	• Connecting to classmates, making friends • Set realistic goals • Memory improvement • Concentration improvement • Still may experience feelings of frustration or being overwhelmed, "Will I ever learn this language?"
	CULTURAL INTEGRATION (OR MARGINALIZATION, SEE BELOW)	
• Basic needs met • Some language competence • Employment and /or economic stability • Family relationship strengthened • Community ties established	• Sense of power and control • Bicultural identity forged • Self-confidence • Pride in self-sufficiency • Sense of success and stable future, "I have a place in this country."	• May disengage from ESL class as self-sufficiency and English competency • Sense that class is no longer needed, that client has moved beyond it • Increased self-study • May transfer to workplace ESL • May focus on college or other adult-education options
	ALIENATION	
• Inability to use (or lack of access to) transportation • Poor physical health • No male escort (if culturally required) • Taking care of small children • Mental health issues • Intergenerational conflict • Possible domestic abuse	• Reluctant to leave home • Not wanting to "take on" the outside world • Isolation and withdrawal • Despair and sadness • Suicidal thoughts • Lamenting loss of old roles	• Attendance very sporadic or student drops out • May have difficulty reaching student by phone • Intends to, but can't manage to come to class • Barriers to attendance, i.e., no transportation, no male escort, childcare, etc. • Overattachment to one teacher, level, or program

(continued)

Table 6.1

PHASES OF IMMIGRANT ADJUSTMENT *(continued)*

STAGES OF ACCULTURATION & POSSIBLE SERVICE IMPLICATIONS		
PHYSICAL EVENTS	**PSYCHO-SOCIAL EXPERIENCE**	**SERVICE IMPLICATIONS**
• Children are not supervised • Especially at risk: older refugees and homebound women	• Fear they cannot succeed in the United States	• Time management, priority setting issues
	MARGINALIZATION	
• Strong involvement with institutions, legal, child welfare, police • Dependence • Unemployment • Legal involvement • Taking on negative roles • Temporary housing or moves often • Seldom leave home • Possible involvement in gangs or crime • Substance or domestic abuse	• Has given up hope of acculturating or having a positive role in the United States • Has resentment/ negative attitude • Hopelessness • Seems unreachable	• Attendance has ceased • May be impossible to locate or contact student

Discrimination, oppression, war, and torture are unique predecessors to immigration because they are the result of targeted, intentional, human action that affects not only the individual, but also the community. Since World War II, there have been 170 armed conflicts resulting in 30 million civilian deaths. Over 140 political regimes are known to use violence to enforce civil law. Often entire racial ethnic, religious, or professional groups are targeted and attacked (Amnesty International, 2007). Obviously, globally, the numbers of people who have survived atrocities is increasing. Amnesty International reports that of refugee populations, 4%–5% will be survivors of torture.

Refugees are individuals or groups who have been forced to escape their country of origin and are currently residing in a second country due to natural disaster or civil/political strife. These individuals have not been offered permanent shelter from the host country to which they have fled (generally a neighboring country with similar challenges). Instead, after a complicated process of verification, they are placed on a list to await resettlement in a third country. This process may extend months, years, and/or generations.

Life in refugee camps is particularly challenging as refugees are often restricted in mobility, employment, and education. Further, resources for the camps are based on a limited supply of international support. Often food, water, medical care, and other basic necessities are sold to the highest bidders. In situations where employment is disallowed, crime, oppression, and traumatic life events abound.

Survivors of targeted individual oppression and torture due to race, ethnicity, religion, political opinion, or social group may not be offered refugee status and may have been forced to leave their country without appropriate documentation and permission. Under current U.S. immigration policy, these individuals are obligated to present themselves in the host country and affirmatively request asylum. Significant proof that identifies the individual as a target of discrimination, oppression, or torture is required to be granted asylum under current U.S. immigration policy. (See the appendixes at the back of this volume for sample affidavits for asylum.)

In many instances the individual who has fled under high risk has only physical and emotional scars to verify his or her story, as official records of torture and oppression are not kept and are often actively denied by perpetrating institutions and governments. Such cases obviously are difficult to prove; the perpetrators of violence may have significant institutional support (often from their government), while the victims have none. Retraumatization from court proceedings (where the individual is obligated to relive the trauma in a sometimes hostile environment) is common, as are long familial separations, lengthy detentions, and extreme economic hardship for asylum seekers (as they are not granted permission to work until they have secured asylum status). Further, federally funded health, mental health, and social service benefits are not offered until asylum status has been procured.

Discrimination, oppression, and torture are practices that target individuals, but are utilized to break down naturally occurring societal supports and create systems of social control that allow a group in power to exercise their undue will (often in brutal ways with unjust consequences) upon the entirety of another group based on a perceived difference between the groups. Trauma resulting from these often complex and closed webs of control affect the physical, emotional, social, and spiritual well-being of their victims.

A major goal of torture is to utilize physical and psychological tactics (by abuse and deprivation) to destroy within the victim any sense of security, reliability, or dependability, relying frequently on isolation and separation to depersonalize the individual targeted (Amery, 1977), and to serve as an example to the rest of the community.

The Triple Trauma Paradigm

Orley (1994) proposed that new immigrants often are in the midst of a chronological interaction of three distinct traumatic periods.

The individual is first affected by the trauma in the country of origin that precipitated their flight from their country. These experiences may include, but are not limited to, oppression, discrimination (refusal of employment, housing, medical care, or basic human rights based on a perceived identification with an undesired group), increased targeting (receiving threats, being watched, having family members or self detained/interrogated, being forced into hiding, etc.), and torture (severe physical actions including but not limited to beatings, mock assassinations, isolation, rape, injury/death to family members, detention, starvation, exposure to extreme conditions, etc.).

Due to the vulnerability of the victims of oppression and torture, the escape/journey of immigration is also fraught with traumatic events. Individuals are often forced to leave family, friends, and all possessions (including legitimate travel documents) as they prepare for escape. They are often exposed to severe travel conditions (walking for days at a time, locked in enclosed spaces, lack of food/water, high/low temperatures, etc.). Many immigrants become victims of crimes; robbery, rape, and extortion are common occurrences in the journeys of new immigrants to safety. Due to the lack of low-cost accessible and legal means for immigration, most individuals are forced to use illegal systems filled with unsavory characters to ensure their voyage. Expediential expenses, high levels of danger, possible detention in a second country, and terror are faced by immigrants as they journey through countries with limited or no permission. Sadly, many victims do not even identify themselves as victims; they often blame themselves for incompetence or immorality in the decisions of survival they are obligated to make under extreme duress.

Lastly, the relocation process is also the stage for a plethora of traumatic events. Indefinite detention, retraumatization by a hostile legal system, poverty, social isolation, forced family separation, the lack of legal status and loss of social role, all are ongoing traumas common in the lives of new immigrants. Further, the experience of trauma-related symptoms may cause the individual to doubt his or her own sanity and competence, adding to stress and disrupting any sense of well-being.

The loss of family identity, community culture, and position is profound for people whose sense of well-being and pride are based on these markers. Difficulties with adjustment to unfamiliar employment, a new language, changes in familial and gender roles, as well as unknown and often isolating social structures in the new country add to the ongoing trauma experienced by the individual (Brody, 1994). Further, there is a real fear of retribution and continuation of country-of-origin conflicts in the host countries for some communities (Pope and Garcia-Peltoniemi, 1991), where members of warring groups are living in small, isolated, homogenous pockets. These factors, combined with the ever-present fear of immigration policy and deportation as well as the increasing conflicts between immigrant communities with local police, child protection officials, and general anti-immigrant attitudes, create a continual parade of traumatic events for new immigrants.

Psychological Consequences of Trauma

There is a variety of ways in which the human psyche adjusts to severe trauma that enhances the ability of the individual to survive without significant psychopathology. Some of these mechanisms may be labeled maladaptive or may even be described as a psychological/psychiatric diagnosis by the posttrauma host community, while others are lauded as positive coping skills. The difference may be determined more on the functionality of the response in the host society than based on an actual objective criterion of symptomology.

It is important to note that coping skills, defense mechanisms, psychological symptoms, and even political, religious, and academic responses to trauma are all culturally bound and are assigned negative or positive polarity based on culture values, traditions, and customs (Stein, 1986).

The most frequent and obvious psychological/psychiatric diagnosis utilized with traumatized populations is that of posttraumatic stress disorder (PTSD) found in the *Diagnostic and Statistical Manual of Disorders* (4th ed.) (DSM-IV) (American Psychiatric Association, 2000). This diagnosis was created specifically for individuals who have experienced an unusual life-threatening event and from which the individual continues to experience symptoms one year after the traumatic incident.

There are three symptom categories that must be present for an individual to receive the diagnosis of PTSD. The first set of symptoms addresses the reexperiencing of traumatic memories in the form of invasive memories/thoughts and flashbacks. Flashbacks are generally short, intense, vivid memories that create physiological effects that mirror those experienced in the initial trauma. The person may experience a raised heart rate, sweating, or difficulty breathing. Unlike the popular media depictions, flashbacks are commonly short in duration (a few minutes long), and the person experiencing them will not generally lose the ability to discern reality and will not necessarily act out traumatic scenes in dramatic and obvious ways.

The second category of symptoms cluster around the desire/need of the survivor to control their own reexperiencing of the trauma by avoiding all thoughts, activities, or triggers of their memories. This may include very specific reactions such as avoiding large crowds, refusing to watch violent material in the popular media, or running away when confronted by uniformed individuals. More frequently, because of the extensive and complex range of traumatic events experienced by survivors of war and oppression, the avoidance responses become generalized. Individuals may distract themselves by working continually, self-medicating with alcohol, or avoiding sleep (so that traumatic dreams cease). Social relationships (including those with intimate partners and close family members) may become distant or conflictual. Outside friendships may be discouraged and new acquaintances mistrusted.

The final grouping of symptoms reflects the physiological changes that often result from trauma. They include hypervigilance, exaggerated startled responses, irritability, and the inability to relax. The parasympathetic nervous system (the fight or flight response), if engaged for an extended period of time without the ability to escape the situation, will become hyperaroused. When these circumstances are repeated with frequency and intensity, the parasympathetic nervous system remains active for longer periods of time and is more difficult to disengage. This heightened stress state results in a feeling of dread and fear, being on the edge, easily angered or upset as well as affecting actual somatic systems such as heightened blood pressure, cardiac arrhythmias, and so forth. As a direct result, the ability to regulate behavior, concentration, learning, and attending to details will be diminished.

A pervasive symptom/coping skill employed (often involuntarily) by survivors of trauma is disassociation. Disassociation is the removal of conscious attention from the current reality to a distracting other thought, memory, and/or physiological reaction. During a crisis, people describe disassociation as the sensation of leaving the body and watching from afar (as a stranger), to what is happening. People may focus on an early memory, or the sound of their own heartbeat. Posttrauma disassociation may appear when a trigger ignites the memory of some incident of trauma. In a more useful scenario, trauma victims often speak of directing their attention from painful/uncomfortable current realities (maybe testifying at an asylum hearing, or being disciplined at work) to a more positive image or dream. This may allow the person to withstand their negative emotion, but also may lead to misunderstanding and confusion.

The disassociated witness may relate the horrific details of their experience of torture with little or no emotion, which is then interpreted by a judge as lacking credibility. A traumatized child may respond to a disciplinarian with a blank look and an inability to react to redirection, which is then interpreted as insolence or stupidity. Disassociation in the general public is frequently an indication of a psychotic process and negative prognosis. In trauma victims, disassociation may be better interpreted as a practical coping skill that needs to be controlled and monitored in nonemergency situations.

Physical and Physiological Consequence of Trauma in New Immigrants

As discussed earlier, new immigrants may have been exposed to extreme violence, malnutrition, severe travel conditions, lack of medical care, and lack of safety, all of which may lead to serious physical symptoms as well as psychological symptomatology. In addition many of the psychological ailments of new immigrants (PTSD, anxiety, and depression) may have component physical symptoms (fatigue, lack of appetite, headache, etc.). Further, cultural factors may make it more likely that a symptom will be perceived or described as somatic and not related to the emotional state of the individual as opposed to being identified as a psychological reaction to stress.

It is of critical importance in such circumstances to investigate both physical and psychological underpinnings of a new immigrant's complaints to ensure that the treatment selected is appropriate and affective. This goal is of course complicated by the limited access that new immigrants have to appropriate medical care and best-practice technology in diagnosis. Many available complex diagnostic procedures (MRI's, brain scans, neurological evaluations, etc.) are not available under Medicaid or the charitable medical services accessible by new immigrants. Undocumented immigrants are particularly at risk, not having access to needed physical and mental health services.

Mediating Factors in Trauma-Based Psychopathology

Not all survivors of war trauma, oppression, or torture respond to their experiences with diagnostic levels of psychological symptoms. There are protective factors within each experience, each individual, and each posttrauma environment that may add positive support and reduce the impact of the trauma, to subclinical reaction. Many of these factors were already mentioned in the discussion on resiliency earlier in this chapter.

Some factors are specific to the trauma experience. The frequency, duration, intensity, and repeated exposure to trauma are known to differentially affect the creation of symptoms. The idea of preparedness also takes place in this discussion. For some individuals, who have made a predetermined and conscious decision to defy an unjust authority, trauma in the form of targeted oppression and even torture may be a consequence for which they are in some way prepared. Individuals who define themselves by a religious, cultural, or political belief that offers an explanation, justification, and compensation for their traumatic experience may perceive that experience differently (fighting for the cause, standing up for justice) and engage actively in returning to their pretrauma functioning. This may mitigate the psychological effects of trauma.

On the other hand, an individual who randomly entered into a traumatic situation (ending up "in the wrong place at the wrong time") with no religious, political, or social frame for the trauma may interpret and generalize their experience to a belief that the world is a chaotic and negative place where bad things randomly happen. This individual is likely to feel hopeless, depressed, and may have little motivation to actively participate in a recovery process.

Lastly, it is important to understand that there is a chronological cycle of natural distress and healing that an individual may follow after trauma and relocation. Many new immigrants at arrival are still functioning in an emergency state. They must find safe housing, access economic means to support themselves and their families (both here and abroad), learn a new language, achieve a permanent legal status, and so on. At that moment, the processing of a traumatic event may move to the psychological back burner until the individual has the stability, attention level, and safety to begin allowing themselves to think about their experiences. Tayabas and Pok (1983) found that generally, new immigrants who had survived traumatic experiences waited one to two years before requesting mental health services.

Treating Vicarious Trauma

A primary challenge in the therapeutic relationship may be the intensity of secondary or vicarious trauma experienced by the mental health professional working with new immigrant communities.

A provider may attempt to minimize or even deny the veracity of the client's experiences that are overwhelming or unfamiliar to them (torture, war, forced exile, etc.). They may be so shocked by the stories they are unable to offer normalization or controlled empathy to the client. Alternatively, some practitioners become attracted to the dramatic and exotic features of their client's experience and focus on these factors to the detriment of the treatment process.

In many circumstances, the mental health practitioner may experience depression, anger, and spiritual questioning in response to a client's experience. The practitioner may become politicized and focus on advocacy to balance the feelings of helplessness that working with the victim may evoke. Secondary trauma experiences are expected and demonstrate a healthy, committed, and compassionate understanding of the new immigrant's experience.

In order to best address this experience, there are steps that mental health providers can take to ensure their own efficacy. Adequate rest, exercise, and good health habits are essential for all mental health care givers. A reasonable balance between work and recreation, supportive social networks, and discovering a level of meaning in existence or work will enhance the provider's energy and passion for such intense work. Personal crisis, including any psychological/addictive symptoms experienced, should be addressed immediately by a mental health professional apart from colleagues.

PSYCHOSOCIAL ASSESSMENT WITH NEW IMMIGRANT INDIVIDUALS

Assessment with any new immigrant community must be undertaken with extreme caution, with appropriate resources, and with a clear and beneficial goal preemptively designated. There are few to no validated and researched measures of mental illness for new immigrant communities. The assessment of mental function is a particularly culture-based activity that utilizes specific societal norms, methods of inquiry, and cultural definitions that exclude even marginalized populations or groups within a society and that may be completely useless when considering immigrant mental health. The same is true for the most part with regard to measures of intelligence, personality, or specific host culture concepts (such as self-esteem).

When attempting to assess for mental illness in new immigrant communities, practitioners must take into consideration the medical/psychological service climate of the country in question. Many new immigrants faced a lack of access to or inability to access appropriate medical and mental health services in their country of origin.

Assessments should be heavily weighted on clinical interviews with culturally competent mental health care providers. Generalization should be limited to unique circumstances mimicking the testing situation. Whenever possible, use multiple information sources, multiple methods, and multiple assessment sessions.

Questions about medical and mental health history, both personal and familiar, should be presented in language that discusses specific symptoms or characteristics in lieu of diagnostics and treatment. They should address very specific, clear, and limited clinical questions that will somehow benefit the client.

Assessments with immigrants will be slower-paced than with other populations. All measures used should be explained to the client, and reliability and validity information should be openly discussed when interpreting any findings. Disclosure about the evaluation (purpose, method, outcome) can give the client a feeling of power, control, and active participation in the process.

Differential diagnosis across cultures, races, and ethnicities needs to be carefully explored within both an individual case and in community-wide interventions. The experience of mental health as defined by general life satisfaction, perception of symptomatology, and expectation of a positive outlook on life is almost entirely culturally defined (Marsella, 1993). How a person explains a particular experience is determined by social learning, expectations from the culture, and their own interpretation of the symptomatology. At the same time, disclosure of the symptom to another may rest on their level of trust, motivation, and expectation of symptom alleviation. Interestingly, but not surprisingly, it is the most organic and chronic mental illnesses that appear most similar in description and prognosis across cultures. Schizophrenia, autism, and mental retardation, for example, have strikingly homogenous presentations across continents, although explanation of etiology and treatment options may vary widely.

Assessment With Asylum Seekers

A critical and practical example is the need of asylum seekers to verify the extent of their physical and psychological distress due to oppression, violence, and torture. In such cases, forensic, medical, and psychological evaluations may be the only "evidence" the individual is able to produce that supports his or her claims of asylum.

In this new area, credibility primarily as well as psychological damage is given weight in identifying true victims. The determination of credibility must be handled delicately in these cases as actual survivors of torture may respond negatively to questions and environments reminiscent of interrogation. Utilizing multiple sources for both individual and country information, extending evaluations overtime to check for consistency, and monitoring internal integrity are all methods for ensuring creditability.

In documenting psychological symptomatology, multiple sources, observation, symptom chronology, and specifically, treatment history and authenticity of symptom description are all important factors in documenting mental illness.

Assessment With Children

Evaluation of immigrant children may also be recommended for appropriate academic placement and special education services. Assessing trauma based on behavioral and emotional patterns in children is particularly difficult. Due to natural resiliency patterns, children may appear to adjust well in most areas, but have symptoms in an area seemingly unrelated to their traumatic experience. Children's experience with a particular academic or mental health service environment may be limited, which affects their performance. Further, pervasive but periodic symptoms of anxiety or depression may mask true ability if placement is determined by a one-session assessment.

INDIVIDUAL INTERVENTION STRATEGIES WITH NEW IMMIGRANTS

Actual social work treatment within new immigrant communities is almost always multimodel in methodology. Services must take into consideration life circumstances, cultural competency, mental health complexities, and medical factors as well as social and spiritual aspects of the individual's life. Woodcock (1997) describes treatment with new immigrants as such a new field that eclecticism and multimethodology are the only ethical and logical choices for practitioners. Kleinman and Kleinman (1991) suggest that the major tasks of the therapeutic alliance between professionals and new immigrants are building a long-term trusting and supportive relationship; recognizing recent stressors; reducing psychiatric-related symptoms; strengthening social ties; and increasing the client's sense of competence, autonomy, and power.

While a variety of specialized methods such as prolonged exposure therapies, biofeedback, and other trauma-specific therapies have been utilized on a small scale and suggested for use with immigrant clients, no controlled study has been conducted to verify their differential effect in newcomer populations. Logically, as in the nonimmigrant population, treatment effectiveness is dependent on the interaction between the treatment method and the individual's belief about his or her own mental health, education, and relationship with the therapist.

A mental health intervention cannot be introduced in isolation to the actuality of the current life situation of the new immigrant client. Concerns about immigration status, safe housing, adequate employment, and appropriate medical cares as well as sufficient food, clothing, and transportation must be addressed as a basis of treatment (Pederson, 2000). While concurrent case management and therapy may be ideal, it is often not available to new immigrant clients with limited access to public benefits.

The most practical solution for those wanting to focus on mental health concerns is to foster relationships with and be well informed about social service: legal, medical, and other charitable services in their geographic area that can assist new immigrant clients with their needs. Utilizing orientation sessions or some part of ongoing sessions to monitor basic needs, provide information and referral concerning community resources, and following up on encountered obstacles or success in obtaining needed services will create a feeling of increased collaboration, trust, and understanding. Further, a client with stable housing, employment, day care, transportation, and basic life needs will be more compliant, cooperative, and motivated to address his or her mental health symptoms.

Despite best intentions and adequate referrals, it may be that the systems encountered by the new immigrant (which may include legal immigration or criminal issues, school districts, Child Protective agencies, County of Federal Relief agencies, employment benefits, and/or charitable medical systems), with their concurrent regulations, bureaucratic obligations, and paperwork, may leave your immigrant client feeling confused, overwhelmed, and frustrated. While it is necessary to create appropriate professional boundaries in lieu of a case coordinator, a mental health practitioner may need to dedicate some time and energy to service coordination and advocacy to ensure that the immigrant client has a base of services that will allow the client to peaceably participate in the mental health treatment.

Establishing the Therapeutic Relationship

As in any client population, the best indication of treatment success will be the therapeutic relationship between the mental health provider and client (Kinzie & Fleck, 1987). This is especially true for immigrants who may be socially isolated, separated from family and friends, and for whom the therapist may be the face of the host culture.

For new immigrant communities, trust is a major theme touching almost all interactions with the host community. Immigrants, especially those who have experienced intentional human violence, or oppression, have seen a side of human nature to which most of us are never exposed. They are aware of the human capacity to harm, to violate human rights and dignity. These experiences certainly may leave survivors with grave doubts about the human condition and little to no faith in social institutions.

Furthermore, for all immigrants, having to address mental health issues with service providers who may be of a different religion, culture, race, or gender than themselves may be significant barriers to trust. This will be discussed later in the section on cultural competence.

Trust will be an especially difficult issue for new immigrants who are exposed to regulations that appear nonsensical (you can live here, but you are not allowed to work; however, your children can receive free education). In these cases, trust is difficult to establish in the face of the fear of violating unknown rules or regulations.

In order to create a trusting therapeutic bond, it may be necessary to be more forthcoming and disclose more personal information with immigrant clients than with those from the host cultures. One issue is the continuation of fear. For many immigrants, distinctions between religions, ethnicities, and classes are conflictual and potentially dangerous. The power differential between most immigrants and their service providers is so great that disclosure of any information may feel risky to a new immigrant. A client anxious to know where you worship, how you vote, or your ethnic background may be ensuring his or her own feeling of safety and ability to confide in you. Disclosure may be as simple as answering the question directly ("Yes, I am of this religious tradition; how do you think that will affect our work together?"), or explaining the parameters of the therapeutic relationship ("I don't believe that my political affiliation will affect our work; is there something specific you are concerned about?"). In many cases, the therapist will serve as a cultural consultant for the new immigrant, who is learning the complexities of the host culture through observation and individual experience.

While disclosure and positive affect may be the basis of the therapeutic relationship, the upkeep of professional boundaries is also educative and important. The role of the mental health practitioner is unique and strange to many cultures. A stranger to whom you tell your most intimate concerns is a bizarre proposition in many communities. New immigrant clients (especially those who are receiving charitable services) may want to offer payment to demonstrate their appreciation and respect of your expertise. Small cultural gifts, food, and souvenirs are appropriate and should be accepted. Expensive gifts, trips, or business gifts should probably be discouraged (explaining about professional boundaries, agency policies, and licensure regulations will help to depersonalize the rejections). Gracious thanks should be offered always in response to an offered gift.

Adoption of the mental health practitioner as an honored family or community member, complete with correspondent title (sister, etc.), is also common and generally not harmful as long as real boundaries are respected. Attendance at significant family or cultural events may be appropriate dependent on practitioner comfort, public level of event (more intimate events should be avoided), and significance (asylum hearing, naturalization ceremony, etc.).

Overcoming Shame and Guilt

Shame is another continual concern in most new immigrant communities. Immigrants may lose status, power, resources, role, and other significant indicators of respect in their move from one culture to another. Further, those who have experienced violence and trauma may perceive that they have in some way created or deserved such an experience. This is enhanced by the fact that in the desperation of war and an immigrant "journey" individuals may have been forced to act in ways they themselves find distasteful or shameful. Finally, new immigrants are often aware that they are not appreciated or respected in their host culture, increasing their feelings of shame and embarrassment. Due to these multiple levels of shame, immigrants may wish to avoid discussing or disclosing their mental health concerns at all costs, leaving service providers without adequate information to offer efficient, effective treatment.

Guilt is the final, almost universal, obstacle to the identification and treatment of mental illness in the new immigrant community. Many immigrants may feel guilty and undeserving when comparing their fates to those community and family members who have been left behind. It is a common response to sacrifice in many areas in order to economically sustain those in the country of origin or assist other members of the community or family to immigrate themselves. Therefore, "complaining" or utilizing valuable resources (time, money, etc.) on identifying or treating the nebulous feelings, emotions, and behaviors of a non-life-threatening mental illness may be discouraged as an American luxury not appropriate for a new immigrant.

Addressing Cultural Issues

In order to sustain therapeutic legitimacy, it is often incumbent upon the mental health professional to address cultural issues and inconsistencies of their own country or people. Unjust immigration policies, racial and linguistic discrimination, forced poverty, inability to access needed services, social isolation, and cultural egocentrism are all potential aspects of a new immigrant's experience that may be addressed in the mental health intervention. For social service practitioners, their own reactions may range from disbelief, guilt, and embarrassment toward their countries or cultures, to anger at the new immigrant for being critical or ungrateful for the host country's generosity. In most circumstances, work with new immigrants will expose the practitioner to a previously unexplored side of his or her own culture.

It takes professional training, supervision, self-exploration, and a true desire to understand the new immigrant's experience to confront these realities in a therapeutic manner that is of assistance to the client. However, denial or avoidance of these issues may lead to a deterioration of the therapeutic alliance.

As in all areas, practitioners themselves should not probe for or focus too exclusively on these themes. The new immigrant client will address them if they feel themselves to be in a supportive and safe environment and when they are relevant. Some new immigrants will be ardent supporters of the ideologies of their new country and will deny that there are any negative aspects in their new homeland. These individuals should also not be challenged about their current beliefs. A dynamic ebb and flow of idealism and cynicism about the host culture is expected.

The concept of acculturation as a goal of treatment or indicator of positive mental health must also be explored as part of the therapeutic relation. Acculturation historically was defined by the adaptation of the new immigrant to the values, lifestyles and economics, and educational and legal system of the host culture. The belief was that by joyfully and gratefully embracing the host country in its entirety, the new immigrant would be accepted, would be successful, and would have little to no grief about leaving their homeland and culture—a psychological version of the American dream.

More recently, alternative models of immigrant adjustment have been proposed that are based on integration, preserving cultural identity, and strengthening global ties. These methods strive to bolster and enhance the immigrant's primary identities (culturally, religiously, etc.) while opening opportunities for economic development, education, and contributions to the tolerant host society and also maintaining social and cultural ties to the country of origin.

However, a practitioner's multiculturalism may be challenged when faced with the actual deep-rooted cultural differences that divide nations, represented in the behaviors, opinions, and values of new immigrant clients. For example, a female client who defers her own academic or professional advancement to support her family; a family with chronic economic struggles who continues to send a significant portion of their salaries abroad; parents who utilize their children as emergency interpreters or child care providers in lieu of making school attendance a priority—all of these may experience negative feedback from a mental health provider who believes in individual rights over collectivism.

This may be further explored as the immigrant client begins to negotiate with the host culture and determine which values, lifestyles, and customs to adopt and which to reject. New immigrants may decide to commit to preserving the primacy of their family, dedicate themselves to strict religious or cultural customs, prioritize family peace over economics, and maintain strict rules of conduct between genders or ages. They may openly criticize the perceived materialism and permissiveness of host culture dress, religiosity, and family relations. They may reject the host society's treatment of the elderly and specialized treatment of animals. New immigrant clients may even question the significance of mental health treatment itself.

An unprepared mental health practitioner may feel defensive and irritated, and may, so to speak, symptomatize the cultural diversity from which these observations and opinions arise.

CULTURALLY COMPETENT MENTAL HEALTH SERVICES

Mental health practitioners in the United States frequently pride themselves on being color-blind and laud themselves for believing that their cultural view can accommodate any level of diversity (Ivey, 1995). Most new immigrant clients however, are highly color-sensitive. They are hyperaware of differences between themselves and the professionals they are exposed to and are frequently uncomfortable with them. Differences in gender, race, religion, culture, education, and class may create barriers for a new immigrant client that are impossible within their cultural perspective to overcome (Freire, 1973). In such cases, a professional's belief about their cultural competence is irrelevant. The immigrant must also be able to benefit from a diverse service provider.

There are many ways to open up mental health prevention, education, and ultimately treatment to new immigrant populations. The first and most obvious is to include representatives from the community, including ethnic-insider mental health professionals in all levels of program design, implementation, and evaluation. Within cultural groups there will always be diversity; however, utilizing ethnically based practitioners will reduce the gap of understanding and increase appropriateness.

Clarifying Treatment Goals

Clarification of treatment goals is also critical in cross-cultural therapies. The alleviation of distress (no matter how defined), the increases in positive life experiences, the ability to complete expected life roles coupled with the increase of resources (personal coping skills, informational, psychoeducational, social, etc.) are all generalized goals that most new immigrant clients will find some resonance with. Therapeutic relations need to be based on mutual respect and dignity with a priority on witnessing, comforting, and creative collaboration as well as having the client express relevant thought and feelings.

For many mental health practitioners confronted for the first time with the stark realities of life in developing nations, war, and immigration, the most difficult task may be the ability to serve as merely a witness to the individual's story. Immigrants often feel (and may have even been told) that no one will understand, believe, or care about their suffering, losses, and struggles. The immigrant client may perceive questioning, confusion, and curiosity on the part of the mental health practitioner as disbelief, or the inability to understand the individual's reality.

Themes such as individualism versus collectivism, gender, age, and educational role differences, and the feeling of a lack of understanding may affect an immigrant client greatly. Positive respectful interactions with members of the host culture are essential for recovery for immigrant clients, who may have lost the feeling of self-efficacy in all other aspects of their lives (Silove, Tarn, Bowles, & Reid, 1991). Using formal titles (Mr., Mrs., Dr.), respecting time limits, and consistently reminding the client of their rights and decision points will assist in this endeavor.

When working with couples or families, demonstrating an understanding or deference to the culturally determined family or gender role, will inspire confidence and reduce concern that you are questioning and challenging your client's cultural beliefs and lifestyles. Immigrant clients may feign acquiescence and respect when in reality they have completely dismissed the service or service provider as incompetent or not able to assist in treatment due to cultural norms and social behavior. Noncompliance in immigrant clients may in fact be an expression of their frustration and termination of culturally inappropriate services.

Linguistic Considerations

Linguistic appropriateness is a minimum requirement of culturally informed mental health services. Clearly the client must have a common language with which to communicate with the service provider. But even this is not sufficient. Individuals who speak English as a second language may be able to communicate in a variety of situations, but not progress adequately in mental health treatment without interpretation. Memories and emotionally laden events are encoded in the language in which they occur. Examining traumatic memories or conflict in communication patterns will be much more challenging and less effective using a second language that is unfamiliar, or in which it does not occur.

The use of interpreters is indicated always when completing a detailed evaluation and in situations where the understanding of the emotional content and context of the information is a focus. Interpreters serve not only as language facilitators, but in the best of circumstances, work as cultural brokers that may add historical context, cultural understanding and normalization of the client presentation in the community.

Concurrently interpreters can be a source of confusion and mistrust in a therapeutic relationship. Within many immigrant communities that are small and insular, the likelihood that the interpreter and client are already acquainted is high. Confidentiality, which may be a new concept for both the client and interpreter, must be stressed at every opportunity, and clear professional boundaries modeled and upheld.

An individual speaking the same language, but with significant differences in geographic locale, gender, religion, class, education, or social group, may be an inappropriate or inefficient interpreter. It is important preemptively to discuss with the client (through a telephonic or neutral interpreter) what parameters they must set on interpreter characteristics and qualifications. It is equally important for the mental health practitioner to remain aware and alert for these issues as treatment proceeds. An astute observer (even with no linguistic skill) can pick up relational or even linguistic difficulties in a session and address the issues utilizing an alternative interpreter or interpretation method.

The primary relationship between immigrant client and mental health practitioner should be created and maintained. England-Dimitrova (1991) suggest the following eight rules for positive interpretation:

1 Use short sentences
2 Isolate complicated or multifaceted concepts

3 Always look directly at the clients when addressing them
4 Ask for verification that the client understands by asking the client to restate instructions or concepts
5 Explain openly and verbally your own appraisals and reaction
6 Use summary statements and check for feedback
7 Don't interrupt the client or interpreter
8 Wait for the complete message to be interpreted before speaking

Traditional Healing Methods

Within the realm of cross-cultural therapies and cultural competence, there has been a movement to include traditional healers and ceremonies in the therapeutic setting for both immigrant and nonimmigrant clients. Although this may, upon occasion, be requested by and appreciated by the client, there is much to be investigated, negotiated, and understood before any such intervention is introduced.

One important caveat is that the impetus of the involvement of traditional healing methods must originate from the new immigrant clients themselves. Individuals within a culture may have vastly different opinions of acceptance of or the practice of traditional healing. For some new immigrants it is something they believe is secret, unique, and not to be shared with noncommunity members. For others such methods are considered sinful, backward, or dangerous. A mental health practitioner may open the discussion by questioning a client about his or her beliefs and utilization of alternative healing methods, with no probing unless the client offers a desire for such an intervention.

If it is determined that the client believes in and desires to integrate traditional healing methods, it is incumbent upon the practitioner to understand what methods are being utilized, for what expected ends, and with what potential interaction affect with other methods utilized. It is essential to seek information assistance from community members who are trustworthy and culturally competent so that one is aware of the procedures, expectations, side effects, and reputations of the traditional healers and methods utilized.

Exploring Alternative Therapies

It is important to meet the diverse clinical needs of new immigrants who may also perceive and experience mental health symptoms in unique ways by utilizing creative and holistic treatment plans. For those who have been victims of violence or sexual violation, and those experiencing chronic pain therapies, incorporating physicality may be of great use. This may include massage therapy, dance and movement therapies, and forms of progressive muscle relaxation and biofeedback as well as traditional medical treatment, including physical therapy.

In order to increase opportunities for expression, particularly in populations where verbalization, either spoken or written, is difficult or underutilized, alternative or creative forms of expressing emotional states such as art therapy, music therapy, recreational therapy, or the use of rituals or photography, may work well. Even engaging in traditional festivals including familiar foods, music, and dances, may have therapeutic value (Kalcik, 1985).

Utilizing Group Therapy

Group therapies have been applied with varying measures to new immigrant communities. Group therapy has, on the surface, much to offer new immigrant clientele. Group therapy may increase feelings of inclusion for this particularly displaced population; it may increase actual social support and socialization when members form friendships and bonds that develop beyond the therapeutic environment. Group therapy may focus on the multiple losses experienced by new immigrants, address cultural adjustments and education, and introduce relevant symptoms and coping skills associated with PTSD or depression. Meeting in a group will tend to regularize many new immigrant concerns (Woodcock, 1997).

However, there are obstacles to creating a positive group therapy experience for new immigrants as well. On a pragmatic note, many new immigrants are employed in base level jobs with little flexibility. Some find themselves filling the most undesired shifts and having their schedules changed frequently. Still others, due to desperate economic need, work at several jobs simultaneously, making attendance at a predetermined and inflexible group meeting almost impossible.

The balance of homogeneity and diversity in new immigrant groups becomes of great importance. Obviously, a group without a common language and using multiple levels of interpretation will become unwieldy and may create barriers to building group cohesion and interrupt the dynamic flow of group process. On the other hand, country-specific groups will likely attract participants from diverse and possibly conflicting political, ethnic, and religious histories that will decrease the level of confidence and comfort of group members. More homogenous groups may be so similar that the therapeutic intent becomes masked by general social interaction and familiar patterns of in-group communication.

FAMILY OR COMMUNITY INTERVENTIONS

Despite the fact that mental health symptoms most frequently present in a particular individual, in many cases the best interventions for working with new immigrants may be addressed the level of family, community, or society.

Family-Level Interventions

In most cultures, the family is the basic social unit of survival. People define their success, well-being, and identity within a family. It may even be a family unit that first identifies or designates an individual as having a difficulty and needing treatment. This becomes complex as family members may be differentially acculturated (different levels of language competence, differential embracing of host culture values, etc.), may utilize distinct and even conflictual coping skills for addressing family trauma (one member who completely represses the memories, while another grieves openly), and may serve as each other's buffer, strength, or trigger in dealing with mental health diagnosis. Further, there may even be multigenerational trauma that affects the entire system. In these cases, Steve Weire suggests utilizing structured family discussions to address trauma, mental health symptoms, and coping skills to create a place for healing within the family unit may help.

Community-Level Interventions

While immigrant clients may well benefit from individual treatment methods (therapy, medication), community interventions may also be appropriate. Further, for many survivors of oppression, war trauma, and torture, who have decided to confront violence and injustice, being treated as an individual victim will be unacceptable. In these situations personal testimonies, class action suits against perpetrators, and participation in truth and reconciliation commissions are appropriate and powerful methods of rehabilitation.

The process of documentation, picture taking, writing a testimonial, recognizing and honoring the stories of others, as well as openly naming perpetrators generally will increase the feelings of meaning and self-efficacy in a "survivor" population.

Participation in such interventions may be preferred by immigrant clients as one does not have to self-identity as symptomatic or define one's self as traumatized to receive the benefit. Rather a positive role as an activist or expert witness is often propagated by these efforts. This process may bind an exiled community together (or increase intergroup conflict); it may strengthen an individual's standing or role in his or her own community. It may also increase memories, fears, and other negative symptoms. Results are varied and all participants should receive information about all possible outcomes before deciding to take part.

Of course it is critical to be aware of a particular client's or community's expectations for the intervention and prepare the client for mixed feedback. On the positive side, community-level programs may result in an increase in actual resources (legal, medical, mental health) for the new immigrant community. Media attention may bring the immigrant communities' experience to the larger society's eyes. However, these programs may also be met with indifference or apathy. Even in the face of overwhelming evidence, little may be done to propagate punishment or justice to powerful institutions or governments who engaged in torture or oppression. Further, inadequate attention in the host-culture media may result in the immigrant community feeling marginalized and unimportant.

A philosophical and possibly religious debate has arisen around the goal of such community interventions. For some, the historical documentation in itself is a reasonable end to efforts in the community. That a fair and objective history will endure creates a sense of justice and a deterrent for future generations. For others, documentation of atrocities is imperative in the struggle for reparation, punishment, and impunity. The feeling that only via actual consequences for perpetrators can community interventions be legitimized is evident in this argument.

More "positive" camps utilize community action to propagate tolerance and diversity in reconciliation efforts, focusing on a future based on collaboration and joint coexistence. Lastly, there are those striving for the goals of forgiveness within groups and individuals within the society, aiming at a mutually beneficial view of allowing bygones to be bygones to ensure peace in future generations.

While individuals may have their own personal beliefs, agendas, or created meaning around their participation in community-based interventions, it is important for the mental health professional to remain neutral as to the desired goal and to play a supportive role to the immigrant client involved.

For many individuals, having their personal pain and symptomology addressed as a community issue may lessen their feelings of embarrassment or responsibility for their current negative stressors. Further, direct comparisons to compatriots may result in an increase of feelings of self-efficacy.

Lastly, community interventions strengthen the ties between the new immigrant populations and their families, friends, and peers left behind. Frequently the process is being simultaneously developed in both home country and immigrant community and is a way for families and social groups to be united in a common experience/struggle and goal. This feeling of unity may decrease the immigrant client's feeling of isolation and distance from homeland and people.

IMMIGRANT CHILDREN AND MENTAL HEALTH

The process of immigration interrupts normal and natural structures of development, physiology (changes in diet, disease processes, change in medical core), social/community interaction, and cognition. Children left in transitional and resource-depleted environments for long periods of time (such as those who have been separated from their parents and families, or lived in refugee camps) may experience a loss of playfulness, creativity, and imagination and have disrupted attachment patterns that follow them into adulthood.

Even upon arrival in the host culture an immigrant child may experience significant distress. As with all children, the adjustment of immigrant children depends greatly on the adjustment of their caretaking adults, the ability of the adults to project/buffer them from the harsher realities of their experience, as well as ability of the caregivers to recognize and help modulate excessive emotional distress with the child.

In reality the quality of caretaking relationships in the immigrant community is of extreme variability. While many immigrant cultures revere and protect children as a symbol of the family's future, in the face of war, trauma, and exile, many protective structures fall to the wayside and leave children in particularly vulnerable positions. Furthermore, new immigrant caretakers may be overwhelmed by the need to learn a new language, find safe housing and steady employment, and navigate cultural systems unknown to them. Parents experiencing mental health or cultural adjustment challenges themselves may have little energy to spend on a child experiencing difficulties.

Children who are left behind face special difficulties. Many children are not given the opportunity to immigrate with a base family unit and instead find themselves in a loosely structured conglomeration of siblings, cousins, and extended family members who are minimally obligated to care for the child. Under stress, these fluid relationships are often terminated and the child may be forced to forge his or her way alone in the next host country.

This is especially true of adolescents who during the time of familial separation were forced to exist as adults, engage in antisocial behavior for their own existence or protection, and who may have formed strong bonds with other youth in similar circumstances. These youth consider themselves adults and are frequently oppositional and skeptical of their parents' attempts to reestablish a disciplinary role in their lives.

For their part, immigrant parents who rightfully feel they have done everything in their power to prioritize and protect their children by arranging care, procuring economic means to provide for their needs, maintaining regular contact (often at high economic and emotional cost), and eventually providing the means for the child to immigrate are often confused and hurt. They may deny or minimize the suffering of their children whom they were forced to leave behind. This dynamic may increase the child's feeling of being unloved and misunderstood by the idealized parent they expected to find upon family reunification. Concordantly, parents are confused and frustrated by children who appear angry, demanding, disrespectful, and not affectionate after waiting so long to be a family.

Obviously, the child's personal history of development, attachment, intellectual ability, academic exposure, and socialization will interact with the current environment. Sadly, the children who have the fewest personal resources, due to multiple losses, environmental neglect, and abuse, may be in situations that call for the highest level of personal strength, flexibility, intellectual flexibility, and self-protection (Kopola, Esquivel, & Baptiste, 1994).

Further, the dissonance between culture of origin and host culture may be most profoundly expressed in the lives of children. School-aged children spend the majority of their day interacting with the host culture, immersed in the values and expectations of the United States and possibly reopening the benefits of a child-indulgent system or of particular adults who make the immigrant child the recipient of excess charity. Quickly children are aware of the tension between the host culture ways and their families' priorities, values, and structures. Immigrant children, in the eyes of their parents, are given an inordinate belief in their individual power through information about child abuse laws (and call 911) and expectations about their individual rights (schooling, protective status, own beds, etc.). Further, in practicality, children who become more quickly bilingual and acculturated are in the precarious position of having to advocate or interpret for their parents in serious adult matters, which may significantly interrupt traditional family roles. These differences in values and lifestyles may become the source of huge rifts between immigrant children and their caretakers.

Children respond to trauma and change in unique ways. While on the surface adjusting well, immigrant children may become withdrawn or depressed (behaviors that go unnoticed in most stressed families), or aggressive and oppositional, which may be defined as disrespectful or insolent by immigrant parents. Many mental health symptoms in immigrant children are left unaddressed until a behavioral, academic, or familial crisis is already at hand.

In initiating mental health interventions with immigrant children, it is necessary to engage the caretakers and complete family system in order to ensure treatment compliance and success. Much energy must be expended in creating a trusting and strong collaboration with the caretakers with the goal of preserving the integration and well-being of the family unit. Utilizing a therapist who can speak the language of the parents (even if the child is fluent in the host culture language) is ideal.

Work with immigrant children may stretch and challenge professional boundaries that must be maintained at all times. Frequently, host cultural mental health providers feel at odds with a parent's or family's cultural definition of childhood. Children in many countries are considered vital and important actors in the family with high expectations of loyalty, respect, social obligations, and morality. Children may be considered investments of the family with seemingly few rights. These beliefs may cause the mental health practitioner to question the parent's love and commitment to the child and to inappropriately offer alternatives to children they deem to be victims of uncaring familial systems. These interventions serve to disassociate children from their primary support group, may increase their expectations in unrealistic ways, and may do grave harm to the family system and to the child as well. In all, serving immigrant children's mental health needs will be best served and maintained at the family and community level while supporting the child in symptom reduction and positive coping skills.

CASE STUDY

The following vignette illustrates an actual case handled by the Liberty Center for Survivors of Torture. You are invited to apply the following questions to the vignette.

1 What social work issues are raised by the vignette?
2 What legal issues are raised by the vignette?
3 As a mental health professional, what would you identify as the presenting problem(s)? What aspects of the experience suggest a crisis, and why? How would you prioritize the immigrant's needs?
4 Conversely, what might you identify as the client's strengths?
5 What short-term mental health interventions and resources do you think would be helpful in this situation? Long-term interventions and resources?
6 What other interventions (beside mental health interventions) might be needed by the client?

Case Study: Ms. X

Ms. X is a 44-year-old female from West Africa. There she joined a party in opposition to the current administration in West Africa. Her family had a long history with the party; her father, who was a party official, had been assassinated. She was quickly identified and targeted as an opposition leader. Her phone was tapped and her apartment watched. She and her family received threatening messages, and her shop was ransacked. Ultimately, for the safety of her family, she was forced to go into hiding and leave her children unprotected. She has not yet been able to reunite with them.

During a peaceful antigovernmental rally, Ms. X was arrested and detained in a tiny cell with 20 other protesters. During her six-month detention, she was regularly beaten, kicked, and assaulted. She was also raped, and suffered a miscarriage due to the beatings. Ultimately, she escaped and came to America as an asylee.

When first seen by mental health professionals, Ms. X displayed a lack of energy, anhedonia, lack of appetite, crying, severe feelings of guilt and worthlessness, nightmares, severe anxiety, and flashbacks. She was unable to concentrate or learn new information. Ms. X also experienced physical symptoms, which included back pain and menstrual irregularities. As a consequence of her forced exile and lack of immigration status, Ms. X was unemployed, had unreliable housing, had no legal representation, was linguistically isolated, and was unable to complete the necessary educational requirements to find adequate employment.

ADDITIONAL RESOURCES

Web Sites

American Psychological Association, Public Policy Office, *The Mental Health Needs of Immigrants:* http://www.apa.org/ppo/ethnic/immigranthealth.html

Bureau of Population Refugees and Migration (agency administers U.S. refugee assistance and refugee admissions programs; site contains key links): www.state.gov/g/prm

Church World Service Immigration and Refugee Program (CWS): www.churchworldservice.org/Immigration/index.html

The Epidavros Project, an excellent site on the INS process of granting asylum: www.wellfoundedfear.org

Grant Makers in Health, *Addressing the Mental Health Needs of Immigrants and Refugees:* www.gih.org/usr_doc/Immigrant_Mental_Health.pdf

Health and Human Development Programs: www.hhd.org

Immigration and Naturalization Service (INS): www.ins.usdoj.gov/graphics/index.html

International Organization for Migration (IOM): www.iom.int/

Migration Policy Institute (MPI has developed substantial expertise relating to the law and practice of protecting refugees and internally displaced people in areas of conflict as well as in the industrialized countries): http://www.migrationpolicy.org/research/refugee.php

National Institute of Mental Health: www.nimh.nih.gov

National Institutes of Health, NLM Gateway: http://gateway.nlm.nih.gov/gw/Cmd

Office of Refugee Resettlement: www.acf.dhhs.gov/

Refugee Council USA: www.rcusa.org

Relief Web (data, legislation, documents, and other information): www.notes.reliefweb.int/w/rwb.nsf

UN Refugee Agency (UNHCR) (created by the United Nations Office for the Coordination of Humanitarian Affairs with the purpose of disseminating information to the international relief community and others): www.unhcr.ch.

U.S. Committee for Refugees (USCR1): www.refugees.org

Books

Harvey, J., & Pauwels, B. E. (2000, June). *Post-traumatic stress theory: Research and application.* New York: Brunner-Routledge.

Harvey, J., & Pauwels, B. E. (2002). *Post-traumatic stress theory: A guide to coping.* Iowa: University of Iowa Publishers.

Hernandez, D. J., & Charney, E. (Eds.). (1998). *From generation to generation: The health and well-being of children in immigrant families.* Washington, DC: National Academies Press.

Kleinman, A., & Good, B. (1985). *Culture and depression: Studies in the anthropology and cross cultural psychiatry of affect disorder.* Berkeley: University of California Press.

Kalick, S., & Jordan, R. (1985). *Women's folklore, women's culture.* Philadelphia: University of Pennsylvania Press.

Lindy, J. D., & Lifton, R. J. (Eds.). (2001). *Beyond invisible walls: The psychological legacy of Soviet trauma (east European patients and their therapists).* New York: Brunner-Routledge.

Nader, K., Dubrow, N., & Slamm, B. H. (1999). *Honoring differences: Cultural issues in the treatment of trauma and loss.* New York: Brunner-Routledge.

Woodcook, J. (1997). Groupwork with refugees and asylum seekers. In T. Mistry & A. Brown (Eds.), *Race and groupwork* (pp. 254–277). London: Whiting & Birch Ltd.

Zinner, E. S., & Williams, M. B. (Eds.). (1998). *When a community weeps: Case studies in group survivorship.* Philadelphia: Brunner/Mazel.

Articles

American Academy of Pediatrics Policy. (1997, July). Healthcare for children of immigrant families. *Pediatrics, 100*(1), 153–156. Available at http://aappolicy.aappublications.org/cgi/content/full/pediatrics;100/1/153.

Amnesty International. (2007, July). AI observations on the report of the working group on human rights protection. 10R61/019/2007.

Driver, C., & Beltran, R. O. (1998). Impact of refugee trauma on children's occupational role as school students. *Australian Occupational Therapy Journal, 45,* 23–38.

Foa, E. B., Keane, M. T., & Friedman, M. J. (2000, October). Guidelines for treatment of PTSD. *Journal of Traumatic Stress, 13*(4), 539–588.

Kwai-Sang Yau, M. (1997). The impact of refugee resettlement on Southeast Asian adolescents and young adults: Implications for occupational therapists. *Occupational Therapy International, 4*(1), 1–16.

Porter, M., & Haslam, N. (2001, October). Forced displacement in Yugoslavia: A meta-analysis of psychological consequences and their moderators. *Journal of Traumatic Stress, 14*(4), 817–834.

Rousseau, C., Drapeau, A., & Corin, E. (1996). School performance and emotional problems in refugee children. *American Journal of Orthopsychiatry, 66*(2), 239–251.

REFERENCES

American Psychiatric Association. (2000). *Diagnostic and statistical manual of disorders* (4th ed., p. 463). Washington, DC: Author.

Amery, J. (1977). Die torture. In J. Avery (Ed.), *Jensits Von Schuld urd Sűhne* (pp. 46–73). Stuttgart: Kletl Cotta.

Brody, E. (1994). The mental health and well-being of refugees: Issues and directions. In A. J. Marsella, T. Bornemann, S. Ekblad, & J. Orley (Eds.), *Amidst peril and pain: The mental health and well-being of the world's refugees* (pp. 57–68). Washington, DC: American Psychological Association.

England-Dimitrova, B. (1991). *Flyktingar och invandrare I sjukvården* [Refugees and immigrants under medical care]. Stockholm, Sweden: Spri.

Escobar, J., Hoyos Nervi, C., & Gara, M. (2000). Immigration and mental health: Mexican Americans in the United States. *Harvard Review of Psychology, 8*(2), 64–72.

Freire, P. (1973). *Pedagogy of the oppressed.* New York: The Seabury Press.

Ginsberg, L., & Ginsberg, R. (1989). *Psychoanalytic perspectives on migration and exile,* trans. N. Festinger. New Haven, CT: Yale University Press.

Guarnaccia, P., & Lopez, S. (1998). The mental health and adjustment of immigrant and refugee children. *Child and Adolescent Psychiatric Clinic of North America, 7*(3), 537–553.

Ivey, A. E. (1995). Psychotherapy as liberation: Toward specific skills and strategies in multicultural counseling and therapy. In J. G. Ponterotto, J. M. Casas, L. A. Suzuki, & C. M. Alexander (Eds.), *Handbook of multicultural counseling* (pp. 53–73). Thousand Oaks, CA: Sage.

Jablensky, A., Marsella, A. J., Ekblad, S., Jannson, B., Levi, L., & Bornemann, T. (1994). Refugee mental health and well-being: Conclusions and recommendations. In A. J. Marsella, T. Bornemann, S. Ekblad, & J. Orley (Eds.), *Amidst peril and pain: The mental health and well-being of the world's refugees* (pp. 1–13). Washington, DC: American Psychological Association.

Kinzie, J. D., & Fleck, J. (1987). Psychotherapy with severely traumatized refugees. *American Journal of Psychotherapy, 41,* 82–94.

Kleinman, A., & Kleinman, J. (1991). Suffering and its professional transformation: Toward an ethnography of interpersonal experience. *Culture, Medicine and Psychiatry, 15*(3), 275–301.

Kopola, M., Esquivel, G., & Baptiste, L. (1994). Counseling approaches for immigrant children: Facilitating the acculturative process. *The School Counselor, 41,* 352–359.

Marsella, A. J. (1993). Counseling and psychotherapy with Japanese Americans: Cross-cultural considerations. *American Journal of Orthopsychiatry, 63,* 200–208.

Murphy, H. B. (1997). Migration, culture and mental health. *Psychological Medicine, 7,* 677–684.

Orley, J. (1994). Psychological disorders among refugees: Some clinical and epidemiological considerations. In. A. J. Marsella, T. Bornemann, S. Ekblad, & J. Orley (Eds.), *Amidst peril and pain: The mental health and well-being of the world's refugees* (pp. 193–206). Washington, DC: American Psychological Association.

Pederson, P. B. (2000). *Handbook for developing multicultural awareness* (3rd ed.). Alexandria, VA: American Counseling Association.

Pope, K. S., & Garcia-Peltoniemi, R. E. (1991). Responding to victims of torture: Clinical issues, professional responsibilities, and useful resources. *Professional Psychology: Research and Practice, 22,* 269–276.

Sachs, L. (1987). *Medicinsk antropologica* [Medical anthropology]. Stockholm, Sweden: Liber Press.

Silove, D., Tarn, R., Bowles, R., & Reid, J. (1991). Psychosocial needs of torture survivors. *Austrian and New Zealand Journal of Psychiatry, 25,* 481–490.

Stein, B. N. (1986). The experience of being a refugee: Insights from the research literature. In C. L. Williams & J. Westermeyer (Eds.), *Refugee mental health in resettlement countries* (pp. 5–23). Washington, DC: Hemisphere.

Tayabas, T., & Pok, T. (1983). The arrival of the Southeast Asian refugees in America: An overview. In *Bridging cultures: Southeast Asian refugees in America* (pp. 3–14). Los Angeles: Asian American Community Mental Health Training Center, Special Services for Groups.

Westermeyer, J. (1989). *Mental health for refugees and other migrants: Social and preventative approaches.* Springfield, IL: Charles C Thomas.

Woodcook, J. (1997). Groupwork with refugees and asylum seekers. In T. Mistry & A. Brown (Eds.), *Race and Groupwork* (pp. 254–277). London: Whiting & Birch Ltd.

7 Avoiding Unintended Consequences in Civil Advocacy for Criminally Charged Immigrants

ALINA DAS

Immigrants who have been criminally charged are subject to numerous and serious consequences that go beyond the criminal penalties. Even a relatively minor interaction with the criminal justice system may jeopardize immigrants' legal status or eligibility for obtaining legal status, thus affecting their ability to live, work, support, and remain with their families in the United States. Many criminal court dispositions may result in immediate detention and the initiation of removal (i.e., deportation) proceedings—even if the immigrant is a long-time lawful permanent resident and has a U.S. citizen family. Civil legal aid organizations and others engaged in civil advocacy on behalf of immigrants should be aware of the consequences of criminal charges. In this article I present an overview of the issue and resources for additional information.

COMMON CRIMINAL GROUNDS THAT TRIGGER NEGATIVE IMMIGRATION CONSEQUENCES

The criminal grounds of deportation, detention, and ineligibility for citizenship and various forms of immigration relief are broad and expansive.

This chapter was first published in 41 Clearinghouse Review: Journal of Poverty Law and Policy, *228 (July–Aug. 2007).*

The Immigration and Nationality Act lists these grounds in several sections, including but not limited to 8 U.S.C. § 1101(f) (grounds that bar a finding of "good moral character" necessary for citizenship and certain forms of relief from removal); 8 U.S.C. § 1182 (grounds of "inadmissibility" resulting in removal of individuals seeking lawful admission or permanent residence status); and 8 U.S.C. § 1227 (grounds of "deportability" resulting in removal of lawfully admitted individuals).

The specific criminal grounds listed under each section overlap to some extent, falling under broad categories such as "crimes involving moral turpitude," "controlled substance offenses," and "aggravated felonies." Several manuals, articles, and resources discuss the definitions of all of these terms, and the circumstances under which an individual's criminal court disposition may fall under one or more of these grounds.[1]

Notably, a criminal court disposition may fall under one of these grounds even if the disposition is not technically a conviction or a crime under state law; the key question is whether the disposition fits into the federal immigration law definitions of criminal grounds triggering negative immigration consequences.[2] A civil legal aid organization or advocate should always consult a qualified immigration law expert whenever a noncitizen client has some interaction with the criminal justice system, however minor, to assess the potential consequences.

Generally, only dispositions arising from criminal court proceedings—or, in some circumstances, in-or-out-of-court statements admitting to the commission of an offense—may serve as criminal grounds that can trigger negative immigration consequences.[3] While civil court findings regarding criminal conduct may also trigger removal on criminal grounds in certain cases, removal proceedings based on such findings are currently uncommon. However, at least one criminal ground of removal is often influenced by civil court proceedings: the "violator of a protection order" ground of deportability under 8 U.S.C. § 1227(a)(2)(E)(ii).[4] This ground applies to violations of orders of protection whether or not the order was initially entered in criminal or civil court. The entry of an order of protection itself will not trigger this ground for removal—the ground is triggered only if a finding shows that the order was violated. Civil legal aid organizations and advocates who work with clients seeking or facing the entry of orders of protection in family court should thus be aware that a subsequent violation of an order of protection might result in the violator's deportation or other negative immigration consequences.

HOW CIVIL LEGAL AID ORGANIZATIONS AND ADVOCATES CAN HELP

Civil legal aid organizations and advocates can help their immigrant clients avoid the unintended consequences of criminal charges by increasing awareness of the triggers, connecting clients to resources, and using civil advocacy to assist clients facing possible immigration proceedings that stem from criminal charges.

Increase Awareness of the Triggers of the Immigration Consequences of Criminal Charges. Civil legal aid organizations and advocates should educate themselves about the triggers of the immigration consequences of criminal charges so that they do not inadvertently put immigrants facing criminal charges at greater risk of deportation and other negative consequences. Many individuals, particularly those with low-level offenses or old convictions, may not realize that they are deportable or subject to other negative immigration consequences until they are screened and identified by the government. Common trigger points that can lead to removal proceedings include (a) renewal of a permanent resident card; (b) submission of an application for adjustment of status, citizenship, or other immigration status or benefit; (c) return to the United States after a trip abroad; (d) any time spent in jail for any reason; and (e) almost any interaction with law enforcement or a government agency (there are some exceptions).[5]

Thus, for example, before civil legal aid advocates tell clients to renew their permanent resident cards to submit with a government benefits application or assist clients in applying for citizenship, the advocates should always consult a qualified immigration expert to find out whether clients' criminal dispositions may put them at risk of deportation and other negative consequences.

Advise Clients and Connect Them to Appropriate Resources. Civil legal aid organizations and advocates can directly advise clients about the immigration consequences of criminal charges and connect them to resources. If clients have an old criminal disposition, they should be informed that the disposition may have negative immigration consequences and understand what actions may trigger such consequences in the future. If they are currently involved in a criminal court proceeding (or, as described above, in a family court proceeding where an order of protection may be entered against them), they must be immediately connected to an immigration law expert who can advise them on how to resolve the situation without getting a disposition or order that may lead to their deportation. A list of useful resources is found below.

Use Civil Advocacy to Assist Clients in Pending or Future Immigration Proceedings Stemming from Criminal Charges. Civil legal aid organizations and advocates can, in some circumstances, use current or new forms of civil advocacy to assist their clients. For example, civil legal aid organizations and advocates may take the following actions:

- *Help clients obtain certificates of rehabilitation.* Civil legal aid organizations and advocates can help immigrants obtain certificates from the state indicating their rehabilitation or good character following a criminal disposition.[6] While these certificates typically do not erase a criminal ground of removal, they maybe helpful if the client is eligible for a discretionary waiver of removal and other forms of discretionary relief.[7]
- *Advocate on behalf of immigrants in family or juvenile court.* Organizations and advocates working in family or juvenile court can help immigrants who have criminal dispositions but who may qualify for certain forms of relief from removal. For example, findings of juvenile delinquency in family or juvenile court generally do not trigger the negative immigration consequences that convictions in criminal court may trigger.[8] Thus advocating for clients' criminal cases to proceed in family or juvenile court rather than criminal court helps them avoid criminal grounds of deportation and may, in some circumstances, help certain young undocumented immigrants gain special legal status.[9] For clients who are survivors of domestic violence and who have committed certain offenses, family court proceedings can help establish whether they qualify for waivers of criminal bars to adjust their status to lawful permanent residents.[10]
- *Develop immigration services.* Civil legal aid organizations can develop or expand immigration units or expert teams in-house to assist directly immigrant clients facing removal or seeking asylum, adjustment of status, and naturalization. Alternatively, civil legal aid organizations can develop partnerships with immigrant service organizations to ensure that they meet the needs of their criminally charged immigrant clients.

NOTES

1. See, for example, Manuel D. Vargas, *Representing Immigrant Defendants in New York* (4th ed.) (New York: New York State Defenders Association, 2006) [hereinafter *Representing Immigrant Defendants*]; Dan Kesselbrenner and Lory D. Rosenberg,

Immigration Law and Crimes (St. Paul, MN: Thompson/West, 2007); Manuel D. Vargas (2006), "Immigration Consequences of Guilty Pleas or Convictions," *New York University Review of Law and Social Change, 30,* 701; Norton Tooby and Katherine A. Brady, *Criminal Defense of Immigrants* (3rd ed.) (Oakland, CA: Law Offices of Norton Tooby, 2003). Charts of the immigration consequences of select federal and state offenses can also be found online at the Defending Immigrants Partnership Web site: http://defendingimmigrants.org/. Note that not all of these charts are up to date.

2. The term *conviction* for immigration purposes is defined at 8 U.S.C. § 1101(a)(48)(A) (2006).
3. Grounds of deportability generally require a conviction (as broadly defined in immigration law), whereas grounds of inadmissibility can be established if an immigrant has a conviction or merely admits to having committed an offense. See Vargas, *Immigration Consequences of Guilty Pleas or Convictions,* supra note 1, at 704–705. Moreover, some categories of inadmissibility do not require the government to have either a conviction or an admission, such as when the government has "reason to believe" that an immigrant is a drug trafficker. See Vargas, *Representing Immigrant Defendants,* supra note 1, at 5.
4. The "violator of a protection order" ground applies to any noncitizen "who at any time after admission is enjoined under a protection order issued by a court and who, the court determines, engages in conduct violating the portion of a protection order that involves protection against credible threats of violence, repeated harassment, or bodily injury to the person or persons for whom the protection order was issued. For purposes of this clause, the term 'protection order' means any injunction issued for the purpose of preventing violent or threatening acts of domestic violence, including temporary or final orders issued by civil or criminal courts (other than support or child custody orders or provisions), whether obtained by filing an independent action or as a *pendente lite* order in another proceeding." 8 U.S.C. § 1227(a)(2)(E)(ii) (2006).
5. Some localities or government agencies may have policies on whether they report individuals with immigration problems to the U.S. Department of Homeland Security. Advocates should learn about these policies and consult local immigration law experts to assess the risk of having a noncitizen client contact a government agency for benefits, housing, and other kinds of assistance.
6. Information about obtaining certificates of rehabilitation can be found at the Legal Action Center's Web site, http://www.lac.org/toolkits/certificates/certificates.htm
7. See, e.g., Vargas, *Representing Immigrant Defendants,* supra note 1, at 89–91.
8. See Vargas, *Representing Immigrant Defendants,* at 124–125; see also *Matter of Devison-Charles,* 22 I&N Dec. 1362 (BIA 2000).
9. Under certain specific circumstances, young undocumented immigrants may be eligible for Special Immigrant Juvenile Status (SIJS) and a special waiver of certain criminal grounds of inadmissibility. More information on eligibility requirements and how to apply may be found at the Immigrant Legal Resource Center's Web site at http://www.ilrc.org/sijs.php; at the New York Online SJIS Guide's Web site at http://quickplace.law.columbia.edu/childimmigrant; and at the National Immigrant Justice Center's Web site at http://www.immigrantjustice.org/content/view/124/96/
10. Certain domestic violence survivors may be eligible to file self-petitions under the Violence Against Women Act (VAWA) or gain "U" nonimmigrant status, and may

receive special waivers of criminal grounds of inadmissibility when adjusting to lawful permanent residence. More information on eligibility requirements and how to apply may be found at Asista's Web site at http://www.asistaonline.org/vawa.asp and http://www.asistaonline.org/u.visa.asp

ADDITIONAL RESOURCES

For more information, civil legal aid organizations, advocates, immigrants, and their families can consult experts and find resource materials from the following organizations:

Immigrant Defense Project of the New York State Defenders Association (telephone 212-725-6422): www.immigrantdefenseproject.org

Immigrant Legal Resource Center (telephone 415-255-9499): www.ilrc.org

The National Immigration Project (telephone 617-227-9727): www.nationalimmigrationproject.org

National Legal Aid and Defender Association (telephone 202-452-0620): www.nlada.org/Defender/Defender_Immigrants

Washington Defender Association Immigration Project (telephone 206-726-3332): www.defensenet.org

8 Immigrants and Employment

MARIELENA HINCAPIÉ

The U.S. culture places a premium on work; a person's identity is often shaped by the type of work he or she does. Work plays an equally important role in the lives of immigrants and refugees[1] who come to the United States. The experience immigrants have looking for work, maintaining jobs that allow them to survive and support their families, contribute to their local communities and society as a whole, and feel that they are valued members of the community will determine how they fare in the United States. Therefore it is critical for social workers to have a solid understanding of the issues affecting immigrant workers and their communities.

It is common for immigrants to work multiple low-paying jobs to make ends meet and send money to their families in their homeland to provide economic support. These remittances are often essential to the survival of families back home and, from a macro economic perspective, raise the standard of living of people worldwide. "Making it" in the United States has a direct correlation to immigrants' ability to find work and support themselves and their family back home. However, immigrants face particular barriers to becoming full participants in society, particularly when it comes to finding and maintaining employment.

This chapter will first provide a profile of low-wage immigrant workers. It will then explain the rights and remedies available to immigrant workers under labor laws and explore the conditions and factors that lead to their abuse and exploitation. The chapter will then illustrate the barriers that prevent employers from enforcing labor and employment laws, including lax enforcement of laws by government agencies, the threat of deportation by immigration agents, and government programs that hinder workers from exercising their rights. It will conclude with some hypotheticals (based on true cases) that will help social work students be better prepared to identify the employment-related issues clients may have and how to assist them individually—while also empowering them to advocate and organize collectively to improve their working conditions.

AN OVERVIEW OF IMMIGRANT WORKERS AND THEIR CONTRIBUTIONS

Migration is a global phenomenon, and the core reason for migration is economic survival. As long as globalization continues, and individuals are forced to leave their home countries out of economic desperation, migration to the United States will increase. It is critical that we look at the root causes of migration, which include economic, political, and environmental forces that "push" people out of their home countries, while also examining the economic and political forces "pulling" immigrants into the United States primarily to fill low-wage jobs.

The United States is now the largest receiving country in the world, with over 37 million immigrants calling this country their new home (Pew Hispanic Center, 2008).[2] While the number of immigrants coming to the United States is at an all-time high, the total percentage of foreign-born individuals is about 12.5% of the total civilian population (Terrazas, Batalova, & Fan, 2007), which is slightly lower than in 1890 when the foreign-born made up 15% of the total population (Gibson & Lennon, 1999).

The 2000 Census confirmed the profound demographic changes that occurred throughout the 1990s (Schmidley, 2001). More recent studies provide further detail about the impact of this demographic change on the U.S. labor force: those termed *new immigrants*—those who entered the United States after 1990—accounted for over 50% of the net growth in the civilian labor force during the last decade (Sum, Fogg, Harrington et al., 2002). That is, between 1990 and 2001, one out of every two new workers in the United States was a new immigrant. New immigrants contributed to at least 60% of the growth in the labor force between 2000 and 2004, and nearly two-thirds of the growth in the male labor force was due to immigrant men (Sum, Fogg, Khatiwada, et al., 2004). Of all foreign-born workers, approximately 37% are from Central America and Mexico, 26% are from Asia, 12% from Europe, 9% from the Caribbean, and 7% from South America (Migration Policy Institute, 2004).

On average, immigrant workers earn less than native-born workers and are more likely to have less than a ninth-grade education. In 2004, about 53% of immigrant workers over age 25 had a high school diploma or less education, compared to almost 38% of native-born workers. Moreover, immigrant workers were more than four times as likely as U.S. workers to lack a high school diploma (American Immigration Law Foundation, 2005).

LOW-WAGE IMMIGRANT WORKERS

As described in chapter 2, there are many different categories of immigration status, and some of these categories impact employment. Some immigrant workers may be documented, meaning that they have federal authorization to work in the United States. For example, asylees and refugees may be granted the right to work (Immigration and Nationality Act, 1952).[3] Immigrants in other categories may be granted temporary work visas solely for employment purposes.[4] Undocumented workers may have entered the country without the government's permission or they may have entered on a temporary visa but overstayed the period of time they were authorized to remain in the United States. The remainder of this section will discuss employment issues faced by undocumented workers, many of whom work in low-wage jobs.

There are an estimated 7.2 million undocumented workers in the United States, and more than 2.5 million of them, or 35%, arrived between 2000 and 2005 (Pew Hispanic Center, 2008). In 2005, the number of undocumented migrants in the United States surpassed that of lawful permanent residents, making up 30% of the total number of foreign-born individuals, while naturalized citizens represented 31%. As of March 2005, there were approximately 11.1 million undocumented migrants in the United States, a majority from Latin America.

Because of their recent arrival in the United States and associated language and cultural barriers, undocumented immigrants face a staggering number of obstacles to obtaining even the basic necessities for survival, much less to participating fully in U.S. society. For example, although undocumented immigrants have high employment rates (Passel, 2005),[5] the average family income of undocumented families is more than 40% below the average income of either legal immigrant or native-born families (Passel, 2005). Indeed, Latinos were the only group who saw their wages decline two years in a row (Kochhar, 2005).

According to the Bureau of Labor Statistics, immigrants comprise a disproportionately large share of workers in many of the less-skilled occupations (Immigration Policy Center, 2005, p. 13). One out of every five low-wage workers is undocumented (Passel, 2006).

Although they comprise about 5% of the workforce (Passel, 2006), undocumented workers are overrepresented in low-wage, high-risk jobs such as agriculture, building maintenance, construction, manufacturing, and food services (Passel, 2005) and in hazardous occupations within those industries (Working Immigrant Safety and Health Coalition, 2002). For example, Latino immigrants constitute 20% of construction workers in California.

Workplace fatalities among U.S. workers who are foreign-born are on the rise, and the rate at which foreign-born workers die as a result of workplace accidents far exceeds that of native-born workers (Gregory & Schiller, 2004). Foreign-born workers accounted for 69% of workplace fatalities in 2002, yet make up 15% of the total workforce (Bureau of Labor Statistics, 2002). Astoundingly, Mexican-born workers in the United States are 80% more likely to die in a workplace accident than native-born workers (Pritchard, 2004).

CONTRIBUTIONS OF IMMIGRANT WORKERS

Notwithstanding the many challenges they face, immigrants are revitalizing many inner-city and first-ring suburban neighborhoods, providing the stimulus behind many of the most successful union and community organizing efforts. They buy homes or rent apartments, establish small businesses, and buy goods, thereby contributing to the economy.

Despite the general misconception that today's immigrants are not assimilating as fast as previous generations of immigrants, especially compared to European immigrants who arrived a century ago, when one examines states (e.g., California) where immigrants have settled for a longer period of time, there is evidence that immigrants are indeed progressing tremendously. A recent study found that about 33% of Latinos who had been in California for less than 10 years were proficient in English, compared with about 74% of Latinos who had been in California for over 30 years (Myers, 2008, p. 6). Similarly, while the rate of poverty among Latinos is severe within their first two decades in the United States, this same study noted a decrease in the poverty level over time (Myers, 2008, p. 7).[6] Finally, first-generation Latino immigrants in California also had high levels of home ownership, which jumped from about 16% of homeowners among those who had been in the country for less than 10 years to about 65% for those who had been here for over 30 years, which was higher than the California homeownership rate of 57% (Myers, 2008, p. 8).

These economic indicators are important to consider when we look at the future of the United States and understand that immigrants are essential to the U.S. economy. New immigration is likely to contribute between one-third and one-half of the growth of the labor force through 2030. Between 2010 and 2030, first- and second-generation immigrants together are projected to account for all growth in the U.S. labor force, while the country will be facing an aging crisis as the Baby Boomer generation begins retiring between 2010 and 2030. We will have a declining number of working-age adults, which may even be below zero in many states (Myers, 2008, p. 8).

Immigrant workers will be essential to keep the economy strong, to serve as caretakers for the aging population, to contribute to the health care and social security systems in place at the time, and to help shape the future of the Unites States. It is critical that we have sound immigration and labor policies that protect these workers' rights to ensure that they can contribute to our country without being exploited and dehumanized in the process.

ARE IMMIGRANT WORKERS PROTECTED BY U.S. LAWS?

The United States has many complex laws at the federal, state, and local level that impact immigrant workers. Federal immigration laws govern who can enter the United States, how individuals can enter the country, who is allowed to stay, and under what circumstances. The Department of Homeland Security (DHS) was created on March 1, 2003, and it includes the Bureau of Immigration and Customs Enforcement (ICE), and the U.S. Bureau of Citizenship and Immigration Services (USCIS) agencies, which enforce immigration laws. The Department of Justice (DOJ) retained jurisdiction over certain immigration policies, and in particular the immigration court system called the Executive Office of Immigration Review is located within DOJ and is therefore independent from DHS.

Labor and employment laws govern individuals' rights at the workplace. For example, the National Labor Relations Act of 1935 (NLRA) gives workers the right to organize, elect, or join a union.[7] Title VII of the Civil Rights Act of 1964 protects workers from employment discrimination based on race, color, national origin, religion, and gender.[8] The Fair Labor Standards Act of 1938 (FLSA) provides workers the right to minimum wage and overtime payment, and the Occupational Safety and Health Act of 1970 (OSHA) provides workers with the right to a safe and healthy workplace.[9] In addition, there are state labor and employment laws that further protect workers. The intersection of immigration with labor and employment laws comes into play when dealing with immigrant workers, and these policies have an effect on all workers' rights. In particular, when determining what rights and remedies are available to immigrant workers, especially undocumented workers, the issue of immigration status may arise.

A worker's immigration status did not factor into his or her employment or civil rights until 1986, when Congress enacted the Immigration Reform and Control Act (IRCA). In an effort to reduce unlawful immigration into the United States, Congress enacted IRCA, making it unlawful for employers to knowingly hire a person who was not authorized to work in the United States.[10] IRCA amended the Immigration and Nationality Act (INA) by creating employer sanctions against employers who violated this new provision.[11] A new employment eligibility verification process—commonly referred to as the "I-9 process"—was created as a means of monitoring the employer sanctions scheme. All employers must complete the I-9 form for all new workers hired after November 6, 1986.[12]

Based on advocacy by civil rights and immigrant rights organizations concerned that the new employer sanctions would result in increased discrimination against "foreign-looking or sounding" U.S. citizens or authorized workers,[13] Congress included antidiscrimination provisions prohibiting citizenship status discrimination and, complementing Title VII of the Civil Rights Act, prohibiting national origin discrimination by small employers.[14] To enforce the INA's antidiscrimination provisions, Congress created the Office of Special Counsel for Immigration-Related Unfair Employment Practices (OSC).[15]

In this context, social service providers may be approached for assistance in employment discrimination. To file a citizenship discrimination claim, a person must be a "protected individual," which only includes

- U.S.-born and naturalized citizens
- U.S. nationals
- lawful permanent residents who file for naturalization within six months of being eligible
- lawful temporary residents
- refugees and asylees

These legal classifications are more fully described in chapter 2. This narrow definition of *protected individual* excludes two large segments of the immigrant population: long-term permanent residents who for a variety of reasons have not applied for naturalization within that six-month window; and the estimated 12 million undocumented persons in the United States.

Under the Immigration Act of 1990, Congress amended the INA's antidiscrimination provisions to prohibit "document abuse" and retaliation.[16] Document abuse occurs when an employer requires workers to present additional or more specific documents than are required by the I-9 employment eligibility verification process. For example, document abuse occurs when an employer requires a newly hired worker to present specific documents, such as an Employment Authorization Document or work permit or a resident alien card or green card, to prove they are authorized to work in the United States. These are considered to be a type of discrimination because the I-9 process was set up to give the worker the choice of which documents to present from a limited list on the back of Form I-9.[17]

Any work-authorized individual can file a document abuse claim. While these claims are not limited to protected individuals, it also does not cover undocumented workers. The reasoning behind this is that IRCA was enacted into law to reduce unlawful immigration and save jobs for U.S. citizens. However, there is widespread agreement that IRCA's employer sanctions have failed to deter employers from recruiting and hiring workers, or to keep undocumented workers from migrating to the United States in search of opportunities for their families. On the other hand, employer sanctions have really become *employee sanctions* where workers are detained by immigration agents and deported while employers often are left unaffected. Moreover, one of the unintended consequences of IRCA has been to force otherwise law-abiding individuals to purchase false documents as a means of finding a job and satisfying the I-9 process.

It is with this backdrop, and the growing anti-immigrant sentiment that ensued after the tragic events of September 11, 2001, that the U.S. Supreme Court issued its decision in *Hoffman Plastic Compounds, Inc. v. N.L.R.B.*[18] In this 2002 decision, the Supreme Court held that an undocumented California factory worker, Jose Castro, who was fired for union organizing activities, could not be awarded back pay.[19] Jose Castro was fired because of his participation in the union organizing campaign in violation of the NLRA. At an administrative hearing before the NLRB, Mr. Castro admitted he was undocumented and that he had used false documents to obtain his job.

In its decision, the Supreme Court distinguished Hoffman Plastic, an "innocent employer" that did not "knowingly" hire an undocumented worker, from Castro, a worker that had used false documents and therefore engaged in "criminal" activity to gain employment. In denying Castro's back pay award, the Court also held that undocumented workers are not entitled to reinstatement, one of the traditional remedies, along with back pay, for such violations. The Supreme Court referred to IRCA as a changed landscape in which Congress created a "comprehensive scheme prohibiting the employment of illegal aliens in the United States."[20] It decided that awarding undocumented workers back pay would compensate them for work they could not have lawfully performed. As a result, while undocumented workers may still join a union, may help organize and vote for a union, and may engage in other activities protected by the NLRA aimed at improving their working conditions,[21] if they are wrongfully terminated, they cannot be reinstated and cannot receive back pay.[22]

Just as with the NLRA, all workers—regardless of immigration status—are protected by most federal and state labor and employment laws. For example, all workers are protected by federal wage and hour law under the FLSA.[23] All workers, regardless of immigration status, have the right to a safe and healthy workplace under the federal OSHA. And unlike the antidiscrimination provisions under the INA discussed above, all workers do have the right to be free from discrimination in the workplace under Title VII of the Civil Rights Act, regardless of their immigration status.[24] However, since *Hoffman,* employers have continuously tried to chip away at the remedies available to undocumented workers but worker advocates have been able to successfully limit the expansion of *Hoffman* into other areas of law.

The area where there have been some inroads into immigrant workers' rights is a person's right to be compensated for work-related injuries. This is of particular concern given the high prevalence of injuries and fatalities on the job suffered by low-wage immigrant workers who toil under some of the most dangerous working conditions. In general, when a worker suffers a work-related injury, she is eligible to receive workers' compensation, which provides the injured worker with medical care, medication, lost earnings, and rehabilitation therapy if she needs to be trained for a new job.[25] For the most part, most state courts have held that *Hoffman* should not be extended to workers' compensation cases because these are state statutes that provide workers with a benefit rather than a remedy for some wrongful act on the part of the employer. However, a couple of states have equated "lost earnings" with the "back pay" remedy the Supreme Court struck down in *Hoffman*.

In Pennsylvania, the state supreme court has held that because a worker is undocumented, his "loss of earning power is caused by his immigration status, not his work-related injury," and therefore the worker should not receive that benefit.[26] In Georgia, the court of appeals has also held that an undocumented worker cannot receive benefits if the worker is only partially disabled because the worker cannot legally seek work.[27] However, if the worker is totally disabled and unable to work, she is entitled workers' compensation benefits even if she is undocumented.[28]

WHAT BARRIERS PREVENT IMMIGRANT WORKERS FROM EXERCISING THEIR WORKPLACE RIGHTS?

Notwithstanding the fact that laws governing the workplace apply to all workers, including undocumented immigrants, there are many barriers that prevent workers from exercising their rights. One of the major barriers is workers' lack of information about their rights and their limited English proficiency. This is why it is so important for providers to be able to properly inform workers about their rights and to give them an appropriate referral. Increasingly, there are many community-based organizations in immigrant communities that have multilingual and multicultural staff, as well as "know your rights" materials in multiple languages. Also, the federal government agencies charged with enforcing the nation's labor and employment laws are required by Title VI of the Civil Rights

Act to ensure that immigrant communities have equal access to their services, which means that the agencies should have multilingual materials (such as complaint forms), plus bilingual staff or interpreters available.[29]

Despite government safeguards and nonprofit advocacy, the unfortunate reality for many immigrant workers is that employer violations of labor and employment laws are rampant, particularly in low-wage industries. Many immigrant workers fear being retaliated against by their employer for asserting their rights. This can include employer intimidation tactics such as threatening workers with deportation or in some cases even physical harm for complaining about their working conditions. As with any worker, for a documented immigrant worker, retaliation may take the form of a demotion, harassment, or termination. For an undocumented worker, all these forms of retaliation pale next to the fear of being deported as a result of exercising their right at work. And employers know all too well the power they hold over workers who do not have authorization to work in the United States.

When workers do exercise their workplace rights by organizing to join a union or by filing claims for unpaid wages with the U.S. Department of Labor (DOL) or a state agency, employers, in an attempt to escape liability, often raise the issue of immigration status, and in some cases contact immigration authorities in the hopes of ridding themselves of problem workers.

The threat of immigration enforcement is one of the most significant barriers facing low-wage immigrant workers trying to assert their labor rights. Increased immigration raids have made the threat of immigration enforcement during a labor dispute very real for immigrant workers. Employers may knowingly hire undocumented workers and only call immigration when those workers file a claim for unpaid wages or join a union campaign.[30]

Finally, increased immigration enforcement and certain governmental programs designed to assist with immigration enforcement at the worksites also prevent workers from exercising and vindicating their rights. Strategies include: increasing immigration raids, the Social Security Administration's (SSA) no-match letter program and the DHS regulations regarding no-match letters, and the DHS electronic employment eligibility verification program called the Basic Pilot Program (recently renamed E-Verify).

Immigration Raids

The United States has witnessed a record number of immigration raids in which immigrant communities have been under attack by the DHS's efforts to get tough on undocumented immigrants. Children have been separated from their parents, left abandoned or placed in foster care while ICE agents have detained their parents. Workers have been taken into custody. Employers have lost production and some of their best workers. Immigrants—or those perceived as immigrants—have been the subject of racial profiling by ICE, and in the process, U.S. citizens and lawful permanent residents have been wrongfully detained and even deported.

Many of these immigration raids are part of worksite enforcement operations that are the method in which ICE enforces the employer sanctions provisions of the federal immigration laws. Beginning in April of 2006, in the midst of the immigration reform debate, ICE announced a new Interior Enforcement Strategy as the second phase of its Secure Border Initiative (SBI) that included a "new" strategy for worksite enforcement. According to ICE, the SBI is a multiyear plan intended to "secure America's borders and reduce unlawful migration" into the United States.[31] This new Interior Enforcement Strategy has resulted in what ICE claims are new steps that the agency has taken to enhance its worksite enforcement in order to combat the unlawful employment of unauthorized workers. ICE touts its worksite enforcement strategy as being in "marked contrast" to previous efforts by the former Immigration and Naturalization Service (INS). ICE's worksite enforcement strategy purportedly aims at promoting national security, protecting critical infrastructure, and ensuring fair labor standards.

Shortly after the attacks on September 11, 2001, ICE focused its worksite enforcement actions on homeland security, thereby targeting national security and critical infrastructure sites. Through a series of operations, and often by working in conjunction with other federal and state agencies, ICE conducted various investigations at nuclear power plants, chemical plants, military bases, defense facilities, airports, and seaports. Several hundred workers were arrested in each of these investigations.[32] Since April 2006, ICE has continued "traditional worksite investigations" by targeting alleged egregious employers who engage in criminal violations by creating unlawful schemes to knowingly hire and exploit undocumented workers.[33]

Under this new Interior Enforcement Strategy, ICE has certainly stepped up its worksite enforcement efforts as has been reported in the press with the large military-style worksite raids of the Swift & Co. plants and the worksite raids in New Bedford, Massachusetts, Van Nuys, California, and Postville, Iowa.[34] However, it is unclear how this increased worksite enforcement and the manner in which ICE conducts the raids are beneficial. While worksite enforcement actions are a mechanism for enforcing employer sanctions, in reality workers are the ones who are more adversely affected—not employers—and these actions rarely have anything to do with ensuring fair labor standards in the workplace. This was most clearly demonstrated with the controversial raid conducted against Agriprocessors kosher plant in Postville, Iowa, where ICE detained 389 immigrant workers.[35] The United Food and Commercial Workers (UFCW) had been leading a union organizing campaign there and advocates allege that this employer engaged in egregious labor violations ranging from child labor to sexual and physical assault of workers. Experience tells us that employers routinely hire and exploit low-wage immigrant workers, violating a number of workplace laws, without any legal repercussion whatsoever. Employers can get away with violating state and federal labor, employment, as well as health and safety laws, by threatening workers with contacting immigration agents should they attempt to exercise their workplace rights, and by retaliating against and firing those workers who do complain about their working conditions, organize to form a union, or otherwise exercise their rights.

Since the creation of employer sanctions under IRCA, the former INS and now its successor, ICE, have had the authority to impose sanctions as well as bring criminal charges against employers who violate immigration law by hiring undocumented workers. Employer sanctions have not had a significant impact upon the unlawful hiring of undocumented workers or on unlawful immigration. Unscrupulous employers often employ and exploit immigrant workers without suffering any liability for violating basic workplace laws. From its inception, the employer sanctions system has failed. This failed system allows employers to manipulate immigration law to circumvent their obligations under labor law, and because of the lack of labor law enforcement, a huge incentive to hire undocumented workers exists.

For comprehensive materials on dealing with immigration raids, see the Additional Resources section at the end of this chapter.

SSA No-Match Letters

Another federal program that was intended to benefit workers but has become a major barrier for those individuals exercising their workplace rights is the SSA no-match letter program. Each year employers are required to file Wage and Tax Statements (Form W-2) with the SSA and the Internal Revenue Service (IRS) to report the wages and taxes for their employees for the previous calendar year.[36] The SSA sends letters to employers and employees notifying them of discrepancies reported in employer wage statements and the SSA's records.[37] The SSA sends out no-match letters when the names or Social Security Numbers (SSN) listed on an employer's W-2 report do not agree with the SSA's records.[38] The purpose of the SSA no-match letter is to notify workers and their employers that the employees are not receiving proper credit for their earnings because of this discrepancy, which can affect future retirement or disability benefits administered by the SSA.

There are many reasons for no-matches, including typographical errors, data entry mistakes, and name changes. SSA no-match letters do not indicate whether a person is authorized to work and have nothing to do with a person's immigration status, nor do the letters prove any wrongdoing by either the employer or employee.[39] Because of employer confusion and misuse of the no-match letters, in 2002, SSA included protective language in its letters warning employers not to discriminate against or take adverse action against workers whose names appeared on a no-match letter.

Despite the warnings to employers in the SSA's no-match letters, many employers continued to mistake no-match letters as notices about their workers' immigration status and fired or suspended workers who received a no-match letter. Many unions challenged such firings of their members under the grievance and arbitration procedure of their collective bargaining agreements. As a result, several labor arbitrators issued decisions finding that employers lacked "just cause" to terminate workers because of a "no-match" letter from the SSA.[40] Notwithstanding favorable labor arbitration decisions, employers continue to misuse the SSA no-match letters and similar information from the SSA when it is convenient, that is, to retaliate against workers for exercising their workplace rights.

Although for years the SSA and other government agencies have made it clear that the letter does not provide information about a worker's immigration status, the DHS is now intent on turning these letters into an immigration enforcement tool. On August 15, 2007, the DHS finalized a rule that expands an employer's legal obligations upon receipt of a no-match letter from the SSA. Under the rule, the ICE could use these letters as evidence that an employer had "constructive knowledge" that an employee is unauthorized to work. The rule includes "safe harbor" procedures that an employer should follow in order to avoid liability under the employer sanctions provisions of the INA.[41] A broad coalition of labor unions, immigrant rights organizations, and businesses filed a lawsuit against the DHS, which resulted in the federal court enjoining the DHS and SSA from implementing the final rule that would have affected millions of U.S. citizens, work-authorized immigrants, and undocumented workers.[42] Despite the injunction and the Court's concerns, at the time of this writing, the DHS has recently reissued the same rule with no substantive changes.[43]

For great resources to deal with SSA no-match letters, see the Additional Resources section at the end of this chapter.

Electronic Employment Verification System

Finally, another federal program that is becoming increasingly problematic for immigrants and may some day soon become an employment barrier for all employees is the Basic Pilot program (recently rebranded the E-Verify program). The Basic Pilot/E-Verify program is a voluntary Internet-based program that was established to allow employers to electronically verify workers' employment eligibility with the DHS and the SSA.[44] To use the Basic Pilot/E-Verify program, employers enter into a Memorandum of Agreement (MOA) with DHS whereby employers agree to follow certain guidelines when using the program. Employers should only use the Basic Pilot/E-Verify to verify the work authorization of new hires, and are prohibited from prescreening job applicants or reverifying the employment authorization of current employees.

The Basic Pilot/E-Verify is often portrayed as the magic bullet that will provide employers with an easier way to verify which documents presented by a worker to satisfy the I-9 process are valid proof of the worker's authorization to work in the United States. However, the program has been plagued by problems since its inception in 1997 when it was created by the Illegal Immigration Reform and Immigrant Responsibility Act of 1996.[45] The program, which is used only by approximately 61,000 employers at the time of this writing, has been hindered by inaccurate and outdated information in the DHS and SSA databases, misuse of the program by employers, and lack of adequate privacy protections.[46]

A 2007 independent evaluation of Basic Pilot/E-Verify commissioned by DHS found that the government databases used for verification are not sufficiently up to date to accurately verify whether someone is authorized to work in the United States.[47] These database errors have a disproportionate impact on foreign-born U.S. citizens, with almost 10% initially being told that they are not authorized to work (versus 0.1% for native-born

U.S. citizens).[48] Between October 2006 and March 2007, about 3,200 foreign-born U.S. citizens were initially improperly disqualified from working by Basic Pilot/E-Verify.[49] Due to database errors, foreign-born lawful workers are 30 times more likely than native-born U.S. citizens to be incorrectly identified as not authorized for employment.[50]

Notwithstanding these major problems, almost every immigration reform bill introduced in Congress over the last couple of years, and many stand-alone bills, aim to make the Basic Pilot/E-Verify program into a mandatory program for all employers to have to verify their workers' employment authorization as a way to enforce the employer sanctions provisions of the INA. This is likely to result in thousands of lawfully authorized workers and U.S. citizens being denied the opportunity to work because of government database inaccuracies. These programs are also likely to lead to greater discrimination because employers are more likely to scrutinize workers they perceive to be foreign-born based on the color of their skin, limited English proficiency, or accent. Finally, a mandatory electronic employment verification system will do nothing to address the undeniable reality that there are approximately 12 million undocumented immigrants in the United States. These workers will simply be pushed deeper into the shadows while their employers pay them off the books and escape liability under federal and state labor and employment laws, thereby depressing working conditions for all workers.

CONCLUSION

In preparing for our collective future, it is clear that all of our lives are intertwined and that a managed immigration system is needed whereby immigrant workers continue playing a central role in helping support this country, while enjoying full labor protections and civil rights, so they can be equal and integrated participants in our society. However, these new workers are less likely to have access to accurate and accessible information about their rights. New immigrants often turn to their local churches, social service agencies, and perhaps a worker center for help, but these institutions and advocates rarely have the resources to provide technical assistance on the complex legal issues that operate in the intersection of immigration laws and policies and labor and employment laws. It is critical for providers to develop a basic understanding of these rights to better serve their clients and to help orient them so that immigrants can learn how to solve their own problems, engage in community organizing efforts, and become full participants in the society they are helping to build through their hard work.

CASE STUDIES

The following cases illustrate employment issues commonly encountered by immigrants. You are invited to discuss the questions following each case.

Case 1: No-Match Letters

You get a frantic call from your client, Teresa, who has just received a letter from her supervisor, Mark. The letter said she had to bring in her Social Security card or immigration documents within 90 days because her employer, John's Janitorial Services (JJS), had received a letter from the Social Security Administration saying Teresa's Social Security number was false. Teresa is afraid of losing her job because she has three children and is a single mother. She has relied on this job for over 10 years to help support her family in Nicaragua. Other workers report that Mark has received these letters in the past, but as far as they know, no one has ever been fired or been questioned about their "papers" before. Mark knows Teresa is undocumented because when he has insisted that she go out with him in the past, he has told her he would protect her from getting fired or being deported. Teresa is very scared.

Teresa is afraid of losing her job and thinks other workers may be fired, too. Earlier this week, a group of her coworkers were suspended without pay until they can bring in new work authorization documents. Rick, the night supervisor at building A, told the group of workers that they had received no-match letters from SSA stating that there are discrepancies with their SSNs. Rick had recently attended a meeting where JJS headquarters informed all supervisors about a recent change in the law where immigration was cracking down on "illegals." Just to be sure that none of these workers were undocumented, Rick has suspended them all until they can correct their records. Most of the workers have been with the company for over six years and JJS has received no-match letters about them in the past without incident.

1. What social work issues does this case raise?
2. What legal issues does this case raise?

3 Are there any potential legal claims the workers may have? What government agencies would you consider contacting?
4 Why do you think that the employer is asking workers to correct their papers based on a no-match letter when it hasn't required this in the past?
5 What initial steps would you advise (a) Teresa and (b) the other workers to take?
6 Are there any mezzo or macro issues that this case raises, such as advocacy aimed at changing organizational systems or policies?

Case Study 2: Back Pay and Reinstatement

A group of 10 workers comes to you. They have been fired, after complaining as a group to their employer that they were not paid for overtime work. Five of the workers are undocumented. Three of these presented work authorization cards to the employer with their correct name, but the documents were false. One of the workers used her sister in-law's work authorization card. One worked under her own name for a time, but after a seasonal layoff, came back to work and used a false name and work authorization card. The workers want to pursue back pay and reinstatement. Each was unemployed or had several months of unemployment, and all are now working, using the same cards that they most recently used with this employer.

1 What social work practice issues does this case raise?
2 What legal issues does this case raise?
3 Can all of the workers get back pay?
4 Can all of them get reinstatement?
5 How will you deal with the workers' use of a false name?

Case Study 3: Labor Organizing

A group of hotel employees is involved in a labor organizing campaign. During the campaign, the employer fires seven immigrants and refuses to pay them for their last two weeks of work. The employer says that they were discharged because it has a policy of verifying Social Security numbers with the Social Security Administration, and the seven workers did not have valid SSNs. You know that at least two of the group of seven who were fired are documented and have good Social Security numbers.

1. What social work issues does this case raise?
2. What legal issues does this case raise?
3. What steps can you take to try to help the workers get their jobs back? Do the undocumented workers have a right to be reinstated?
4. What claims can they potentially file?
5. Can they get back pay for the work they performed?

Quiz: Myths and Facts About Immigrant Workers

For each statement, decide whether it is a myth (false) or a fact (true).

1. You need to either be a U.S. citizen or have a green card to legally work in the United States.
2. All workers have the right to be paid for work performed... even if they are undocumented.
3. Employers are only required to verify the work authorization of workers who are not citizens.
4. If an undocumented worker is injured on the job, she is out of luck and cannot get medical care.
5. Undocumented immigrants do not have the same employment rights as all other workers.
6. It is illegal for an employer to report a worker to the immigration authorities because the worker filed a complaint against the company.
7. If a worker gets an SSA no-match letter, it means he is undocumented and the employer can fire him.
8. Employers cannot use the E-Verify program to screen job applicants and make sure they are hiring only citizens and legal workers.
9. If the E-Verify program cannot confirm that a worker is authorized to work, that means she is undocumented.
10. If there is an immigration raid, all workers have the right to remain silent and not provide incriminating information.

Answers: 1-myth; 2-fact; 3-myth; 4-myth; 5-myth; 6-fact; 7-myth; 8-fact; 9-myth; 10-fact.

NOTES

1. Note that this chapter will use the term *immigrant* to refer to all individuals who have made the United States their new home, whether they arrived as immigrants or as refugees who were fleeing persecution in their home country.

2. *Statistical Portrait of the Foreign-Born Population in the United States, 2006,* Table 1—Population by Nativity: 2000 and 2006 (Pew Hispanic Center, January 23, 2008), http://pewhispanic.org/factsheets/factsheet.php?FactsheetID=36
3. Immigration and Nationality Act of 1952, Sec. 208.
4. See, for example, INA (cite to H-1B, H-2A, H-2B as examples).
5. Ninety-two percent of undocumented males between the ages of 18–64 participate in the labor force. Jeffrey S. Passel, *Unauthorized Migrants: Numbers and Characteristics* (Pew Hispanic Center, June 2005).
6. Dowell Myers's study found that in 2005, the poverty rate among Latino immigrants in California dropped from 28.7% for those who had been in the United States for less than 10 years to 11.8% for those who had been in the country for more than 30 years.
7. The NLRA is enforced by the National Labor Relations Board (NLRB). To learn more about the NLRA, visit the NLRB's Web site at www.nlrb.gov
8. Title VII is enforced by the Equal Employment Opportunity Commission (EEOC), which also enforces the Age Discrimination in Employment Act of 1967, Americans with Disabilities Act of 1990, and the Equal Pay Act of 1963. To learn more about the EEOC and the laws under its jurisdiction, visit www.eeoc.gov
9. The U.S. Department of Labor (DOL) enforces the FLSA, as well as the Migrant and Seasonal Agricultural Worker Protection Act and the Family Medical Leave Act. DOL also oversees the Occupational Safety and Health Administration. To learn more about the DOL, its agencies, and the laws under its jurisdiction, visit www.dol.gov
10. Immigration Reform and Control Act of 1986, Pub. L. No. 99–603, § 101(a)(1), 100 Stat. 3359 (Nov. 6, 1986), codified at 8 U.S.C. § 1324a (2000) amended the Immigration and Nationality Act. INA § 274A.
11. 8 U.S.C. § 1324a(a) (2008).
12. 8 C.F.R. § 274a.7 (2008).
13. See Government Accountability Office, Pub. No. GAO/GGD-90–62, *Immigration Reform: Employer Sanctions and The Question of Discrimination* (1990) (finding a "serious pattern of discrimination" resulting specifically from employer sanctions but attributing the problem primarily to employer confusion regarding the array of documents employees could present to satisfy the I-9 employment verification requirements and a lack of awareness of the new law among employers). For a discussion of employment discrimination, see "Pursuing Racial Justice (Part 2): Growing Immigrant Communities Face Increased Employment Discrimination," *Clearinghouse Review—Journal of Poverty Law and Policy, 36*(3/4), July–August 2002.
14. 8 U.S.C. § 1324b(a)(1)(B) (2001) (prohibiting citizenship status discrimination); ibid., § 1324b(a)(2)(A)-(B) (prohibiting national origin discrimination by employers with 4 to 14 employees). Title VII of the Civil Rights Act prohibits employment discrimination by employers with more than 15 employees.
15. For more information about OSC, visit www.usdoj.gov/crt/osc
16. Immigration Act of 1990, Pub. L. No. 101–649, 104 Stat. 4978 (codified at INA, 8 U.S.C. §§ 1101 et seq. (2001)) (adding § 274B(a) of the INA).
17. The Form I-9, which applies to every employee hired in the United States, was revised on November 7, 2007, to reflect recent changes in immigration law and procedures. The Form I-9 is available at http://www.uscis.gov/files/form/i-9.pdf
18. 535 U.S. 137 (2002).
19. The remedy of back pay refers to compensation a worker can receive for the wages she would have earned had she not been wrongfully terminated.

20. *Hoffman Plastic Compounds, Inc., supra,* 535 U.S. at 147.
21. See *Sure-Tan v. NLRB,* 467 U.S. 883 (1984) (pre-IRCA decision holding that undocumented workers are covered "employees" under NLRA).
22. For a more detailed discussion, see Catherine L. Fisk and Michael J. Wishnie, *The Story of Hoffman Plastic Compounds, Inc. v. NLRB: Labor Rights Without Remedies for Undocumented Immigrants,* in Laura J. Cooper and Catherine L. Fisk (Eds.), *Labor Law Stories* (Foundation Press, 2005).
23. See *Reyes, et al. v. Van Elk, Ltd., et al.,* 148 Cal. App. 4th 604, 613 (2007) (holding that "if the FLSA did not cover undocumented aliens, employers would have an incentive to hire them"), citing *Patel v. Quality Inn South,* 846 F.2d 700 (11th Cir. 1988) (undocumented worker is employee for purposes of the [FLSA] and may sue for unpaid wages and liquidated damages).
24. See *Rivera, et al. v. NIBCO, Inc.,* 364 F.3d 1057 (9th Cir. 2004) (holding that *Hoffman* does not make immigration status relevant to the determination whether a defendant has committed national origin discrimination under Title VII).
25. Lost earnings is compensation for the wages the worker would have earned had she not been injured on the job.
26. See *The Reinforced Earth Co. v. Workers Comp Appeal Bd,* 810 A.2d 99, 107–108 (Pa. 2002).
27. See *Martines v. Worley & Sons Construction,* 628 S.E. 2d 113, 114 (Ga. Ct. App. 2006).
28. See *Wet Walls v. Ledezma,* 598 S.E. 2d 60 (Ga. Ct. App. 2004).
29. For more information about access to federal agencies, see *Limited English proficiency—A federal interagency Web site,* available at http://www.lep.gov
30. See e.g., *Corinthian Vigor Ins. Brokerage, Inc.,* 25 F.Supp.2d 1053, 1056 (N.D. Cal. 1998) (finding that employer who called INS in retaliation for worker's claim for unpaid wages was retaliation in violation of FLSA); *Singh v. Julta, et al.* 214 F.Supp.2d 1056 (N.D. Cal. 2002) (Jury awarded $200,000 in damages to worker who had been trafficked into the United States and reported to INS in retaliation for wage claim). For more information about how advocates can assist workers who may be the victims of immigration enforcement during a labor dispute, see *Issue Brief: Immigration Enforcement During Labor Disputes,* National Immigration Law Center, available at http://www.nilc.org/immsemplymnt/IWR_Material/Advocate/labor dispute_infobrief_2007–04–23.pdf
31. For more information on the SBI's interior enforcement strategy, see "ICE Announces a New Interior Enforcement Strategy," *Immigrants' Rights Update, 20*(2), May 23, 2006; available at http://www.nilc.org/immsemplymnt/wkplce_enfrcmnt/wkplcenfrc022.htm
32. See *Overview of Issues Affecting Low-wage Immigrant Workers,* National Immigration Law Center (March 2003), available at http://www.nilc.org/DC_Conf/dc-conf2003/Updated_Mats/Ovrvw_Issues_Affecting_LW_ImmWrkrs.pdf
33. See for example, *ICE agents arrest seven managers of nationwide pallet company and 1,187 of the firm's illegal alien employees in 26 states,* available at http://www.ice.gov/pi/news/newsreleases/articles/060420washington.htm. This article relates to the ICE raid at IFCO Systems North America, Inc. ("IFCO"). Note that the criminal complaints included information that 53.4% of the workers' Social Security numbers were invalid, did not match the Social Security Administration's (SSA) records, or

belonged to children or deceased persons, and that SSA had sent the employer approximately 13 written notices of such discrepancies in 2004 and 2005.

34. See "Raid an 'Outrageous Use of Force,' Union Says," CNSNews.Com (December 13, 2006); "Inhumane Raid Was Just One of Many," *Boston Globe,* March 26, 2007.
35. See "Immigration Raid Jars a Small Town," *Washington Post,* May 18, 2008. For a sobering account of this raid from the perspective of a court interpreter, see "Interpreting after the Largest ICE Raid in U.S. History: A Personal Account," Erik Camayd-Freixas, PhD, Florida International University (June 13, 2008). Retrieved from http://thesanctuary.soapblox.net/showDiary.do?diaryId=269
36. Social Security Administration, *Social Security Online, Employer W-2 Filing Instructions & Information,* available at http://www.ssa.gov/employer/gen.htm
37. For more information, see *Facts About the Social Security No-Match Letter,* National Immigration Law Center, available at http://www.nilc.org/immsemplymnt/SSA-NM_Toolkit/factsaboutno-matchletter_2008–03–26.pdf. For a sample no-match letter sent directly to employees at their home address, see http://www.nilc org/immsemplymnt/SSA-NM_Toolkit/DECOR_Employee_ltr.pdf. For letters sent by SSA to employers about a particular worker, see http://www.nilc.org/immsemplymnt/SSA-NM_Toolkit/DECORE_Employer_ltr.pdf. For letters sent by SSA to employers about multiple workers, see http://www.nilc.org/immsemplymnt/SSA-NM_Toolkit/ssa_no-match_prototypeletter_2007–08.pdf
38. Id.; see also Social Security Administration, *Social Security Online, Questions?* No. 20 (updated March 15, 2007), available at http://ssa-custhelp.ssa.gov/cgi-bin/ssa.cfg/php/enduser/std_alp.php
39. For a sample no-match letter sent directly to employees at their home address, see http://www.nilc.org/immsemplymnt/SSA-NM_Toolkit/DECOR_Employee_ltr.pdf. For letters sent by SSA to employers about a particular worker, see http://www.nilc.org/immsemplymnt/SSA-NM_Toolkit/DECORE_Employer_ltr.pdf. For letters sent by SSA to employers about multiple workers, see http://www.nilc.org/immsemplymnt/SSA-NM_Toolkit/ssa_no-match_prototypeletter_2007–08.pdf
40. For a summary of labor arbitration decisions on the no-match issue, see Monica Guizar, "Social Security Administration No-Match Letters and Collective Bargaining Agreements," *California Labor & Employment Law Review, 20*(2) (April 2006). See also, *Aramark Facility Services v. SEIU, Local 1877,* 2008 U.S. App. LEXIS 12704 (9th Cir. 2008) (holding that no-match letters do not provide constructive knowledge of workers' immigration status and therefore employer does not have just cause to fire workers).
41. See 8 U.S.C. § 1324a(a)(2).
42. See *American Federation of Labor and Congress of Industrial Organizations, et al. v. Chertoff, et al.,* Case No. C07–04472 CRB, U.S.D.C.
43. See *Summary of U.S. Dept. of Homeland Security Supplemental Proposed Rule,* National Immigration Law Center (March 27, 2008), available at http://www.nilc.org/immsemplymnt/SSA_Related_Info/DHS_Final_Rule/SSA_no-match_summary_3–26–08.pdf
44. For more information, see *Basic Information Brief: DHS Basic Pilot Program* (National Immigration Law Center, January 2008).
45. Pub. L. 104–208, 110 Stat. 3009 (September 30, 1996).
46. For a detailed discussion of these problems, see *How Errors in Basic Pilot/E-Verify Databases Impact U.S. Citizens and Lawfully Present Immigrants* (NILC,

April 2008), available at http://www.nilc.org/immsemplymnt/ircaempverif/e-verify_impacts_USCs_2008–04–09.pdf

47. See *Findings of the Web Basic Pilot Evaluation* (Westat, September 2007), www.uscis.gov/files/article/WebBasicPilotRprtSept2007.pdf, at xxi. The U.S. Citizenship and Immigration Services Web page, "Findings of the Web-Based Basic Pilot Evaluation," which links to related files, is at www.uscis.gov/portal/site/uscis/menuitem.5af9bb95919f35e66f614176543f6d1a/?vgnextoid=89abf90517e15110VgnVCM1000004718190aRCRD&vgnextchannel=a16988e60a405110VgnVCM1000004718190aRCRD
48. Ibid. at 50.
49. Nicholas Riccardi, "Arizona Slams Door on Illegal Immigrants: Some Citizens Have Been Bruised, Too, as the State Cracks Down," *Los Angeles Times*, April 5, 2008, www.latimes.com/news/nationworld/nation/la-na-arizimmig5apr05,1,6970275,full.story.
50. See *Findings of the Web Basic Pilot Evaluation*, supra (note 67), at xii-xiii.

ADDITIONAL RESOURCES

Employment Web Sites

America's Union Movement (AFL-CIO): www.aflcio.org
Change to Win: http://www.changetowin.org/
Council for Occupational Safety and Health, Immigrant Worker Resources and Links: www.coshnetwork.org/immigrant_worker_resources.htm
Equal Employment Opportunity Commission (EEOC): www.eeoc.gov
Form I-9: http://www.uscis.gov/files/form/i-9.pdf
Limited English Proficiency—A Federal Interagency Web site: http://www.lep.gov
National Employment Law Project: www.nelp.org
National Immigration Law Center: www.nilc.org
National Immigration Law Center, *Classes of Immigrants Authorized to Work in the United States:* http://www.nilc.org/immsemplymnt/IWR_Material/Attorney/Classes_of_Immigrants.pdf.
National Immigration Law Center, *Immigration & Immigrant Workers: The Basics:* http://www.nilc.org/immsemplymnt/IWR_Material/Attorney/The_Basics.pdf
National Labor Relations Board (NLRB): www.nlrb.gov
Social Security Administration, *Social Security Online, Employer W-2 Filing Instructions & Information:* http://www.ssa.gov/employer/gen.htm
United States Citizenship and Immigration Service: www.uscis.gov
United States Department of Labor (DOL): www.dol.gov
U.S. Department of Labor—Bureau of Labor Statistics: www.bls.gov

Judicial Decisions

American Federation of Labor and Congress of Industrial Organizations, et al. v. Chertoff, et al., Case No. C07–04472 CRB, U.S.D.C.
Aramark Facility Services v. SEIU, Local 1877, 2008 U.S. App. LEXIS 12704 (9th Cir. 2008).
Contreras v. Corinthian Vigor Ins. Brokerage, Inc., 25 F.Supp.2d 1053, 1056 (N.D. Cal. 1998).

Hoffman Plastic Compounds, Inc., supra, 535 U.S. at 147.
Martines v. Worley & Sons Construction, 628 S.E. 2d 113, 114 (Ga. Ct. App. 2006).
Reyes, et al. v. Van Elk, Ltd., et al., 148 Cal. App. 4th 604, 613 (2007).
Rivera, et al. v. NIBCO, Inc., 364 F.3d 1057 (9th Cir. 2004).
The Reinforced Earth Co. v. Workers Comp Appeal Bd, 810 A.2d 99, 107–108 (Pa. 2002).
Singh v. Julta, et al. 214 F.Supp.2d 1056 (N.D. Cal. 2002).
Sure-Tan v. NLRB, 467 U.S. 883 (1984).
Wet Walls v. Ledezma, 598 S.E. 2d 60 (Ga. Ct. App. 2004).

Immigrant Labor Organization and Advocacy

Bacon, D. (1998). Paolo Freire hits L.A.'s mean streets: Organizing day laborers. http://dbacon.igc.org/immigrants/03daylab.htm (1–10).

Bacon, D. (2001). Why labor needs to organize and defend the rights of immigrant workers. http://dbacon.igc.org/imgrants/26whylaborneedstodefend.htm (1–11).

Fine, J. (2006). *Worker centers: Organizing communities at the edge of the dream.* Ithaca, NY: Cornell University Press.

Frank, L., & Wong, K. (2004). Dynamic political mobilization: The Los Angeles County Federation of Labor. *Working USA—The Journal of Labor and Society, 8*(2), 155–181.

Gordon, J. (2005). *Suburban sweatshops: The fight for immigrant rights.* Cambridge, MA: Belknap Harvard University Press.

LeDuff, C. (2001). "At a slaughterhouse, some things never die," in *How race is lived in America: Pulling together, pulling apart.* New York: Times Books.

Lerner, S. (2003). An immodest proposal: A new architecture for the house of labor. *New Labor Forum, 12*(2), 9–30.

Milkman, R. (2006). *L.A. story: Immigrant workers and the future of the U.S. labor movement.* New York: Russell Sage Foundation.

Milkman, R., & Wong, K. (2000).Organizing the wicked city: The 1992 Southern California drywall strike. In R. Milkman (Ed.), *Organizing immigrants: The challenge for unions in contemporary California* (pp. 169–198). Ithaca, NY: Cornell University Press.

Waldinger, R., Erickson, C., Milkman, R., Mitchell, D. J. B., Valenzuela, A., Jr., Wong, K., & Zeitlin, M. (1997). Helots no more: A case study of the Justice for Janitors Campaign in Los Angeles. In K. Bronfenbrenner et al. (Eds.), *Organizing to win* (pp. 142–167). Ithaca, NY: Cornell University Press.

Wong, K. (2004). Don't miss the bus: The immigrant workers' freedom ride. *New Labor Forum, 13*(2), 60–66.

Immigrants, Employment, and the Economy

Ahlstrand, A. L., Laurie, J., Bassi, L. L. J., & McMurrer, D. P. (2001). *Workplace education for low-wage workers.* Alexandria, VA: American Society for Training and Development.

Alba, R. D., and Nee, V. (2003). *Remaking the American mainstream: Assimilation and contemporary immigration.* Cambridge, MA: Harvard University Press.

Altonji, J., & Card, D. (1991.) The effects of immigration on the labor market outcomes of less-skilled natives. In J. Abowd & R. Freeman (Eds.), *Immigration, trade, and the labor market* (pp. 201–234). Chicago: University of Chicago Press.

Bates, T. (1987). Self-employed minorities: Traits and trends. *Social Science Quarterly 68,* 539–551.

Bernhardt, A., Morris, M., Handcock, M. S., and Scott, M. A. (2001). *Divergent paths: Economic mobility in the new American labor market.* New York: Russell Sage Foundation.

Borjas, G. J. (1999a). *Heaven's door: Immigration policy and the American economy.* Princeton, NJ: Princeton University Press.

Brown, I. (Ed.). (1999). *Latinas and African American women at work: Race, gender, and economic inequality.* New York: Russell Sage Foundation.

Bureau of Labor Statistics. (2002). *National census of fatal occupational injuries.* Washington, DC: U.S. Department of Labor, Author.

Butcher, K. F., & Piehl, A. M. (2000). The role of deportation in the incarceration of immigrants. In G. J. Borjas (Ed.), *Issues in the economics of immigration* (pp. 351–386). Chicago: University of Chicago Press.

Card, D. E. (2001). Immigrant inflows, native outflows and the local labor market impacts of higher immigration. *Journal of Labor Economics, 19,* 22–64.

Crane, K. W., Asch, B. J., Heilbrunn, J. Z., & Cullinane, D. C. (1990). *The effect of employer sanctions on the flow of undocumented immigrants to the United States.* Washington, DC: Urban Institute Report 90–8.

Duleep, H. O., & Regets, M. C. (1992). Some evidence on the effects of admissions criteria on immigrant assimilation. In B. R. Chiswick (Ed.), *Immigration, language and ethnic issues: Canada and the United States* (pp. 410–439). Washington, DC: American Enterprise Institute.

Espenshade, T. J., & Hempstead, K. (1996). Contemporary American attitudes toward U.S. immigration. *International Migration Review 26*(4), 1144–1167.

Friedberg, R. M., & Hunt, J. (1995, Spring). The impact of immigration on host country wages, employment and growth. *Journal of Economic Perspectives, 9,* 23–44.

Gianmarco, I. P. O., & Peri, G. (2006, July). *Rethinking the effects of immigration on wages.* NBER Working Paper 12497. Cambridge, MA: National Bureau of Economic Research.

Gibson, C. J., & Lennon, E. (1999, February). *Historical census statistics on the foreign-born population of the United States: 1850–1990.* Population Division Working Paper No. 29.

Green, D. A. (1999). Immigrant occupational attainment: Assimilation and mobility over time. *Journal of Labor Economics, 17,* 49–79.

Harrington, P. E., & Sum, A. (2006). As jobs go off the books, immigrants edge out some native-born workers. *Commonwealth, 11*(2), 83–90.

Jasso, G., Rosenzweig, M., & Smith, J. P. (1998). The changing skill of new immigrants to the United States: Recent trends and their determinants. NBER Working Paper 6764. Cambridge, MA: National Bureau of Economic Research.

Johnson, H. P. (1997). *Undocumented immigration to California: 1980–1993.* San Francisco: Public Policy Institute of California.

Khatiwada, I., Sum, A., & Barnicle, T. (2006). *New foreign immigrant workers and the labor market in the United States.*

Kooker, N. R. (2006, April). Hospitality immigrant quandary. *Boston Business Journal.*

Levine, L. (2007, January). *Immigration: The effects on low-skilled and high-skilled native-born workers.* Report prepared for Members and Committees of Congress by the Congressional Research Service, Order Code 95–408.

Light, I. (1979). Disadvantaged minorities in self-employment. *International Journal of Comparative Sociology, 20,* 31–45.

Mattoo, A., Neagu, I. C., and Çalar. (2005, April). *Brain waste? Educated immigrants in the U.S. labor market.* World Bank Policy Research Working Paper 3581.
Mehta, C., Theodore, N., Mora, I., & Wade, J. (2002). *Chicago's undocumented immigrants: An analysis of wages, working conditions, and economic contributions.* Chicago: UIC Center for Urban Economic Development.
Mountford, A. (1997). Can a brain drain be good for growth in the source economy? *Journal of Development Economics, 53,* 287–303.
Murray, J., Batalova, J., & Fix, M. (2006, July). *The impact of immigration on native workers: A fresh look at the evidence.* Washington, DC: Migration Policy Institute, Insight No. 18.
National Association of Manufacturers. (2003). *Keeping America competitive: How a talent shortage threatens U.S. manufacturing.* Washington, DC: Author.
National Employment Law Project. (2001). *Temp work and unemployment insurance—helping employees at temporary staffing and employee leasing agencies.* New York: Author.
Paral, R. (2005). *Essential workers: Immigrants are a needed supplement to the native-born labor force.* Washington, DC: Immigration Policy Center.
Passel, J. S. (2006). *The size and characteristics of the unauthorized migrant population in the U.S.: Estimates based on the March 2005 current population survey.* Washington, DC: Pew Hispanic Center.
Pitts, S. (2007, Fall). The race question and building labor power in the context of the immigrant upsurge. *Labor and Working-Class History Association (LAWCHA) Newsletter.*
Powers, M. G., & Seltzer, W. (1998). Occupational status and mobility among undocumented immigrants by gender. *International Migration Review, 32*(1), 21–55.
Reitz, J. G. (1998). *Warmth of the welcome: The social causes of economic success for immigrants in different nations and cities.* Boulder, CO: Westview Press.
Reitz, J. G., Frick, J. R., Calabrese, T., & Wagner, G. C. (1999). The institutional framework of ethnic employment disadvantage: a comparison of Germany and Canada. *Journal of Ethnic and Migration Studies, 25,* 397–443.
Sassen, S. (1995). Immigration and local labor markets. In A. Portes (Ed.), *The economic sociology of immigration: Essays on networks, ethnicity, and entrepreneurship.* New York: Russell Sage Foundation.
Schmidley, D. (2001, December). *Profile of the foreign-born population in the United States: 2000, current population reports—Special Studies.* Series P23–206. Washington, DC: U.S. Census Bureau.
Smith, J. P., & Edmonston, B. (1997). *The new Americans: Economic, demographic and fiscal effects of immigration.* Washington, DC: National Academies Press. http://books.nap.edu/catalog/5779.html
Stark, O., Helmenstein, C., & Prskawetz, A. (1998). Human capital depletion, human capital formation, and migration: A blessing or a curse? *Economics Letters, 60,* 363–367.
Sum, A., Fogg, N. & Harrington, P. (2002). *Immigrant workers and the great American job machine: The contributions of new foreign immigration to national and regional labor force growth in the 1990s.* Boston: Northeastern University, Center for Labor Market Studies.
Terrazas, A., Batalova, J., & Fan, V. (2007). *Frequently requested statistics on immigrants in the United States.* Washington, DC: Migration Policy Institute.

Tobar, P. (2004). *The employment experiences of teens in central city labor markets: The influence of demographic/human capital traits, family background, and environmental factors.* M.A. Workshop Paper, Department of Economics, Northeastern University, Boston, MA.

Waldinger, R. (1999). Network, bureaucracy, and exclusion: Recruitment and selection in an immigrant metropolis. In F. D. Bean and S. Bell-Rose (Eds.), *Immigration and opportunity: Race, ethnicity, and employment in the United States* (pp. 228–259). New York: Russell Sage Foundation.

Immigration Raids

Brochure: Rights During Immigration Raids, CASA de Maryland: http://www.nilc.org/ce/nonnilc/raidsrights_dwn&nlg&casa.pdf

From Raids to Deportation: A Community Resource Kit, National Immigration Project: http://www.nationalimmigrationproject.org/commresourcekit.html

How to Be Prepared for an Immigration Raid, National Immigration Law Center: http://www.nilc.org/ce/nilc/immraidsprep_2007–02–27.pdf

Know Your Rights Cards, National Immigration Law Center: http://www.nilc.org/ce/nilc/rightscard_2007–03–15.pdf

"Know Your Rights," video regarding immigration raids, Coalition for Humane Immigrant Rights of Los Angeles (CHIRLA): www.chirla.org/mediarights.mp4

No-Match Letters

The Low-Wage Immigrant Worker Coalition's efforts to "Stop the Social Security Administration (SSA) No-Match Letter Campaign": www/lwiw.org.

Social Security Administration "No-Match" Letter Toolkit (3rd ed.). National Immigration Law Center: http://www.nilc.org/immsemplymnt/SSA-NM_Toolkit/index.htm

REFERENCES

American Immigration Law Foundation. (2005, November). *Economic Growth & Immigration: Bridging the Demographic Divide.* Special Report of the Immigration Policy Center of the AILF. Washington, DC: Author.

Bureau of Labor Statistics. (2002). *National census of fatal occupational injuries.* Washington, DC: U.S. Department of Labor, Author.

Fisk, C. L., & White, M. J. (2005). *The story of Hoffman Plastic Compounds, Inc. v. NLRB:* Labor rights without remedies for undocumented immigrants. In Laura J. Cooper and Catherine L. Fisk (Eds.), *Labor law stories* (Foundation Press, 2005).

Gibson, C. J., & Lennon, E. (1999). *Historical census statistics on the foreign-born population of the United States: 1850–1990.* Population Division Working Paper No. 29, U.S. Bureau of the Census, Washington, DC.

Gregory, V., & Schiller, J. (2004, October 4). Fatality rate is 25% higher for Latino workers: Immigrants face greatest risks of death at jobs. *Alameda Times-Star.*

Guizar, M. (2006). Social Security Administration No-Match letters and collective bargaining agreements. *California Labor & Employment Law Review, 20*(2).

Immigration and Customs Enforcement. *ICE agents arrest seven managers of nationwide pallet company and 1,187 of the firm's illegal alien employees in 26 states.* Available at http://www.ice.gov/pi/news/newsreleases/articles/060420washington.htm

Inhumane raid was just one of many. (2007, March 26). *Boston Globe.*

Journal of Poverty Law and Policy, *Growing Immigrant Communities Face Increased Employment Discrimination,* Clearinghouse Review—Journal of Poverty Law and Policy, Pursuing Racial Justice (Part 2), Vol. 36, Numbers 3–4, July-August 2002.

Kochhar, R. (2005). *Latino labor report 2004: More jobs for new immigrants but at lower wages.* Washington, DC: Pew Hispanic Center.

Migration Policy Institute. (2004). *What kind of work do immigrants do? Occupation and industry of foreign born workers in the United States.* Washington, DC: Author. [Online newsletter, no. 3.] http://72.14.205.104/search?q=cache:06LfarSNOSgJ:www.migrationpolicy.org/pubs/Foreign%2520Born%2520Occup%2520and%2520Industry%2520in%2520the%2520US.pdf+What+Kind+of+Work+Do+Immigrants+Do%3F+Occupation+and+Industry+of+Foreign+Born+Workers+in+the+United+States,+Migration+Policy+Institute&hl=en&ct=clnk&cd=1&gl=us

Myers, D. (2008). *Thinking ahead about our immigration future: New trends and mutual benefits in our aging society.* Washington, DC: Immigration Policy Center, American Immigration Law Foundation.

National Immigration Law Center. (2008, January). *Basic information brief: DHS basic pilot program.* Washington, DC: Author.

National Immigration Law Center, *Issue Brief: Immigration Enforcement During Labor Disputes* (NILC, Apr. 2007), available at http://www.nilc.org/immsemplymnt/IWR_Material/Advocate/labordispute_infobrief_2007–04–23.pdf

National Immigration Law Center, *Overview of Issues Affecting Low-wage Immigrant Workers* (NILC, Mar. 2003) available at http://www.nilc.org/DC_Conf/dc-conf2003/Updated_Mats/Ovrvw_Issues_Affecting_LW_ImmWrkrs.pdf

National Immigration Law Center, *Facts About the Social Security No-Match Letter* (NILC, Mar. 2008), available at http://www.nilc.org/immsemplymnt/SSA-NM_Toolkit/factsaboutno-matchletter_2008–03–26.pdf

National Immigration Law Center, *Summary of U.S. Dept. of Homeland Security Supplemental Proposed Rule* ((NILC, Mar. 2008), available at http://www.nilc.org/immsemplymnt/SSA_Related_Info/DHS_Final_Rule/SSA_no-match_summary_3–26–08.pdf

National Immigration Law Center, *How Errors in Basic Pilot/E-Verify Databases Impact U.S. Citizens and Lawfully Present Immigrants* (NILC Apr. 2008), available at http://www.nilc.org/immsemplymnt/ircaempverif/e-verify_impacts_USCs_2008–04–09.pdf

National Immigration Law Center, sample no-match letter sent directly to employees at their home address, *see, http://www.nilc.org/immsemplymnt/SSA-NM_Toolkit/DECOR_Employee_ltr.pdf.* For letters sent by SSA to employers about a particular worker, *see,* http://www.nilc.org/immsemplymnt/SSA-NM_Toolkit/DECORE_Employer_ltr.pdf. For letters sent by SSA to employers about multiple workers, *see,* http://www.nilc.org/immsemplymnt/SSA-NM_Toolkit/ssa_no-match_prototypeletter_2007–08.pdf

Nicholas Riccardi, "Arizona Slams Door on Illegal Immigrants: Some Citizens Have Been Bruised, Too, as the State Cracks Down," *Los Angeles Times,* Apr. 5, 2008, www.latimes.com/news/nationworld/nation/la-na arizimmig5apr05,1,6970275, full.story.

Passel, J. S. (2005). *Unauthorized migrants: Numbers and characteristics.* Washington, DC: Pew Hispanic Center.

Pew Hispanic Center. (2008). *Statistical Portrait of the Foreign-Born Population in the United States, 2006,* Table 1—Population by Nativity: 2000 and 2006. Washington, DC: Author.

Pritchard, J. (2004, March 13). *Mexican worker deaths rise sharply.* Associated Press.
Pursuing racial justice (Part 2): Growing immigrant communities face increased employment discrimination. (2002, July/August). *Clearinghouse Review—Journal of Poverty Law and Policy, 36*(3/4).
Schmidley, D. (2001). *Profile of the foreign-born population in the United States: 2000, current population reports—Special Studies.* Washington, DC: U.S. Census Bureau, Series P23–206.
Social Security Administration. (2007, March 15). *Social Security Online, Questions?* 20. Retrieved from http://ssa-custhelp.ssa.gov/cgi-bin/ssa.cfg/php/enduser/std_alp.php
Pew Hispanic Center. (2008, January). *Statistical portrait of the foreign-born population in the United States, 2006.* Table 1—Population by Nativity: 2000 and 2006. (Pew Hispanic Center, Jan. 2008).Washington, DC: Author.
Sum, A., Fogg, N., Harrington, P., et al. (2002, August). *Immigrant workers and the great American job machine: The contributions of new foreign immigration to national and regional labor force growth in the 1990s* (pp. 16–17). Boston, MA: National Business Roundtable, Center for Labor Market Studies, Northeastern University.
Sum, A., Fogg, N., Khatiwada, I., and Palma, S. (2004, July). *Foreign immigration and the labor force of the U.S.: The contributions of new foreign immigration to the growth of the nation's labor force and its employed population, 2000 to 2004.* Boston, MA: Center for Labor Market Studies, Northeastern University.
Terrazas, A., Batalova, J., & Fan, V. (2007). *Frequently requested statistics on immigrants in the United States.* Washington, DC: Migration Policy Institute.
Working Immigrant Safety and Health Coalition. (2002, November). *Improving health and safety conditions for California's immigrant workers.* Berkeley, CA: Author.

Statutes

Immigration Act of 1990, Pub. L. No. 101–649, 104 Stat. 4978 (codified at INA, 8 U.S.C. §§ 1101 et seq. (2001)).
Sections § 274B(a) of the INA); 101(a)(15) H-1B, H-2A, H-2B; 8 U.S.C. § 1324a(a) (2008).

Regulations

8 C.F.R. § 274a.7 (2008).
Immigration Reform and Control Act of 1986, Pub. L. No. 99–603, § 101(a)(1), 100 Stat. 3359 (Nov. 6, 1986), codified at 8 U.S.C. § 1324a (2000) amended the Immigration and Nationality Act. INA § 274A.

Children and Family Issues

PART III

9 Immigrant Children and Education

LEN RIESER

Immigrant families with children face a number of challenges, but also bring many strengths. The children of immigrants can be today's science competition winners, and tomorrow's entrepreneurs, nurses and doctors, teachers, homeowners, and taxpayers. However, some newcomer families with children face special difficulties within the U.S. educational system.

Because of the particular challenges facing newcomer children in the area of access to education, this chapter discusses ways in which social workers can help families get their children into school and obtain the educational services they need. The main focus is on public elementary and secondary schools, although the chapter includes some discussion of other educational alternatives (independent schools, religious schools, home schooling). The chapter also briefly addresses preschool services.

EXPECTATIONS OF SCHOOL AND EDUCATION: AN OVERVIEW

School and *education* are, of course, familiar concepts—so much so that one might assume that all people share the same understanding of what is meant by them. The reality, however, is different. What children learn, and how schools operate, are matters that vary enormously from place to place and culture to culture.

In some countries, schools are secular; in others, they are closely managed by religious authorities. Access to school is universal in some places, but limited to children from well-to-do families, or children of favored ethnic backgrounds, or boys, or those who can pay school fees, in others. The age range a child *may* attend school varies greatly from place to place, as does the age range during which the child *must* attend.

Teachers wield nearly absolute authority in certain societies. Elsewhere, teaching is an unprestigious, civil-service job. Students in some countries achieve at significantly higher levels than do American students; in other places, the situation is quite the opposite.

For all of these reasons, immigrant families bring attitudes, expectations, and experiences in regard to schooling that may align only in part, if at all, with their experiences in the United States. Challenges for the social worker include understanding the family's educational background, as well as their wishes and hopes for their children and the children's *own* wishes and hopes, which may be very different. The social worker must determine what choices an immigrant family has with respect to their children's schooling, and help them exercise those choices. Tasks include facilitating communication between the family and the new school, and solving problems of enrollment, grade and course assignment, and school adjustment.

A special challenge is to do all this in a way that actually empowers families during the years their children are in school. During these years, issues and questions will inevitably continue to arise. It will be important that the family have its own understanding of how to do as much as possible on its own, and when and where to seek additional help.

Working with families on school problems is thus a complex task, requiring a multitude of abilities, perspectives, and contacts. Social workers are most effective in this field when they have relationships with a network of community leaders, teachers, administrators, health and mental health professionals, advocates, and others who can offer, in one way or another, insight into understanding issues and resolving educational problems. For any social worker who deals with children in school, developing such a network becomes a high priority.

This chapter does not attempt to substitute for the ongoing advice of such a collection of individuals, who can offer much more help with specific situations than can any written account. The purpose, instead, is to describe the legal and policy framework within which American public schools operate, because that framework provides the starting point for efforts to work with an individual child or family.

Since immigrant students typically go to the same schools that native-born children attend, much of the information provided here applies to students generally. On some points, however, there are special rules and policies that apply especially, or exclusively, to immigrants.

Education laws and policies vary from state to state; policies, indeed, vary even from school district to school district. Social workers must remember that all general rules have their exceptions, and should take care to obtain more specific information when needed.

EDUCATION LAW AND POLICY IN THE UNITED STATES

It is often said that education is primarily a state and local matter. It is true that many important aspects of our educational system, such as school age and attendance requirements, residency rules, course requirements, and graduation criteria, are governed by state and local laws, rules, and policies. However, federal law—which has always been important on questions of discrimination, freedom of expression, and other matters relating to constitutional rights—is of increasing significance as well. The elaborate requirements of the No Child Left Behind Act with respect to student testing and school improvement are an example.

Because laws and policies in this area come from multiple sources, and interact in complex ways, it can be confusing to sort out what the rules are in any particular situation. Thus, it makes sense to maintain a healthy skepticism about whether what one is told is actually correct. Teachers and administrators will sometimes speak with great authority and the best of intentions, and still be wrong.

Especially if the question is an important one affecting a child's rights (for example, whether a child living with a relative is eligible to attend school in the relative's district), it may be important to consult with someone with expertise in the area. Needed information might come from a different teacher or administrator, or from another social worker who is experienced with the school system. Alternatively, assistance might come from a parent or student advocacy group, which might have education as its sole focus or might be a multipurpose organization.

As a last resort, for problems that cannot be resolved in another way, it may be necessary to consider making a formal complaint—for example, to a state department of education or human relations agency, or to a court. Sometimes, complaint procedures are relatively simple and quick; in other contexts, they are expensive. Legal consultation can be helpful in sorting out the options, and the pros and cons of each. Consultation may be available from an attorney connected to one's own agency, an advocacy group or legal services agency, or a *pro bono* lawyer. At the end of this chapter, we return to the question of when and how to get help with education problems.

Types of Schools

Elementary and secondary schools in the United States may be public (operated by a governmental agency, most often a "school district" or town or city), religious, or independent. Unless a court has intervened, for example, via an adjudication of dependency, parents have an absolute right to choose a public, religious, or independent school for their child. In most states, parents also have the right to choose *no* school for their child, and instead to educate him or her at home—although such home schooling arrangements typically require compliance with some governmental standards. These schooling options differ in some crucial respects, and there are even variations within each category.

Public Schools

Every child of school age belongs, by virtue of his or her address, to a school district (or the equivalent), and has a right to attend a public school, assuming certain age and residency requirements are met. The question of *which* public school(s) within a district a child has the right to attend may be complex. We will discuss the important question of school choice *within* public school districts in more detail in the section below titled "Enrollment and School Placement."

A school-district-operated school may not, however, be the family's only option. A relatively new variety of public school, often governed by a body such as a board of trustees, is the public charter school. Charter schools may coexist in the same area with school-district-operated schools. They often have specific themes, and may or may not have specific admissions requirements.

Not all public schools operate in a traditional school building. Some charter schools, for example, function through distance learning, in which the student stays home (or goes to some other setting) and takes courses online.

All public schools, including district-operated and charter schools, are free of charge. They are also subject to many laws, regulations, and policies, including, for example, requirements concerning the content of the curriculum, the qualifications of teachers, and the rights of parents and students.

Religious and Independent Schools

Religious and independent schools provide additional schooling options. These schools typically charge tuition fees; actual amounts, as well as policies on scholarships and financial aid, vary drastically. Religious and independent schools may be selective in their admissions policies, and may, depending on the circumstances, be permitted to exclude children on grounds that would be impermissible in the public education setting. In general, these schools are subject to much less governmental control and regulation than are public schools.

Home Schooling

Home schooling is yet another option. Typically, home schooling arrangements require either that the parent serve as teacher (in which case she or he must meet specific requirements), or that a family or group of families secure a teacher for their children. There may also be requirements concerning curriculum and documentation of children's progress.

The social worker can help an immigrant family by making sure that the family is aware of, and able to navigate among, these various educational options. Often, no one will have told the family about options other than the local school-district-operated school, much less what the pros and cons of those other options may be or how one might go about pursuing them.

For any particular child, of course, the neighborhood public school may turn out to be the best choice. But it is also possible that another school within the district might be available and a better fit, or that a charter, religious, or independent school is within reach and is an even better option. Social workers can help families by making sure that they know about these possibilities, not only when the child first enters school but as his or her needs develop and change.

Because most children in the United States attend public schools, the balance of this chapter will focus primarily on the public educational system. *Thus, from this point forward, the term* school *refers to* public school. Again, however, it is important to remember that for any specific child, other options may exist.

ROLES AND RESPONSIBILITIES OF PARENTS

Parents have important rights and responsibilities in the educational system of the United States. Besides choosing the school the child will attend, the parent has the right, and sometimes the duty, to be involved in many aspects of the educational process. We will touch on many of these areas of parental involvement in subsequent sections.

Special rules apply when a child is living apart from his or her parent. This situation is not uncommon, of course, among immigrant children, who may, for example, be living with relatives because the parents are still in the country of origin.

If the child has an actual legal guardian, that is, an individual appointed by a court to function as the child's parent, the guardian simply substitutes for the parent in all respects. However, while it may be desirable in some situations to arrange for the appointment of a guardian, that may not be necessary for school purposes. In many states, a relative or other caregiver with whom the child lives may be legally viewed as the parent with regard to the child's schooling. In addition, a child who has reached a certain age and lives independently may have the right to manage his or her own education.

These laws, which vary somewhat from state to state, are important, because they involve the fundamental question of who is in charge of the child's education. It is unusual to find a law that gives a child's *social worker* (as opposed to parent, guardian, or other caregiver) the right to make decisions concerning a child's schooling.

If the child has no parent living in the United States, and is undocumented, U.S. immigration law allows children to obtain lawful permanent resident status or a green card through Special Immigrant Juvenile Status (SIJS). As briefly described in chapter 2, juveniles under the jurisdiction of a juvenile court who are eligible for long-term foster care due to drug abuse, abandonment, or neglect may qualify for lawful permanent resident status.

A first step in this process is to have the state family court adjudicate the child dependent. Typically SIJS is granted to children in juvenile dependency court who are placed in foster care. Once the child has been adjudicated dependent, SIJS is a way for a dependent of juvenile court to become a permanent resident of the United States (i.e., get a green card). If the juvenile applies for this status and is successful, she or he may remain in the United States, work legally, qualify for in-state tuition at college, and in five years apply for U.S. citizenship. However, if the application is denied, the child might be deported (8 U.S.C. § 1101(a)(27)(J); 8 C.F.R. § 204.11(c)). The social worker should collaborate with the child welfare agency so as to get the child recognized as dependent. After this process is completed, the social worker should work with an immigration attorney to ensure that the minor becomes a lawful permanent resident.

LANGUAGE ACCESS

Schools and parents communicate about all sorts of issues, from initial enrollment to questions of placement, progress, behavior, access to special services and activities, and much more. This is, of course, a problematic area for immigrant families because of language barriers.

In general, when a parent's native language is not English, the public school has a duty under federal civil rights laws, and sometimes state law as well, to communicate effectively with that parent (Title VI of the Civil Rights Act of 1964, 42 U.S.C. § 2000d). This means that significant written notices and letters to the parent must be translated, and that interpretation services must generally be available for such school-sponsored events as meetings to discuss a child's progress and parent meetings concerning schoolwide issues.

SCHOOL AGE

The issue of the child's age comes up in two distinct ways in the context of elementary and secondary education. There is, first, an age range within which a child has the *right* to go to school. This varies from state to state, but often begins at age 5 or 6 and continues to 20 or 21, or the point at which the student graduates from high school, whichever occurs first. Children within this age range have the right to attend a public school. Independent and religious schools, by contrast, are not required to cover any specific age range.

It is worth noting that most public school systems offer kindergarten, and some offer preschool programs. Head Start programs are also widely available for preschool youngsters. These programs, of course, may be open to children at ages considerably below 5 or 6.

Further, the Individuals with Disabilities Education Act, the federal special education law, requires that states provide early intervention services to children from birth onward. This is a significant expansion, for children who have developmental delays and disabilities, of the usual age range for educational services. While an extended description of early intervention programs is beyond the scope of this chapter, these programs may be of enormous value to immigrant children. Moreover, since access to early intervention services is an entitlement for qualifying children, it is important that the social worker know how these services are delivered in his or her area, and how to assist families in applying for them.

There is, in addition, a second age range relevant to schooling: the age for compulsory attendance, that is, the age range during which the child has the *obligation* to attend school. This varies from state to state, but often runs from 6 or 7 to 17 or 18. A child whose age falls within the compulsory attendance age range must attend school, but as we have noted, can attend either a public or some other sort of school.

The social worker can assist a family in understanding the age ranges for school admission (including admission to preschool and, for children with delays or disabilities, early intervention services) and compulsory attendance. Both sets of age limits are likely to be different here from what they were in the home country. Indeed, the very fact that school attendance is required will be new for some families.

The social worker may need to sort out instances in which the two age ranges become confused. Thus, for example, a 19-year-old student may be told that she is no longer *permitted* to attend school when the reality is that she is no longer *required* to attend school. The several "extra" years of schooling that are generally available to students above compulsory attendance age can make a significant difference to immigrants whose education has been interrupted, or who have had difficulty catching up in a new language. The social worker can help by encouraging the family to consider whether the student should stay in school for an additional period.

Finally, the problem of documenting the age of a child who does not have the necessary papers is addressed in the next section.

ENROLLMENT AND SCHOOL PLACEMENT

Enrollment requirements for public school are typically set by state law. They ordinarily include documentation of identity, age, and residency. Sometimes, additional documentation, such as proof of immunizations, is also required.

The question of the child's legal right to be in the United States sometimes surfaces as an issue in the educational enrollment process. This is improper, since the Supreme Court has made clear that an immigrant child who meets the normal residency requirements for school attendance is entitled to attend school—regardless of the child's immigration documents or, indeed, whether the child has *any* immigration documents at all (*Plyler v. Doe*, 457 U.S. 202 (1982)). (Residency requirements will be discussed later in this section.) As a general rule, therefore, schools have no authority to ask for any immigration information or documentation as part of the enrollment process.

Proof of Identity and Age

Documentation of a child's identity and age is easy, of course, when the family has the necessary papers (such as birth certificate, passport, or the like), but can sometimes be problematic if those papers are unavailable. Newcomer families sometimes have passports and visas (which may have expired) or no passport or visa at all. Generally, state law and policy allow the use of various alternative methods for establishing identity and age, for example, submission of an affidavit of a medical professional concerning the child's age. Documentation problems can almost always be resolved through persistence, so it never makes sense to accept the suggestion that a child will not be able to attend school because papers are missing. Social workers can help by assisting immigrant families in obtaining these documents.

Residency

As used in the enrollment context, *residency* refers to whether the child meets requirements regarding physical residency in the school district, rather than to the child's immigration status. Again, residency requirements are set by state law and policy. The simplest case is that of a child who lives with his parent or parents within the physical boundaries of the school district. A child in that situation should ordinarily have no difficulty meeting the residency requirement, so long as the parents provide documentation (lease or deed, utility bills, driver's license, and the like) showing that they do, in fact, live in the district. If the family is living with relatives, and are not themselves named on the deed or lease, it should still be possible to enroll the child based on some alternative documentation that the family actually lives where they claim to live (such as a letter from the landlord).

School districts occasionally deny admission on the ground that the family's living arrangements are irregular in some way, for example, inconsistent with local codes because too many people are living in one residence. Ordinarily, this should not be a permissible basis for denying enrollment, since school districts do not have the authority to enforce housing or zoning codes. The question for the school district should be simply whether or not the family actually lives within the district.

The situation can become more complex when the child is living apart from his or her parents. State laws vary on this point, but most include provisions allowing a child who lives with another adult (legal guardian, relative, caregiver) to attend school in the district in which that adult resides. Similar state laws protect children living in foster homes, group homes, and institutional placements.

There are also state laws allowing older children who are living entirely independently (sometimes referred to as "emancipated minors") to enroll in the district in which they reside. Finally, the McKinney Vento Act, a federal law, entitles homeless families to send their children to school in the district in which they last resided before becoming homeless, or in the district in which they are currently living (42 U.S.C. § 11431 et seq.).

As mentioned earlier, a child's immigration status does not affect eligibility for enrollment, and should *not* be confused with residency. An immigrant child who meets the normal residency requirements for school attendance is entitled to attend school—regardless of the child's immigration documents or, indeed, whether the child has *any* immigration documents at all.

Nevertheless, there are a few ways in which immigration status may be relevant to school enrollment. In the case of a foreign exchange student, for example, the school will know about the child's immigration status, because it will have supplied information in connection with the child's application for a foreign exchange student visa. (In this situation, the student may also be required to pay tuition to the school.) As described in chapter 2, persons can enter the United States legally as foreign students on an F visa. In this situation, the school will have admitted the student and issued the student the necessary forms (an Immigration Form I-20), which may help the student obtain a visa to enter the United States.

Another case might be that of a family who visits the United States as tourists. While the school has no right to view the family's visa, the family does bear the burden of showing that they are truly residing in the district—which, depending on state law, may require that they must demonstrate intent to remain. This might be difficult if the truth is that the family plans to return to its home country after a short visit.

Social Security Number

There is no law authorizing schools to require that a family provide social security numbers as a condition of enrollment. Thus, a child who meets other relevant criteria for enrollment has a right to be admitted, even without a Social Security number. Moreover, while Social Security numbers may be *requested* as part of the application process for certain services, such as the school lunch program, the law provides that the number cannot be *required*.

Language Access During the Enrollment Process

We have already discussed the obligation of the school to communicate effectively with parents in their native language where necessary. This requirement applies, of course, to the communication that must occur during the enrollment process as well as to other important communications between family and school.

Choice of School

State or local law and policy may allow families some choice among schools *within* the public school system. Sometimes, the family need not meet any specific criteria in order to enroll the child in a school of their choice; in other situations, admission may be based on the child's achievement or behavioral record, interest in a specific program, or other factor (such as race, in those few districts that are still governed by some sort of judicial desegregation order). The federal No Child Left Behind Act has created some additional choice options, including the right to transfer from a school that has failed to make adequate yearly progress (AYP) for several years running to a school that has achieved AYP, and the right to transfer from a "persistently dangerous" school to a school not in that category (20 U.S.C. § 6316).

As we have noted, immigrant families may be less familiar than non-immigrant families with the school choice options that they may have, even within the public education system. Moreover, they may be less likely to know much about schools outside their neighborhood, or about application forms, deadlines, and the like. The social worker can help by helping immigrant families obtain that information and make the best possible choices for their children.

In summary, most immigrant children do not encounter difficulty in enrolling in school, but for those that do, the situation can obviously be serious. Missing documentation, alternative living arrangements, and language barriers can all cause problems, as can conscientious school employees who may be demanding more than what the law actually requires. It is important, therefore, that the social worker be fully informed about the laws and policies of his or her state, and be persistent when the school district seems to be imposing requirements that are not found in official policy.

The social worker can also help by deflecting any effort, on the part of school staff, to inquire into a child's immigration status; by asking that a translator be provided when necessary; and by making sure that the family understands all of the options they may have with respect to choosing a school for their child.

COURSE PLACEMENT AND INSTRUCTION

As a general rule, schools will assign a child to a grade on the basis of the child's chronological age. There may or may not ordinarily be some choice of courses at the child's grade level. Courses are typically aligned with state academic standards that define the knowledge and skills that the child is expected to acquire. Tests and assessments are typically aligned with these standards as well.

This somewhat standardized approach may or may not fit the needs of the immigrant student. Fortunately, the laws require that schools make certain modifications to their programs when that is necessary to meet a child's special needs.

Services for Children Who Are Learning English

Two federal laws, Title VI of the Civil Rights Act of 1964, 42 U.S.C. § 2000d, and the Equal Educational Opportunities Act, 20 U.S.C. § 1703(f), as well as many state laws, require that school districts make special arrangements for children whose native language is not English. See U.S. Department of Education, Office for Civil Rights, "The Provision of an Equal Educational Opportunity to Limited-English Proficient Students" (2007).

First, schools are legally required to assess the child's English proficiency—to determine, for example, whether the child is at beginning, intermediate, or advanced level in terms of reading, writing, listening to, and speaking the language. Careful assessment is important, especially because quick judgments about a child's English ability can often prove to be wrong. The child who can speak enough English to get by on the playground, for example, or even to converse with his peers, may be only partially able—or completely unable—to understand academic material presented in the language.

Second, assuming that the assessment shows that the child is not yet proficient in English, he or she must be provided instruction in the language. This program must be based on sound professional judgment, which ordinarily means that the child will receive English as a Second Language instruction from a teacher with qualifications in the field of second-language learning. (The teacher usually need not be bilingual, however, since the focus is on teaching English—not on translating from another language.)

Because mere immersion in an English-language environment is rarely viewed as a professionally defensible form of instruction, except possibly for very young children or those who are nearing English proficiency, it makes sense to be skeptical when a child with limited English is simply placed in regular classes on the theory that he or she will gradually pick up the language. The same can often be said of situations in which the child is simply placed in a regular English class, since instruction in these classes ordinarily presupposes that the child is already as proficient in the language as other students of the child's age.

Third, depending on the child's level of English proficiency, he or she may have difficulty making sense of academic classes (math, science, history, and so on) that are taught in English. This, of course, is the reason that some schools offer bilingual instruction, in which children are taught academic content in their native language. The more typical situation is that the child's coursework is delivered in English; in that situation, schools are required to find ways of adjusting the instruction so that the child can benefit from it to the same degree that a native speaker would benefit.

How this is done will depend on the child's level of English proficiency. For example, the teacher may need to deliver some instruction in simplified English, use more nonverbal approaches, offer extra help or tutoring, enlist the help of the English as a Second Language teacher, or take various other possible steps. The point is that, for a child who needs extra help because of a language barrier, extra help must be provided.

Schools must also make adjustments to their testing procedures so that students who are English language learners can be fairly assessed. This principle applies both to locally developed tests and assessments and to standardized and statewide tests. Depending on the student's English level, adjustments may include the provision of extra time, translation or the use of a language dictionary, modified questions, modified grading standards, and more. The point is that, if the test is intended to measure the student's mastery of a subject such as science or history, steps must be taken to ensure that this is in fact what is measured—not the student's English proficiency.

In summary, students who are learning English are not legally required to sink or swim in school. Rather, schools have the obligation to provide help both in learning English and in mastering academic content that is delivered in English. While the nature and extent of the assistance that must be provided will depend on the student's level of English proficiency, the demands of the coursework, and other factors, the social worker should ask questions if it appears that the child seems to be receiving no, or inadequate, help.

Special Education

Under the federal Individuals with Disabilities Education Act (IDEA), and state laws, special education services are available for students who, because of a disability, need such assistance (20 U.S.C. § 1400 *et seq.*). Of course, limited English proficiency is not a disability, and the law requires that care be taken not to classify a child as in need of special education solely because he or she is learning English. But for those English language learners who have learning disabilities, emotional disturbances, mental retardation, autism, hearing or visual impairments, or other disabilities, special education can be essential.

Special education is an area in which the law prescribes especially detailed rights and procedures. These begin with an evaluation, designed to determine whether the child is eligible for special education. Parents have a right to obtain such an evaluation on written request, within a specified time period. Requesting an evaluation does not commit the parents to agreeing to special education for their child; the evaluation is simply designed to determine whether, in the view of the evaluation team, special education is needed.

IDEA requires that evaluation materials and procedures be selected and administered so as not to be discriminatory on a racial or cultural basis, and also mandates that the evaluation be "provided and administered in the child's native language native language or mode of communication, unless it clearly is not feasible to do so" (20 U.S.C. § 1414(a)(6)). This means, in general, that evaluation procedures and personnel must be culturally and linguistically competent to assess the child—a point on which advocacy may be needed, given the shortage, in many places, of such personnel.

Assuming the evaluation concludes that the child needs special education, and that the parents agree, the next step is a conference to design a program of specialized instruction that is appropriate to the child's needs. The program is described in a written individualized education program (IEP), and may also include related services such as counseling, speech therapy, and the like.

A decision is then made concerning the child's placement, which must be as inclusive as possible, as much within the regular educational environment as is possible in light of the child's needs and the services that he or she is to receive. For most children, this means placement in a regular school, mostly or fully in regular classes with some specialized services. For some children with more complex impairments, placement in special classes or even in a special school serving only children with disabilities may be considered; however, the law strongly disfavors these sorts of noninclusive placements. For some parents of immigrant children with complex disabilities, the legal preference for inclusion may be a source of concern. For other parents, who come from backgrounds where students with disabilities are routinely educated with other children, there may be no issue at all.

Special education law also provides mechanisms for resolving disagreements between the family and the school. Virtually every decision concerning the child—beginning with the decision as to whether the child has a disability and needs special education, and continuing on through decisions concerning the content and implementation of the child's IEP as well as decisions concerning his or her placement—can be contested by the family. The procedures include both mediation and actual legal hearings and appeals. While the details are too extensive to include here, the important point is that a family that is dissatisfied with a school's decisions concerning special education is not required simply to accept those decisions, but has some recourse.

Finally, as noted in the section above entitled "School Age," all states must provide preschool early intervention services to children, from birth to age 5, who have certain delays and disabilities. The procedures for accessing these services are similar, though not identical, to those described above for school-age children.

Schools are also required to modify their programs and services to meet the needs of children with disabilities who, while not requiring special education, do need some special arrangements—such as access to an elevator, or a change in the daily schedule to accommodate health concerns (29 U.S.C. § 794, "Section 504 of the Rehabilitation Act"; 42 U.S.C. § 12131 *et seq.*, Americans with Disabilities Act).

Other Special Programs and Services

School systems offer a wide variety of other special programs and services, such as preschool programs, tutoring programs, after-school and extracurricular programs, advanced placement classes, vocational and technical programs, magnet programs, and summer programs. As a general rule, under Title VI of the Civil Rights Act and many state laws, immigrant students should have equal access to these programs.

Equal access begins with adequate notice to the student and the family that the program exists, and of the steps that must be taken to access it; here as in other important school communications, information must be provided in the family's native language. Equal access also generally means that, if the immigrant student meets the other requirements for admission to the program, the fact that she or he is an English language learner should not be a basis for exclusion, nor should the student be admitted only on the condition that she or he receive no special help. On the contrary, services such as English as a Second Language instruction must ordinarily be provided *within* the program.

Social workers should be familiar with the special programs and services that the school makes available, including special education, access to vocational-technical programs, tutoring, and other such services. If immigrant families are not receiving information about the availability of these services, the school should be asked to provide information in families' native languages. And if immigrant students are being told that they are ineligible for special services and programs, the social worker should be skeptical, because immigrants in general have the same right of access to school services as all other students—even if special arrangements must be made on account of a child's need for help with English.

STUDENT RIGHTS IN SCHOOL

Students, including newcomer students, have a number of additional rights in public schools in the United States. In this section, we discuss First Amendment freedoms (expression, religion); nondiscrimination; the right to safety in school; and the right to fairness in discipline.

Freedom of Expression

Under the First Amendment to the U.S. Constitution, students have a right to express their ideas and opinions in school. At the same time, this right is limited in some important ways. For example, speech that causes a substantial disruption of the educational process can be prohibited (although the mere fact that other people take offense at what is said does not necessarily constitute disruption). Schools can also prohibit speech advocating the use of illegal drugs, or lewd speech. This area can be complicated; the important point is that students do have substantial free speech rights, and that policies that infringe on those rights may be illegal.

The First Amendment also protects students from being forced to say things with which they disagree. Thus, for example, the courts have held that students cannot be required to say the Pledge of Allegiance (*West Virginia Board of Education v. Barnette,* 319 U.S. 624 (1943)).

Freedom of Religion

Yet another set of First Amendment protections involves religion. Under the Free Exercise Clause of the Amendment, students are generally free to maintain their own religious beliefs, to pray, and to wear religious items. Again, there may be some limitations on these rights. Under the

Establishment Clause, public schools are prohibited from teaching religious beliefs, conducting school-sponsored prayers, or endorsing particular religious holidays or symbols. Schools may, on the other hand, teach *about* religion and religions, include religious music in school concerts (so long as the effect is not to promote a specific religion).

Discrimination and Equal Access

Under federal law and most states' laws as well, public schools are prohibited from discriminating on the basis of race, ethnicity, national origin, religion, and gender. This means that, in general, none of these grounds may be the basis for excluding a student from a school program or providing him or her with services that are inferior to those provided to others. All students, regardless of race, ethnicity, national origin, religion, and gender, have a right of equal access to school programs and services.

Discrimination on the basis of disability is also prohibited by federal and state laws. This similarly means that a student with disabilities must generally have equal access to school programs, with the caveat that equal access is not required where the student could not participate successfully in the program even with reasonable accommodations and adjustments.

Discrimination on the basis of sexual orientation may also be prohibited. Here, federal law is generally silent, so one must look to state and local laws and policies for relief—and only some states or localities have them.

Safety

Schools have a legal duty to protect students from harm, but that duty can be difficult to enforce. Most schools and districts have procedures for reporting threats as well as actual harm to students; obviously, it is important to know how these procedures work in one's own locality. School officials are less likely to allow a dangerous situation to continue if they have been fully notified of its existence.

Schools also frequently operate mediation programs, bullying-intervention programs, and other services that can help resolve conflict, including intergroup conflicts. These services may also be available from the local municipality, social service agency, or state program.

Finally, under the No Child Left Behind Act, a student who is the victim of a violent crime has the right to transfer to another school in the district (20 U.S.C. § 9532). This provision can be of benefit to some students, although it has the obvious drawback that it can only be requested after the fact, and is useful only if the district operates more than one school at the student's grade level.

Fairness in Discipline

Under court decisions interpreting the Due Process Clause of the U.S. Constitution, schools must notify students, generally in writing, concerning school rules and penalties for violations. As noted earlier, translation must be provided for non-English-speaking students and their families.

The Supreme Court has interpreted the Fourth Amendment as allowing school officials to search a student's possessions, and in some circumstances the student's person, if there is a reason to suspect that the student has violated a school rule. In general, the extent of the permissible search will depend on the nature and strength of the suspicion. Random drug testing may also be permitted, even in the absence of suspicion of specific students, at least in connection with after-school and extracurricular activities. Finally, it is worth noting that lockers and desks are not considered to be students' possessions, but rather to belong to the school; thus, school officials have an unlimited right to search these items.

Under the Due Process Clause, students accused of violating school rules are entitled to fair procedures to determine whether the accusation is valid. The extent of the procedure will depend on the severity of the punishment; generally, short suspensions from school require only a relatively informal meeting or hearing with a school staff member, while longer exclusions may require a more formal hearing before an individual or board not involved in the controversy. Specific rules vary from state to state. There are additional rules applicable to students with disabilities; the purpose of these rules is to ensure that students are not unfairly punished for behavior that is a manifestation of their disability. Some disciplinary decisions are appealable to court.

Students who are disciplined may have the right to continuing educational services. For example, a student who is transferred to some sort of disciplinary alternative program will continue his or her schooling within that program. Even a student who is expelled may have the right to continue to receive some school services, and return to regular school after a certain period.

In summary, students are entitled to basic fairness in the school setting. This includes freedom in the areas of speech and religion, freedom from discrimination, the right to a safe environment, and the right to fairness in discipline. All of these freedoms have limitations; however, the social worker should be alert to situations in which the school seems to have gone beyond the bounds of basic fairness, and take steps to find out whether the school's actions are permissible.

These protections may be especially important to immigrant students, who may be more likely than others to be mistreated in school because of cultural, linguistic, and religious differences. Immigrant students may also get into disciplinary trouble when they do not fully understand school rules, or when they misinterpret the actions of fellow students or respond in ways that might make sense in their culture but are unacceptable here.

SCHOOL RECORDS AND THE RIGHT TO INFORMATION

Obtaining copies of a child's school records can be crucial to solving problems concerning the child's program. This is especially true when there are concerns over the child's program and academic progress; reason to believe that the child may have a disability; disciplinary problems; or similar concerns.

The Federal Education Rights and Privacy Act and many state laws entitle parents and guardians, and students themselves if they are over 18, to view school records (20 U.S.C. § 1232g). There are a few exceptions, such as notes made by law enforcement personnel. Schools can take up to 45 days to make the records available (or less time if state law provides otherwise); in general, however, families will be given prompt access to records on request. The same is true of a social worker or other professional who has a signed release. While schools are not always required to provide actual copies of records, most will do so on request.

The same federal law also prohibits schools from releasing a student's school records to third parties without the written consent of the parent or guardian (or student, if over 18). However, consent is not required if the disclosure is to another school to which the student is seeking admission.

The law also provides for public access to information of a broader nature, not specific to the individual student, such as information on overall achievement levels of students in a specific school or district, teacher qualifications, safety violations, dropout rates, and more. (See, for example, 20 U.S.C. § 6316, the No Child Left Behind Act.) Also generally available are school improvement plans, school policies, and school rules.

Helping a family with school problems becomes easier when one has the whole picture. School records can provide valuable information that the family may not be able to supply, and are usually relatively easy to obtain. It makes sense to make it a routine to request the child's school file—or at least the most current records—whenever one is attempting to assist a family with a difficult school situation.

PARENTAL INVOLVEMENT IN SCHOOL ACTIVITIES

Most schools conduct activities designed to educate parents about their children's schooling, involve parents in school events and activities, and give parents the chance to participate in school and district governance. Some of these "parent engagement" activities are voluntary on the part of the school. Others—including allowing parents to visit their child's classroom—are legally mandated in many circumstances by the federal No Child Left Behind Act and state laws.

For many reasons, immigrant parents may be less likely than native-born parents to participate in these activities. The reasons include language barriers, concerns regarding immigration status, cultural differences (such as the assumption that parents do not have a legitimate role to play in schools), and the demands of work and child care. Yet it is well known that parental participation can make a tremendous difference to a child's education. An active parent is better able to help his or her child with schoolwork, monitor progress and identify problems as they arise, communicate effectively with teachers and administrators, and in many other ways support the child's learning. Active parents may also become advocates for school improvements that can benefit all children.

Social workers can assist by helping families understand that it is their right to become involved in their child's schooling, and that their child is likely to benefit if they do so. Social workers can also help parents obtain the translation and interpretation services that they may need in order to participate effectively in parent-engagement activities, and inform parents that meetings with teachers and participation in school activities should not be affected by their immigration status.

CONCLUSION

The issues of school law and policy that may confront an immigrant family are many and varied. It bears repeating that the best way to approach these problems is with the help of a network of people—educators, parent and student groups, other social workers, education and immigration advocates—who know the school system, the rules, and key insiders. Most problems can be resolved informally, though some will require specialized consultation and external pressure.

Parent and student organizations with a focus on primary and elementary education are found in major school districts, as well as many smaller ones. Even groups that primarily provide services within schools, such as some Parent Teacher Associations, often promote useful relationships with teachers and administrators. Other, more advocacy-oriented parent and student organizations are experienced in helping parents resolve problems, both for individual families and for groups.

Every state has a statewide, federally funded protection and advocacy organization that advocates for the rights of persons with disabilities. A link to the national association of protection and advocacy agencies is found in the references section of this chapter. Advocacy groups serving other populations, such as immigrant students, also exist on the national level and in many local areas. For legal services, the local or state bar association can be helpful, as can the local legal aid agency, the public defender service, and law school clinical projects. Legal organizations that specialize in education, or in children's issues generally, can also be found.

Finally, it is worth emphasizing that social workers, like other people, went to school themselves, and tend to view school personnel as authority figures. Of course, they are; but as we have noted, that does not mean that they are always right, that they have always exhausted all of the options for helping a family, or that they necessarily understand—literally, in the case of immigrants—where the family is coming from. Social workers can perform a unique service to immigrant families by helping them adjust to authority while also questioning it when appropriate; and by finding families the help they need while also encouraging them to advocate for the educational needs of their children.

CASE STUDIES

1. The J family, recently arrived from another country, has two children—a 17-year-old girl and a 13-year-old boy. In their home

country, only the boy attended school; the girl was taught at home. What advice, and what sort of help, might you offer them in relation to each of the following questions? To the extent that you might need additional information in order to assist the family, how might you obtain it?

- **a** Are the children *entitled* to attend school in their new location? If so, how do they go about enrolling?
- **b** Are the children *required* to attend school?
- **c** Do the children have any schooling options *other than* their neighborhood public school?
- **d** What schooling arrangements would be *best* for the children?

2 The family has decided to send their children to the local public schools. The boy, V., is placed in seventh grade. There are no adults in the school who speak his language, but there is one other student—another seventh-grader—who does, and who also speaks good English. The school assigns the other student to help V., but even so, you have the impression that V. is having serious difficulty. You are also aware that V.'s parents cannot offer him much help, since they understand even less English than he does. Despite your misgivings, V.'s parents seem quite satisfied with the situation. They point out that the school seems to be safe, and that V. appears to be picking up English rapidly from his classmates—so rapidly, indeed, that he can now act as their interpreter in stores and on the street.

- **a** How should you handle your concerns about V.'s academic progress?
- **b** Is V. entitled to services from the school in addition to (or instead of) those that he is currently receiving? If so, what are they?
- **c** You decide that V. is, in fact, entitled to additional services, and you decide to help him obtain them. How do you go about that? What obstacles might you anticipate, and how might you address them?

3 Z., the girl, also experiences some difficulty in school. For one thing, she is told not to wear a religious symbol that is important to her. (The school notes that it has banned all religious activities, so there is no discrimination against her specific religion.) Also, although Z. is an accomplished dancer, she is told that she cannot apply to the district's special school for the performing arts, because there is no English as a Second Language class at that school. In a year or so, school officials tell the family, her English will be better and she can apply at that point.

a Z.'s parents, as well as Z. herself, feel strongly about the religious symbol. They are also hesitant to push the issue, however, because Z. is clearly in a religious minority. Can you help them, and if so, how?

b Z. tells you that, if she cannot attend the performing arts program, she will probably drop out of school. Can you help her, and if so, how?

ADDITIONAL RESOURCES

General Web Sites

National Association for Bilingual Education: www.nabe.org
National Parent-Teacher Association: www.pta.org
Public Education Network (national network of local "public education funds," working to improve public schools): www.publiceducation.org
Teachers of English to Speakers of Other Languages: www.tesol.org
U.S. Department of Education: www.ed.gov

Selected National Legal Advocacy Organizations:

American Civil Liberties Union: www.aclu.org
Asian American Legal Defense and Education Fund: www.aaldef.org
Center for Human Rights and Constitutional Law (information on Special Immigrant Juvenile Status): http://immigrantchildren.org/cases/
Lambda Legal (advocacy on behalf of lesbians, gay men, bisexuals, transgender people and those with HIV): www.lambdalegal.org
Mexican American Legal Defense and Education Fund: www.maldef.org
NAACP Legal Defense and Education Fund (legal arm of the National Association for the Advancement of Colored People): www.naacpldf.org
National Council of La Raza (Latino civil rights advocacy organization): www.nclr.org
National Disability Rights Network (information, resources, and links involving services to persons with disabilities, including special education): www.ndrn.org

Legal References

Constitutional Provisions, Statutes, and Regulations

United States Constitution, First Amendment
United States Constitution, Fourth Amendment
United States Constitution, Due Process Clause (Fourteenth Amendment)
8 U.S.C. § 1101(a)(27)(J)
20 U.S.C. § 1232g
20 U.S.C. § 1703(f)
20 U.S.C. § 1400 *et seq.*
20 U.S.C. § 1414(a)(6)
20 U.S.C. § 6316
20 U.S.C. § 9532

29 U.S.C. § 794
42 U.S.C. § 2000d
42 U.S.C. § 11431 *et seq.*
42 U.S.C. § 12131 *et seq.*
8 C.F.R. § 204.11(c)

Cases

Plyler v. Doe, 457 U.S. 202 (1982)
West Virginia Board of Education v. Barnette, 319 U.S. 624 (1943)

Other Materials

U.S. Department of Education, Office for Civil Rights. (2007). *The provision of an equal educational opportunity to limited-English proficient students.* Washington, DC: Author.

10

Women, Gender-Based Violence, and Immigration

SUJATA WARRIER AND JENNIFER ROSE

I will break open the story and tell you what is there. Then, like all the others that have fallen out onto the sand, I will finish with it, and the wind will take it away.

Shostak (1981)

We have stories to tell. Just like Nisa who begins her narration of her stories with the above lines, the work of the violence against women or gender-based violence (GBV) movement worldwide began with stories of women's experience of violence at the hands of their loved ones. Violence against women in all its forms is a worldwide phenomenon that affects one in three women. As acknowledged by the Secretary General of the United Nations, it is one of the most basic violations of human rights. Despite progress on many fronts and in many parts of the world, the true dimensions of the problems remain unacknowledged. Women and women's groups who have worked to end violence against women acknowledge that the problem not only destroys lives but fractures communities and stalls any form of development. According to the World Health Organization:

- In every country where reliable, large-scale studies have been conducted, results indicate that between 15% and 71% of women report they have been physically or sexually abused by an intimate partner in their lifetime.

- Population-based studies report between 12% and 25% of women have experienced attempted or completed forced sex by an intimate partner or ex-partner at some time in their lives.
- Both the 2002 and the 2005 Multi-Country study found that intimate-partner violence had a serious impact on women's health and well-being, and was linked to HIV, increased STDs, and serious mental health consequences for women.

Immigrant and refugee women experience domestic, sexual, and other forms of violence in ways that are both similar and dissimilar to that experienced by women who are born in the United States, including those from marginalized communities. Immigrant and refugee women face many systemic barriers and internal community realities that make it harder for them to find safety, support, and empowerment.

During the 1991 "Dreams Lost, Dreams Found" conference (hosted by a number of organizations that collaborated to create the agenda), immigrant and refugee women's advocates stressed that the experiences of domestic and sexual violence within the immigrant and refugee populations in the United States were both similar and dissimilar to those of women born and raised in the country.

There was strong agreement that refugee and immigrant women face myriad vulnerabilities and challenges in navigating and accessing service delivery systems. History and current knowledge indicate that immigrant and refugee women access the full range of services when provided in a linguistically and culturally appropriate manner. Unlike native-born women, battered immigrant women may need to seek legal services in order to gain immigration status and safety from abusive U.S. citizen spouses. The numbers of women who have sought legal immigration relief through the 1994 landmark Violence Against Women Act (VAWA) provision to protect immigrant domestic violence victims is staggering. None of this could have been achieved if domestic violence advocates, immigrant rights practitioners, and concerned social service providers had not networked and collaborated to challenge barriers and create safety for all immigrant and refugee women.

This chapter will examine violence against women in immigrant and refugee communities; the particular dynamics, risk factors, and consequences of violence against immigrant women.

VIOLENCE AGAINST WOMEN IN IMMIGRANT AND REFUGEE COMMUNITIES

There is wide acceptance that the definition of violence against women should include "any act of gender-based violence that results in, or is likely to result in, physical, sexual or mental harm or suffering to women, including threats of such acts, coercion or arbitrary deprivation of liberty, whether occurring in public or in private life" (United Nations General Assembly, 1993). This encompasses physical, sexual, and psychological violence occurring in the family and in the general community, including battering; sexual abuse of children; dowry-related violence; rape; female genital mutilation and other traditional practices harmful to women; nonspousal violence and violence related to exploitation, sexual harassment, and intimidation at work, in educational institutions, and elsewhere; trafficking in women; forced prostitution; and violence perpetrated or condoned by the state.

While this is the accepted definition of violence against women, the evolution of the movement in the United States has given rise to assumptions and practices that have narrowed and fragmented both the definition and the issues. Thus the domestic and sexual violence are often treated as separate issues and concerns; domestic violence is seen only as interpersonal and all efforts are directed to the victim or survivor leaving the relationship.

The results of these efforts have meant that there are systemic barriers that make it hard for immigrant and refugee women to access services and protective laws. For the most part, the services are not designed to be culturally and linguistically appropriate. To begin with there are innumerable barriers for immigrant and refugee communities as they try to navigate life in the United States.

Immigrants and Refugees: Differences and Similarities

In many ways immigrants and refugees may appear similar in that they were not born in the United States, but there are critical differences between the two categories. The overall difference in a legal sense stems from their immigration status and the benefits that these statuses convey (as discussed in chapter 2).

As described in chapter 2, under the 1980 U.S. Congressional Refugee Act, a refugee is a person who has fled his or her country of origin because of past persecution or a well-founded fear of persecution based upon race, religion, nationality, political opinion, or a membership in a particular social group. If the person is not in the United States, he or she may apply overseas to *enter already recognized* as a refugee. If the person is already within the United States, having for example entered as a visitor, or a student, or even entered with documents, he or she may apply for asylum. Regardless of the location, applicants must prove a "well founded fear, of persecution on the grounds of race, religion, nationality, political opinion, or a membership in a particular social group" (1980 U.S. Refugee Act).

Women fleeing abusive situations, from female genital mutilation to domestic violence, may be able to claim protection under the Refugee Act, claiming fear of persecution based on their social group—their status as women. However, this remains a very controversial area as to whether women constitute a social group or not. It is possible that the social worker may be able to help by drafting an affidavit to submit to the government, using his or her credentials to help the client prove the first part of the refugee test: that the applicant is indeed afraid to go back to the country of origin and that the social worker is providing the necessary therapy to alleviate the fear of past (and future) persecution if deported to the country of origin. The only way that this works for the clients as a means of support is if the social worker collaborates closely with other providers and women's rights advocates who may be helpful in assisting with research on women's rights and human rights abuses to support the second part of the definition: persecution as substantiated through reported human rights violations. The social worker may also collaborate with the legal representative by testifying, in person or through an affidavit, regarding the applicant's state of mind—for example, fear of persecution if returned to the country of origin.

When it comes to gender-based violence (GBV), there are more similarities than differences between immigrants and refugees. The need to assimilate and be a part of the American dream, a better life for the children—all create conditions that lead to denial of the issue. Sharing family secrets and resurrecting difficult issues from the past are matters of great shame. For both the immigrant and the refugee community, the need to fit in and become the model minority means that difficult and potentially disastrous issues and concerns such as domestic violence and sexual assault should be silenced, denied, or articulated as only related to the stress of immigration.

Because of the urgency for assimilation, many immigrant communities do not readily see the seriousness of domestic violence. They may consider it a private matter and unimportant compared to more pressing needs such as decent housing and employment. For many refugee communities who have fled horrendous conditions in their home as well as transit countries, the priority remains to adjust to a new life and make it in the new home country.

A thorough understanding of the context from which immigrants and refugees arrive in this country is a must for advocates working on the issue of violence against women in either the refugee or immigrant community.

DYNAMICS, RISK FACTORS, AND CONSEQUENCES OF VIOLENCE AGAINST IMMIGRANT WOMEN

Immigration Status and Systems as Tools of Control

Although gender-based violence cuts across racial, ethnic, and cultural boundaries, there are certain sociocultural issues that need to be taken into account when working on GBV.[1] One notable aspect within domestic violence is the ways in which the partner uses immigration status to control women. The women's vulnerability is further exacerbated by current U.S. immigration policies. In the provision of the Marriage Fraud Act Amendment of 1986 (8 U.S.C. (§ 1186a)), a foreign spouse of a U.S. citizen is granted a two-year conditional residency status, requiring that the U.S. citizen petition on behalf of his/her foreign spouse in order for the latter to obtain permanent residency. This policy affords partners the license to abuse (Anderson, 1993; Bau & Tamayo, 1991).

There are many such examples of how abusive partners use women's immigration status to instill fear in them and control them. For example, a partner may threaten to divorce his wife, or not petition for her permanent residency. Fear of losing legal status and facing deportation or deportation in the case of women who have no papers or are undocumented could prevent a woman in this situation from seeking outside help (Crandall, Senturia, Sullivan, & Shiu-Thornton, 2005; Dutton, Orloff & Hass, 2000; Hogland & Rosen, 1990; Klein & Ofloff, 1993; Orloff, Jang, & Klein, 1995; Raj, Liu, McCleary-Sills, & Silverman, 2005). This may be especially traumatic for women who have children who are American citizens and thus risk separation from them. The Immigrant

Power & Control Wheel provides a good overview of multiple ways in which immigration status can be used as part of a system of power and control.[2]

In addition to immigration status, disparities in other areas, such as English proficiency and knowledge of the U.S. laws and systems, can place immigrant/refugee women in a vulnerable position; abusive partners may use the system to reinforce their abuse. For example, if a police officer arrives at the scene because either she calls or someone calls for her, the English-speaking partner may talk the police officer into believing that it was the woman who perpetrated the violence.

The following types of marriage or relationships contribute to the vulnerability of foreign-born women:

- Women who immigrate to the United States through their marriage/engagement to U.S. military service personnel (Erez & Bach, 2003).
- Mail-order brides. An increasing number of civilian men in the United States utilize picture/mail-order-bride services from such parts of the world as Asia and Eastern Europe (Anderson, 1993; Crandall et al., 2005; Lai, 1986; Narayan, 1995; Vergara, 2000).
- Women who marry men of the same ethnic background who had been living in the United States. Within many immigrant and refugee communities, a practice of marrying foreign-born women of the same ethnic and/or cultural background is common; bachelors (sometimes married men, as well) often return to their country of origin for the specific purpose of finding a bride (Ayyub, 2000; Chin, 1994; Dasgupta & Warrier, 1996; Sullivan, Senturia, Negash, Shiu-Thornton, & Giday, 2005).

All of the above relationships, whether commercially arranged or not, may involve disparities in economic and social resources between the couple, such as the level of English proficiency; levels of formal education or no education; knowledge of U.S. civil, legal, medical, and social systems; and the availability of personal and social networks for support and access to support from family within the home country. Such uneven social and economic resources can make foreign-born women vulnerable to their partners' power and control. Many of these types of marriages are predicated upon the stereotypical views of women from these countries as subservient and passive as compared to the "liberated American woman." Many foreign-born brides enter the United States not knowing their rights and often are not told about them or are provided misinformation about their rights or what might happen if they choose to use these rights; they are isolated, often intentionally, and deprived of opportunities to make social connections on their own and may be financially dependent on the men and often forced to remain this way.

As discussed above, women who marry military personnel or come as mail-order brides may sometimes find themselves in abusive situations. The abusive partners then use women's immigration status to instill fear in them and control them. However, as discussed in chapter 2, through the immigration provisions of the Violence Against Women Act, newcomer women, married to lawful permanent residents or U.S. citizens, can self-petition without needing the support of the abusive sponsor/husband. Therefore immigrant women may be able to safely flee the violence and even prosecute their abusers if they have access to lawyers, social workers, and advocates.

As with asylum petitions, social workers, in collaboration with other service providers and immigration attorneys, can assist women who have been victims in proving abuse by helping the client put together the evidence required to prove a case of abuse that may ultimately result in lawful permanent residence. The abused woman can now self-petition if married to a U.S. citizen or lawful permanent resident. Unmarried children under the age of 21 who have not filed their own self-petition may be included in petitions as *derivative beneficiaries.* Social workers can assist in proving abuse, through affidavits and other documents, by:

- Arranging and working with their client to write their own testimony in a chronological and linear order for the immigration officials to follow the trajectory of the story—this in fact is the single most important document needed to file a self-petition
- Submitting affidavits from others that the marriage was a bona fide one or ended within the past two years for reasons connected to domestic violence
- Getting copies of the Order of Protection From Abuse
- Obtaining hospital records, if any, of medical treatment because of the abuse
- Obtaining police records to show that the police had been called
- Submitting an affidavit that the social worker is providing counseling (this is necessary and needed for empowerment)

In many rural areas across the country where the availability of immigration attorneys providing legal assistance on VAWA, gender-based asylum, and refugee cases is extremely limited, social workers and advocates are critical players in evidence collection for abused newcomer women. Identifying immigration and family law attorneys who are willing to collaborate and develop expertise on issues of violence against women is often a key component of good advocacy in geographic locations where legal resources are scarce. The strategy of building collaborative relationships and providing cross-training on issues related to violence against women should be included as part of the social worker's overall goal of assisting the newcomer woman in securing appropriate legal remedies that will ensure her safety.

Issue of Multiple Perpetrators

Although domestic violence is typically conceptualized in the United States as violence perpetrated by one intimate partner against the other, studies of Asian Pacific Islander (API) populations reveal that it is not uncommon for members of the affinal family and other extended family members to perpetrate violence against their daughters-in-law directly or indirectly with very little or no support from the natal family (Dasgupta, 2000; Grewal, 2007; Fernandez, 1997; McDonnell & Abdulla, 2001; Mehrotra, 1999; New Visions Korean Committee, 2004; Shiu-Thornton, Senturia, & Sullivan, 2005; Yoshihama, 2000). As mentioned above, for refugee women from these communities, claims for asylum can be submitted if they can provide evidence of persecution. The persecutor need not be a government agent, but can be an agent the government is "unwilling or unable to control" such as spouses or parents-in-law in the case of domestic violence, or grandmothers in the case of female genital mutilation. Again, in collaboration with other providers and an attorney, the social worker's role can be crucial in helping the applicant for asylum gather the necessary evidence to support the claim.

Knowledge, Attitudes, and Beliefs of General Community

Attitudes and beliefs regarding gender-based violence affect how services are rendered and what services women will seek. As many immigrant/refugee battered women rely on support from family, friends, and fellow community members, social workers working with this population must have knowledge of and address the attitudes, beliefs, and behaviors of community members as expressed by their clients and incorporate strategies in their work that can deal with the woman's response to community shaming tactics and her fear of loss of community (Torres 1987). Some of these attitudes, as shown in a number of studies, exert a strong influence on the women's coping and help-seeking behaviors, for example, gossiping and making fun of victims and blame, hostility, and criticism for exposing the violence to those outside the family/ethnic community especially to a hostile and often racist society. A recent study of Ethiopian women provides this information:

> If the victims call the police or speak out about their abuse, they may face loss of support or direct intimidation from the community.... For refugee and immigrant women whose only social support comes from other Ethiopians, community disapproval or sanction may be too much to bear.

Sociocultural and Sociopolitical Context

There are many issues that affect immigrant/refugee women's experiences with GBV in the United States. It is often tempting to identify the immigrant or refugee culture as the main cause of GBV, but a great deal of caution has to be exercised in jumping to such conclusions. As stated at the start of this chapter, GBV is a worldwide phenomenon—the rates are not that dissimilar in the United States and GBV has been recognized as stemming from the various manifestations of patriarchal attitudes. Therefore, it is critical to view cultural values and practices both of the immigrant and refugee culture as one of the many factors that may influence various aspects of IPV in immigrant/refugee communities and being aware that there are many intracultural diversities. A just outcome in cases of GBV within immigrant and refugee communities for victims of GBV can be achieved only when social workers recognize both the reality of internal diversity and the institutional barriers created by U.S. social and legal systems and the impact of both of these on the lives of immigrant and refugee women. For example, the immigration and refugee settlement process, and the experience of racism and other forms of discrimination, are likely to reinforce certain cultural values and practices among immigrants and usually these are the more conservative attitudes toward women. It is therefore incumbent on the social worker to recognize that language, culture, and so on, are all realities that the immigrant or refugee woman lives with and barriers are those that are created by systems to help but can end up being a stumbling block when confronted by issues and concerns that the system cannot address adequately. It is often easy to see the barriers as existing within communities and not in the systems that then make access for women much harder.

Therefore, there are many dynamic and interactive influences among factors on individual, interpersonal, familial, organizational, community, and policy levels. The attitudes and behaviors of an immigrant/refugee batterer, survivor, or community bystander are continuously shaping, and are shaped by, sociocultural and political contexts.

Economic factors may serve to drive some women from their country of origin to the United States to work. Guided under the false impression that they may be coming to work, let's say, in a restaurant, some women find themselves instead being trafficked for sex or working under exploitative factory conditions. In many cases, duress or coercion is involved in the harboring or transporting of the women, who are then either imprisoned or provided very limited mobility by the traffickers. In these situations, if there is a raid and trafficked women are discovered, the government may designate such a person a victim of trafficking. She may then be given a document, or in her passport (if she has one) may be stamped the letter T, which is a designation that she has been classified as a victim of trafficking and is allowed to remain in the United States legally similar to that of newcomers achieving refugee status. As in the application for lawful permanent status based on abuse, or in the application for asylum based on persecution, the social worker's role is crucial, in collaborating with other agencies, and connecting the victim of trafficking to other providers who can meet her basic as well as legal needs. The development of a coordinated advocacy plan is particularly important when the social worker interfaces with a victim of trafficking prior to government intervention and classification of legal status. Unless and until a government entity certifies that the victim has been trafficked, lack of protection from the trafficker and lack of government benefits creates incredible vulnerability for the trafficked woman. The social worker should engage in ongoing safety planning and assistance in prioritizing social- and health-related needs. Another key element of advocacy should include proper training of the social worker and other service providers on how to properly identify human trafficking.

Cultural Practices, Values, and Norms

Cultural values and practices impact the ways in which GBV manifests itself and how individuals, families, and community members and organizations respond to it. Many cultural values can be both oppressive and nurturing at the same time and must be understood within the context of the woman's own interpretation:

- Rigid and hierarchal patriarchal values—the roles are assigned to men, and women are expected to defer to men.
- Face saving, importance of family, role of fate—there is strong pressure to keep the family together in order to save face and this hinders any independence or help-seeking on the part of the victim unless it is in limited ways within the community. Religion and fate often play a critical role in how the issue is discussed and the inevitability of accepting religious precepts and fate. These values, while inhibiting women, can also be a source of strength for them.
- Leaving home to come to a foreign country—whether by choice or by circumstance—is not easy and often leads to the experience of loss of social capital, disruption, personal loss, isolation, and trauma. Limited English proficiency and lack of familiarity of the system in the United States can exacerbate all of these feelings.
- Institutionalized racism, xenophobia, and the impact of U.S. social policies on the lives of immigrant and refugee survivors cannot be overlooked. These affect both men and women but do not cause gendered violence. However, it does affect how the survivors' experiences with discrimination will allow them to access help. Since September 11, 2001, this has meant that women from many immigrant and refugee communities hesitate to seek any service because they are not sure how it will impact the perpetrators of violence (Raj, Silverman, McLeary-Sills, & Liu, 2004). With an increase in the rates of deportations and raids, the concerns among survivors of using any system or helping agency has been heightened—and many of the U.S. policies such as the Welfare Reform Act, the Illegal Immigration and Immigrant Responsibility Act, the Patriot Act, and the Marriage Fraud Act all contribute to the vulnerability of immigrant and refugee women.
- The passage of the Violence Against Women Act of 1994 and its subsequent reauthorizations of 2000 and 2005 have helped some immigrant and refugee women access both immigration relief and public benefits. Close to 5,000 applications have been approved by the U.S. Citizen and Immigration Services (USCIS). Tireless efforts by advocates helped bring about these changes.
- The experiences of immigration and resettlement may lead to the imposition of rigid values and normative behavioral expectations from the country of origin in a complex process known as cultural

freezing. When the pressure to assimilate is high, as it is in the United States, a more rigid adherence may be practiced because of the fear of the loss of cultural values. What is most interesting is that the freeze is usually around values that govern relationships with women and children.

- The need to survive and maintain a positive image can lead to denial of gendered violence in the community, especially in the face of racism and xenophobia. On the one hand, the model minority myth can stifle dissent and silence those working on gender-based violence; but on the other hand, it has often led to success in many immigrant and refugee communities.

IMPLICATIONS FOR SOCIAL WORKERS AND SOCIAL SERVICE AGENCIES

Immigrant and refugee women's access to agency, the response of the agencies designed to help women, and women's own help-seeking are all connected to the current conditions within the United States. On the whole, many immigrant and refugee survivors are:

- Reluctant to contact formal institutions—they are never sure of what the responses are likely to be and whether or not the professionals or advocates will contact USCIS. Although there is some evidence that Latina immigrants may contact law enforcement at higher rates than other immigrant women, what is not clear is whether this is the result of a desire to contact the police or whether the police are the only resource in poor communities.
- Overall the preference is to use informal sources of support from within the community. Members of the faith-based groups and friends within the social networks are relied on to help women through turbulent times.

The willingness to seek help is associated with access to services. Access can be hindered by limited English proficiency, availability of and access to transportation, narrow eligibility criteria among social service agencies, high cost, lack of knowledge of and familiarity with services, denial within the community, racism, discrimination, fear of negative response, fear of USCIS, and fear of government agencies. All of these or a combination of these can impact access. Additionally, expectations regarding gender roles, family concerns, shame, and saving face, plus fear of community reactions, can add to the burden faced by survivors. Help-seeking seems to be linked to the length of stay in the country, the generation status, and the availability of support. Social workers do need to be aware of the constraints and how they can also be perceived by immigrant and refugee women as being part of a service provision that is linked to governmental systems. It is the responsibility of social workers to break down the barrier.

However, seeking help does not always result in desired outcomes. While many in social service agencies may be well-meaning, they may impose their values or beliefs on the presenting situations and deny or minimize the suffering of immigrant women. In some situations they may even blame the women and be insensitive toward those considered foreigners. For example, a well-meaning social worker who is very concerned about the safety of an abused immigrant woman may immediately be insistent that she leave her abuser without trying to understand about the cultural background of the family, thereby failing to support the self-determination capabilities of her client, an important social work principle. Strengthening mainstream agencies' capacity to respond to the needs of immigrant/refugee battered women is critical, and front-line social workers are often in a unique position to identify the primary barriers for newcomer women in seeking assistance. Social workers should consider the organizational barriers that are experienced by newcomer women attempting to access the services of their agency. Often it is a matter of identifying the various points of entry that may be culturally and/or linguistically inaccessible for limited English proficient newcomer women and developing a language access plan for the organization. In addition, increasing organizational accessibility requires a proper mapping and assessment of the immigrant and refugee populations and the internal diversity within them that are emerging within the organization's service area. Therefore, thinking that all Latino/a communities are the same does not work. The particular community may be from Guatemala or Peru or from Mexico; they could be indigenous and not speak Spanish. They could be from a rural community and, simply referring them to a Latino/a organization or social worker, may not meet the needs of the particular women. Engaging in such organizational capacity-building will help the social worker determine which immigrant/refugee populations are the most marginalized from the agency's services.

Beyond individual and organizational advocacy approaches to better serving immigrant/refugee survivors of abuse, social workers should also consider the important work of community organizing—both as a strategy to outreach to more marginalized newcomer populations within the agency's service area as well as to help build the capacity of those communities in addressing violence against women. Given the importance of informal help sources in the lives of battered immigrant/refugee women, changing community members' attitudes and social norms is critical to lessening victim-blaming, and promoting help-seeking is essential.

Many immigrant and refugee communities are addressing the issue within their communities and others should support that effort. Incorporating community organizing strategies into the larger frame of advocacy work creates an opportunity for the communities that are most impacted by gender-based violence to develop a sense of ownership of the issue, and may be the best hope of changing social norms. In addition, the leadership of the immigrant and refugee survivors of abuse has emerged as a key strategy to building community capacity to address gender-based violence. Social workers play a key role in identifying former clients and other immigrant/refugee women who are emerging leaders and assisting them to engage their own communities in strategies that address barriers in accessing services or create more effective public awareness regarding gender-based violence.

What has become increasingly clear is that working on the issue of gender-based violence requires collaboration between all those who are trying to change conditions within the immigrant and refugee communities. Social workers can be catalysts in identifying key stakeholders, both within the social service systems as well as the grassroots immigrant/refugee communities they seek to serve.

CASE STUDIES

The following case depicts a scenario of domestic violence against an immigrant woman. You are invited to discuss the questions that appear immediately following the case.

Case Scenario 1: Ana and Christina

Ana

Born in Mexico, Ana now lives outside a small city in the Midwest with her U.S. husband Blake, their son, David, born in January 2005, and

Cristina, Ana's Mexican-born 15-year-old daughter from a previous relationship.

Ana entered the United States without inspection in March 2001. She eventually moved to this city, _____, where she has worked various jobs so that she can send money to Mexico to help support her parents, siblings, and Cristina, who had remained in Mexico with Ana's parents.

Ana and Blake met in September 2003 at work. They began dating soon after, and fell in love. In January 2004, Blake proposed to Ana, and promised to arrange for Cristina to come to the United States, and to adopt her. Blake and Ana were married in February 2004. In March 2004, Ana asked Blake when Cristina could come live with them. Blake became very angry and insulted Ana for having had Cristina out of wedlock. He called Ana a whore and Cristina a bastard. He slapped Ana across the face and walked out of the house. He returned that night and apologized, promising that he wouldn't hurt her again, and that he would arrange for Cristina to come there as soon as possible. He also promised to file an I-130 relative petition for Ana so she could become a legal permanent resident. Ana accepted Blake's apology and "things were fine" until the following month.

In April 2004, Ana became pregnant with David. Blake accused her of having slept with somebody else and said he was not the father. He began to punch her in the face, choke her, and strike her repeatedly in the stomach. Ana passed out and slept until the following morning.

During the next few months, Blake became very controlling of Ana, and tried to isolate her from her friends. He made her go to work and straight home; he did not permit her to go elsewhere unless he was with her. When Ana asked Blake when Cristina would be coming, Blake again called Ana and Cristina insulting names, punched Ana several times in the face, and told her to stop bothering him about it.

Cristina

Cristina finally arrived at the family home on December 1, 2004. She told her mother that a smuggler who said he knew Blake had brought her to the United States.

Blake refused to allow Cristina to attend school. Instead he got her a job, and said that she had to turn over all her income to him, because he had made the arrangements for her to be brought to the United States, had paid his friend to bring her, and therefore she had to work off the debt. Prior to Cristina's coming to the United States, Blake had never told Ana or Cristina about paying a smuggler or that Cristina would have to work for him and give him all her earnings.

Cristina continued to work and turn over her income to Blake. She became increasingly withdrawn, and seemed frightened of Blake.

In September 2005, Ana asked Blake how much longer Cristina would have to work to pay back the money he spent to bring her to the United States. Blake became angry, and told her that Cristina would work for him for as long as he said so.

They Access the System

In March 2006, Ana again confronted Blake about how long he expected Cristina to work for him. Blake beat Ana and then left the house. Ana took Cristina and David to a neighbor's house. The neighbor took Ana to you. The neighbor speaks Spanish; Ana isn't saying much, but seems to be speaking Spanish too.

Questions

1. What social work issues are raised by this case?
2. What legal issues are raised by this case?
3. What would you do if you were the first person Ana or Cristina approached? What services could you provide?
4. Who else do you need to help them? What other people or organizations could help in this scenario?
5. How would you communicate with Ana and Cristina? Who is most likely to be able to communicate with them well, and get their story?
6. Do you think Cristina and Ana are eligible for immigration status? If so, what kinds of applications could they file? What could you do to help with this? Who else do they need to help them?
7. What kind of help may they need in the civil system? How can you help? Who else do you need to help with this? What might be helpful in a protection order?
8. How would you work with immigration attorneys if the need arises?
9. In what other ways can you help Ana and Christina? Can you help both of them? Will there be ethical issues that are raised if you worked with both of them?

Case Study 2: Johanna

Johanna is a citizen of Jamaica. She met Christopher, a U.S. citizen and a disc jockey at a dance club. They started dating and fell in love. Later they moved in together. Three years later they married, but Christopher never filed immigration papers for Johanna.

Christopher began controlling Johanna from the beginning. He would call her frequently to make sure he was aware of her whereabouts. He would not let her see her few friends. He purchased a cell phone for her to make it easier for him to access her.

Johanna became pregnant and the abuse escalated, with Christopher's violence often directed at Johanna's abdomen. Within a few months, Johanna suffered a miscarriage. She was upset and depressed after the miscarriage, but this did not stop Christopher from continuing his sexual abuse of Johanna. She became pregnant again but continued to be depressed.

Johanna carried the pregnancy to term, but had a very difficult labor and was warned by the doctor that she should not resume any sexual relationship soon. An enraged Christopher forced Johanna to have sex, which led to her hospitalization. The social worker from the hospital staff met with Johanna, talked to her, and put her in touch with the local domestic violence services.

Questions

1. What social work issues are raised by this case?
2. What legal issues are raised by this case?
3. Is Johanna eligible for domestic violence services? Which ones?
4. Can Johanna obtain medical benefits to pay for her hospitalization?
5. What other forms of public assistance is Johanna going to need in order to leave the relationship?
6. Which of these public benefits is she eligible for and when?
7. Can Johanna obtain a civil protection order against Christopher?
8. What systemic barriers might she encounter if she goes to court to seek a protection order?
9. What would you do if you were the first person Johanna approached? What services could you provide?
10. Who else do you need to help them?

11 How would you communicate with Johanna? Who is most likely to be able to communicate with her as well, and get her story?
12 Do you think Johanna is eligible for immigration status? If so, what kinds of applications could she file? What could you do to help with this? Who else does she need to help her?

Case Scenario 3: Lupe

Lupe is a citizen of El Salvador who entered the United States on a visitor's visa in 1991. Her landlord introduced her to Enrique, who is also a citizen of El Salvador. Enrique gained his permanent residency through his mother. Enrique and Lupe lived together for many years and had two American citizen daughters. They married in 1998.

Lupe suffered both physical and mental abuse throughout the course of their relationship. Enrique was extremely controlling and possessive. He picked her clothes for her, and he told her where and when she could work, whom she could talk to, and what and when she could eat. There were several incidents of physical violence, which has been escalating over the years. Many times neighbors have intervened to try to stop Enrique's violence against Lupe. Enrique's mother has also intervened. Some of the injuries Lupe has suffered have required hospitalization. She has also lost hearing in one of her ears as a result of being hit on that side. At the hospital the medical personnel asked whether her spouse had hurt her and told her that she could get help about the domestic violence. But Lupe was too afraid, because Enrique kept telling her that if she speaks about the abuse to any one he will gain legal custody of the children and keep her from seeing them again. He also tells her that if she calls the police he will have them deport her.

On this particular day, Enrique decided that his mother should move in with them and that Lupe should take care of her. Lupe felt that this was not a good idea since their two-bedroom apartment was already crowded. An enraged Enrique began beating Lupe. A frightened neighbor called the police. Lupe is terrified that when the police show up they will not speak to her, but only to Enrique, the children, and the neighbors.

Questions

1 What social work issues are raised by this case?
2 What legal issues are raised by this case?
3 How should the police respond to Lupe?

4. What advice can the police offer Lupe?
5. Why might Lupe be afraid to speak to the police? Are there other possible communication problems?
6. What kinds of safety plans should be offered to Lupe? Will they be the standard ones or should they be different?
7. Should the police response be different if the victim has a different ethnic background and/or is from a different nation?
8. Would Lupe be able to obtain legal custody of the children?
9. What problems might she face and what resources would she need?

Case Scenario 4: Sima

Sima is a citizen of India. She met her husband Rashid in India when he was visiting his extended family in India. Rashid is working in the United States at a well-known computer firm in New Jersey. Against the wishes of her parents she married him in 1997.

Rashid became physically, emotionally, and sexually abusive to Sima immediately after marriage. Initially he refused to bring her to the United States, saying that she would find it difficult to adjust to life here. After a year, he brought her on a fiancée visa, telling her that this was the best way. He also told her that she is not to tell anyone that they were married. Sima was confused and could not understand why she had to lie to members of her community about their marital status. Once she came here, the abuse worsened. She was not allowed to talk to anyone or do anything without his permission.

Within three months of coming to the United States, Rashid brought his parents to live with them for a six-month period. The abuse worsened; Sima was expected to wait on her in-laws and meet all their demands. If they complained to Rashid when he got back from work, Rashid would punish her for her "bad behavior."

One of her neighbors called the police after a particularly brutal incident. The police came and arrested Rashid. They offered to take Sima to the local shelter after communicating with great difficulty with her. Sima spoke very little English.

At the shelter, Sima would not eat, change her clothes, or even go out. All she wanted to know was if Rashid had been allowed to go home. When the staff suggested that she talk with someone from a local program that served women from her community, she refused. The staff thought she was depressed.

Questions

1. What social work issues are raised by this case?
2. What legal issues are raised by this case?
3. What are some of the issues confronting Sima?
4. What strategies are needed to help her?
5. What about her immigration issues? If Sima were told that she would be able to stay in this country if she cooperated in pressing criminal charges against her husband, do you think she would?
6. How could you convince her that it would be in her best interests?
7. What collaborations would enhance your work with Sima?

NOTES

1. This section has been adapted from a report prepared by The Family Violence Prevention Fund for the Robert Wood Johnson Foundation and written by Mieko Yoshihama.
2. The original power and control wheel was developed by battered women participating in support groups at the Domestic Abuse Intervention Project in Duluth, MN. It explains the different ways in which batterers using their power, privilege, and sense of entitlement use various socially sanctioned methods to control and abuse their partners. Since then, the wheel has been used to explain abuse in other groups such as immigrants, elders, etc. There is also an equality wheel. These wheels can be found on www.ncdsv.org.

ADDITIONAL RESOURCES

American Civil Liberties Union, *Human Trafficking: Modern Enslavement of Immigrant Women in the U.S.:* www.aclu.org/womensrights/humanrights/29998res20070531.html

Family Violence Prevention Fund, *Immigrant Women:* www.endabuse.org/programs/immigrant

Legal Momentum—Advancing Women's Rights, *Immigrant Women Program:* www.legalmomentum.org/site/PageServer?pagename=iwp_main

Migration Information Source, *Immigrant Women:* www.migrationinformation.org/Feature/display.cfm?id=2

National Network to End Violence Against Immigrant Women: www.immigrantwomennetwork.org

REFERENCES

Anderson, M. J. (1993). A license to abuse: The impact of conditional status on female immigrants. *Yale Law Journal, 102,* 1401–1430.

Ayyub, R. (2000). Domestic violence in the South Asian Muslim immigrant population in the United States. *Journal of Social Distress and the Homeless, 9,* 237–248.

Bau, I., & Tamayo, W. R. (1991). Immigration Marriage Fraud Amendments of 1986 (Marriage Fraud Act) and other related issues. In Domestic Violence in Immigrant and Refugee Communities (Ed.), *Family Violence Prevention Fund* (VII-1–VII-16). San Francisco: Family Violence Prevention Fund.

Chin, K. L. (1994). Out-of-town brides: International marriage and wife abuse among Chinese immigrants. *Journal of Comparative Family Studies, 25,* 53–69.

Crandall, M., Senturia, K., Sullivan, M., & Shiu-Thornton, S. (2005). "No way out": Russian speaking women's experiences with domestic violence. *Journal of Interpersonal Violence, 20,* 941–958.

Dasgupta, S. D. (2000). Charting the course: An overview of domestic violence in the South Asian community in the United States. *Journal of Social Distress and the Homeless, 9,* 173–185.

Dasgupta, S. D., & Warrier, S. (1996). In the footsteps of "Arundhati": Asian Indian women's experience of domestic violence in the United States. *Violence Against Women, 2,* 238–259.

Dutton, M. A., Orloff, L. E., & Hass, G. A. (2000). Characteristics of help-seeking behaviors, resources, and service needs of battered immigrant Latinas: Legal and policy implications. *Georgetown Journal on Poverty Law & Policy, 7,* 245–305.

Erez, E., & Bach, S. (2003). Immigration, domestic violence, and the military: The case of military brides. *Violence Against Women, 9,* 1093–1117.

Fernandez, M. (1997). Domestic violence by extended family members in India. *Journal of Interpersonal Violence, 12,* 433–455.

Grewal, M. (2007). A communicative perspective on assisting battered Asian Indian immigrant women. In S. D. Dasgupta (Ed.), *Body evidence: Intimate violence against South Asian women in America* (pp. 164–178). New Brunswick, NJ: Rutgers University Press.

Hogland, C., & Rosen, K. (1990). *Dreams lost, dreams found: Undocumented women in the land of opportunity: A survey research project of Chinese, Filipina, and Latina undocumented women.* San Francisco: Coalition for Immigrant and Refugee Rights and Services, Immigrant Women's Task Force.

Klein, C. F, Ofloff, L. E. (1993). Providing legal protection for battered women: An analysis of state statutes and case law. *Hofstra Law Review, 21,* 801–1020.

Lai, T. A. (1986). Asian women: Resisting the violence. In M. C. Burns (Ed.), *The speaking profits us: Violence in the lives of women of color* (pp. 8–11). Seattle, WA: Center for the Prevention of Sexual and Domestic Violence.

McDonnell, K. A., & Abdulla, S. E. (2001). *Project AWARE: Research project.* Washington, DC: Asian/Pacific Islander Domestic Violence Resource Project.

Mehrotra, M. (1999). The social construction of wife abuse: Experiences of South Asian women in the United States. *Violence Against Women, 5,* 619–640.

Narayan, U. (1995). "Male-order" brides: Immigrant women, domestic violence and immigration law. *Hypatia, 10,* 104–119.

New Visions Korean Committee. (2004). *Results of surveys.* Ann Arbor, MI: New Visions, Alliance to End Violence in Asian/Asian American Communities.

Orloff, L. E., Jang, D., & Klein, C. F. (1995). With no place to turn: Improving legal advocacy for battered immigrant women. *Family Law Quarterly, 29,* 313–329.

Raj, A., Liu, R., McCleary-Sills, J., & Silverman, J. G. (2005). South Asian victims of intimate partner violence more likely than non-victims to report sexual health concerns. *Journal of Immigrant Health, 7,* 85–91.

Raj, A., Silverman, J. G., McLeary-Sills, J., & Liu, R. (2004). Immigration policies increase South Asian immigrant women's vulnerability to intimate partner violence. *Journal of the American Medical Women's Association, 60,* 26–32.

Shiu-Thornton, S., Senturia, K., & Sullivan, M. (2005). "Like a bird in a cage": Vietnamese women survivors talk about domestic violence. *Journal of Interpersonal Violence, 20,* 959–976.

Shostak, M. (1981). *Nisa: The life and words of a !Kung woman.* New York: Vintage.

Sullivan, M., Senturia, K., Negash, T., Shiu-Thornton, S., & Giday, B. (2005). "For us it is like living in the dark": Ethiopian women's experiences with domestic violence. *Journal of Interpersonal Violence, 20,* 922–940.

Torres, S. (1987). Hispanic-American battered women: Why consider cultural differences? *Response, 10,* 20–21.

United Nations General Assembly. (1993). The Declaration on the Elimination of Violence Against Women, 85th Plenary Meeting, December 20, 1993. A/RES/48/104.

Vergara, V.B.M. (2000). Abusive mail-order bride marriage and the thirteenth amendment. *Northwestern University Law Review, 94,* 1547–1600.

Yoshihama, M. (2000). Reinterpreting strength and safety in socio-cultural context: Of domestic violence and experiences of women of Japanese descent. *Children and Youth Services Review, 22,* 207–227.

11 Working With Lesbian, Gay, Bisexual, and Transgender Immigrants

RACHEL B. TIVEN AND VICTORIA NEILSON

According to the 2000 U.S. Census, at least 36,000 same-sex binational couples are living in the United States. Many of those couples are raising young children: More than 58% of female binational families and more than 33% of male binational families include children under the age of 18.

Families are the lynchpin of the American immigration system. Two-thirds of legal migrants to the United States come on family-based petitions, sponsored by a spouse, parent, adult child, or sibling. Sponsorship by an immediate relative is a uniquely privileged category: Only immediate relatives are not limited by an annual numerical cap, and only immediate relatives can sponsor someone who has fallen out of legal status. For gay and lesbian families, however, spouses are not recognized. No matter how long the family has been together or how many children they have, under American immigration law they have no recognition and no rights.

This chapter will review the history of how U.S. immigration laws have treated LBGT newcomers, why sponsorship by a same-sex partner is not an option, how lesbian, gay, bisexual, and transgender people may be able to apply for asylum, issues related to transgender immigrants, challenges facing newcomers, and challenges facing social work providers.

HISTORICAL BACKGROUND

In 1952, a sweeping revision to American immigration law imposed a ban on lesbian and gay people. The language barred "aliens afflicted with psychopathic personality, epilepsy or mental defect."[1] Congress explicitly intended this language to cover "homosexuals and sex perverts."[2] The law was amended in 1965 to more specifically prohibit the entry of persons "afflicted with... sexual deviation."[3]

Until 1990, "sexual deviation" was grounds for exclusion from the United States, and anyone who admitted being a homosexual was refused entry. While lesbian and gay individuals are no longer banned from the United States outright, for same-sex couples the ban has not ended.

Boutilier v. Immigration Service, 1967

In 1967, the Supreme Court affirmed that "psychopathic personality" was intended to refer to lesbian and gay people. Twenty-one-year-old Clive Boutilier, a Canadian, had moved to the United States in 1955 to join his mother, stepfather, and three siblings who already lived there. In 1963, he applied for U.S. citizenship, admitting that he had been arrested on a sodomy charge in 1959.[4] He was ordered deported.

He challenged his deportation all the way to the Supreme Court, which, in a 6–3 decision, affirmed Congress's right to bar gay people from entering the country. The majority found that "Congress was not laying down a clinical test, but an exclusionary standard which it declared to be inclusive of those having homosexual and perverted characteristics... Congress used the phrase 'psychopathic personality' not in the clinical sense, but to effectuate its purpose to exclude from entry all homosexuals and other sex perverts."

Boutilier was torn from his partner of eight years. According to one historian, "Presumably distraught about the Court's decision... Boutilier attempted suicide before leaving New York, survived a month-long coma that left him brain-damaged with permanent disabilities, and moved to southern Ontario with his parents, who took on the task of caring for him for more than twenty years." He died in Canada on April 12, 2003, only weeks before that country moved to legalize same-sex marriage (Long, Stern, & Francoeur, 2006).

Even while the ban was in force, gay and lesbian people did manage to visit the United States, especially to be with the person they loved. In the mid-1970s, an Australian national named Anthony Sullivan was living in Boulder, Colorado, with his American partner, Richard Adams. When Sullivan's visitor's visa was about to expire, they managed to persuade the county clerk to issue them a marriage license, with which Sullivan applied for a green card as Adams's spouse. They received a written reply from the Immigration and Naturalization Service:

> Your visa petition...for classification of Anthony Corbett Sullivan as the spouse of a United States citizen [is] denied for the following reasons: *You have failed to establish that a bona fide marital relationship can exist between two faggots.* (Immigration and Naturalization Service, 1975) (emphasis added)

Sullivan and Adams sued, and in 1980, the Ninth Circuit Court of Appeals concluded that because Congress intended to restrict the term "spouse" to opposite-sex couples, and because Congress has extensive power to limit access to immigration benefits, the denial was lawful.[5]

The ban was finally repealed in 1990, but without making any provision for gays and lesbians to be treated equally with regard to family-based immigration sponsorship.

IMMIGRATION BASED ON FAMILY REUNIFICATION: DENIAL OF FAMILY RECOGNITION

Two-thirds of legal immigrants to the United States arrive on family-based petitions—sponsored by a fiancé, spouse, parent, adult child, or sibling. "Family reunification" lies at the heart of the U.S. immigration system. In the words of one Republican Congressman, "Prolonging the separation of spouses from each other...is inconsistent with the principles on which this nation was founded."[6] However, separating same-sex couples is a principle Congress favors. In 1996, Congress passed the Defense of Marriage Act, which forbids recognizing same-sex partners as spouses or family members for any federal purpose, including immigration. Despite the gains that same-sex couples have made on the local level in some states, same-sex couples are not eligible for immigration benefits. Immigration recognition is completely controlled by the federal government, and federal law does not recognize same-sex couples for any reason, even if they are married in Massachusetts, California, or abroad.

Binational same-sex couples are treated as legal strangers under American immigration law, no matter the length of their relationship or the seriousness of their commitment. These couples—in which one partner is a U.S. citizen or permanent resident and the other partner a foreign national—live in every state, and represent approximately 6% of the gay and lesbian couples in this country.

Gay and lesbian relationships are the only family relationships that are categorically denied recognition by the immigration system, even if they have a valid marriage license and extensive proof of the validity of their commitment. This is particularly frustrating when compared to the extensive recognition the immigration system affords heterosexual couples. Opposite-sex married couples are a rare category of family relationships whose visa applications are not subject to a numerical limit—as many heterosexual couples who apply for spousal benefits every year can get them, unlike nearly every other family category. With very few exceptions, heterosexual binational couples can claim the right to enter the United States even without a marriage license. They must show a U.S. consulate abroad that they have a bona fide intention to marry and have met at least once before—and the latter condition is waivable.

Lesbian and gay couples, on the other hand, cannot win any recognition at all. Even if they have a "bona fide intention to marry," their marriage will not be recognized by U.S. law. Gay couples are caught in a bind—they can't win equal benefits because they're not legally married, but they aren't allowed to marry, or their valid marriages are unrecognized.

Same-sex binational couples who manage to stay together in the United States do so by patching together student or employment visas, or by going underground to become undocumented and at constant risk of deportation. A foreign national who falls in love with an American while in the United States on a tourist visa, for example, might then enroll in a university and apply for a student visa, which lasts for the duration of the degree program. After graduation, he or she has to find a job that will provide employment sponsorship, but these employment visas are often short-term. The vast majority of employment visas require that one's time in the United States be temporary, not permanent, so the stress and anxiety of finding a new job and a new visa never ends. Heterosexual couples can get off this treadmill by applying for a fiancé visa, and later a green card based on marriage. For gay and lesbian couples, there is no way out. A foreign national on a temporary visa may have that visa revoked if immigration officials learn of the relationship: The existence of a loving partner can be used as evidence of unlawful intent to remain in the United States.

Legislation pending in Congress, in the form of a bill called the Uniting American Families Act, would change the immigration law to give gay and lesbian couples an equal opportunity to prove their relationships are bona fide and green card–worthy. Instead of creating a separate domestic partnership or marriage-like status that would be nullified by the Defense of Marriage Act, the bill simply amends the immigration law to include same-sex couples where the law refers to spouses. There is significant international precedent for this approach—of the at least 19 countries that offer immigration benefits to same-sex couples, 14 of them do so via legislation, not by recognizing equal marriage rights.[7]

If the foreign national in the couple is living with HIV, he or she may not be able even to visit the United States. HIV-positive foreign nationals are almost completely banned from entering the United States. The travel ban applies to visitors seeking permission to enter the country on nonimmigrant visas, and the adjustment bar forbids anyone HIV-positive who is already here from becoming a legal permanent resident, even if he or she is otherwise qualified. (Part of the application procedure for legal permanent residence includes a medical examination, which includes an HIV test.)

Waivers are available to both the ban and the bar, but they are difficult to get.[8] The travel ban waiver applies to trips of 30 days or less, and requires proving that the applicant is currently asymptomatic and poses no danger to the U.S. public health, and is able to cover medical bills if he or she becomes sick while in the United States. A waiver to the adjustment bar requires proving all of those things, but is only available to people with a qualifying relative. A qualifying relative is a U.S. citizen or permanent resident (green card holder) parent, child, or opposite-sex spouse. As a result, gay and lesbian couples without a suitable parent or child are barred from seeking a waiver where a similarly situated straight couple would be able to win one.

IMMIGRATION BASED ON ASYLUM

Asylum is a unique promise—and a particular challenge—for LGBT and HIV-positive foreign nationals. Immigration courts have recognized sexual orientation, transgender identity, and HIV-positive status as grounds for asylum in the United States.

Asylum can be granted to someone present in the United States who meets the definition of a refugee. A refugee is "any person who is outside any country of such person's nationality…and who is unable or unwilling to return to, and is unable or unwilling to avail himself or herself of the protection of that country because of persecution or a well-founded fear of persecution on account of race, religion, nationality, membership in a particular social group, or political opinion."[9] Of the five grounds on which a claim for asylum can be based, membership in a particular social group provides the best basis for asylum based on sexual orientation or gender identity. There is no statutory definition of "membership in a particular social group," but it is frequently described in case law as "a group of persons who share a common, immutable characteristic that the members of the group cannot or should not be required to change."[10]

In 1994, Attorney General Janet Reno certified as precedent a case called *Matter of Toboso-Alfonso.*[11] The case was pivotal in establishing that a well-founded fear of persecution on the basis of one's sexual orientation is a valid basis on which to claim asylum in the United States. Since then, nearly a dozen precedential cases have further established the right to seek asylum based on lesbian, gay, bisexual, transgender, or HIV-positive identity. Although no precedential decision recognizes transgender people as members of a particular social group, many successful asylum claims have been brought on behalf of transgender refugees (Immigration Equality and National Immigrant Justice Center, 2006).

While persons living with HIV or AIDS face challenges in attempting to immigrate to the United States, for the purposes of asylum, there is the possibility that people facing HIV persecution in their own country may be considered members of a particular social group. In 1996, the Immigration and Naturalization Service (INS) Office of General Counsel issued a memorandum that recommended that the INS and the Executive Office for Immigration Review should grant asylum based on the social group category of HIV-positive individuals, assuming that the applicant in question meets all of the other elements required for asylum. Although there are no precedential cases that recognize HIV status as creating membership in a particular social group, asylum has been granted in some cases where HIV persecution was an essential element of the application.[12] While HIV is grounds for inadmissibility to the United States, asylees can apply for a humanitarian-based waiver of this law and this waiver (called an I-602) is routinely granted.

In 1996, Congress passed the Illegal Immigration Reform and Immigrant Responsibility Act, which generally restricted access to asylum protection. This legislation created additional bars to asylum, the most restrictive of which was a one-year filing deadline. In order to be granted asylum, an applicant must file for asylum within one year of his or her arrival in the United States. Although exceptions exist, this deadline has created unique hardships for LGBT and HIV-positive asylum seekers because they are often unaware that their sexual orientation, gender identity, or HIV status can form the basis of an asylum claim, and are often afraid to disclose these intimate aspects of their identity to a government official given the persecution they faced in their own country.[13]

SPECIAL ISSUES RELATING TO TRANSGENDER IMMIGRANTS

For transgender immigrants, the immigration challenges are somewhat different than for lesbian and gay immigrants, and significantly more complex.

Transgender immigrants face a broad array of issues in securing legal status and immigration documents that correctly reflect their identity. This area of the law is so specialized that LGBT civil rights attorneys often lack the immigration expertise to properly advise transgender immigrants, and immigration practitioners lack the cultural competence and understanding of transgender legal issues to adequately represent these clients.

Issues for transgender immigrants and their family members include marriage, identity documents, asylum, and detention.

Marriage

Binational couples in which one or both partners are transgender may be able to win immigration benefits if they have a valid "straight" marriage in the state or country where they were married. However, the right to recognition has had a shaky history over the past decade. On April 16, 2004, U.S. Citizenship and Immigration Services (USCIS) issued a policy memorandum stating that USCIS would not recognize marriages for immigration purposes where one or both of the spouses "claims to be transsexual." In May of 2005, however, court challenges coordinated by civil rights groups led to a positive decision from the Board of Immigration Appeals (BIA). In *Matter of Lovo-Lara,* the court held that as long as the marriage is valid where performed, it should be valid for immigration purposes. While the *Lovo-Lara* decision was good news for the transgender community, it is still unclear in many states and countries whether or not transgender individuals can legally marry. (For more information, visit http://www.immigrationequality.org/template.php?pageid=172.)

Identity Documents

A policy memorandum from USCIS issued April 16, 2004, states that transsexual individuals should be issued identity documents (such as employment authorization cards, green cards, etc.) that reflect "the outward, claimed and otherwise documented sex of the applicant at the time of CIS document issuance." In spite of this stated policy, transgender individuals may still have difficulty obtaining documents that match their corrected gender. It also remains unclear what level of medical intervention USCIS will require before they recognize sex change. (For more information, visit http://www.immigrationequality.org/template.php?pageid=171.)

Asylum

If a transgender individual fears returning to his or her home country based on gender identity, the individual may qualify for asylum in the United States. The person will have to demonstrate having suffered past persecution (harm directly from the government or from others that the government was unable or unwilling to control) or prove a well-founded fear of future persecution. Transgender people who suffered persecution in their own country because others assumed they were gay or lesbian may also have grounds to apply for asylum.

Detention

When Immigration and Customs Enforcement (ICE) takes a person into custody, it is referred to as *immigration detention*. The reasons an individual might end up in immigration detention range widely. As a result of a series of harsh immigration laws that were passed in the 1990s, persons with minor visa violations, even asylum seekers, often end up in detention for months or years. ICE currently detains about 200,000 immigrants a year. All indications show that this number will rise. Although many detainees are not being held for criminal violations, the majority of them are confined in county jails and contract facilities under jail-like conditions. LGBT and HIV-positive detainees are particularly vulnerable in these environments. They are often the subjects of discrimination, harassment, and outright abuse. HIV-positive detainees suffer additionally from the substandard health care in place at many of these facilities.

In addition to respect and access to basic health care that can be life-saving, transgender detainees have specific concerns in immigration detention. Safety in sex-segregated facilities is a serious issue. Transgender detainees are almost always housed with inmates of their birth sex; many detainees have reported that when they expressed fears for their safety they were placed in solitary confinement for 23 hours a day. Safe accommodations that do not punish the victim for harassment are necessary. In addition to routine medical needs, access to hormone therapy is a need for many transgender detainees, who are literally trapped in a system that insists such treatment is elective. Sudden withdrawal of hormone treatment places transgender immigrants at risk for serious medical conditions, including cardiovascular illness, diabetes, depression, anxiety, chest and breast pain, high/low blood pressure, and withdrawal symptoms including hot flashes, nausea, and dizziness. These conditions can in turn lead to attempts at self-treatment such as auto-castration, which can cause serious harm and extensive, costly hospitalizations.

CHALLENGES FACING LGBT NEWCOMERS

LGBT newcomers face unique challenges in accessing the social service system, beyond the universal hardships of language barrier and culture shock.

LGBT people are more likely than other immigrants to arrive in the United States without close family ties; they may have left their home country to distance themselves from rejecting or abusive family members. Even those who have relatives already settled in the United States may not be able to come out to them about their sexual orientation, and may be afraid to come out in any setting closely tied to family or community of origin. For example, a Pakistani man sought resources for his asylum case from a legal services agency, which provided him with information on country conditions for gay men in Pakistan. When advised to discuss the information with his attorney, he replied, "I can't tell my attorney I'm gay. He's from my community."

Extensive resources for LGBT immigrants are available in big cities and on the Internet (see resources section), but newcomers who speak neither English nor Spanish may not be able to access those resources, and those who are alienated from their own gay identity may not know how to seek them out. Immigrant aid groups based in religious communities may not have information about LGBT issues, or clients may assume they do not. Gay and lesbian organizations may seem unfriendly, upper-class, or otherwise unwelcoming to newcomers.

For those who may be eligible to seek asylum, such ignorance can have a very high cost. The one-year filing deadline requires asylum-seekers to file a claim within 365 days of their arrival in the United States—even though it may take much longer for a closeted LGBT person to learn that sexual orientation or gender identity is something they should reveal to, not hide from, the government. Given that not two decades ago, homosexuality was grounds for exclusion from the United States, this is hardly an unreasonable misconception. Likewise, frightened asylum-seekers may give incomplete or contradictory information when they first enter the United States that can be used against them when they learn that it is safe to reveal their sexual orientation.[14] For asylum-seekers living with HIV/AIDS, the paradox is acute: HIV infection is still grounds for exclusion and removal (deportation), and people with AIDS can be tested on demand at the border. Yet HIV can be a positive factor in an asylum case, and a successful asylee is entitled to a special, humanitarian HIV waiver.

For LGBT immigrants living with HIV/AIDS, asylum and an accompanying humanitarian waiver may be the *only* way to remain legally in the United States, because without a qualifying relative, their HIV status will permanently preclude them from getting a green card.

The denial of an HIV waiver is just one of the collateral harms of nonrecognition that same-sex immigrant families face. Not only are American citizens denied the right to sponsor their foreign-national partners for a green card, they cannot sponsor them for an HIV waiver if the foreign partner manages to procure a green card through employment. LGBT foreign nationals navigating the American immigration system are treated unequally in other ways, most crucially in the denial of dependent visas to partners and nonbiological children. A heterosexual person arriving in the United States on a student visa, an employment visa, or after winning asylum or the green card lottery, for example, has the right to bring spouse and minor children in too. Not so for spouses of the same sex, or for children not related to the primary visa-holder by biology or adoption. In contrast, a heterosexual businesswoman entering the United States on a work visa would be able to bring her husband and stepchildren with her in the same visa status.[15]

The final irony gay and lesbian couples face when navigating the immigration system is that the loving, committed relationship they are building must often be kept secret. Nonimmigrant visa holders—those present in the United States for temporary reasons such as school, work, or travel—may not possess any intent to remain in the United States permanently. Customs officials and consular officers may take anything as a sign of forbidden "immigrant intent"—even hand-holding or a vacation snapshot. Evidence of the relationship can be seen as proof that the visitor intends to remain in the United States unlawfully. This is particularly ironic, given that opposite-sex couples are eligible for full immigration benefits upon proof that their relationship is genuine and sincere. For lesbian and gay foreign nationals, a serious, long-term relationship with an American can cost them their visa.

CHALLENGES FACING THE PRACTITIONER IN A SOCIAL SERVICE SETTING

The biggest challenges facing practitioners in social service settings include knowledge of the law and cultural competence. Knowledge of the overlapping options (and nonoptions) for LGBT individuals and couples is crucial; for example, it is vital to know that a Massachusetts or California marriage or a state-based civil union does not qualify for green card sponsorship—and can even hurt someone in the United States on a temporary visa by creating evidence of immigrant intent. For transgender couples, however, the options can be quite different, and vary state by state.

No practitioner would be expected to memorize each state's rules for recognition of transgender marriages, but it is crucial that they know where to look for that information. Knowing that asylum is an option, and where to find a gay or gay-friendly immigration lawyer who can capably represent an asylum-seeker, is important. By the same token, practitioners must be aware of what is not acceptable: marriage fraud ("green card marriage") is a serious crime and not a solution even for a same-sex couple facing systemic discrimination.

Knowing where to look for information presupposes that practitioners are culturally competent to ask the right questions in the first place. Immigrants may fail to disclose their sexual orientation due to fear, or to not understanding its relevance. The ability to draw out a potential asylum-seeker or a transgender couple is an important skill.

Social workers affiliated with religious or ethnic institutions may be viewed warily by LGBT people, especially if those communities perpetuated discrimination or persecution against them in their home country.

An open, nonjudgmental attitude that involves recognizing and respecting client individuality is the key to a successful relationship with LGBT/HIV clients through the proceedings because sexual minorities and people with HIV/AIDS are individuals as diverse as their heterosexual or HIV-negative counterparts. Do not make assumptions about a client's experiences based merely on stereotypical profiles such as appearance, dress, and physical features (e.g., gay men as effeminate and probably HIV-positive; lesbians as masculine). Questions laden with stereotypes or judgments not only might injure the client's self-esteem but might inhibit the client from building a trusting working relationship.

Common stereotypes to avoid include: that a person's sexual orientation or HIV-status is the central defining feature of his or her identity; that homosexuals are promiscuous, lonely, self-hating people; that a homosexual no longer practices or believes in her religion since most religions reject homosexuality; that homosexuality is caused in men by overbearing, controlling mothers and absent fathers; that lesbians are trying to be men, or always dress in a masculine or androgynous manner; that an ostensibly effeminate character means that the male homosexual plays a woman's role in a romantic relationship; that in order to define himself or herself as a transgender, a transgender individual must have had surgery or be contemplating medical interventions.

Regarding people with HIV/AIDS, there are many judgmental assumptions about how they contracted HIV (e.g., that they contracted HIV through willful or reckless conduct); their celibacy (e.g., that they are or should be celibate now); medical treatment regimens (e.g., that they should be pursuing Western medical treatment and the protease inhibitor "cocktail"); social support needs (e.g., that they should be involved in individual or group therapy). Additionally, there is the negative assumption that a client is somehow self-hating when he is not completely out, or open, about his sexual orientation, gender identity, and/or HIV status to family, friends, employer, and so forth.

The diversity of how clients construct, understand, and live their identities is the evidence that contradicts these stereotypes and judgmental perspectives. Conscious, close attention to one's own communication and interaction with the client can evince an open, nonjudgmental attitude.

RECOMMENDATIONS FOR WORKING WITH TRANSGENDER CLIENTS

If a professional has never worked with a transgender client before, it is most important to be respectful and nonjudgmental. The term *transgender* can have different meanings to different people. For some, being transgender simply means not conforming to rigid gender norms, and thus some people, for example, very butch lesbians or effeminate gay men, may identify as transgender although they do not believe that their bodies do not match their gender identity.

For others, the term *transgender* means that the individual feels that the anatomical sex with which he or she was born does not match his or her gender identity. Transgender people who feel this way often take medical steps to make their anatomy match their gender identity.

Transgender people often refer to the anatomical sex that was assigned to them at birth as their *birth sex*. The process of taking medical steps, such as hormone therapy, electrolysis, and/or surgery, to give an outward appearance that matches gender identity, is often called *transitioning*. When referring to a client's gender or sex after transitioning, the phrase "corrected gender" or "corrected sex" is often used.

When working with a client, it is important to address him or her by the pronoun he or she prefers. Most transgender people prefer to be addressed with the pronoun of their chosen gender from early in their transition process; some people eschew traditional pronouns altogether, preferring to use their proper name in all situations, or neologisms like "ze" or "hir." If unsure, ask.

When referring cases to attorneys, and then working in partnership with the client's representation, it is important to ask about any problems that occurred during childhood. Maybe the client was perceived as particularly effeminate or overly masculine and suffered mistreatment as a result. One needs to find out when the client first realized he or she was transgender and when he or she began living in a gender role different from the birth sex. Part of the history should also include finding out if the individual has taken any medical steps to transition and whether there are any plans in the future to transition further.

Most transgender people never have genital reassignment surgery. Surgery is expensive and rarely covered by health insurance. For transgender men (F–>M) the surgical techniques are not as advanced as they are for transgender women. Gender identity comprises much more than anatomy, and some transgender people never choose to undergo any medical steps to transition. However, the validity of a marriage certificate for immigration purposes may depend on how the state or country in which the marriage took place defines gender transition.

It is also important to understand that gender identity and sexual orientation are different aspects of a person's identity. Transgender individuals, like nontransgender individuals, may consider themselves heterosexual, homosexual, or bisexual. One should not make assumptions about a client's sexual orientation based upon gender identity. On the other hand, even if a client identifies as heterosexual, he or she may be perceived as gay or lesbian in their country of origin and may fear persecution on this basis. For example, if an F–>M transgender man had a relationship with a woman in his country in the past, people in his community may have considered the relationship lesbian, even if the applicant and his partner viewed the relationship as heterosexual.

CASE STUDIES

The following case studies illustrate life experiences commonly encountered by LBGT immigrants. You are invited to discuss the following questions about each vignette.

1. What social work issues are raised by this vignette?
2. What legal issues are raised by this vignette?
3. What would you identify as the presenting problem(s)? How would you prioritize the immigrant's needs?
4. What legal options might the immigrant have?
5. What is the role and function of the social worker working with the client and/or family in this vignette?
6. What short-term interventions and resources do you think would be helpful in this situation? Long-term interventions and resources?

Case Study 1: Ahmed

Ahmed, an immigrant who has lived and worked in New York City illegally for many years, is only weeks away from deportation. Ahmed's employer has agreed to sponsor him for legal permanent residence, and Ahmed was about to get his green card… until he learned he was HIV positive. Ahmed has an American partner, but the federal government's refusal to recognize same-sex couples means that his partner cannot sponsor him for the waiver.

Case Study 2: Mark and Fabien

Mark and Fabien have been partners for over 17 years. They have a beautiful home in small-town Pennsylvania and are the proud parents of John, 8, and Claire-Marie, 4, whom they adopted from foster care. Fabien, a Frenchman, has been able to stay in the country through student and work visas. His current work visa is coming to an end without the possibility of renewal, and they face dire choices.

In France, Fabien could sponsor Mark for immigration benefits, but French law does not recognize adoption by same-sex couples, and the children would have to leave and reenter every six months. The family would prefer to stay in the United States, but because Fabien is on a student visa he cannot work, so Mark's salary must support them. The expense of tuition for Fabien's previous student visa forced them to sell their home to keep Fabien in the United States. Mark's sister suffers from debilitating multiple sclerosis, and he shares her care with their elderly parents. Mark explains, "We are in an impossible situation. We are running out of money and options. We cannot leave our family and friends here, but Fabien can't stay. Now we may not even have France as an option. A straight couple would not be in this situation."

Case Study 3: Ojo

In 2003, Ojo fled his native Nigeria, fearing for his life after an angry mob murdered his partner upon discovering the two were romantically involved. Ojo came to the United States, arrived in New York without proper entry documents, and was immediately detained in an Immigration and Customs Enforcement (ICE) facility. Immigration Equality met with Ojo in detention and secured pro bono representation for him. Ojo wishes to stay in the United States; he fears for his life if he returns to Nigeria.

Case Study 4: Olivia

Olivia is a lesbian from Uganda. In high school she fell in love and began a secret relationship with another female student. When Olivia's cousin discovered the relationship, he told her family, who brought a stranger into their home to rape her while they watched. Olivia did not seek protection from the police because homosexuality is illegal in Uganda. Olivia fled to the United States. She is desperate to stay and fears what will happen if she returns to Uganda.

Case Study 5: Melissa

Melissa has been a U.S. citizen for over a decade. After naturalizing, Melissa completed sex reassignment surgery and legally changed her name. Living her life completely as a female, and even having a U.S.-issued passport in the female gender and in the name of Melissa, she applied to the U.S. Citizenship and Immigration Service (USCIS) to have her naturalization certificate amended to include her new name and corrected gender. She was stunned when she received a denial notice.

Melissa is very concerned about the denial, especially since she is currently sponsoring her foreign-born husband for his green card. "It's just incredible to me that they could deny me this. I've been living as a female for years, using this name, and I even have a U.S. passport that says I'm female." With her husband's green card interview coming up soon, Melissa is terrified of what might happen. "My biggest fear is just for my husband. What if they deny our application and he has to leave the United States? I'd be devastated," she said.

Case Study 6: Victoria Arellano

The true case of Victoria Arellano exhibits, to an extreme degree, the medical challenges often faced by transgender immigrants. On July 20, 2007, Victoria, a transgender woman, died while under the care of ICE's San Pedro Detention facility. She died shackled to her bed, her body overcome with pneumonia and meningitis that could have been cured in any medical facility in the United States with inexpensive and readily available medical assistance. Instead, Victoria was deliberately denied access to medical attention.

When Victoria was taken into ICE custody she was managing her HIV through the use of a common antibiotic called dapasone. Victoria notified officials at the San Pedro facility of her need for the medication and was denied proper treatment despite the well-known medical consequences of any lapse in treatment. Her health began to rapidly deteriorate and soon Victoria was so ill that she could not move without pain. Her condition was so dire that other detainees began advocating on her behalf. "We made requests to the infirmary asking for help because she was so sick. She wasn't eating, she had constant diarrhea, and she was vomiting blood. The nurse who responded was totally inhumane," states Oscar Santander, fellow detainee at San Pedro, as reported in an August 9 report in the *Daily Journal.* "The nurse said, Oh, is that the same person you complained to us about before? The doctor hasn't approved any medication. Just give her Tylenol and water, and it'll go away."

"It" did not go away. Another detainee at the San Pedro, Abel Gutierrez, told the *Daily Journal,* "Victoria was so sick and they wouldn't do anything. One night, 80 of [us] defied the order to line up for evening head count, and staged a protest on Arellano's behalf." A week before her death Victoria was finally taken to the hospital but was returned to the facility within 24 hours. By the time she was taken to another hospital it was too late, and Victoria died shackled to her bed. The men who tried to speak out on Victoria's behalf were transferred in retribution for trying to help her.

NOTES

1. Immigration and Nationality Act, § 212(a)(4), 66 Stat. at 182.
2. The Senate Judiciary Committee had recommended in 1950 that "the classes of mentally defectives" barred from entry in existing legislation "should be enlarged to include homosexuals and other sex perverts" (S. Rep. NO. 1515, 81st Cong., 2d Sess., p. 345). The proposed Immigration and Nationality Act thus originally contained an additional phrase expressly providing for the exclusion of aliens "who are homosexuals or sex perverts." These words were omitted from the law as passed, because—as the Senate Judiciary Committee explained—"The Public Health Service has advised that the provision for the exclusion of aliens afflicted with psychopathic personality or a mental defect…is sufficiently broad to provide for the exclusion of homosexuals and sex perverts. This change of nomenclature is not to be construed in any way as modifying the intent to exclude all aliens who are sexual deviates" (S. Rep. No. 1137, 82d Cong., 2d Sess., p. 9). See *Boutilier v. Immigration Service,* 387 U.S. 118 (1967). *Family, Unvalued: Discrimination, Denial, and the Fate of Binational Same-Sex Couples under U.S. Law,* Human Rights Watch and Immigration Equality, 2006, p. 25, fn 53.
3. 1965 Amendments, Pub. L. No. 89–236, 79 Stat. 911 (1965).
4. Sodomy charges were once commonly used by the police to harass gay people. The prosecution of private consensual sex between adults was ruled unconstitutional in 2003. *Lawrence v. Texas,* 539 US 558 (2003).
5. *Adams v. Howerton,* Ninth Circuit, 673 F.2d 1038 (1980).
6. Rep. Raymond McGrath, quoted in C. Duenas, (2000), "Coming to America: The Immigration Obstacle Facing Binational Same-Sex Couples," *Southern California Law Review, 73,* 811–841.

7. For a full list of countries that provide equal immigration rights, see *Family, Unvalued,* Appendix B, at http://hrw.org/reports/2006/us0506/10.htm#_Toc132691986.
8. In July 2008, the Senate removed HIV/AIDS from the immigration law, a necessary first step to ending the HIV travel and immigration ban. For now, HIV remains on the list of communicable diseases which bar entry to the United States. In addition, in November 2007 the Bush administration proposed changes to the travel ban waiver, which if approved will make it even more difficult for people with HIV to enter the country. For updates, see http://immigrationequality.org/.
9. INA § 101(a)(42)(A), 8 USC § 1101(a)(42(A).
10. *Matter of Acosta* (and the rest of Asylum Manual, fn 4).
11. 20 I & N Dec. 819 (BIA 1990).
12. Immigration Equality and National Immigrant Justice Center (2006, p. 3).
13. Ibid.
14. Recently the Seventh Circuit Court of Appeals held that it is reasonable for someone seeking asylum based on sexual orientation not to disclose that to authorities at their port of entry, given the persecution such information has caused them in their home country. *Moab v. Gonzalez,* 207 U.S. App. Lexis 21893 (7th Cir. 2007).
15. A minor loophole allows same-sex partners of nonimmigrant visa holders to enter on a tourist visa, but the visa must be renewed frequently and does not allow the same rights and privileges a proper derivative visa would provide. See http://immigrationequality.org/template.php?pageid=155.

ADDITIONAL RESOURCES

Books

Cantu, L., & Luibheid, E. (2005). *Queer migrations: Sexuality, U.S. citizenship, and border crossings.* Minneapolis: University of Minnesota Press.

Lambda Legal & Immigration Equality. (2005). *HIV and immigration law: The basics.* New York: Author. Available in English and Spanish at http://www.immigrationequality.org/template.php?pageid=200)

Lambda Legal & Immigration Equality. (2005). *Sexual orientation and immigration law: The basics.* New York: Author. Retrieved from http://www.immigrationequality.org/template.php?pageid=199AAAAa

Luibheid, E. (2002). *Entry denied: Controlling sexuality at the border.* Minneapolis: University of Minnesota Press.

Transgender Immigration Manual—forthcoming from Immigration Equality and Transgender Law Center, published by the American Immigration Lawyers Association.

Film

Through Thick and Thin, Sebastian Cordoba, director, 2007. *Through Thick and Thin* examines the trials of gay and lesbian binational couples as they struggle against U.S. immigration laws. California: Hear No Evil Films.

Web Sites

Asylum Law.org provides very useful information about asylum law in the United States and internationally, with a new database of sexual orientation–related materials. Has a section on sexual minorities and HIV status: http://www.asylumlaw.org/

Center for Gender and Refugee Studies. Has great primary source materials on gender-based asylum claims, including domestic violence, female genital mutilation, rape, and sexual orientation issues: http://cgrs.uchastings.edu

Immigration Equality. A national organization that works to end discrimination in U.S. immigration law, to reduce the negative impact of that law on the lives of lesbian, gay, bisexual, transgender, and HIV-positive people, and to help obtain asylum for those persecuted in their home country based on their sexual orientation, transgender identity or HIV-status: http://www.immigrationequality.org

Sylvia Rivera Law Project. A New York–based legal services organization providing free legal services to transgender individuals. It includes information on transimmigrants living in New York: http://www.srlp.org/

Transgender Law Center. A national organization that engages in litigation, education, and advocacy to secure equal rights for transgender individuals: http://www.transgenderlawcenter.org

REFERENCES

Feinberg, L. (2007, September 8). Death of trans immigrant in detention forged United States. New York: Worker's World.

Immigration and Naturalization Service. (1975). Letter to Richard Adams, November 24, 1975. Quoted in S. Long, J. Stern, & A. Francoeur, *Family, unvalued: Discrimination, denial, and the fate of binational same-sex couples under U.S. law.* New York: Human Rights Watch, 2006. Retrieved from http://hrw.org/reports/2006/us0506/

Immigration Equality and National Immigrant Justice Center. (2006). *LGBT/HIV asylum manual.* New York: Author. Retrieved from http://www.immigrationequality.org/manual_template.php

Immigration Equality and Transgender Law Center. (2006, January). *Immigration Law and Transgender People.* San Francisco: Author. Retrieved from http://transgenderlawcenter.org/Immigration%20Law%20%20English%20fact%20sheet.pdf

Immigration Law and Transgender People. (2006). New York: Immigration Equality.

Long, S., Stern, J., & Francoeur, A. (2006). *Family, unvalued: Discrimination, denial, and the fate of binational same-sex couples under U.S. law.* New York: Human Rights Watch. Retrieved from http://hrw.org/reports/2006/us0506/

12 Older Adult Immigrants in the United States: Issues and Services

PATRICIA BROWNELL AND
ROBIN CRESWICK FENLEY

Social work began to emerge as a professional discipline during the Progressive Era in the late nineteenth century in the United States. At that time the focus of social workers was immigrant families, particularly mothers and children. At the beginning of the twenty-first century, gerontological social work is coming into its own (Greene & Choi, 2008).

Despite this trend, scholarship on immigrant older adults is still in its infancy. The purpose of this chapter is to provide an overview of sociodemographics on older adult immigrants, as well as current social work scholarship on issues, assessments, and interventions related to older adult immigrants and their families. Current trends and their implications will also be discussed.

SOCIODEMOGRAPHICS OF OLDER ADULT IMMIGRANTS IN THE UNITED STATES

The sociodemographics of older adult immigrants in the United States, defined by the U.S. Census Bureau as foreign-born and 65 years of age and older, is shaped by immigration policy, so a brief history is provided here.

The Naturalization Act of 1790, the first immigration law of the United States, clearly stated that only "whites" could become naturalized citizens (Takaki, 1998). Reflecting the needs and attitudes of a developing nation, three distinct periods of U.S. immigration policy were identified by Martin and Midgley (1999) in Kilty (2002).

The laissez-faire period from 1780 to 1875, recognizing the value of cheap labor, permitted an influx of largely Chinese immigrants for construction of the transcontinental railroads, farming, and manufacturing, but without the benefits of naturalization (Martin & Midgley, 1999). The years 1875 through 1920 saw a time of qualitative restrictions applied to groups such as convicts, prostitutes, and the mentally ill (Kilty & deHaymes, 2000). From the 1920s through the present, U.S. immigration policy has been characterized by quantitative restrictions, imposing limits on the total numbers of immigrants allowed in the country, regardless of ethnicity or nationality. A visible manifestation of this is the Bush administration's proposal to build fences along the U.S. and Mexican borders in order to reduce the numbers of illegal immigrants crossing from Mexico into the United States.

The 1924 Immigration and Naturalization Act established national origin quotas, totaling 150,000 immigrants (Kilty & deHaymes, 2000). These national origin quotas favored northern and western European immigrants, and set bars for Asian-born immigrants. Japanese immigrants were prohibited, while by comparison, northern and western European immigrants were permitted entry in liberal numbers (Kilty & deHaymes, 2000). It was not until 1952 that U.S. policy permitted naturalization of Asian immigrants (Kilty, 2002). As a result, historically the older immigrant population has been of European origin, a pattern that continues today.

Immigration became a greater concern after the Civil War, reflecting racist and exclusionary policies that were fueled by fears of an alien element, those who allegedly were determined to undermine this country's institutions, leading to societal disintegration and decay (Portes & Rumbaut, 1996, in Kilty, 2002). The Alien and Sedition Act of 1798, the only prominent piece of legislation authorized in response to these fears, stipulated that "any 'alien' who represented a 'danger to the peace and security of the nation' could be expelled" (Quiroz-Martinez, 2001, p. 18, in Kilty, 2002). With nascent social work practiced in largely immigrant communities, early responsibilities for the worker included vigilance and interprofessional cooperation to ensure fair implementation of this act. In today's post-9/11 climate, that attention and collaboration remain necessary.

The Immigration and Nationality Act Amendments of 1965 and later amendments eliminated the national quota system and opened U.S. immigration to the world. This resulted in an increasing number of Asian and Latin American immigrants, as well as a more modest increase in immigration from other parts of the world such as the continent of Africa, Oceania, and other regions.

According to the 2000 Census, among the 3.1 million older people residing in the United States who were foreign-born, 1.2 million or almost 39% were born in Europe. In contrast, over 31% were born in Latin America and over 22% born in Asia. As the foreign-born population in the United States shifts from European origin to Latin American and Asian origin, this will be reflected in subsequent shifts in national origins of foreign-born older adults in subsequent years (He, 2002).

Also reported in the 2000 Census, almost two-thirds of older immigrants have resided in the United States for more than 30 years. As a result, older immigrants are almost twice as likely to be naturalized citizens compared with immigrants of all ages. Older immigrants from Europe, however, have the highest proportion of naturalized citizens when compared with Asian and Latin American older adult immigrants (He, 2002). Geographic distribution of older immigrants is different than that of native-born older adults as older immigrants tend to choose their location of residence based on the presence of family, immigrant networks, and ethnic communities. For example, the West has the highest proportion of older adult immigrants while the Midwest has the lowest, when compared with native-born older adults (He, 2002).

There are a number of older immigrants, however, who have never applied for citizenship, possibly because of fear of passing the citizenship test. Elderly people, who are over 65 and have resided in the United States as permanent residents for at least 20 years, have reduced requirements for history and government knowledge and may be tested in the language of their choice other than English. Social workers may want to inform their older noncitizen clients about this law and explore with them the advantages of citizenship in conveying rights to apply for certain government benefits that are discussed later in this chapter; and also to participate in voting for candidates most responsive to their concerns.

SOCIOECONOMIC CHARACTERISTICS OF OLDER ADULT IMMIGRANTS IN THE UNITED STATES

Compared with native-born older adults, the older immigrant is more likely to lack a high school education (almost 45% as compared with 29% of native-born elders), yet in contrast, almost 19% have a bachelor's degree or higher, a figure that is 15% in native-born elders. While immigrant older adults are more likely than native-born elders to have a low educational attainment, this cannot be assumed to be the case for all older foreign-born adults (He, 2002). Many young-old immigrants in the Russian community, for instance, have immigrated to this country with professional degrees but are unable to practice their respective professions due to language barriers and licensing requirements.

Immigrant older adults are more likely to live with families than native-born older adults (over 62% compared with almost 53% native-born elders). Foreign-born elders are also more likely than their native-born counterparts to live in large family households (over 20% compared with 9% native-born elders). While less likely to live alone than native-born older women, older immigrant women are more likely to live alone than older immigrant men.

With marriage rates almost identical for immigrant older men and women (97%), the factor that distinguishes the genders is loss of a spouse. Almost 46% of older immigrant women are widows, compared with only about 14% of their male counterparts (He, 2002). This discrepancy is due to a combination of factors, including the tendency of women to marry men who are older than themselves, higher remarriage rates for older widowers, and higher life expectancy for women than men.

Not surprisingly, the poverty rate is higher for older adult immigrants than native-born elders. In 1999, the poverty rate for older adult immigrants was almost 14%, as compared with over 9% of native-born elders (He, 2002). However, there was also a difference in poverty rate between foreign-born elderly who were naturalized citizens as compared with those who were not citizens (over 11% as compared with over 19% for noncitizens). More households including or headed by immigrant older adults participated in noncash programs (over 29%) than cash programs (almost 17%). Noncash programs include school lunches, food stamps, housing assistance, and Medicaid; cash assistance includes Temporary Assistance for Needy Families (TANF), General Assistance, and Supplemental Security Income (SSI).

According to the 1999 Census, 94% of the older immigrant population in the United States had health insurance for all or part of the year, as compared with over 99% of the older native-born population (He, 2002). However, the older foreign-born population had a disproportionately large percentage with no health insurance coverage, and older noncitizens had the lowest rate of coverage by Medicare and other insurances except Medicaid. Labor force participation by older immigrants was over 12%, slightly lower than native-born elders (almost 14%).

ISSUES RELATED TO OLDER ADULT IMMIGRANTS IN THE UNITED STATES

Adaptation to American culture is considered a factor in quality of life and well-being among immigrant older adults. It could be hypothesized that immigrant older adults of European origin may find adapting to the dominant Anglo culture of the United States easier than immigrant older adults of African, Asian, or Latin American origin. However, these immigrants come from very diverse countries and cultures, a fact that historically has not been acknowledged in health, mental health, and social service practice literature.

Increasingly, efforts are being directed toward the development of culturally responsive services and a culturally competent workforce, particularly in urban areas. Understanding eligibility of older adult immigrants for government benefits and services must go hand-in-hand with increasing the cultural competency of social workers and social service, health, and mental health agencies.

Eligibility for Government Programs and Services Based on Immigration Status

One major barrier to obtaining needed services for immigrant older adults lacking full citizenship status in the United States is the passage of the Personal Responsibility and Work Opportunity Reconciliation Act of 1996. This law disentitled noncitizens from receiving Supplemental Security Income (SSI), Medicaid, Temporary Assistance to Needy Families (TANF), and food stamps. In particular, Medicaid provides access to health and mental health services to many indigent and low income older adults. While the Balanced Budget Act of 1997 restored federal eligibility for some Medicaid funded services and SSI for categorically and financially legal immigrants, many government benefits and entitlements remain out of reach for noncitizen elderly immigrants (Binstock & Jean-Baptiste, 1999).

To be fully eligible for federal benefits, applicants must be citizens, or have qualified alien status (Weiner, 2007). Qualified aliens include lawful permanent residents, refugees, asylees, persons granted withholding of removal, Cuban/Haitian entrants, persons paroled into the United States for at least one year, certain battered spouses, and parents of U.S. citizens. Examples of government-funded programs open to all older adults regardless of immigration status include emergency Medicaid, adult protective services, and select components of the National Family Caregivers Support Program.

Federal means-tested programs that are restricted to qualified immigrants who meet additional criteria include SSI, Medicaid, food stamps, and TANF cash assistance. Social workers serving immigrant older adults and their families may need to work collaboratively with legal service providers who have expertise in this complex area of immigration law to ensure their clients are receiving all benefits and services allowable under the law, without risking sanction and deportation (Weiner, 2007).

Most Older Americans Act–funded services continue to remain available for immigrants at least 60 years of age and older who do not have full citizen status. These include senior centers and nutrition programs, National Family Caregiving Program resources and services, and case management services. County and state administered adult protective services are also provided to eligible older adults regardless of citizenship status. However, Older Americans Act–funded case management and adult protective services assist with linkage to government benefits programs such as Medicaid and cash grant assistance, which may continue to be inaccessible for immigrant older adults who lack adequate documentation. Access to health and mental health care based on citizenship for indigent immigrant older adults depends on local and state policies as well (Weiner, 2007).

Acculturation, Mental Health, and Health

Ms. Singh immigrated to the United States after the death of her husband in India to be close to her son and daughter-in-law and her grandchildren. She anticipated that she would be cared for by her family in the United States. However, after she arrived Ms. Singh realized that she was expected to care for her grandchildren while her children worked, and to look after the household. She became despondent and was unable to perform the duties her children expected of her. However, she did not want to share her feelings with the doctor or staff at the Indian American clinic where her children took her to be examined, out of concern that her family would be stigmatized and the memory of her late husband dishonored.

For Asian Indians, adapting to the English-speaking culture may be less challenging than adapting to different family structures and social expectations. Older immigrants who came to the United States to seek educational opportunities may experience greater opportunities for acculturation as well, but family members including spouses may have different experiences, particularly if they had not had exposure to western culture prior to migration (Nandan, 2005). Family proximity and congruity of social and religious values also may serve as predictors of adaptation (Nandan, 2005) and help-seeking behavior.

Separate chapters of this text will deal with health and mental health issues, but it is worth mentioning some salient points here. Acculturation stress and depression has been recognized as adverse mental health outcomes when older immigrants fail to adapt to their new culture. Acculturation stress has been defined as an acculturation gap between an older adult immigrant and his or her adult children (Mui & Kang, 2006). This can predict depression, which is an often undiagnosed but serious form of mental illness among older adults, particularly older Asian women. One study found differences in adaptation, acculturation, and psychological well-being among diverse groups of Asian older adult immigrants, suggesting the need for service delivery systems to be sensitive to within-group variations (Mui & Kang, 2006).

Grief associated with loss and change can also result in depression among older Chinese American immigrants (Casado & Leung, 2001). Factors such as acculturation, length of time in the United States, living arrangements and degree of contact with family, frequency of visits to country of origin, and English-language proficiency were all associated with depression and grief responses (Casado & Leung, 2001).

Physical health as well as mental health status may be influenced by factors related to country of origin and culture for older adult immigrants. Degree of social integration is also related to health status for older adult immigrants (Diwan & Jonnalagadda, 2001). In one study of Asian Indian older adult immigrants, positive health outcomes were associated with strong perceived social support and proximity of family, while negative health outcomes were associated with body weight, gender, length of time in the United States, and old age (Diwan & Jonnalagadda, 2001).

Studies of older adults in countries of origin for older adult immigrants can provide insight into the impact of native culture on mental health and well-being, apart from factors related to acculturation for immigrants. Physical conditions, functional ability, and financial sufficiency can contribute to chronic life strain (Boey, 2001). In a study of Chinese older adults in Hong Kong, physical health and availability of family network supports were important factors in mental health, depressive symptoms, and life satisfaction (Boey, 2001).

> Mr. Xiu is a 91-year-old immigrant from China who lives alone in a fourth-floor walk-up apartment in a large urban city. His wife passed away over 10 years ago and their only child, a married son in another state, died last year from a heart attack. There are no family members nearby. Mr. Xiu has limited contact with his daughter-in-law and two teenage granddaughters. He has expressed to his mahjong partners that he feels lonely since the deaths of his family members. Neighbors notice that the lights are rarely on at night. Mr. Xiu's hearing has increasingly worsened but he refuses to wear any assistive device. The health of Mr. Xiu seems to have been good up until recently with complaints of pain in his knees. He hasn't seen a doctor for many years and doesn't trust them. A life-long heavy smoker, Mr. Xiu has a chronic cough and a pronounced raspiness in his voice. Mr. Xiu's mahjong partners are beginning to notice that he is becoming disorganized in his thinking and has frequent and uncharacteristic episodes of anger and irritability.

Chronic illnesses can contribute to depression as a form of mental illness with Chinese immigrant older adults. One study demonstrated that arthritis is associated with depressive symptoms in Chinese immigrant elders, and found gender differences in older adult Chinese immigrants' response to the pain of arthritis and back and neck ailments (Wu, Tran, & Amjad, 2004).

Caregiving Issues

Caregiver stress and burden has been extensively studied with native-born older adults and their families. Less is known about caregiving issues related to families of immigrant older adults. For older Chinese immigrant caregivers, family and individual economic conditions were associated with caregiver depression and subjective perception of burden (Zhan, 2005). Caregiving stress and perception of burden were found to be similar for Korean American caregivers of older adult relatives with dementia as for native-born caregivers; however, the expression of burden and stress was different, suggesting the need for alternative intervention strategies (Zhan, 2005). Ethnic and racial diversity among caregiver families can also predict differences in resource utilization and perceptions of familial responsibility for an elderly and impaired immigrant family member (Scharlach et al., 2006).

> A native of Bogotá, Columbia, Ms. Juarez obtained a tourist visa to visit her only child, a physically disabled and alcoholic daughter who resided in the United States for many years. After some time in the United States, Ms. Juarez's visa expired. The daughter's physical condition worsened and required hospitalization followed by extensive subacute care. During this time, it became apparent to facility staff that Ms. Juarez was becoming increasingly confused and was unable to care for herself properly; hospitalization for Ms. Juarez was required. Staff at both facilities were in contact with each other and recognized that Ms. Juarez, now in an undocumented status, was no longer able to live unattended in the community and that neither the daughter nor Ms. Juarez were able to provide the care or support they each required.

Attribution of dementia can vary among diverse immigrant populations. One study of Vietnamese caregivers suggested that folk idioms, religious or spiritual beliefs, and culturally determined perceptions of age-normal conditions of older adults can influence immigrant caregivers' perceptions of and responses to dementia in older adult family members (Yeo, Uyen Tran, Hikoyeda, & Hinton, 2001).

Cognitive impairment among older Chinese and Hispanic immigrants in particular is strongly stigmatized. The individual with dementia is thought to be crazy, with dementia-related behaviors often viewed as an embarrassment to the family. Locking the impaired older adult in the extended family's shared apartment while the adult child goes to work is not uncommon. Formal supportive services are not sought for multiple reasons: lack of culturally competent services, unfamiliarity with services, lack of affordable services, inadequate or no medical insurance, limited income, and legal status of the older immigrant.

The relationship among health status, cultural patterns in caregiving, and housing resources has been studied for older Puerto Ricans and their families both in their country of origin and as immigrants to the United States. Living arrangements are linked to cultural patterns, and can influence stress and burden of both caregivers and immigrant older adults. For example, the multigenerational housing patterns found in

Latin American cultures and countries like Puerto Rico can support the cultural value of family caregiving. Housing policies in the United States that are intended to promote the independence of the elderly can serve as a barrier to familial caregiving relationships that depend on proximity of caregiver and older adult, and reflect deeply held and experienced cultural values linked to country of origin for immigrant families and older adults (Ramos, 2007). While Puerto Rican older adults are considered citizens of the Untied States and are eligible for government benefits, older adults from other Latin countries lacking citizenship status may not have eligibility status, which may place greater caregiving burdens on family members.

SPECIAL ELDERLY IMMIGRANT POPULATIONS

Grandparents Raising Grandchildren

Census data show the increase in numbers of households in which grandparents are raising grandchildren. However, few studies have examined cultural differences in grandparenting for older immigrant grandparent caregivers. Many immigrant older adults provide supplementary care for grandchildren while adult children are at work. In particular, Asian American older adult grandparents are found to provide a significant amount of childcare without being the legal guardians of their grandchildren or being the primary caregivers (Yoon, 2005).

Since the 1990s, attention has been focused on the change from older people in traditional grandparental roles to grandparents as caregivers for grandchildren (Park & Greenberg, 2007). However, family caregiving has become increasingly common for people in later life (Montgomery, Rowe, & Kosloski, 2007). In African American households, extended families provide support for both relatives and nonrelatives (Taylor, Chatters, & Celious, 2003). Grandmothers who serve as caregivers can experience economic as well as health challenges, demonstrating interactive effects among age, gender, caregiving status, health, and economic well-being (Park, 2006).

> Mr. Chou, a chain smoker, was hospitalized with second-degree burns to his hands and arms. He lived with his son-in-law, daughter, and grandchild. The son-in-law and daughter worked long hours; the grandchild was in kindergarten. Mr. Chou's daughter noticed deterioration in her father's

memory but attributed it to old age. Changes in her father's personal hygiene, such as not bathing or changing his clothes regularly, were similarly attributed to age. Mr. Chou was needed by his daughter and son-in-law to walk the granddaughter to and from school, and care for her until the daughter returned from work. Grandfather and granddaughter got along very well.

Immigrant grandparents from various communities, functioning as primary caregivers of grandchildren while the biological parents work very long hours, are often charged with the responsibility for transporting the grandchildren to and from school and caring for them until the parents return home. In some instances, it becomes necessary for these grandchildren to direct the grandparent home because cognitive impairment has disoriented the grandparent.

According to 2000 Census data, Latinos are more likely to assume caregiving responsibilities for grandchildren than Asians (Simmons & Dye, 2003). For example, nationally, Central American grandparents are more likely than noncaregiving peers to be raising grandchildren. These caregiving grandparents are more likely than peers to be younger, to be married, to have not completed high school, to be out of the labor force, and to live below the poverty line than noncaregiving peers (Minkler, 2007).

Latino grandparents with primary caregiving responsibility for grandchildren were found to define behaviors of grandchildren toward them as abusive, as opposed to disrespectful or normal, more frequently than African American custodial grandparents (Brownell, Berman, Nelson, & Fofana, 2003). Perceptions of elder abuse and tolerance toward behaviors that may be construed as abusive can be mediated by culture and country of origin for Asian Americans (Moon, Tomita, & Jung-Kamei, 2001).

The 2000 Census has shown that in New York City, there are over 84,000 grandparent-headed households. Proportionately, Newark, New Jersey has the largest number of grandparent-headed households in the country. Grandparents often assume the full-time responsibility of raising the grandchild due to various causes including the death, incarceration, addiction, or abandonment on the part of the biological parent.

The unique concerns of grandparents are often overlooked by social service provider agencies. Unless the agency is specifically mandated to work with grandparents either directly or by extension, social workers may not be cognizant of the types of questions to ask, as with investigating reported elder abuse. It is incumbent upon agency leadership and specifically social work supervisors to ensure that staff members receive adequate training on the wide array of service issues within the cultural context of the client presenting to their agency. Such awareness and knowledge allows for a more comprehensive and global assessment of clients, empowering both client and worker.

Grandparents raising grandchildren face numerous legal challenges based on individual state statutes related to eligibility for government benefits and entitlements for their grandchildren and themselves, and on ability to make decisions for their grandchildren related to health care, school enrollment, and other aspects of grandchildren's lives. Immigrant grandparents, some of whom may be nondocumented, face more daunting challenges than native-born grandparents with full citizenship status. Social workers serving grandparent-headed families are advised to work closely with custodial grandparents and specialized legal counsel on these issues (Daig & Stangl, 2006).

> Seventy-four-year-old Ms. Li secured a temporary visa and came to the United States from her native China to care for the 10-year-old child of her recently widowed oldest son. Ms. Li was ambivalent about the trip, feeling pressured by her son, anxious about leaving China, and yet wanting to help. Ms. Li stayed considerably longer than she had expected and discovered that she enjoyed watching her grandchild grow up. When her son announced that he no longer needed her assistance and told her she was free to return to China, Ms. Li was surprised at how empty she began to feel. Just days before her scheduled departure, Ms. Li woke up feeling dizzy, had difficulty speaking, and was disoriented. Her son wanted to call for medical help, but Ms. Li, now undocumented, refused.

For the older Asian immigrants, as well as those from other countries brought to the United States to live with their adult children in order to care for the grandchildren, the new duties can be met with mixed feelings. In a foreign environment, non-English-speaking grandparents may feel they have lost the lifelong familiar sights, sounds, and smells of their native country. Friends may be hard to cultivate as family responsibilities supersede opportunities for socialization, and living conditions may be cramped. Official status may slide into undocumented when the visitor visa expires and is not renewed because of unfamiliarity with language, procedure, transportation, and a host of other reasons.

Initially containing the seeds of a mutually reciprocal relationship, changes for the elder immigrant as the grandchild grows up and the importance of their role recedes may precipitate alterations in mental health, compounded by social isolation. Physical illness may also occur; and without financial resources or linguistic competency, the older immigrant often delays treatment, potentially worsening the health situation. Fearful memories of government intervention and reprisals, carried with some elder immigrants from experiences in their country of origin, compounded by undocumented status, can be counterproductive when health care services are warranted. As the immigrant ages and care needs become evident, how do they get the necessary care, who advocates for them, and who pays for it?

Immigrant Elder Abuse Victims

A growing body of research has developed to examine the link between culture and ethnicity with elder abuse. In 1997, the California-based Archstone Foundation funded a groundbreaking conference in Los Angeles, bringing together scholars in aging and elder abuse to present papers and discuss issues related to elder abuse in immigrant and diverse cultural communities in the United States. Much of this work was summarized by Tatara (1998), in his edited book: *Understanding Elder Abuse in Minority Populations.*

Among the studies that have focused on immigrant older adult elder abuse victims, Moon (1998) provides a historical overview of Korean immigration to the United States, and suggests that Korean elders are vulnerable to mistreatment because they have a difficult time adjusting to the American culture, language, and social system. According to Moon, the traditional transfer of property to the adult son may contribute to the vulnerability of this immigrant population to financial abuse (Moon, 1998). Cultural perspectives may influence Korean American older adults' perceptions and tolerance of abuse as compared with non-abusive familial behavior toward themselves and others. Cultural valuation of family over individuals, fear of bringing shame to the family, and avoiding conflict are identified as factors that may keep elder abuse hidden in the Korean American community.

According to Sanchez (1998), elder abuse is correlated with aging and dependency in the Mexican American community. Cultural norms of patriarchy and *machismo* may carry over into old age for long-term partners and spouses in this community. Poverty, ageism, and the concept of *familismo* may continue to place older women at greater risk of abuse by male partners.

Tomita (1998) finds that risk factors including dependency, social obligation, filial piety, and family conflict may be correlated with elder abuse in the Japanese American community. Myths about the invulnerability of Asian older adults to familial abuse because of cultural norms revering older adult family members may get in the way of detecting elder abuse in this ethnic population. Research on Vietnamese elders and their families identified dependency and feelings of personal indebtedness as cultural factors associated with elder abuse (Lee, 1997).

Among eastern European elders, research suggests that both victims' and perpetrators' characteristics are relevant to elder abuse risks. These include dependency on the part of older adults, and substance abuse and unemployment on the part of perpetrators. Being a new immigrant was found to be a significant predictor of physical abuse for Israeli immigrants (Iecovich, 2005).

ASSESSMENT INSTRUMENTS FOR OLDER ADULT IMMIGRANTS AND MENTAL HEALTH

Stress, coping, and depression have been identified as negatively related to successful acculturation and caregiving for older adult immigrants in the United States. The Geriatric Depression Scale (GDS) has been used to examine the factors related to depression for older Japanese American immigrants. Mild depression was identified in almost 20% of study respondents, with health, fear of placing burden on family members, and availability of close friendships and emotional support as factors associated with depression in this population (Shibusawa & Mui, 2001).

Depression screening is used in health and social service settings to identify depression in older adults, including immigrant elders. When used in a senior center for one study, over 29% of Mandarin-speaking Chinese older adult immigrants were found to be depressed. The instrument used was a translation of the original Geriatric Depression Scale into Chinese (Shibusawa & Mui, 2001).

The Culturagram is an instrument developed to assess the level of acculturation of immigrants of all ages in the United States. It can be used to assess the cultural triggers for elder abuse with at-risk older adult immigrants (Brownell, 1998). The Culturagram can be useful as a guide for social workers to obtain culturally relevant information on immigrant families including older members (Brownell, 1998).

Components of the Culturagram that can assist social workers to make culturally sensitive assessments of older immigrants and their families include reasons for immigration, length of time in the United States and in their current community of residence, legal or nondocumented status, age at time of immigration, fluency and literacy in English and language of origin, contact with cultural or religious institutions, health beliefs, holidays and special events observed, impact of crisis events, and values concerning family, education, and work (Congress & Kung, 2005). Assessments using the Culturagram can inform service planning as well as predict risk and intervention outcomes, regardless of the cultural identity of social workers who may be utilizing the instrument. For further information on the Culturagram, see Congress & Kung (2005).

Access to mental health and health services are limited for nondocumented and legal immigrants, particularly those who have not contributed to Social Security or are not legally married to partners who may be eligible for Social Security and Medicare benefits. Eligibility for entitlements can best be determined by a social worker in collaboration with an immigration attorney. The Violence Against Women Act of 2005 may provide a remedy against deportation and access to public assistance benefits for abused older adults, but only if the abuse rises to the level of a crime as defined by the penal code and the victim is legally married to the abuser.

INTERVENTIONS FOR OLDER ADULT IMMIGRANTS IN THE UNITED STATES

Older adults move into old age with differential social, health, and mental health needs based on cognitive, psychological, and physical characteristics, family, community and social network supports, and culturally determined preferences. While a number of studies have examined the fit between these characteristics and service and health and mental health interventions, only a relative few have focused specifically on these aspects of older adult immigrant needs and intervention models and services.

Older adult immigrants who are physically and cognitively intact can benefit from leisure activities that assist them to both acculturate to their new country, and link to their country and culture of origin. A study of leisure activity that is intended to preserve older adults' sense of ethnic identification and cultural integration found that for a group of Korean American older adult immigrants, leisure activity was used more for ethnic preservation than cultural integration (Kim, Kleiber, & Kropf, 2001). The gerontological social worker in settings that provide older adult immigrants with opportunities for leisure activity, like community and senior centers, can recognize the value of leisure activities as culturally specific (Kim, Kleiber, & Kropf, 2001).

Social group work, a traditional social work method of practice, has been identified as relevant for the Asian American older immigrants. Group work practice evolved during the settlement house movement of the Progressive Era, and is a core method of social work practice with immigrant populations. It is particularly relevant to practice within senior centers for work with immigrant older adults. The group provides a venue for discussion of sensitive issues, builds on the strengths of older adult participants, and is an intervention that is socially acceptable and adapts to the language and social limitations and needs of participants, including older Asian Americans with limited English-language capabilities (Chung, 2004).

Senior Centers

Attempts to bring individual mental health services to senior centers have been met with mixed results. For some centers with a population largely of European descent and greater acculturation, appointments with the social worker were seen as something of a status symbol, resulting in waiting lines. Issues generally brought to the social worker were not of a personal nature, but largely revolved around finances and entitlements. However, in response to a suicide, members of a more ethnically diverse senior center were reticent to offer opinions to the larger group, but were willing to talk in small groups about the deceased and share their thoughts and feelings about the suicide.

Senior centers serve as focal points for leisure activities and service needs for older Americans, including those who are native and those who are foreign-born. However, senior centers can be an underutilized resource for older adult immigrants. While elderly Chinese immigrants use senior centers regularly for leisure activities, they may underutilize the available support services, including task assistance (Lai, 2001). New immigrants in one Canadian study used more acculturation services than those who were in their new country for a longer period of time. Moreover, immigrants from mainland China used support services less frequently than Chinese immigrants from Hong Kong or Taiwan. However, older immigrants from mainland China were more likely to use acculturation services to facilitate their integration into mainstream culture (Lai, 2001).

Senior centers do not only provide leisure and group programs and services for immigrant older adults, but also provide congregate and home-delivered meals, an important nutrition supplement for older adult immigrants with limited incomes and resources. However, older Asian and Latin American immigrants are underrepresented in these programs in many localities. Barriers to participation in nutrition supplement programs for frail Asian and Latino older immigrants have been studied, with lack of English language proficiency identified as the key barrier to participation for these immigrant groups (Choi, 2001).

Food reflecting cultural preferences is one component to successful service delivery, attracting elderly immigrants to senior centers. Identification and engagement of at-risk older adult immigrants, in addition to culturally and linguistically appropriate outreach, are seen as key to preventing poor health based on nutritional deficits for these groups (Choi, 2001). Older immigrants attending senior centers located within or affiliated with nearby multiservice agencies benefit from communication between senior center staff and agency social workers when care needs are identified.

Reminiscence Groups and Intergenerational Activities

Reminiscence groups can have therapeutic effects on older adults, including older adult immigrants (Chong, 2000). A Hong Kong–based study on the use of reminiscence groups for older adult Chinese attending a social center suggests that this technique can be useful for engaging older adult Chinese immigrants in a social group process (Chong, 2000).

Intergenerational activities, when available, are beneficial to both young and old participants. One creative use of the intergenerational model and the elderly immigrant has been for youngsters to help the older adult prepare for citizenship.

Service barriers for older adult immigrants can adversely affect their health and mental health status. Older Chinese immigrants to Canada were surveyed and the finding suggested that barriers related to administrative problems, personal attitudes, and circumstantial problems were predictors of physical and mental health (Lai & Chau, 2007). Implications for social work include the need to recruit and educate more social workers with diverse language capabilities and cultural competencies (Lai & Chau, 2007).

Older adult Latino immigrants were found to seek mental health assistance in later life in response to grief and losses. However, barriers to successful engagement were identified as lack of adequate financial resources and transportation, lack of knowledge about mental health symptoms and services of primary physicians, lack of information on available resources, and personal and cultural characteristics like stigma and shame related to cultural differences between older adult immigrants and mental health professionals (Choi & Gonzalez, 2005). Special outreach efforts and availability of concrete and culturally competent services were identified as essential to link immigrant elderly to needed mental health services.

Caregiver Support, Nursing Home, and Home Care Services

Caregivers of older adult immigrants with dementia are challenged to provide needed care and obtain culturally and linguistically appropriate supportive services for their care-dependent family members. Dementia-specific outreach and services programs targeted to immigrant groups, like Latinos, can provide needed community-based, culturally sensitive, coordinated delivery of care to older adult immigrants with dementia and their family caregivers (Aranda, Villa, Trejo, Ramirez, & Ranney, 2003). Ethnically sensitive consortium service models can bring together public and nonprofit agencies to engage in effective and linguistically appropriate outreach, education, and service delivery to underserved immigrant populations (Aranda, Villa, Trejo, Ramirez & Ranney, 2003).

> Mr. Ortiz is a 69-year-old restaurant worker, residing in the United States for over 30 years, who lost his job after the attacks of September 11, 2001. He has been struggling to keep his diabetes under control for much of his adult life and was recently diagnosed with high cholesterol and an elevated blood pressure. His supportive family is concerned with the cognitive changes they've noticed over the past few years. Mr. Ortiz has lost his way on several occasions when traveling home from familiar locations, is unable to consistently report that he has eaten, and has experienced a dramatic weight loss. His family members work several jobs to make ends meet, so Mr. Ortiz is on his own for much of the time.

Home care services are not only provided by family members to immigrant elders, but are also provided by home care and home health care agencies as well. In one study, Asian/Pacific Islander elders received home care after being discharged from nursing home rehabilitation with more care dependency needs, a greater proportion of dual eligibility for Medicare and Medicaid (suggesting lower household income and resources), and more home health care service hours approved than their White counterparts (Lee & Peng, 2001).

Trauma experienced in their country of origin can affect older adult immigrants' acculturation, adjustment, and willingness to accept needed social, health, and mental health services. Comparisons between Holocaust survivors and older people who did not experience the Holocaust identified more similarities than differences in willingness to enter nursing home care (Letster-Pouw & Werner, 2003). For example, attitudes about nursing home care were predictive of unwillingness to enter nursing homes for both groups. However, financial concerns were more salient for Holocaust survivors, while living situations and education were of greater significance for other older adults. Holocaust survivors in one study who tried not to relive their Holocaust experiences were less likely to accept nursing home services than those who were more willing to work through these memories. This suggests that social work services employed in working through traumatic Holocaust memories may similarly benefit the older Holocaust survivor in need of nursing home services (Letster-Pouw & Werner, 2003).

Older adult immigrants who require nursing home services, as well as their families, may be concerned about the cultural sensitivity of the nursing home environment. One study sought to examine whether ethnic-specific nursing home facilities improved the quality of care for older adult immigrant residents by studying Japanese American older women in Japanese and non-Japanese long-term care residences (Hikoyeda & Wallace, 2001). This included examining the effect of factors like food, language used by staff and administration, and attitudes of administration on quality of life satisfaction of residents. The study found that cultural factors alone did not lead to quality of life satisfaction of residents and their families, as individual characteristics also affected residents' perceptions of quality of life (Hikoyeda & Wallace, 2001).

Elder Abuse Programs and Services

Juan S. emigrated from Puerto Rico 24 years ago at the age of 40, and recently had to stop working due to a back ailment, precipitating heavy drinking. He is abusive to his wife, Yolanda S., who emigrated from Mexico 10 years ago at the age of 50. They have been living together for 8 years and do not have children. Recently they separated due to the abusive behavior

> of Juan toward Yolanda. Juan receives Social Security and will be eligible for Medicare in six months. Yolanda does not have citizenship and has been working since arriving in the United States as a manicurist off the books. She has arthritis and is unable to continue her work as a manicurist. Juan refuses to give her money unless she returns to live with him. She is afraid of him, but does not see an alternative for herself.

Elder abuse programs and services provide social work, health, mental health, and legal services to both older victims and their abusers. When the victims and/or the abusers are immigrants, this presents even more complex challenges for social workers in health, mental health, and legal settings than work with older victims and their families who are citizens.

According to the National Research Council (2003), few elder abuse program interventions have been evaluated, and of those that have, none specifically addressed issues related to immigrant elderly. Research on elder abuse with culturally diverse populations generally does not distinguish between immigration status and culture. However, there is a growing and significant body of research on elder abuse and how culture mediates perceptions of abusive behavior, types of elder abuse manifested in different cultural communities, and help-seeking among elder abuse victims and family members of diverse cultural identities (Chang & Moon, 1997; Moon, 1998; Tatara, 1998; Tomita, 1998).

> In the case of Ms. Juarez, the older adult immigrant from Colombia whose daughter was unable to care for her, Adult Protective Services (APS) was called to initiate a Medicaid application for nursing home placement. APS reported that Ms. Juarez had erroneously received Medicaid benefits for approximately six months with questionable supporting documentation. As a result of further investigation, Ms. Juarez was found to be ineligible for Medicaid by federal law and regulation. Therefore, even though Ms. Juarez was stabilized and ready for discharge, she could not return to her daughter's apartment and had no ability to pay for placement of any sort. Deportation was not an option because there were no living relatives other than the daughter to assume responsibility for her care.

In the case of Ms. Juarez, discussed earlier in this chapter, interventions can remain elusive. Even with the involvement of protective interventions of government-administered adult protection programs like adult protective services, nondocumented older adult immigrants without capacity have few remedies available to them. Systems do not currently exist to respond to this type of situation and the financial drain on health care institutions will be significant as the population ages and social supports fail to meet the increased care requirements. In the case of Ms. Juarez, after much negotiating and discussion with representatives from government, health, social services, and the for-profit and not-for-profit sectors of long-term care, it was decided that placement would be secured for Ms. Juarez as a victim of elder abuse and neglect, as her daughter was unable to properly respond to her care needs. The receiving facility offered to underwrite the care and is not being reimbursed.

Some authors, notably Sanchez (1998) and Malley-Morrison & Hines (2004), discuss legal barriers to immigrant elder abuse victims obtaining needed services, such as shelter, health, and mental health services that may require documentation of citizenship. These and other authors also address issues beyond cultural norms that may prevent elder abuse victims from seeking and obtaining needed assistance. According to Malley-Morrison and Hines (2004), for example, elder abuse victims and their families may not seek help due to mistrust of majority cultural services and the strong cultural role of the family.

Services such as nursing home services, medical care, and home care are accepted more readily by elder abuse victims and their families after counseling to relieve stress, anxiety, and depression (Nahmiash & Reis, 2000). However, older adults who lack documentation of citizenship may have difficulty qualifying for these services if funded by government entitlements. Older adult victims of abuse with refugee status may be distrustful of government authority, including law enforcement, because of negative experiences in their countries of origin (New York City Elder Abuse Training Project, 2004).

There is growing interest in evidence-based practice in the social work profession, as well as interdisciplinary practice with law. This suggests that in the future more research on immigrant elders will focus on intervention outcomes research, as well as research that examines the effect of immigration status, as well as cultural factors, on service uptake and the challenges on social work service delivery with foreign-born older adults in the United States.

CONCLUSION

Gerontological social work has begun to achieve a high profile in the United States and North America, but within this field of practice, social work with older adult immigrants must gain prominence as well. A survey of the sociodemographics of aging in the United States makes clear that the older adult population is not only becoming increasingly diverse, but that the diversity is reflecting ethnicities and cultures in countries of origin that are considered nontraditional in American culture.

Not only is the proportion of European-born older adult immigrants shrinking, but the proportion of diverse Asian and Latin American older adult immigrants is growing. This provides a unique challenge to U.S. health, mental health, and social service delivery systems to achieve cultural, linguistic, and ethnic sensitivity and balance. The small but growing body of practice experience and scholarship on issues and needs related to the immigrant elderly population and their families and communities, as well as useful assessment instruments and intervention strategies, can serve to inform social work practitioners and policy makers about the needs of diverse older adult immigrants as the population ages.

Increased life expectancy and reduced lifetime fertility are driving a demographic transition (United Nations, 2007). This transition has three stages: The first stage is a rejuvenation of the age distribution as the proportion of children rises because of increased survival of the young; the second stage—due to fertility declines—begins a decline of the proportion of children with a concomitant rise in adults of working age; and in the third stage, proportions of both children and working-age adults decline, with the proportion of older people increasing.

Developed countries are already at the third stage of the demographic transition, with most of the developing countries still at the second stage. However, according to the UN population report cited earlier, the majority of the world's older people age 60 years and above live in developing countries and by 2050, almost 1.6 billion people will be at least 60 years and older. Because women live longer than men, developing countries in particular will be less likely to experience what is being seen in the developed countries as the reduction in the gender advantage, that is, gender differences are expected to continue to widen in old age.

The United States as a developed country is expected to continue to increase its population of immigrants from the developing world, and this population will in turn move into old age. It is essential that the health, mental health, social service, and legal service delivery systems are ready to serve them.

Given the complex issues related to health, safety, cognitive capacity, and culture that are reflected in the case examples in this chapter, it appears that at least some of the problems faced by elderly immigrants and their families cannot be remedied under current U.S. federal law. An undocumented older adult with dementia and no one able or willing to provide needed care may not be able to apply for citizenship or may be deported to their country of origin. Recent legislation limiting access to citizenship for even elderly and disabled refugees suggests that social workers and lawyers face daunting challenges in seeking assistance for nondocumented elderly (Refugees in the Cold, 2008).

One remedy to be contemplated for the future is that of a Convention for the Human Rights of Older Persons (personal communication, Susan B. Somers, Secretary General, International Network for the Prevention of Elder Abuse, January 4, 2008). With more people living longer, ensuring the protection and promotion of the health and security of older adults is a matter of human rights, as well as public policy. While the UN General Assembly has adopted the United Nations Principles for Older Persons, the need for an international treaty confirming governments' obligations for ensuring the human rights of older adults across international borders remains unaddressed (Mahabali, 2004). Social workers and lawyers working together in states and localities, as well as the United Nations, can promote a future where all immigrant older adults are able to obtain needed benefits and services to ensure protection and well-being.

CASE STUDIES

The following cases previously introduced in this chapter illustrate life experiences commonly encountered by elderly immigrants. You are invited to discuss the questions following each case.

Case 1: Mr. Xiu

Mr. Xiu is a 91-year-old man living alone in a fourth-floor walk-up apartment in New York. His wife passed away many years ago and their only son died last year from a heart attack. His daughter-in-law and two teenage granddaughters have limited contact with Mr. Xiu.

Mr. Xiu has expressed to his mahjong partners that he feels lonely since the deaths of his family members. Feelings of hopelessness are evident as Mr. Xiu frequently sighs and says he is living too long.

Mr. Xiu's hearing has increasingly become impaired but he refuses to wear any assistive device. As a result, misunderstanding and conflict often characterize his interactions.

Otherwise, the health of Mr. Xiu has been fine up until now, although he complains of pain in his knees and an occasional cold. He hasn't seen a doctor for many years, and doesn't especially trust them. A heavy lifelong smoker, Mr. Xiu has a chronic cough and an increasing raspiness in his voice. Mr. Xiu's mahjong partners are beginning to notice that he is becoming disorganized in his thinking and disruptions in routine are reacted to with uncharacteristic anger and irritability.

Mr. Xiu has also become suspicious of his neighbors, saying that they are stealing his Social Security checks. A trusted friend, invited in to help repair a leak in the kitchen, found two checks in the freezer while getting ice for their drinks. He laughed and gave the checks to Mr. Xiu.

1. What social work issues are raised by this vignette?
2. What legal issues are raised by this vignette?
3. How is Mr. Xiu to be engaged to seek help? Is it enough to play mahjong or would Mr. Xiu benefit from activities of some other kind?
4. There appears to be a serious illness developing in Mr. Xiu's throat and lungs. If this is a cancer and there are no family supports, how can Mr. Xiu access palliative care services?
5. Mr. Xiu is expressing his depression and it seems to be complicated by paranoid ideation. What will it take for a person like Mr. Xiu to seek or accept assistance?
6. What might be the cause(s) of his disorganized thinking and irritability?
7. Recalling that Mr. Xiu doesn't trust doctors, how can advanced directives or estate planning be addressed with him?

Case 2: Ms. Juarez

Ms. Juarez is an 88-year-old woman who came to the United States from Colombia in 1996 to visit her daughter on a tourist visa. Ms. Juarez's daughter, with whom she had lived, has multiple sclerosis (MS) and is an alcoholic. The daughter has been hospitalized for exacerbation of the MS symptoms compounded by alcoholism, and now has been transferred for extensive subacute care. During this time, Ms. Juarez was also hospitalized with profound deterioration in cognition, disorganized thinking and behavior, and poor self-care.

The tourist visa has expired and Ms. Juarez is now in the country illegally. She is no longer in need of acute care but does require a supportive setting. The hospital can no longer afford to keep her and nursing homes will not accept her because she does not have skilled nursing needs, insurance, or ability to pay. Ms. Juarez is not eligible for Medicaid. She wants to live with her daughter, who also requires additional support.

1 What social work issues are raised by this vignette?
2 What legal issues are raised by this vignette?
3 What care options are available to Ms. Juarez?

Case 3: Mr. Ortiz

Mr. Ortiz, the 69-year-old former restaurant worker with diabetes, high cholesterol, high blood pressure, and impaired cognition, has two sons and one daughter; he lives with his wife and oldest son, who both work several jobs to make ends meet. A younger son and daughter live one state away with their own families. Overall, the family is very caring and supportive.

The family noticed a change in Mr. Ortiz's cognition about three years ago. While traveling to or from familiar locations, Mr. Ortiz occasionally lost his way, requiring assistance to arrive at his destination. Mr. Ortiz would forget if he ate or not, which impacted his blood glucose levels. Although he is not employed, Mr. Ortiz has recently begun waking in the middle of the night and dressing for work. Mrs. Ortiz sees the changes in her husband, including a dramatic weight loss, and is not sure what to do.

Sometimes Mr. Ortiz feels frustrated and irritable because he recognizes that he has difficulty recalling recent events, yet his memory of his youth and young adulthood seem to be intact. Increasingly, Mr. Ortiz stays inside the house by himself during the day, refusing to go outside to socialize with neighbors.

1 What social work issues are raised by this vignette?
2 What legal issues are raised by this vignette?
3 How can the physician help the family address the changes seen in Mr. Ortiz?
4 Mr. Ortiz is isolating himself. How can this pattern be broken?
5 Had Mr. Ortiz received a thorough work-up for Alzheimer's disease, how would he and his family be better prepared to cope with the cognitive and physical changes?

6. Should Mr. Ortiz consider a health care proxy? Why or why not?
7. Had Mr. Ortiz attended a medical/social model day care, how could his sudden weight loss and withdrawn behavior have been addressed?

Case 4: Ms. Li

Seventy-four-year-old Ms. Li secured a temporary visa and came to the United States from her native China to care for the 10-year-old child of her recently widowed oldest son. Ms. Li was ambivalent about the trip, feeling pressured by her son, anxious about leaving China because she co-owned a restaurant with her brother-in-law, and yet wanting to help. Ms. Li stayed considerably longer than she had expected and discovered that she enjoyed watching her grandchild grow up. When her son unexpectedly announced that he no longer needed her assistance and told her she was free to return to China, Ms. Li was surprised at how empty she began to feel. Just days before her scheduled departure, Ms. Li woke up feeling dizzy, had difficulty speaking, and was disoriented. Her son wanted to call for medical help, but Ms. Li, who had overstayed her visa and was now undocumented, refused.

1. What social work issues are raised by this vignette?
2. What legal issues are raised by this vignette?
3. The death of Ms. Li's daughter-in-law was very sudden and obviously detrimental to the son. What could have been some options for both son and grandson to help cope with this loss? Mindful of the cultural context, who would be the optimum provider of these options?
4. It appears that the son is ambivalent about his mother. How is this to be addressed?
5. Ms. Li could have modest financial resources if she decided to sell her interest in the restaurant. If she were to do so, how should she be advised given her unexpected care needs? Would or should her son be included in the discussion?
6. Is there a role that the grandchild can play in healing or harming the grandmother-son relationship? What about the grandchild's needs?
7. How is the fear of Ms. Li, who is now undocumented, to be overcome in accessing the needed care?

ADDITIONAL RESOURCES

General Resources

Administration on Aging: www.aoa.gov

The American Immigration Law Foundation, *Immigration and the Elderly:* www.ailf.org/ipc/infocus/ipc_infocus_0708.shtml

Coalition of Limited English Speaking Elderly: www.clese.org

NPR—National Public Radio, *Elderly Immigrants Flow Into California:* www.npr.org/templates/story/story.php?storyId=88402850

Elderly Immigrants and Welfare

Binstock, R. H., & Racheal, J. B. (1999). Elderly immigrants and the saga of welfare reform. *Journal of Immigrant Health 1*(1), 31–40.

Bean, E. D., Van Hook, J. V. W., & Glick, J. E. (1997). Country of origin, type of public assistance, and patterns of welfare recipiency among U.S. immigrants and natives. *Social Science Quarterly, 78*(2), 432–451.

Estes, C. L., Goldberg, S., Wellin, C., Linkins, K. W., and Shostak, S. (2006). Implications of welfare reform on the elderly: A case study of provider, advocate, and consumer perspectives. *Journal of Aging and Social Policy, 18*(1), 41–63.

Freidland, R. B., & Veena, P. (1997). *Welfare reform and elderly legal immigrants.* Washington, DC: Henry J. Kaiser Family Foundation.

Hu, W.-Y. (1998). Elderly immigrants on welfare. *The Journal of Human Resources, 33*(3), 711–741.

Matloff, N. (1997, June 25). *Welfare use among elderly immigrants.* Testimony before the U.S. Senate Judiciary Committee, Subcommittee on Immigrants, 103rd Congress.

Van Hook, J. (2000). SSI eligibility and participation among elderly naturalized citizens and noncitizens. *Social Science Research 29*(1), 51–69.

Elder Abuse

Anetzberger, G. J., Korbin, J. E., & Tomita, S. K. (1996). Defining elder mistreatment in four ethnic groups across two generations. *Journal of Cross-Cultural Gerontology, 11*(2), 187–212.

API Elder Abuse Center: http://www.apilegaloutreach.org/elder.html

Archstone Foundation and the National Center on Elder Abuse (1997). *Understanding and combating elder abuse in minority communities.* Long Beach, CA: Author. This publication is a collection of the keynote addresses, presentations, and discussions of the "Understanding and Combating Elder Abuse in Minority Communities" conference. For information regarding the publication, contact the Archstone Foundation, 401 E. Ocean Blvd., Suite 1000, Long Beach, CA 90802, telephone (562) 590–8655.

Chang, J., & Moon, A. (1997). Korean-American elderly's knowledge and perceptions of abuse: A qualitative analysis of cultural factors. *Journal of Multicultural Social Work, 6*(1/2), 139–154.

Clearinghouse on Abuse and Neglect of the Elderly (CANE): http://db.rdms.udel.edu:8080/CANE/index.jsp

Le, Q. K. (1997). Mistreatment of Vietnamese elderly by their family members in the United States. *Journal of Elder Abuse and Neglect, 9*(2), 51–62.

Moon, A., & Benton, D. (2000). Tolerance of elder abuse and attitudes toward third-party intervention among African American, Korean American, and White elderly. *Journal of Multicultural Social Work, 8*(3/4), 283–303.

Moon, A., & Evans-Campbell, T. (1999). Awareness of formal and informal sources of help for victims of elder abuse among Korean-American and Caucasian elders in Los Angeles. *Journal of Elder Abuse & Neglect, 11*(3), 1–23.

National Center on Elder Abuse: www.elderabusecenter.org

Pablo, S., & Braun, K. (1997). Perceptions of elder abuse and neglect and help-seeking patterns among Filipino and Korean elderly women in Honolulu. *Journal of Elder Abuse and Neglect,* 9(2), 63–76.

San Francisco Consortium for Elder Abuse Prevention: http://www.ioaging.org/services/special/program_elder_abuse/

Tatara, T. (Ed.). (1998). *Understanding elder abuse in minority populations.* Philadelphia, PA: Brunner/Mazel Taylor & Francis Group.

Tomita, S. The consideration of cultural factors in the research of elder mistreatment with an in-depth look at the Japanese. (1994). *Journal of Cross-Cultural Gerontology* 9, 39–52.

REFERENCES

Aranda, M. P., Villa, V. M., Trejo, L., Ramirez, R., & Ranney, M. (2003). El portal Latino Alzheimer's project: Model program for Latino caregivers of Alzheimer's disease-affected people. *Social Work, 48*(2), 259–271.

Binstock, R. H., & Jean-Baptiste, R. (1999). Elderly immigrants and the saga of welfare reform. *Journal of Immigrant Health, 1,* 31–40.

Boey, K. W. (2001). Contribution of chronic life strain to mental health status of Chinese older adults. *Journal of Gerontological Social Work, 35*(1/2), 39–52.

Brownell, P. (1997). The application of the Culturagram in cross-cultural practice with victims of elder abuse. *Journal of Elder Abuse and Neglect,* 9(2), 19–33.

Brownell, P., Berman, J., Nelson, A., & Fofana, R. C. (2003). Grandparents raising grandchildren: the risks of caregiving. *Journal of Elder Abuse and Neglect, 15*(3/4), 5–31.

Casado, B. L., & Leung, P. (2001). Migratory grief and depression among elderly Chinese American immigrants. *Journal of Gerontological Social Work, 36*(1/2), 5–26.

Chang, J., & Moon, A. (1997). Korean-American elderly's knowledge and perceptions of abuse: a qualitative analysis of cultural factors. *Journal of Elder Abuse and Neglect, 6*(1/2,) 139–154.

Choi, N. G. (2001). Frail older persons in nutrition supplement programs: A comparative study of African American, Asian American, and Hispanic Participants. *Journal of Gerontological Social Work, 36*(1/2). 187–207.

Choi, N. G., & Gonzalez, J. M. (2005). Barriers and contributors to minority older adults' access to mental health treatment: perceptions of geriatric mental health clinicians. *Journal of Gerontological Social Work, 44*(3/4), 115–135.

Chong, A. (2000). Reminiscence group for Chinese older people—a cultural consideration. *Journal of Gerontological Social Work, 34*(2), 7–22.

Chung, I. (2004). The sociocultural reality of the Asian immigrant elderly: Implications for group work practice. *Journal of Gerontological Social Work, 44*(3/4), 81–93.

Congress, E. P. (1997). Using the Culturagram to assess and empower culturally diverse families. In E. P. Congress & M. J. Gonzalez (Eds.), *Multicultural perspectives in working with families* (2nd Ed.) (pp. 3–21). New York: Springer Publishing Company.

Congress, E., and Kung, W. (2005). Using the culturagram to assess and empower culturally diverse families. In E. P. Congress and M. J. Gonzalez, *Multicultural perspectives in working with families* (2nd ed.) (pp. 3–21). New York: Springer Publishing.

Diag, J., & Stangl, T. L. (2006). *Grandparents raising grandchildren: Common legal issues.* Port Huron, MI: Lakeside Legal Aid. Retrieved December 31, 2007, from http://www.lakeshorelegalaid.org/docs/grg.pdf

Diwan, S., & Jonnolagadda, S. S. (2001). Social integration and health among Asian Indian immigrants in the United States. *Journal of Gerontological Social Work, 36*(1/2), 45–62.

Greene, R. R., & Choi, N. (2008). Gerontology: A field of practice. In B. W. Whire, K. M. Sowers, & C. M. Dulmus (Eds.), *Comprehensive handbook of social work and social welfare* (pp. 283–314). Hoboken, NJ: John Wiley & Sons, Inc.

He, W. (2002). *The older foreign-born population in the United States: 2000.* U.S. Census Bureau Current Population Reports, Series P23–211. Washington, DC: Government Printing Office.

Hikoyeda, N., & Wallace, S. P. (2001). Do ethnic-specific long term care facilities improve resident quality of life? Findings from the Japanese American community. *Journal of Gerontological Social Work, 36*(1/2), 27–44.

Iecovich, E. (2005). Elder abuse and neglect in Israel: A comparison between the general elderly population and elderly new immigrants. *Family Relations, 54*(3), 436–447.

Kilty, K. (2002). Race, immigration, and public policy: The case of Asian Americans. *Journal of Poverty, 6*(4), 23–41.

Kilty, K. M., & deHaymes, M. (2000). Racism, nativism, and exclusion: Public policy, immigration, and the Latino experience in the U.S. *Journal of Poverty, 4*(1/2), 1–25.

Kim, E., Kleiber, D. A., & Kropf, N. (2001). Leisure activity, ethnic preservation, and cultural integration of older Korean Americans. *Journal of Gerontological Social Work, 36*(1/2), 107–129.

Lai, D. W. (2001). Use of senior center services of the elderly Chinese immigrants. *Journal of Gerontological Social Work, 35*(1/2), 59–79.

Lai, D. W., & Chau, S. B. (2007). Effects of service barriers on health status of older Chinese immigrants in Canada. *Social Work, 52*(3), 261–269.

Lee, J. S., & Peng, T. R. (2001). A profile of Asian/Pacific Islander elderly in home health care. *Journal of Gerontological Social Work, 36*(1/2), 171–186.

Lee, Q. K. (1997). Mistreatment of Vietnamese elderly by their family members in the United States. *Journal of Elder Abuse and Neglect, 9*(2), 51–62.

Letster-Pouw, S., & Werner, P. (2003). The willingness to enter a nursing home: A comparison of Holocaust survivors with elderly people who did not experience the Holocaust. *Journal of Gerontological Social Work, 40*(4), 87–103.

Mahabal, K. B. (2004). *Healthy aging and human rights.* Mumbai, India: Healthcare Management. Retrieved January 12, 2008, from http://www.expresshealthcaremgme.com/20041130/healthandhumanrights01.shtml

Malley-Morrison, K., & Hines, D. A. (2004). *Family violence in a cultural perspective: Defining, understanding, and combating abuse.* Thousand Oaks, CA: Sage.

Martin, P., & Midgley, E. (1999, June). Immigration to the United States. *Population Bulletin, 54,* 1–44.

Minkler, M. (2007). Central American grandparents raising grandchildren. *Hispanic Journal of Behavioral Science, 29*(1), 5–18.

Montgomery, R. J., Rowe, J. M., & Kosloski, K. (2007). Family caregiving. In J. A. Blackburn & C. N. Dulmus (Eds.), *Handbook of gerontology: Evidence-based approaches to theory, practice, and policy* (pp. 426–454). Hoboken, NJ: Wiley.

Moon, A. (1998). Elder abuse and neglect among the Korean elderly in the United States. In T. Tatara (Ed.), *Understanding elder abuse in minority populations* (pp. 109–118). Philadelphia, PA: Taylor & Francis.

Moon, A., Tomita, S. K., & Jung-Kamei, S. (2001). Elder mistreatment among four Asian American groups: An exploratory study on tolerance, victim blaming and attitudes toward third-party intervention. *Journal of Gerontological Social Work, 38*(1/2), 153–169.

Mui, A. C., & Kang, S. Y. (2006). Acculturation stress and depression among Asian immigrant elders. *Social Work, 51*(3), 243–255.

Nahmiash, D., & Reis, M. (2000). Most successful intervention strategies for abused elders. *Journal of Elder Abuse and Neglect, 12*(3/4), 53–70.

Nandan, M. (2005). Adaptation to American culture: Voices of Asian Indian immigrants. *Journal of Gerontological Social Work, 44*(3/4), 175–203.

National Research Council. (2003). *Elder mistreatment: Abuse, neglect, and exploitation in an aging America.* Washington, DC: The National Academies Press.

New York City Elder Abuse Training Project. (2004). *Elder abuse training guidelines for law enforcement.* New York: New York City Department for the Aging.

Refugees in the cold. (2008, January 12). *New York Times,* Editorial Section, A14.

Park, H. H. (2006). The economic well-being of households headed by a grandmother as caregiver. *Social Service Review, 80,* 264–294.

Park, H. H., & Greenberg, J. S. (2007). Parenting grandchildren. In J. A. Blackburn & C. N. Dulmus (Eds.), *Handbook of gerontology: Evidence-based approaches to theory, practice, and policy* (pp. 397–425). Hoboken, NJ: Wiley.

Portes, A., & Rumbaut, R. G. (1996). *Immigrant America: A portrait* (2nd ed.). Berkeley, CA: University of California Press.

Quiroz-Martinez, J. (2001). Missing link. *Color Lines, 4*(2), 17–21.

Ramos, B. M. (2007). Housing disparities, caregiving, and their impact for older Puerto Ricans. *Journal of Gerontological Social Work, 49*(1/2), 47–64.

Sanchez, Y. (1998). Elder abuse and mistreatment in Mexican American communities: the Nevada and Michigan Experiences. In T. Tatara (Ed.), *Understanding elder abuse in minority populations* (pp. 67–77). Philadelphia, PA: Taylor & Francis.

Scharlach, A. E., Kellam, R., Ong, N., Baskin, A., Goldstein, C., & Fox, P. J. (2006). Cultural attitudes and caregiver service use: lessons from focus groups with racially and ethnically diverse family caregivers. *Journal of Gerontological Social Work, 47*(1/2), 133–156.

Shibusawa, T., & Mui, A. C. (2001). Stress, coping, and depression among Japanese American elders. *Journal of Gerontological Social Work, 35*(1/2), 63–81.

Simmons, T., & Dye, J. L. (2003). *Grandparents living with grandchildren: 2000.* Washington, DC: U.S. Census Bureau.

Takaki, R. (1998). *Strangers from a distant shore: a history of Asian Americans* (rev. ed.). Boston: Little, Brown.

Tatara, T. (1998). Introduction. In T. Tatara (Ed.), *Understanding elder abuse in minority populations* (pp. 1–9). Philadelphia, PA: Taylor & Francis.

Taylor, R. J., Chatters, L. M., & Celious, A. (2003). Extended family households among Black Americans. *African American Research Perspectives, 9*, 133–151.

Tomita, S. K. (1998). Exploration of elder mistreatment among the Japanese. In T. Tatara (Ed.), *Understanding elder abuse in minority populations* (pp. 119–139). Philadelphia, PA: Taylor & Francis.

United Nations. (2007). *World economic and social survey 2007: Development in an aging world.* New York: Department of Public Information.

Weiner, B. (2007). *Restrictions on eligibility of non-citizens in New York State for certain Federal and State public benefits.* Albany, NY: Empire Justice Center.

Wu, B., Tran, T. V., and Amjad, Q. A. (2004). Chronic illnesses and depression among Chinese immigrant elders. *Journal of Gerontological Social Work, 43*(2/3), 79–95.

Yeo, G., Uyen Tran, J. N., Hikoyeda, N., and Hinton, L. (2001). Conceptions of dementia among Vietnamese American caregivers. *Journal of Gerontological Social Work, 35*(1/2), 131–152.

Yoon, S. M. (2005). The characteristics and needs of Asian-American grandparent caregivers: A study of Chinese American and Korean-American grandparents in New York City. *Journal of Gerontological Social Work, 44*(3/4), 75–94.

Zhan, H. J. (2005). Social-economic context of parent care: Explaining Chinese caregivers' psychological and emotional well-being. *Journal of Gerontological Social Work, 45*(4), 83–100.

PART IV

Immigration Policy

13

Overview of Immigrant Eligibility for Federal Programs

TANYA BRODER

Low-income immigrants in the United States have faced substantial restrictions on access to public benefit programs since the enactment of the 1996 welfare and immigration laws.[1] Even where eligibility for immigrants was preserved by the 1996 laws or restored by subsequent legislation, many immigrant families hesitate to enroll in critical health care, job-training, nutrition, and cash assistance programs due to fear and confusion caused by the laws' chilling effects.

The 1996 laws also attempted to transfer to state and local government certain powers traditionally held by the federal government. In addition to restricting a range of federal benefits, the welfare law allows states to offer or deny eligibility to most immigrants for three federal programs as well as many state benefit programs.[2] The withdrawal of federal resources makes it difficult for states to serve significant portions of their low-wage population, at a time when growing numbers of immigrants are settling in communities throughout the United States.[3]

Overview of Immigrant Eligibility for Federal Programs © *2007 National Immigration Law Center (www.nilc.org). Reprinted from* Resource Manual: Low-Income Immigrant Rights Conference 2007 *by permission. The author thanks Sonal Ambegaokar, NILC health policy attorney; Jonathan Blazer, NILC public benefits policy attorney; and Dinah Wiley, NILC public benefits policy attorney, for their helpful comments and suggestions.*

Despite these pressures, most states have chosen to continue providing services to low-income immigrants. Following the passage of the 1996 laws, nearly every state elected to provide benefits to immigrants wherever federal funding was available. Over half of the states spend their own money to cover at least some of the immigrants who are ineligible for federally funded services. A growing number of states or counties provide health coverage to children and/or pregnant women, regardless of their immigration status. But funding for some of the state programs is temporary and has been threatened or eroded in state budget battles. Some state and local governments have enacted measures attempting to further limit access to services for immigrant families, while others have chosen to invest in immigrant communities.[4]

During the past decade, immigrants have organized to an unprecedented degree, naturalized and voted in record numbers, and forged coalitions to advocate for restoring equal treatment. Immigrants and their allies succeeded in reversing some of the federal restrictions, demonstrating that the voices of newcomers are increasingly powerful and reflecting a recognition by Congress that the 1996 laws went too far.

Immigrants comprise one-fifth of the nation's low-wage workforce.[5] Although some immigrants do well economically, many others work long hours at low-wage jobs with no health insurance or other benefits. In fact, nearly half of immigrant workers earn less than twice the minimum wage,[6] and only 26% of immigrants have job-based health insurance.[7]

IMMIGRANT ELIGIBILITY RESTRICTIONS

Categories of Immigrants: "Qualified" and "Not Qualified"

The 1996 welfare law created two categories of immigrants for benefits eligibility purposes: "qualified" and "not qualified." Contrary to what these names suggest, the law excluded most people in *both* groups from eligibility for many benefits, with a few exceptions. The qualified immigrant category includes:

- Lawful permanent residents, or LPRs (persons with green cards).
- Refugees, persons granted asylum or withholding of deportation/removal, and conditional entrants.

- Persons granted parole by the Department of Homeland Security (DHS) for a period of at least one year.
- Cuban and Haitian entrants.
- Certain abused immigrants, their children, and/or their parents.[8]

All other immigrants, including many persons lawfully present in the United States, are considered not qualified.[9]

In 2000, Congress established a new category of non–U.S. citizens, *victims of trafficking*, who, while not listed among the qualified immigrants, are eligible for federal public benefits to the same extent as refugees.[10] In 2003, Congress clarified that "derivative beneficiaries" listed on trafficking victims' visa applications (spouses and children of adult trafficking victims; spouses, children, parents, and minor siblings of child victims) also may secure federal benefits.[11]

Federal Public Benefits Denied to Not-Qualified Immigrants

The law prohibits not-qualified immigrants from enrolling in most federal public benefit programs.[12] However, there are important exceptions to these bars. Federal public benefits include a variety of safety-net services paid for by federal funds.[13]

But the welfare law's definition does not specify which particular programs are covered by the term, leaving that clarification to each federal benefit-granting agency. In 1998, the U.S. Department of Health and Human Services (HHS) published a notice clarifying which of its programs falls under the definition.[14] The list of 31 HHS programs includes Medicaid, the State Children's Health Insurance Program (SCHIP),[15] Medicare, Temporary Assistance for Needy Families (TANF), Foster Care, Adoption Assistance, the Child Care and Development Fund, and the Low-Income Home Energy Assistance Program.

The HHS notice clarifies that not every benefit or service provided within these programs is a federal public benefit. For example, in some cases not all of a program's benefits or services are provided to an individual or household; they may extend, instead, to a community of people—as in the weatherization of an entire apartment building.[16]

The welfare law also attempted to force states to pass additional laws, after August 22, 1996, if they choose to provide state public benefits to not-qualified immigrants.[17] Such micromanagement of state affairs by the federal government is potentially unconstitutional under the Tenth Amendment.

Exceptions to the Restrictions

The law includes important exceptions for certain types of services. Regardless of their status, all immigrants remained eligible for emergency Medicaid, if they are otherwise eligible for their state's Medicaid program.[18] The law did not restrict access to public health programs providing immunizations and/or treatment of communicable disease symptoms (whether or not those symptoms are caused by such a disease). School breakfast and lunch programs remain open to all children regardless of immigration status, and every state has opted to provide access to the Special Supplemental Nutrition Program for Women, Infants and Children (WIC).[19] Also exempted from the restrictions are in-kind services necessary to protect life or safety, as long as no individual income qualification is required. In January 2001, the attorney general published a final order specifying the types of benefits that meet these criteria. The attorney general's list includes child and adult protective services; programs addressing weather emergencies and homelessness; shelters, soup kitchens, and meals-on-wheels; medical, public health, and mental health services necessary to protect life or safety; disability or substance abuse services necessary to protect life or safety; and programs to protect the life or safety of workers, children and youths, or community residents.[20]

Verification Rules

When a federal agency designates a program as a federal public benefit for which not-qualified immigrants are ineligible, the law requires the state or local agency to verify all applicants' immigration and citizenship status. But many federal agencies have not specified which of their programs provide federal public benefits. Until they do so, state and local agencies are under no obligation to verify immigration status. Also, under an important exception contained in the 1996 immigration law, nonprofit charitable organizations are not required to "determine, verify, or otherwise require proof of eligibility of any applicant for such benefits." This exception relates specifically to the immigrant benefits restrictions in the 1996 laws.[21]

Eligibility for Major Federal Benefit Programs

Congress restricted eligibility even for qualified immigrants by arbitrarily distinguishing between those who entered the United States before or "on or after" the date the law was enacted, August 22, 1996. The law barred most immigrants who entered the United States on or after that date from federal means-tested public benefits during the five years after they secure qualified immigrant status.[22] Federal agencies clarified that federal means-tested public benefits are Medicaid (except for emergency care), SCHIP, TANF, food stamps, and Supplemental Security Income (SSI).[23]

TANF, Medicaid, & SCHIP

States can receive federal funding for TANF, Medicaid, and SCHIP to serve qualified immigrants who have completed the federal five-year bar.[24] "Humanitarian immigrants"—refugees, persons granted asylum or withholding of deportation/removal, Cuban/Haitian entrants, Amerasian immigrants, and victims of trafficking—are exempt from the five-year bar, as are "qualified" immigrant veterans, active duty military, and their spouses and children.

Over half of the states use state funds to provide TANF, Medicaid, and/or SCHIP to some or all of the immigrants who are subject to the five-year bar on federally funded services, or to a broader group of immigrants.[25] Some of these programs have been threatened by state budget shortfalls.

Food Stamps

Although the 1996 law severely restricted immigrant eligibility for food stamps, subsequent legislation restored access for many of these immigrants. Qualified immigrant children, the humanitarian immigrant and veterans groups described above, lawful permanent residents with 40 quarters of work history, certain Native Americans, lawfully residing Hmong and Laotian tribe members, and immigrants receiving related assistance[26] are now eligible regardless of their date of entry into the United States. Qualified immigrant seniors who were born before August 22, 1931, may be eligible if they were lawfully residing in the United States on August 22, 1996. Other qualified immigrant adults, however, must wait until they have been in qualified status for five years before they can secure critical nutrition assistance.

Eight states provide state-funded food stamps to some or all of the immigrants who were rendered ineligible for the federal program.[27]

Supplemental Security Income

Congress imposed its most harsh restrictions on immigrant seniors and immigrants with disabilities who seek assistance under the SSI program.[28] Although advocacy efforts in the two years following the welfare law's passage achieved a partial restoration of these benefits, significant gaps in eligibility remained. SSI, for example, continues to exclude not-qualified immigrants who were not already receiving the benefits, as well as most qualified immigrants who entered the country after the welfare law passed[29] and seniors without disabilities who were in the United States before that date. "Humanitarian" immigrants (refugees, persons granted asylum or withholding of deportation/removal, Amerasian immigrants, or Cuban and Haitian entrants) can receive SSI, but only during the first seven years after having obtained the relevant status.

A few states provide cash assistance to seniors and persons with disabilities who were rendered ineligible for SSI; some others provide much smaller general assistance grants to these immigrants.[30]

Sponsored Immigrants

Under the 1996 welfare and immigration laws, family members and some employers eligible to file a petition to help a person immigrate must become financial sponsors of the immigrant by signing a contract with the government (an affidavit of support). Under the enforceable affidavit (Form I-864), the sponsor promises to support the immigrant and to repay certain benefits that the immigrant may use.

Congress imposed additional eligibility restrictions on immigrants whose sponsors sign an enforceable affidavit of support. When an agency is determining a lawful permanent resident's financial eligibility for a program, in some cases the law requires the agency to deem the income of the immigrant's sponsor or the sponsor's spouse as available to the immigrant. The sponsor's income and resources are added to the immigrant's, which often disqualifies the immigrant as over-income for the program. Previously, fewer programs imposed deeming, and when they did, it was applied for only three years. By contrast, the 1996 laws impose deeming rules until the immigrant becomes a citizen or secures credit for approximately 10 years of work history in the United States,[31] in the TANF, food stamps, SSI, nonemergency Medicaid, and SCHIP programs.[32] Domestic violence survivors and immigrants who would go hungry or homeless without assistance can get benefits without deeming for at least 12 months (the indigence exemption).[33] The U.S. Department of Agriculture (USDA) issued helpful guidance on the indigence exemption and other deeming and liability issues, including exceptions from liability for sponsors who are also receiving food stamps.[34] HHS also issued guidance on deeming in the TANF program, for immigrants with enforceable affidavits of support who reach the end of the five-year ban and become potentially eligible for the federal program.[35]

OVERVIEW OF BARRIERS THAT IMPEDE ACCESS TO BENEFITS FOR IMMIGRANTS

Confusion about Eligibility

Confusion about eligibility rules pervades benefit agencies and immigrant communities. The confusion stems from the complex interaction of the immigration and welfare laws, differences in eligibility criteria for various state and federal programs, and a lack of adequate training on the rules as clarified by federal agencies. Consequently, many eligible immigrants have assumed that they should not seek services, and eligibility workers mistakenly have turned away eligible immigrants.

Public Charge

The misapplication of the public charge ground of inadmissibility has contributed significantly to the chilling effect on immigrants' access to services. The "public charge" provision in the immigration laws allows officials to deny applications for permanent residence if the authorities determine that the immigrant seeking permanent residence is "likely to become a public charge." In deciding whether an immigrant is likely to become a public charge, immigration or consular officials look at the "totality of the circumstances," including an immigrant's health, age, income, education and skills, and affidavits of support. The law on public charge did not change in 1996, and the use of programs such as Medicaid or food stamps had never weighed heavily in public charge determinations. Yet shortly after enactment of the welfare law, immigration officials and judges began to prevent immigrants from reentering the United States or obtaining LPR status, unlawfully demanding that they repay benefits such as Medicaid, and denying green cards until the applicants withdrew from programs such as WIC.[36]

Immigrants' rights advocates, health care providers, and state and local governments organized to persuade federal agencies to clarify the limits of the laws. In May 1999, the Immigration and Naturalization Service (INS) issued guidance and a proposed regulation on the public charge doctrine.[37] The guidance clarifies that receipt of health care and other noncash benefits will not jeopardize the immigration status of recipients or their family members by putting them at risk of being considered a public charge.[38] Immigrants' rights advocates have been monitoring the implementation of this guidance and its effect on immigrants' willingness to seek services. Several years after the issuance of this guidance, widespread confusion and concern about the public charge rules remain.

Affidavit of Support

The 1996 laws also enacted rules that make it more difficult to immigrate to the United States to reunite with family members. Effective December 19, 1997, relatives (and some employers) must meet strict income requirements and must sign a long-term contract—an affidavit of support—promising to maintain the immigrant at 125% of the federal poverty level and to repay any means-tested public benefits the immigrant may receive.[39] Although the federal benefits for which sponsors may be liable have been named (TANF, SSI, food stamps, nonemergency Medicaid, and SCHIP), few immigrants with enforceable affidavits of support have been eligible for these federal services. Federal agencies have issued little guidance on these provisions. Recently issued regulations on the affidavits of support make clear that states are not obligated to pursue sponsors and that states cannot collect reimbursement for services used prior to public notification that they are considered means-tested public benefits for which sponsors will be liable.[40]

Most states have not designated the programs that would give rise to sponsor liability, and the National Immigration Law Center (NILC) is aware of only one state that has attempted to pursue reimbursement.

However, the specter of sponsor liability already has deterred eligible immigrants from applying for benefits, based on concerns about exposing their sponsors to government collection efforts.

Language Policies

Many immigrants face significant linguistic and cultural barriers to obtaining benefits. Almost 20% of the U.S. population (5 years of age and older) speak a language other than English at home.[41] Although 97% of long-term immigrants to the United States eventually learn to speak English well, many are in the process of learning the language.[42] Almost 8% of the people living in the United States speak English less than very well.[43] These limited-English proficient (LEP) residents cannot effectively apply for benefits or meaningfully communicate with a health care provider without language assistance.

Title VI of the Civil Rights Act of 1964 prohibits recipients of federal funding from discriminating on the basis of national origin, an obligation that includes taking reasonable steps to provide language assistance to LEP persons. Recipients' compliance with this requirement has been limited. In August 2000, the White House issued an executive order directing federal agencies, by December 11, 2000, to submit to the U.S. Dept. of Justice (DOJ) plans to improve language access, and to publish guidance for programs receiving federal financial assistance regarding compliance with the Title VI requirement to take "reasonable steps" to assure "meaningful access" to federally funded services.[44] DOJ published guidance emphasizing that agencies, programs, and services receiving federal funds must ensure that persons with limited English proficiency can participate effectively and explaining that failure to do so may constitute national origin discrimination prohibited by Title VI.[45] The DOJ published final guidance to its recipients on June 18, 2002.[46] Several agencies, including HHS, developed and published guidance for public comment, but many remain delinquent.

Advocates will continue to monitor agencies' development of guidance, which is posted on the federal interagency language access Web site, www.lep.gov, as it is issued. They are encouraging states to take advantage of federal funds available for the reimbursement of language assistance services provided through Medicaid and SCHIP. And they are urging states to take language and cultural needs into account in providing benefits and implementing welfare-to-work and job-training programs.

Verification and Reporting

Rules that require benefit agencies to verify immigration and citizenship status[47] have been misinterpreted by some agencies as allowing benefit personnel to act as immigration enforcers. Because some federal agencies still have not determined which of their programs provide federal public benefits that require verification of immigration status, some institutions are confused about their duty to screen applicants. As a condition of eligibility, some agencies demand immigration documents or Social Security numbers (SSNs) even when applicants are not legally required to submit such information. Lack of federal clarification in the reporting and verification areas led some state and local agencies to ask unnecessary questions on application forms and even to issue unnecessary warnings to immigrants in notices on the walls of agency waiting rooms. And increased scrutiny of immigrant communities in the name of national security, as well as publicity generated by proposals that would require hospitals to inquire about immigration status, raised additional privacy concerns for immigrant families, who may avoid applying for services.[48]

Verification

In 1997, DOJ issued an interim guidance for federal benefit providers to use in verifying immigration status until DOJ issues final regulations governing verification.[49] The guidance, which remains in effect, directs providers that benefit agencies already using DOJ's computerized Systematic Alien Verification for Entitlements (SAVE) program continue to do so. It recommends that agencies make financial and other eligibility decisions before asking the applicant for information about his or her immigration status. The guidance also directs agencies to seek information only about the person applying for benefits and not about his or her family members.

Questions on Application Forms

In September 2000, HHS and USDA issued guidance recommending that states delete from benefits application forms questions that are unnecessary and may chill participation by immigrant families.[50] The guidance confirms that only the immigration status of the applicant for benefits is relevant. It encourages states to allow family or household members who are not seeking benefits to be designated as nonapplicants early in the application process. Similarly, under Medicaid, TANF, and the Food Stamp Program, only the applicant must provide an SSN. SSNs are not required for persons seeking only emergency Medicaid. In June 2001, HHS indicated that states providing SCHIP through separate programs (rather than through Medicaid expansions) are authorized, but not obligated, to require SSNs on their SCHIP applications.[51]

Reporting to DHS

Another source of fear in immigrant communities is the occasional misapplication of a 1996 reporting provision that is in fact quite narrow in scope.[52] The reporting requirement applies to only three programs—SSI, public housing, and TANF—and requires the administering agency to report to the INS (now the DHS) only persons whom the agency *knows* are not lawfully present in the United States.[53]

In September 2000, federal agencies issued a joint guidance outlining the limited circumstances under which the reporting requirement may be triggered.[54] The guidance clarifies that only persons who are actually seeking benefits (not relatives or household members applying on their behalf) are subject to the reporting requirement. Agencies are not required to report such applicants unless there has been a formal determination, subject to administrative review, on a claim for SSI, public housing, or TANF. The conclusion that the person is unlawfully present also must be supported by a determination by the immigration authorities, "such as a Final Order of Deportation."[55] Findings that do not meet these criteria (e.g., a DHS response to a SAVE computer inquiry indicating an immigrant's status,[56] an oral or written admission by applicants, or suspicions of agency workers) are insufficient to trigger the reporting requirement. Finally, the guidance stresses that agencies are not required to make determinations about immigration status that are not necessary to determine eligibility for benefits. Similarly, agencies are not required to submit reports to DHS unless they have knowledge that meets the above requirements. USDA has confirmed that this knowledge standard is consistent with a preexisting reporting requirement in the Food Stamp Program.[57]

DEVELOPING A STRATEGY FOR CHANGE

The post-1996 restorations of immigrant benefits eligibility primarily affected individuals who were present in the United States on

August 22, 1996. The impact of the restorations has diminished as new entrants arrive without access to services, and the exclusionary legacy of the 1996 laws remains.

A strategy for change would challenge the United States to return to the traditional principle of equal treatment for citizens and lawfully present immigrants, a principle that generally prevailed in public benefits programs before August 22, 1996.[58] A multiyear approach could also seek opportunities to advance equal access to critical services for all members of our communities, regardless of their immigration status—for example, by ensuring that all persons have access to preventive health services. Finally, the extent to which immigrants are served by public benefit programs depends in large part on the general effectiveness of such programs, signaling the need for immigrants to work in concert with broader networks of low-income families and their allies struggling to preserve and strengthen the safety net for all.

NOTES

1. Personal Responsibility and Work Opportunity Reconciliation Act of 1996 (hereinafter "welfare law"), Pub. L. No. 104–193, 110 Stat. 2105 (August 22, 1996); and Illegal Immigration Reform and Immigrant Responsibility Act of 1996 (hereinafter "IIRIRA"), enacted as Division C of the Defense Department Appropriations Act, 1997, Pub. L. No. 104–208, 110 Stat. 3008 (September 30, 1996).
2. A state's denial of benefits to lawfully present immigrants may be unconstitutional, even if apparently authorized by the 1996 welfare law. See *Aliessa v. Novello,* 96 N.Y.2d 418 (N.Y. Ct. App. June 5, 2001), which rules that New York law denying state-funded medical services to a subgroup of immigrants violates the Equal Protection Clause of the U.S. and New York State Constitutions and Article 17 of the New York State Constitution. See also *Ehrlich v. Perez,* 908 A.2d 1220 (MD. Ct. App, October 12, 2006), applying strict scrutiny review to governor's budget cuts to state medical services for qualified immigrants. But see *Soskin v. Reinertson,* 353 F.3d 1242 (10th Cir. 2004), upholding Colorado's law terminating Medicaid to immigrants whose benefits are not mandated by federal law, but finding that the state failed to provide pretermination hearings to some recipients, as required by the Medicaid Act.
3. During the 1990s, for example, the immigrant population in "new immigrant" states grew twice as quickly (61% vs. 31%) as the immigrant population in the six states that receive the greatest numbers of immigrants. Michael Fix, Wendy Zimmermann, and Jeffrey Passell, *The Integration of Immigrant Families in the United States* (Washington, DC: Urban Institute, July 2001). See also *A Description of the Immigrant Population* (Washington, DC: Congressional Budget Office, Nov. 2004).
4. See *State and Local Policies on Immigrant Access to Services: Promoting Integration or Isolation?* (Los Angeles: National Immigration Law Center, May 2007); *Pro-immigrant Measures Available to State or Local Government: A Quick Menu of*

AffirmativeIdeas (Los Angeles: National Immigration Law Center, September 2007). The National Immigration Law Center will hereafter be referred to as NILC.

5. Randy Capps and Michael Fix, *Tabulations of Current Population Survey* (Washington, DC: Urban Institute, November 2001).
6. Randy Capps, Michael Fix, et. al., *A Profile of the Low-Wage Immigrant Workforce* (Washington, DC: Urban Institute, November 2003).
7. Leighton Ku and Shannon Blaney, *Health Coverage for Legal Immigrant Children: New Census Data Highlight Importance of Restoring Medicaid and SCHIP Coverage* (Washington, DC: Center on Budget and Policy Priorities, October 2000).
8. To fall within the battered spouse or child category, the immigrant must have an approved visa petition filed by a spouse or parent, a self-petition under the Violence Against Women Act (VAWA) that sets forth a prima facie case for relief, or an application for cancellation of removal under the VAWA. The spouse or child must have been battered or subjected to extreme cruelty in the United States by a family member with whom the immigrant resided, or the immigrant's parent or child must have been subjected to such treatment. The immigrant must demonstrate a "substantial connection" between the domestic violence and the need for the benefit being sought. And the battered immigrant, parent, or child must have moved out of the household of the abuser. Benefit agencies are encouraged to process these applications preliminarily, to inform immigrants of the resources that might become available to them should they decide to move.
9. Before 1996, some of these immigrants were served by benefit programs under an eligibility category called "permanently residing in the U.S. under color of law" (PRUCOL). PRUCOL is not an immigration status, but a benefit eligibility category that has been interpreted differently depending on the benefit program and the region. Generally, it means that DHS is aware of a person's presence in the United States but has no plans to deport or remove him or her from the country. Some states continue to provide services to these immigrants using state or local funds.
10. The Victims of Trafficking and Violence Protection Act of 2000, Pub. L. No. 106–386 § 107 (October 28, 2000). Federal agencies are required to provide benefits and services to individuals who have been subjected to a "severe form of trafficking in persons," without regard to their immigration status. To receive these benefits, the victim must be either under 18 years of age or certified by the U.S. Department of Health and Human Services (HHS) as willing to assist in the investigation and prosecution of severe forms of trafficking in persons. In the certification, HHS confirms that the person either (a) has made a bona fide application for a T visa that has not been denied, or (b) is a person whose continued presence in the United States is being ensured by the attorney general in order to prosecute traffickers in persons.
11. Trafficking Victims Protection Reauthorization Act of 2003, Pub. L. No. 108–193, § 4(a)(2)(December 19, 2003).
12. Welfare law § 401 (8 U.S.C. § 1611).
13. "Federal public benefit" is described in the 1996 federal welfare law as (a) any grant, contract, loan, professional license, or commercial license provided by an agency of the United States or by appropriated funds of the United States, and (b) any retirement, welfare, health, disability, public or assisted housing, postsecondary education, food assistance, unemployment, benefit, or any other similar benefit for which payments or assistance are provided to an individual, household, or family

eligibility unit by an agency of the United States or appropriated funds of the United States.

14. HHS, Personal Responsibility and Work Opportunity Reconciliation Act of 1996 (PRWORA), "Interpretation of 'Federal Public Benefit,'" 63 FR 41658–61 (August 4, 1998).
15. SCHIP (Title XXI of the Social Security Act) was created in § 4901 *et seq.* of the Balanced Budget Act of 1997 (hereinafter "BBA"), Pub. L. No. 105–33, 111 Stat. 552 (August 5, 1997).
16. HHS, Division of Energy Assistance, Office of Community Services, Memorandum from Janet M. Fox, Director, to Low Income Home Energy Assistance Program (LIHEAP) Grantees and Other Interested Parties, re Revision-Guidance on the Interpretation of "Federal Public Benefits" Under the Welfare Reform Law (June 15, 1999).
17. Welfare law § 411 (8 U.S.C. § 1621).
18. Welfare law § 401(b)(1)(A) (8 U.S.C. § 1611(b)(1)(A)).
19. Welfare law § 742 (8 U.S.C. § 1615).
20. U.S. Dept. of Justice (DOJ), "Final Specification of Community Programs Necessary for Protection of Life or Safety under Welfare Reform Legislation," A.G. Order No. 2353–2001, published in 66 FR 3613–16 (January 16, 2001).
21. IIRIRA § 508 (8 U.S.C. § 1642(d)).
22. Welfare law § 403 (8 U.S.C. § 1613).
23. HHS, Personal Responsibility and Work Opportunity Reconciliation Act of 1996 (PRWORA), "Interpretation of 'Federal Means-Tested Public Benefit,'" 62 FR 45256 (August 26, 1997); U.S. Dept. of Agriculture (USDA), "Federal Means-Tested Public Benefits," 63 FR 36653 (July 7, 1998). The SCHIP program, created after the passage of the 1996 welfare law, was later designated as a federal means-tested public benefit program. See Health Care Financing Administration, "The Administration's Response to Questions about the State Child Health Insurance Program," Question 19(a) (September 11, 1997).
24. States were also given an option to provide or deny federal TANF and Medicaid to most qualified immigrants who were in the United States before August 22, 1996, and to those who enter the United States on or after that date, once they have completed the federal five-year ban. Welfare law § 402 (8 U.S.C. § 1612). Only one state, Wyoming, denies Medicaid to immigrants who were in the country when the welfare law passed. Colorado's proposed termination of Medicaid to these immigrants was reversed by the state legislature in 2005 and never took effect. In addition to Wyoming, six states (Alabama, Mississippi, North Dakota, Ohio, Texas, and Virginia) do not provide Medicaid to all qualified immigrants who complete the federal five-year ban. Five states (Indiana, Mississippi, South Carolina, Texas, and Wyoming) fail to provide TANF to all qualified immigrants who complete the federal five-year ban.
25. See *Guide to Immigrant Eligibility for Federal Programs,* 4th ed. (Los Angeles: National Immigrant Law Center, 2002), and updated tables at www.nilc.org/pubs/Guide_update.htm. See also Shawn Fremstad and Laura Cox, *Covering New Americans: A Review of Federal and State Policies Related to Immigrants' Eligibility and Access to Publicly Funded Health Insurance* (Washington, DC: Kaiser Commission

on Medicaid and the Uninsured, November, 2004). Retrieved from www.kff.org/medicaid/7214.cfm.

26. For this purpose, disability-related programs include: SSI, Social Security disability, state disability or retirement pension, railroad retirement disability, veteran's disability, disability-based Medicaid, and disability-related General Assistance, if the disability determination uses criteria as stringent as those used for SSI.
27. See NILC's updated tables on state-funded services, at www.nilc.org/pubs/Guide_update.htm.
28. Welfare law § 402(a) (8 U.S.C. § 1612(a)).
29. Most new entrants cannot receive SSI until they become citizens or secure credit for 40 quarters of work history (including work performed by a spouse during marriage, persons "holding out to the community" as spouses, and by parents before the immigrant was 18 years old).
30. See *Guide to Immigrant Eligibility for Federal Programs,* 4th ed. (Los Angeles: NILC, 2002), and updated tables at www.nilc.org/pubs/Guide_update.htm.
31. That is, until the immigrant has credit for 40 quarters of work history.
32. Welfare law § 421 (8 U.S.C. § 1631).
33. IIRIRA § 552 (8 U.S.C. § 1631(e) and (f)). The domestic violence exemption can be extended for a longer period if the abuse has been recognized by U.S. Citizenship and Immigration Services (USCIS), a court, or an administrative law judge. The indigence exemption may be renewed for additional 12-month periods.
34. 7 C.F.R. § 274.3(c); USDA, "Non-Citizen Requirements in the Food Stamp Program" (January 2003), www.fns.usda.gov/fsp/rules/Legislation/pdfs/Non_Citizen_Guidance.pdf. See also USDA's Proposed Rule, "Food Stamp Program: Eligibility and Certification Provisions of the Farm Security and Rural Investment Act of 2002," 69 FR 20723, 20758–9 (April 16, 2004).
35. HHS, "Deeming of Sponsor's Income and Resources to a Non-Citizen," TANF-ACF-PI-2003–03 (April 17, 2003), www.acf.hhs.gov/programs/ofa/pi2003–3.htm.
36. Claudia Schlosberg and Dinah Wiley, *The Impact of INS Public Charge Determinations on Immigrant Access to Health Care* (Washington, DC: National Health Law Program and NILC, May 22, 1998).
37. DOJ, "Field Guidance on Deportability and Inadmissibility on Public Charge Grounds," 64 FR 28689–93 (May 26, 1999); see also DOJ, "Inadmissibility and Deportability on Public Charge Grounds," 64 FR 28676–88 (May 26, 1999); U.S. Dept. of State, INA 212(A)(4) Public Charge: Policy Guidance, 9 FAM 40.41.
38. The use of all health care programs, except for long-term institutionalization (e.g., Medicaid payment for nursing home care), was declared to be irrelevant to public charge determinations. Programs providing cash assistance for income maintenance purposes are the only other programs that are relevant in the public charge determination. The determination is based on the "totality of a person's circumstances" and therefore even the past use of cash assistance can be weighed against other favorable factors, such as a person's current income or skills or the contract signed by a sponsor promising to support the intending immigrant.
39. Welfare law § 423, amended by IIRIRA § 551 (8 U.S.C. § 1183a).
40. U.S. Department of Homeland Security, "Affidavits of Support on Behalf of Immigrants," 71 FR 35732, 35742–43 (June 21, 2006).

41. American Community Survey table, "Percent of People 5 Years and Over Who Speak a Language Other Than English at Home" (2006).
42. James P. Smith and Barry Edmonston (Eds.), "The New Americans," p. 377 (Washington, DC: National Research Council, 1997).
43. Id.
44. Executive Order No. 13166, "Improving Access to Services for Persons with Limited English Proficiency," 65 FR 50121 (August 16, 2000).
45. DOJ, Civil Rights Division, "Enforcement of Title VI of the Civil Rights Act of 1964—National Origin Discrimination Against Persons with Limited English Proficiency; Policy Guidance," 65 FR 50123 (August 16, 2000).
46. "Guidance to Federal Financial Assistance Recipients Regarding Title VI Prohibition against National Origin Discrimination Affecting Limited English Proficient Persons," 67 FR 41455 (June 18, 2002).
47. Welfare law § 432, amended by IIRIRA § 504 (8 U.S.C. § 1642). The Deficit Reduction Act of 2005's citizenship verification requirement, which applies only to U.S. citizens, did not change the verification rules for immigrants. However, the provision has generated a great deal of confusion in immigrant communities and among the public. Health care advocates, providers, and state agencies are working to limit the harm to Medicaid applicants and recipients who are citizens, as well as the chilling effect for immigrants caused by states' implementation of the new law. Yet the requirement has prevented tens of thousands of U.S. citizen children from securing Medicaid. Donna Cohen Ross, "New Medicaid Citizenship Documentation Requirement Is Taking a Toll: States Report Enrollment Is Down and Administrative Costs Are Up" (Center on Budget and Policy Priorities, March 13, 2007). Proposals to reduce the burden imposed by these documentation requirements are pending in Congress. However, Congress also has proposed to apply the strict documentation requirement to the State Children's Health Insurance Program. See, for example, Section 211 of The Children's Health Insurance Program Reauthorization Act (CHIPRA) (H.R. 976) (vetoed by the president).
48. Health care providers and advocates worked to minimize the harm stemming from Section 1011 of the Medicare Prescription Drug, Modernization and Improvement Act. Section 1011 provides limited reimbursement to hospitals and health providers for emergency services to certain uninsured immigrants, including undocumented immigrants. Patients seeking emergency services are *not* required to provide immigration documents or to disclose information about their immigration status in order to receive treatment or to be claimed for section 1011 reimbursement. However, advocates and providers were concerned that the forms and procedures recommended by the Centers for Medicare and Medicaid Services (CMS) would lead to intrusive or intimidating questions, which could deter immigrants and their family members from seeking care.
49. DOJ, "Interim Guidance on Verification of Citizenship, Qualified Alien Status and Eligibility Under Title IV of the Personal Responsibility and Work Opportunity Reconciliation Act of 1996," 62 FR 61344–416 (Nov. 17, 1997). In August 1998, the agency issued proposed regulations that draw heavily on the interim guidance and the Systematic Alien Verification for Entitlements (SAVE) program. See DOJ, "Verification of Eligibility for Public Benefits," 63 FR 41662–86 (August 4, 1998). Final regulations have not yet been issued. Once the regulations become final, states

will have two years to implement a conforming system for the federal programs they administer.

50. Letter and accompanying materials from HHS and USDA to State Health and Welfare Officials: "Policy Guidance Regarding Inquiries into Citizenship, Immigration Status and Social Security Numbers in State Applications for Medicaid, State Children's Health Insurance Program (SCHIP), Temporary Assistance for Needy Families (TANF), and Food Stamp Benefits" (September 21, 2000).
51. HHS, Health Care Financing Administration, Interim Final Rule, "Revisions to the Regulations Implementing the State Children's Health Insurance Program," 66 FR 33810, 33823 (June 25, 2001).
52. Welfare law § 404, amended by BBA §§ 5564 and 5581(a) (42 U.S.C. §§ 608(g), 611a, 1383(e), 1437y)).
53. Id. See also H.R. Rep. 104–725, 104th Cong. 2d Sess. 382 (July 30, 1996). In other contexts, the knowledge requirement has been interpreted to apply only where an agency discovers that a person is "under an order of deportation." See *Memorandum of Legal Services Corporation General Counsel to Legal Services Corporation Project Directors* (December 5, 1979) (knowledge of unlawful presence includes only instances involving an "immigrant against whom a final order of deportation is outstanding").
54. Social Security Administration, HHS, U.S. Dept. of Labor, U.S. Dept. of Housing and Urban Development, and DOJ—Immigration and Naturalization Service, "Responsibility of Certain Entities to Notify the Immigration and Naturalization Service of Any Alien Who the Entity 'Knows' Is Not Lawfully Present in the United States," 65 FR 58301 (Sept. 28, 2000).
55. Id.
56. SAVE, or Systematic Alien Verification for Entitlements, is the DHS process currently used to verify eligibility for several major benefit programs. See 42 U.S.C. § 1320b-7. DHS verifies an applicant's immigration status through a computer database and/or through a manual search of its records. This information is used only to verify eligibility for benefits and cannot be used to initiate deportation or removal proceedings (with exceptions for criminal violations). See the Immigration Reform and Control Act of 1986, 99 Pub. L. 603, § 121 (November 6, 1986); DOJ, "Verification of Eligibility for Public Benefits," 63 FR 41662, 41672, and 41684 (August 4, 1998).
57. USDA, "Food Stamp Program: Noncitizen Eligibility, and Certification Provisions of Public Law 104–193, as Amended by Public Laws 104–208, 105–33 and 105–185," 65 FR 70166 (November 21, 2000).
58. See Ron Haskins, Mark Greenberg, and Shawn Fremstad, *Federal Policy for Immigrant Children: Room for Common Ground?* (Washington, DC: Brookings Institution Press, Summer 2004).

14

Social Workers and Immigrant Advocacy

JASMEET KAUR SIDHU

America is a nation of immigrants, but which immigrants do we accept? Which do we resent? Which do we fear? To which ones are we willing to extend basic civil rights and social services? These are the questions we face as a nation struggling with its demographic identity. What role will social workers play in this debate?

This chapter explores advocacy tools for the social worker community, whether acting as individuals, volunteers, and/or members of social service organizations. Equipped with the skills and guidelines for effective advocacy, social workers can provide a lasting voice for their underrepresented clients, and the burgeoning immigrant community at large.

Social workers often advocate on behalf of their clients through direct service representation. In this chapter, we will refer to such activities as "*micro* advocacy." However, when individuals or organizations engage in strategies directed not at individual clients, but rather at *systems,* we will call this "*macro* advocacy." Macro advocacy may attempt to change policies in any number of ways: for example, the way a hospital treats new patients; the policies of a welfare agency; the way a public school offers services to English language learners; the way landlords treat their nonresident tenants, or the way employers treat undocumented employees.

This chapter will begin by discussing the importance of advocacy work to social workers engaged with immigrant clients. It will then discuss individual and micro advocacy strategies. Finally, it will discuss macro advocacy strategies, and the laws that impact them.

THE IMPORTANCE OF IMMIGRANT ADVOCACY

> *Never doubt that a group of thoughtful committed citizens can change the world. Indeed it's the only thing that ever has.*
>
> —Margaret Mead

Margaret Mead's quotation is an important reminder that thoughtful, committed citizens can help make their communities better, more just, and more equitable. Social workers, in particular, have consistently been the voice of the unheard, the powerless, the poor, and those most in need of assistance. Since the very beginning of the profession, when Jane Addams founded Hull House for needy clients (including immigrants) in Chicago, social workers have had a long history of advocating for vulnerable populations.

In today's changing social and political climate, immigrants are one of the fastest-growing groups who need a voice. In 2007 alone, there were approximately 182 immigration-related laws passed in 43 states (Gillam, 2007).[1] Many of these state laws are decidedly anti-immigrant. For example, a law was recently implemented in Oklahoma making it illegal to hire, transport, or house an illegal immigrant and authorizing local police in Oklahoma to assist federal immigration authorities in enforcing U.S. immigration law. The law also denies state services to undocumented aliens and imposes penalties on employers who hire them (Gillam, 2007).

At the local level, cities have also been quick to pass immigrant-related ordinances in the wake of a failed federal solution. In one such case, Hazelton, Pennsylvania's City Council passed the Illegal Immigration Relief Act, which suspends the license of any business that "employs, retains, aids, or abets" illegal immigrants; the act imposes a fine of $1,000 per day on any landlord renting property to an illegal immigrant; and declares that all official city business be written in English only. People wishing to rent apartments in Hazleton will be required to apply for city residency licenses, which will only be granted after establishing citizenship (Powell & Garcia, 2006).

At the opposite end of the spectrum, there are a handful of towns like New Haven, Connecticut, that are *reaching out* to the immigrant community and offering perks, such as an ID card. Besides serving as valid identification for bank services and law enforcement, the card can be used at municipal locations such as libraries, beaches, and parks—and even as a debit card for city parking meters and local shops. The goal of this type of policy is to integrate undocumented immigrants into the community, protect them from crime that may result from a lack of documentation, and encourage them to be more willing to report crimes to police (Matos, 2007; McKinley, 2007; and Medina, 2007).

When social workers assist immigrants in finding fair housing, health care, education, benefits, and wages equal to American-born citizens, they are not only doing their job, but they are also advocating for the rights of countless immigrant communities struggling to become a part of the American fabric.

The National Association of Social Workers has recognized immigrants' needs, as illustrated in a recent editorial (2008) on Immigrant Rights in *Social Work* and in the publication of an Immigrant Policy Tool Kit (2007) that contains materials related to immigrant policy issues across the United States. The NASW Board of Directors (2008) also recently voted to add to their Code of Ethics that social workers should work to eliminate discrimination against any person or group based on their "immigration status."

Such efforts underscore the point that social workers must come together to advocate on micro and macro levels and affect policy change that will not only help their clients but the community at large. We will now explore how social workers can assist their clients on a micro level.

INDIVIDUAL ADVOCACY FOR IMMIGRANT CLIENTS

There are many ways in which social workers can act in their individual capacities to assist the immigrant communities with which they work.

Educate Immigrant Clients About Their Rights

In the areas of housing, social services, health care, labor, among others, there are ongoing changes and new procedures that would be confusing even to native-born English speakers. Hopefully the information in this volume has made the reader more aware of immigrant rights and procedures. Simply being familiar with policies and helpful resources and passing along information to clients can be extremely helpful and effective.

Educate Others About Immigration Issues

With the growing number of immigrants in America, immigrants' rights issues and the policies and reform agendas tied to those rights will remain part of the national debate for years to come. As of this writing, immigration ranks in the top 10 issues of importance to voters in the 2008 election. But beyond the national agenda, immigrants have represented and will continue to represent a large percentage of the population served by social workers in the United States. It is imperative that social work students, professionals, and volunteers remain educated on the issues affecting their communities.

The best way to remain educated and active is through organizing and participating in discussions, forums, debates, and panels on immigrants' rights issues. Students can volunteer with local nonprofit organizations advocating on behalf of immigrants, and can perhaps organize an educational session at their school. Practicing social workers can invite local agencies and community members to train their chapters on everything from new ordinances or policies affecting local immigrants to react to events like raids, hate crimes, and civil rights violations. Getting to know the immigrant advocacy groups operating in your community is an important way to get involved and effect systematic change.

Provide Input on Legislation and Policy

As an individual, you can provide input by commenting on regulations or providing testimony on the effects of various policies and procedures on the communities you serve. Often, the most crucial moment for individuals and groups to make a difference in policy is when regulations are being formulated. Social workers should, therefore, understand the legislation and policies of local agencies and administrative bodies and use their input into those documents as another way to advocate for immigrants' rights.

While individual advocacy efforts are valuable and important, macro advocacy is an important tool for any successful organization seeking to effect change (Grant & Crutchfield, 2007), but especially for those organizations whose membership includes social workers. The remainder of this chapter will show how macro advocacy, undertaken at the organizational level, can be a powerful tool for change.

MACRO ADVOCACY FOR SOCIAL CHANGE

Organizations that focus on immigrants' rights have the structure, resources, and manpower to make significant changes in their communities. In just a few recent examples:

- The New York Civic Participation Project (NYCPP) guided the passing of a new municipal law in 2007 requiring that New York City's welfare, food stamps, and Medicaid offices provide translation and interpretation services to those not proficient in English.
- The Tennessee Immigrant and Refugee Rights Coalition (TIRRC) helped defeat 19 bills in the Tennessee state legislature in 2006 and 40 bills in 2007 that would have negatively impacted thousands of immigrant families and caused unintended harm to all Tennesseans.
- The National Council of La Raza's (NCLR)'s efforts helped to make comprehensive immigration reform a topic at the forefront of the federal legislative agenda in 2007.

These are just a few examples of how organizations can help shape governmental policy and inspire individuals to become advocates for their cause (Grant & Crutchfield, 2007). Advocacy can involve any activity through which an organization and its members support, oppose, or educate others regarding an issue tied to their mission.

CREATING AN EFFECTIVE ADVOCACY STRATEGY

When advocating on behalf of immigrants' rights, what are the necessary steps in creating an effective game plan? How do we take great ideas and turn them into successful advocacy strategies?

The first step in creating a successful strategy is understanding the basics of advocacy. Unlike other areas of work, like direct services, advocacy work is not easily measured and can often take months or many years to see resolution. Advocacy requires:

- *Systems Knowledge*—having a sense of the inner workings of the local government, administrative agencies, legislature, and courts.

- *Creative Evaluation of Influence*—being able to identify strengths and connections of your friends, colleagues, and coalition members, and assign value to those connections; and knowing how to tell your story.
- *Patience*—comprehending that long-term systematic change takes time.
- *Flexibility*—being able to change strategies when one approach is not working.
- *Bravery*—the ability to take risks and accept failures.

By approaching advocacy from the right frame of mind, it is easier to develop a game plan. Advocates should ask themselves four key questions (adapted from Schultz, 2003): (a) *What do you want?* (b) *Who can provide it?* (c) *To whom will they listen?* (d) *What do they need to hear?*

What Do You Want?

What problem do you want to solve? Is a complete solution feasible in a reasonable amount of time? If not, are there smaller steps that move in the right direction?

Before embarking on the planning stage of any advocacy campaign, it is important to identify meaningful yet realistic goals. For example, a meaningful goal might be to get all currently undocumented immigrants in America valid citizenship within the next three months. But, how realistic is that? Would it even be possible for our current infrastructure to support that goal? Obviously not. On the other hand, another goal might be to get all currently undocumented immigrants valid citizenship within the next 30 years. This goal is clearly more realistic—yet how meaningful would it be to the immigrant communities who need support now?

A better goal—one which is both meaningful *and* realistic—might be to advocate for passage of comprehensive immigration reform at the federal level in the next two years, to prevent state and local governments from creating their own limited solutions to larger problems.

As another example, a few years ago, several public libraries in low-income immigrant communities in Brooklyn faced potential closure because of budget cuts under the local political administration. The problem was simple: Without public libraries, many immigrant children in these communities would be deprived of vital access to educational resources. The New York Civic Participation Project (NYCPP) determined that a meaningful and realistic solution was to keep the library facilities open to the public.

Who Can Provide It?

To continue the above example, the NYCPP needed to know who to work with to provide the solution. NYCPP organized parents and children in the low-income immigrant communities in Brooklyn to protest the closure. Together their voices resonated. The right people—those with budgetary responsibility—heard their message, and the libraries remained open.

As with the NYCPP example, it is important to ask early on: *To whom should we target our message?* Who has the power to grant us a solution? Will we achieve success through lobbying and attempts to influence legislation? Will we make the most impact through the voting public and nonpartisan electoral efforts? Will bringing civil rights lawsuits create change through enforced judicial decisions? Or, will commenting on regulations and other policies be most fruitful? Which avenue of change will result in a solution? Will it be a combination of these efforts or is it best to focus on one?

As another example: Muslim Advocates, a public charity, is concerned with issues of fairness and justice for the Muslim-American community. In the months and years following the attack on the World Trade Center of September 11, 2001, they were concerned with civil rights violations against members of the Muslim-American community. By participating in meetings with senior officials of the U.S. Department of Justice, the U.S. Department of Homeland Security, and the FBI, Muslim Advocates was able to articulate the Muslim community's civil rights concerns to the executive branch officials and agencies that created and enforced government policies. They felt that a solution could best be provided by the officials and agencies creating and enforcing policies in that crucial time.

To Whom Will They Listen?

Identifying the entity or individual with the power to fix a problem or create a solution is usually not the most challenging part of the advocacy process. The most crucial and sometimes frustrating part of the process is *getting* those people to listen to the message. Who will the legislators or courts or agencies listen to? Will it be the general public, who votes them into office? Opinion leaders? Special constituencies, such as tobacco or dairy farmers? What about children who want to be educated?

The National Korean American Services and Education Consortium (NAKASEC) was part of a coalition to pass the DREAM Act, ensuring a way for immigrant children to gain access to public education. As part of their efforts, NAKASEC created a minidocumentary video entitled *DREAM*. The documentary portrays the story of a child's hopes expressed while awaiting the outcome of the contested federal legislation. The video, told through the voice one young girl, explained how a student's life can change because of opportunities for a better education. The message was powerful, and one that affected the opinions of legislators, community organizers, and the public.

What Do They Need to Hear?

One of the greatest weaknesses passionate individuals sometimes have is the inability to see things from another's perspective. Activists tend to get so wrapped up in their cause that they lose sight of the lens through which others may view the same issue. How can advocates make their issues relevant to the legislators or the general public?

Different individuals respond to different appeals. For some, it takes quantitative data, such as objective polls illustrating the number of civil rights violations against immigrant workers, or statistics that show decreases in crime, despite increases in immigration rates. Others may respond to a compelling message, like the *Day Without Immigrants* campaign in 2006, where mass rallies were staged across the United States as immigrants boycotted work or school and avoided spending money as a way of showing their worth to the economy. Still others respond to sheer numbers, such as the sight of thousands of immigrant advocates demonstrating in front of legislatures. Immigrant advocacy groups may need to rethink their messaging—or may need to create several different types of messages—to gain broader public support or get the attention of legislators.

PLANNING AN EFFECTIVE ADVOCACY CAMPAIGN

Once advocates have defined their goals and strategy, the next step is planning an advocacy campaign.

Assessing Advocacy Capacity

Organizations that wish to undertake advocacy work must first address their *advocacy capacity.* This is an essential initial step to planning a campaign, seeking grant funding, and organizing a staff.

Things to consider when making the assessment are:

- *Operations*—Is advocacy part of how you operate? Does your board of directors already have an advocacy policy? Do you have systems in place to manage record keeping and accounting practices?
- *Staff*—Do you have experienced staff (consultants, lobbyists, marketing/public relations, fundraisers) already working for your organization? If not, is it crucial that you hire such staff?
- *Network*—Whom do you know? Do your staff, board, or supporters have connections in local government, agencies, or media?
- *Skills*—What advocacy skills, knowledge, and experience does your organization have? Have you been trained on the rules regarding advocacy activity?
- *Technology*—Do you need specific technology programs to forward your advocacy efforts (such as a Web site, e-mail alerts, a database of supporters, etc.)?
- *Funding*—What resources are available? Are private foundations willing to fund your work? (Restrictions and regulations regarding funding will be discussed in more detail later in this chapter.)
- *Messaging*—Do you have staff skilled in creating advocacy messages and campaigns?

If an organization does not have much advocacy capacity, it should make efforts to increase its advocacy capacity through grant writing, fundraising, commitments from the board, and hiring more staff or consultants with expertise in developing advocacy processes. After an organization has assessed and made plans to increase its advocacy capacity, it has laid the groundwork for good strategic planning around the goal itself.

Strategic Considerations

There are many strategic considerations to take into account in successfully carrying out an advocacy game plan, including timing, relationships, opposition, and negotiation.

Depending on the type of advocacy activity pursued, the *timing* may affect your outcome. Legislative sessions vary. The regulatory process is complex. Litigation can be a slow and often deadline-driven effort. If your strategy involves election-related activity such as voter education, campaign season starts early, and it is important to be ahead of the game. As was evident with the failure of the Comprehensive Immigration Reform Act (which was defeated in 2007), systematic and long-lasting change takes months and sometimes years to come into fruition.

Your network of *relationships,* both within and without the organization, is a key element in advocacy campaigns. Knowing the right people can equal success in getting in to see a legislator or having someone from the media write an article or air a broadcast about your cause—and these events can make or break your efforts.

Remember that no one is unimportant to your efforts—everyone from the receptionist to the chief of staff has power and can either help or hinder you. It is important to identify who your staff, board, and volunteers know (both personally and professionally), and to always work to strengthen and increase your relationships. One important way to do this is by joining or creating a coalition of organizations. Coalitions confer breadth; even if you do not have access to certain people in the legislature, local government, or media, your coalition members may. By sharing resources and influence, coalition members can support a common goal. Developing connections and partners on which your organization can depend gives you an automatic springboard on the next advocacy campaign. You are no longer starting at ground zero; *you have built advocacy capacity.*

When building a network, it is important to focus energy where it counts. You must proclaim your message and goals to the community that supports you, but if you only focus on legislators and community leaders that agree with you, you won't make much headway toward effective and long-term change. However, there are some individuals who will never agree with or support your advocacy goals, so you should not expend much energy on them, either.

The Tennessee Immigrant and Refugee Rights Coalition (TIRRC) is a good example of the power of networking. TIRCC helped found the Southeast Immigrants' Rights Network, a group that increases cooperation and learning between immigrant rights organizations in the entire southeastern United States. Through its networking efforts, TIRRC has brought together one of the most diverse immigrant rights coalitions in the country and has expanded its organization's reach significantly.

TIRRC has become a model and mentor for newer immigrants' rights networks.

Identifying and anticipating the views of the *opposition* (current or potential) allows successful advocates to make arguments that are well-reasoned and persuasive. No matter how benevolent and great your cause, your organization likely has an enemy—organizations that are opposed to your mission, for example. What will they say in debates, op-eds, meetings with legislators, or communications with the public? What weaknesses exist in their arguments, and how can you neutralize them? For example, many immigrant advocacy groups have taken the arguments of their opponents—that immigrants drive up crime rates or that immigrants do not pay taxes—and have funded research and substantive reports chronicling why those arguments hold no weight (Rumbaut & Ewing, 2007).

Effective advocates always consider in advance that they may have to *negotiate* in the final hours of their struggle. Accordingly, advocacy groups should build in give-aways (points that they are willing to concede, in order to gain other advantages), and be willing to accept minor changes. Above all, as an advocate you must know your bottom line. Whatever the bottom line is—whether it is as broad and sweeping as immigration reform at the federal level or as specific as allowing all immigrants to hold valid drivers' licenses—it is important to start there and build out.

Also, be prepared to walk away from or switch strategies that are not working. Perhaps the best way to get valid driver's licenses is not by lobbying local legislators. Maybe it is by getting more immigrants registered to vote so that they can elect legislators who will enact fair policies and procedures.

Whatever your strategy, advocates and advocacy organizations should appreciate the efforts of staff, volunteers, and supporters; and regularly evaluate the outcomes of the strategy. Remember, advocacy activities must be evaluated differently than other services. When telling your advocacy story (whether though a grant report, annual report, article, newsletter, or other publication) it is important to include incremental progress. You may not have numerical data to back up your efforts, but connections you made in key offices, education and outreach efforts, increases in your volunteer base, and lobbying and election activities are all just as important to your efforts as passing legislation or achieving other concrete goals.

The following sections will discuss types of advocacy organizations, and specific advocacy activities that they may take part in.

TYPES OF ADVOCACY ORGANIZATIONS

There are several different types of nonprofit tax-exempt organizations through which advocates can effect change. Internal Revenue Code section 501 (c) lists over 26 different types. Some of the most common types of organizations—those in which social workers are most likely to find employment—will be briefly explained here.

Public Charities

The most common type of nonprofit is the 501(c)(3) *public charity*. Public charities are defined under the tax code and associated regulations as groups that engage in religious, scientific, literary, or other charitable activities. Examples of well-known 501(c)(3) public charities are the National Council of La Raza, Planned Parenthood, Habitat for Humanity, the United Way, and the American Red Cross.

There are many benefits to being a 501(c)(3) public charity. One is that 501(c)(3) charities are tax-exempt, meaning they do not pay most federal taxes. Additionally, contributions to 501(c)(3) public charities are tax deductible; donors can deduct a contribution up to 50% of their adjusted gross income if they itemize. Therefore, people are usually more willing to donate to a 501(c)(3) public charity as opposed to other tax-exempt organizations.

Public charities often receive grants from private foundations and other public charities like community foundations (sometimes referred to as public foundations) that support their work. These grants can represent a large portion of a public charity's funding. It is important to understand the rules related to funding sources for 501(c)(3) charities so organizations writing grant proposals will know whom to approach and what types of funding they can provide. Public charities may engage in advocacy generally and may even lobby as long as they remain within their limits. Public charities may also engage in nonpartisan election-related activity but may not endorse candidates. These rules will be discussed in more detail in the subsequent sections.

Private Foundations

Private foundations are another type of 501(c)(3) organization. While public charities are supported by a variety of financial sources, private foundations are generally funded from a single source. For example, many private foundations are created by families or corporations (e.g., the Mary Reynolds Babcock Foundation, the Gates Foundation, and the Robert Wood Johnson Foundation). Also, private foundations usually get ongoing funding from investment income rather than donations.

Because private foundations are often funded by a single source, Congress determined there was greater potential for abuse of their tax-exempt status. As a result, private foundations are subject to more stringent rules than 501(c)(3) public charities and must follow special rules governing the way they may grant money. Private foundations are required to spend a certain percentage of their net investment assets every year for charitable purposes. The mandatory payout for private foundations was instituted to ensure that these tax-exempt entities would operate for charitable purposes.

Other Types of Advocacy Organizations

While 501(c)(3) public charities and private foundations are the most common types of nonprofit organization, there are other types of tax-exempt nonprofit structures that are powerful vehicles for policy change as well. 501(c)(4) organizations are *social welfare organizations* that, like 501(c)(3)s, are tax-exempt (meaning they do not pay any income tax to the federal government), but contributions to 501(c)(4)s are not tax-deductible and they are not as likely to receive grants from private foundations.[2] Examples of such social welfare organizations are the Sierra Club and the Human Rights Campaign (HRC).

Because 501(c)(4) organizations receive less tax benefits than public charities, they are also less restricted in the types of activities in which they may engage. Unlike public charities, 501(c)(4) organizations can engage in an *unlimited* amount of lobbying activity. (Lobbying will be discussed later in this chapter.) Further, 501(c)(4) organizations may also engage in *some* partisan political activity—supporting or opposing candidates for public office—provided such activity is secondary in nature to the organization. Accordingly, the primary purpose of a 501(c)(4) organization cannot be to engage in partisan political activity.[3]

Other entities include 501(c)(5) *labor unions* and 501(c)(6) *trade associations,* which follow the same rules as 501(c)(4) social welfare organizations. Like social welfare organizations, labor unions and trade associations *may* engage in some partisan political activity as long as such activity is secondary in nature, and not the primary purpose or function of the organization.[4] Organizations under 501(c)(4), (c)(5), and (c)(6) that engage in such partisan political activity should be careful to follow either state or federal election law.[5]

The National Association of Social Workers (NASW), for example, is a 501(c)(6) trade association, and NASW can engage in unlimited amounts of lobbying activity as well as some secondary partisan political activity.

Finally, tax-exempt 527 organizations, like federally registered *political committees* (organized under section 527 of the tax code), are usually created for the sole purpose of getting a candidate or party elected to office. Section 527 is where all political organizations reside, including political parties, candidate committees, federally registered political committees, and so forth. Section 527 organizations may engage in partisan political activity with no limitation under the tax code and regulations.

The remainder of the chapter will look at macro-level advocacy efforts that can be undertaken by various advocacy organizations.

PARTISAN ELECTION-RELATED ACTIVITIES

Under federal tax law, 501(c)(3) public charities—the most common type of nonprofit organization—cannot engage in ANY partisan political activity. Specifically, these organizations and their members can never engage in activity that supports or opposes a candidate for any public office.[6] (Staff, volunteers, and board members of these organizations may support or oppose candidates or parties for office *as long as they are acting in their own capacity and not as officers or representatives of the organization.* In other words, if an individual affiliated with or working for a public charity wishes to engage in partisan political activity, he/she should be off the clock or on personal leave. It is good practice for these organizations to have a policy on this matter and prohibit the use of organizational e-mail, phone, or other resources for personal partisan political communications or efforts.)

Public charities may engage in unlimited amounts of *nonpartisan* election-related activity.[7] These activities include issue advocacy, voter education, voter registration, "get out the vote" activities, and candidate education.[8]

Generally, these activities are seen as nonpartisan in nature. Prior to the 2004 elections, however, the IRS began a new program, the Political Activities Compliance Initiative (PACI), which investigated allegations of partisan election-related activity by 501(c)(3) public charities. While few organizations have lost their tax-exempt status as a result of PACI investigations, it is still vitally important to know the standards by which the IRS determines permissible nonpartisan activity.[9] The IRS uses a "facts and circumstances" test: For example, if a public charity organizes a candidate debate, the IRS may look at not only the debate itself, but also at the circumstances surrounding the debate, for example: whether the event was open to the general public or targeted at a particular audience; where the event was held; who the moderator was; which candidates were invited; and when the debate took place. As a result, 501(c)(3) public charities coordinating such activities should consider such facts and circumstances and whether they are in keeping with permissible nonpartisan activity.[10]

Issue Advocacy

Issue advocacy is one example of a nonpartisan, election-related activity. For example, the American Immigration Law Foundation put out a series of public service ads encouraging the public to learn more about immigration issues. One of the ads states:

> Immigration is good for American workers because most Americans and immigrants don't compete for the same jobs. As the American work force grows older and better educated, fewer workers are willing and able to take jobs that require little education. As Americans acquire more education and training, immigrant workers fill the gaps in our workforce, taking jobs as groundskeepers, busboys, construction workers and agricultural workers. At the same time, immigrants start new businesses and spend hundreds of dollars on housing and consumer foods each year, which creates new jobs for Americans and immigrants alike. The U.S. economy benefits in immeasurable ways from the innovation and creativity of highly skilled immigrants in fields such as engineering, medicine and computer science. As a nation of immigrants and a nation of laws, we owe it to ourselves to create an immigration system that is good for families, good for business and good for America. Learn more about immigration reform. (http://www.ailf.org/psa/)

This is an example of acceptable, nonpartisan issue advocacy.

Permissible 501(c)(3) election-related issue advocacy should be nonpartisan in nature and focus on issues related to the organization's purpose. The issue advocacy should never be coordinated with a candidate or political party, should not contain any express advocacy or code words (such as: "Vote for the *progressive* candidate"), and should not contain content that "could only be interpreted by a reasonable person as advocacy for or against the election of a clearly identified candidate."[11]

Some elements that may affect whether the communication is seen as partisan include: (a) whether the statement identifies a candidate; (b) whether the statement expresses approval or disapproval of the candidate's positions or actions; (c) whether the statement references the election or is timed to coincide with the election; (d) whether the statement targets voters in a particular election, and whether the issue is one that distinguishes candidates.[12] It is never a bad idea for a 501(c)(3) organization to include a disclaimer on their issue ad stating that the group is not taking any position or expressing any preference about the candidates displayed on the ad, and that the group does not support or oppose candidates or political parties.

Voter Education

Another area where many public charities are becoming increasingly active is through voter education. As entities dedicated to specific causes, 501(c)(3)s often have the resources to educate the public and bring issues to the forefront of an election. Public charities may engage in voter education through issuing candidate questionnaires and creating voter guides, facilitating candidate debates or forums, or even through having candidates appear at their events. As with issue advocacy, these activities are *generally permissible* nonpartisan election activities for public charities, but public charities engaging in voter education should be aware of the guidelines within which they must operate.

For example, the Massachusetts Immigrant and Refugee Advocacy Coalition (MIRA) provided voter education materials to over 20,000 people through a statewide advocacy campaign around immigrants, rights issues. Additionally, United for Peace and Justice, a 501(c)(3), recently put out a voter guide and a call to get involved through their Voter Engagement Project. The voter guide focuses on the war in Iraq and its effect on the economy, as well as its social and political ramifications.

Candidate Questionnaires

Candidate questionnaires are another useful tool for exploring and presenting candidates' feelings and beliefs around certain issues. When putting together a candidate questionnaire, public charities should attempt to cover a broad range of issues and steer clear of biased questions (questions that suggest the answer to the question in the question itself) and pledges.[13] So, for example, a public charity focused on the rights of U.S.-born children of immigrants wouldn't want to ask candidates a question like:

> Don't you agree that the raids of immigrants in New Bedford had serious psychological and traumatic impact on the children of those deported? If you are elected governor, do you promise to stop all future raids in the New Bedford community?

Instead, the group may ask:

> What is your position on the raids that occurred in New Bedford and the effect they have on U.S.-born children of immigrants? What policies would you develop as governor to address the immigration issues in our community?

Similarly, the groups would not want to just focus on one issue, like the raids, or access to health care or civil rights, but cover a broad range of issues, like civil rights, immigration, economic issues, access to health care, youth, education, and so forth.[14]

Candidate Debates

501(c)(3) public charities may wish to educate voters through live candidate debates. As with other activities, there are rules that must be followed: The charity must invite all viable candidates (viability can be determined by any objective criteria, like polling data or funds raised). The debate should have an impartial moderator (e.g., the executive director of the charity should *not* be the moderator); unbiased audience; and no contextual favoritism.[15] Just as with candidate questionnaires, debate questions should cover a broad range of issues and be unbiased in nature.

A good way to ensure an unbiased audience is to hold the debate in a venue where all feel comfortable attending, such as a school or university, or open the event to the general public or give each candidate an equal number of tickets to distribute. The procedure for the debate itself should be equitable, as well. If the moderator gives one candidate two minutes extra to answer a specific question, he/she must extend the same time to other candidates answering that question.[16]

A debate is different than an event with an invited speaker. For example, let us assume that Al Gore is a candidate for presidency and a 501(c)(3) environmental organization wishes to invite him to their annual fundraising luncheon to speak about global warming. Since the organization is inviting Gore to address his role as an environmental advocate rather than a candidate for office, it would not have to invite any of the other presidential candidates to the luncheon. Organizations holding these types of events should be very clear however, that the event is not campaign-related, and that the candidate should avoid mentioning his/her candidacy; furthermore, the event should not be timed to coincide with the election. The closer the event is to the election the more it looks like the candidate has been invited because of his or her candidacy.

Legislative Scorecards

Legislative scorecards are another tool some 501(c)(3)s use to educate the public on certain issues. Legislative scorecards track the votes of legislators in the previous session. A 501(c)(3) working on immigrants and labor issues, for example, may issue a legislative scorecard that focuses on the way city council members voted on: existence of worker centers, employer sanctions for hiring undocumented workers, mandatory minimum wage laws and employee benefits, and so on.

Public charities issuing a legislative scorecard should not time the release of a scorecard to coincide with the election; rather the scorecard should coincide with the legislative cycle. Do not do it for the first time in an election year. A 501(c)(3) legislative scorecard should include all legislators, but may focus on a broad range of issues important to the organization, and commentary is allowed.[17]

Get Out the Vote and Voter Registration Drives

In the months preceding the 2008 elections, many researchers reported on the large pool of immigrants and their children who will soon be eligible to join the U.S. electorate, and the effect these new voters will have on future elections. As of June 2006, there were nearly 9.5 million immigrants who were eligible to naturalize, become U.S. citizens, and vote. Furthermore, 1 million U.S.-born children of immigrants will reach 18 by the 2008 elections (Hoyt, 2006). These statistics are fueling unprecedented efforts in the immigrants' rights community to create voter registration and get out the vote (GOTV) campaigns targeting this new voting population. Advocacy organizations are realizing that systematic change at the government level cannot occur without educating, organizing, and empowering the underrepresented to vote and elect good leaders.

The Latino and Arab-American communities, for example, spearheaded GOTV campaigns in anticipation of the 2008 election targeted at their underrepresented voting members: *Ya Es Hora* and *Yalla* Vote![18]

Section 501(c)(3) organizations can enlist unregistered voters through voter registration and get people to the polls through GOTV efforts, but they should keep in mind the permissible goal for this activity: *encouraging people to exercise their right to vote.*[19] Messaging should have no reference to any candidate or political party and no suggestion of who to vote for or with which party to register.

With regard to targeted GOTV or voter registration efforts by a 501(c)(3), it is permissible to target activities as long as the rationale remains nonpartisan. So, for example, a group could target a particular location, like Orange County, North Carolina, because it was where most of the organization's members reside, but not because it is an important electoral district. Similarly, a 501(c)(3) could target a particular audience—like voters with historically poor voter turnout—but not voters who support a particular candidate.

Candidate Education

The final area through which 501(c)(3) public charities can participate in election-related activities is candidate education. It is quite common for a 501(c)(3) specializing in a certain topic area to receive requests for information, research, or opinion on a particular issue from a candidate's campaign. 501(c)(3)s wishing to provide materials and information to candidates may offer information about the organization's program, goals, issues, and agenda and provide information that is already gathered.[20] Organizations wishing to proactively provide information to candidates should just make sure that they offer the information to all candidates equally or make the resources available online so that any of the candidates could access it.

LOBBYING

Lobbying is a powerful strategy for advocacy organizations. 501(c)(3) public charities can and should advocate for policy change, but there are some limits on the amount of *lobbying* activity in which they can engage. For more detailed information on these limits and the two tests (Insubstantial Part Test *or* 501(h) Expenditure Test) under which public charities can determine their limits, please see Exhibits 14.1 and 14.2.

Exhibit 14.1 Guidelines for 501(c)(3) Public Charities

Public Charities Can Lobby:
Guidelines for 501(c)(3) Public Charities

501(c)(3)s public charities (including public foundations) CAN lobby within the generous limits allowed by federal law. How much lobbying the organization can do depends on which of two sets of rules the organization chooses to fall under -- the "501(h) expenditure test" or the "insubstantial part test." In issuing regulations on lobbying, the Internal Revenue Service stated that, under either test, public charities "may lobby freely" so long as lobbying is within specified limits (*see* Lobbying by Public Charities). Private foundations that lobby create a taxable expenditure for their foundation. Consequently private foundations do not engage in any lobbying activity (*see* Lobbying by Private Foundations, 55 Fed. Reg. 35,579 (June 29, 1990).

Remember These Key Points

► Electing to use the 501(h) expenditure test can maximize the organization's lobbying activity.

- The organization only counts lobbying activity that it spends money on. Cost-free activities, such as volunteer time, do not count against the organization's lobbying limits because an organization does not pay its volunteers.
- 501(h) provides a clear dollar limit on the amount of money an electing 501(c)(3) can spend on lobbying. The limits vary depending on the size of the organization's budget. Small organizations that spend less than $500,000 a year can often expend as much as 20% of their budget on lobbying.
- An electing 501(c)(3) may spend up to a quarter of its overall lobbying limit on "grass roots" lobbying (urging the general public to communicate the organization's position on legislation to legislators) or up to the entire amount on "direct" lobbying (telling legislators or their staff to support or oppose legislation or urging the organization's members to do so).
- An electing 501(c)(3) can take advantage of some specific exceptions for activities that otherwise might appear to fit the definition of lobbying. Among these exceptions is a "nonpartisan analysis, study or research" or a substantive report that fully discusses the pros and cons of a legislative proposal.
- A 501(c)(3) may elect the 501(h) expenditure test to govern its lobbying activity by filing the simple Form 5768 once with the IRS.

► If the 501(c)(3) has not elected 501(h), it may still lobby as long as its lobbying activities do not become a "substantial" part of the 501(c)(3)'s overall activities.

► Working on or contributing to a ballot measure campaign is permissible lobbying activity under these rules. 501(c)(3) organizations are able to engage in a wide range of advocacy regarding these ballot measures, so long as they do not exceed their lobbying limits.

► If a 501(c)(3) wishes to engage in more lobbying than is permitted for 501(c)(3) organizations, consider creating an affiliated 501(c)(4) organization. A 501(c)(4) can engage in an unlimited amount of lobbying.

11 Dupont Circle, N.W., 2nd Floor
Washington, D.C. 20036
Phone: 202-822-6070
Fax: 202-822-6068

ALLIANCE FOR JUSTICE
www.allianceforjustice.org
advocacy@afj.org
866-NPLOBBY

519 17th Street, Suite 560
Oakland, CA 94612
Phone: 510-444-6070
Fax: 510-444-6078

Exhibit 14.2 Electing the 501(h) Expenditure Test

Election-related activity: You can do it, as long as you follow the rules.

Discuss the following examples to determine whether you think they would be permissible for 501(c)(3)s? 501(c)(4)s? 501(c)(6)s?

1. Deport Arnold Not My Homies (DANMH) is a nonprofit organization based in California. DANMH wants to plan a voter registration campaign through which they will create a list for subsequent use in a GOTV drive. The list will note not only the name of the individual being registered but also which party they are registered with. DANMH hopes to host GOTV trainings through which they encourage volunteers and staff members to call individuals who are registered Democrats and encourage them to get to the polls on election day.

2. *Noting down what party individuals registered with is not an acceptable activity for a 501(c)(3). 501(c)(3) organizations should not have voter registration lists that indicate party affiliation because they cannot support or oppose candidates or parties for election—their activity must remain nonpartisan.*

   501(c)(4)s and 501(c)(5) s and (c)(6)s, however, may engage in the activity because they can engage in some partisan political activity as long as it is secondary in nature to the overall activity of the organization.

3. United We Stand (UWS), a Texas-based nonprofit organization, is hosting its annual conference in Austin, Texas, in August 2008. Ravi, the president of UWS is extremely upset about the fact that neither the president, nor any of the Texas representatives and senators, were able to pass Comprehensive Immigration Reform Legislation in 2007. During a speech at the United We Stand Conference, Ravi criticizes the president and the Texas congressman and senators who failed to support the bill. Two of the congressmen mentioned are running for reelection in November. Before this speech, UWS had never publicly criticized any of the aforementioned legislators.

501(c)(3)s cannot engage in any partisan political activity but they may *criticize sitting legislators. As such, the 501(c)(3) could criticize the president who is not running for reelection, as a sitting legislator. The key issue here is whether the 501(c)(3) could criticize the two congressmen running for reelection. Because UWS did not previously criticize the legislators, criticizing them within three months of the election may look as if UWS is opposing the candidates. Remember that when criticizing incumbents key points to consider are whether the (c)(3) has previously criticized the individual while he or she was a sitting legislator, ramping up criticism near an election and the timing of the criticism as it relates to the election. There are no black and white answers here, only facts and circumstances and whether the activity appears to be nonpartisan.*

4. We Hate Immigrants (WHI) is a religious nonprofit church organization based in Oklahoma. The minister of WHI is well known in the community. A month before the gubernatorial election, the minister invites Jim, a candidate for governor, to speak from the pulpit to the membership about his candidacy. No other candidates are invited by WHI. As he is introducing Jim, the minister states, "I know WHI is a nonprofit and I'm not telling you all how to vote on election day, but rest assured, I'll be voting for Jim, because he understands our message and will lead Oklahoma to greatness."

   Churches and auxiliaries of churches are 501(c)(3) organizations. Accordingly, any staff or representative of the church should not be engaging in activity on the church's behalf that is impermissible for 501(c)(3) organizations. The minister of WHI could in his individual capacity support Jim for governor, but he would probably not want to do so during a sermon or from the pulpit as it gives the implication that the church is in some way endorsing a candidate. The activity is impermissible.

5. Bobby is running for state senator in Illinois. He is pro-immigrants' rights and believes every immigrant, even ones that are undocumented, deserve to be treated with dignity and respect. Many of Bobby's opponents, however, continually lash

out at him during debates and public forums, claiming that immigrants take jobs from Americans who are willing to work, drive up crime rates, and do not pay taxes. Bobby, frustrated with his opponents and their willful ignorance, approaches your organization, Welcome to America (WTA), a local nonprofit. Two years ago, WTA published several substantive reports on immigration issues addressing all of Bobby's opponents' points. The reports were titled *Jobs Americans Don't Want: Immigration Up, Crime-Rates Down* and *Immigrants and Taxes: Myth vs. Fact*. Bobby asks if WTA can update the research in the three reports before the next debate so that he can have a fighting chance at silencing the weak arguments of his opponents. Much has changed in the past two years and he knows if he uses the old reports, his opponents will question the report's validity. WTA had no plans to update the reports, and would have to pull staff off of other projects to get the job done. But, the debate will be broadcast on local television stations and they could educate a wide audience, and get people interested in their organization if they were to get the information to Bobby in time.

501(c)(3) organizations may educate candidates on issues that are important to their members and the public at large, but they may not create information for a candidate. For example, WTA could educate Bobby and the other candidates about the plight of immigrants and the hatred the opposition might be spreading about the immigrant population, but they should make the information available to all of the candidates (they can still meet with Bobby, but the information should be on their Web site or accessible to other candidates as well), and they cannot create reports or information that they were not already planning to create simply because a candidate requests it. Doing so would in essence make the 501(c)(3) part of the candidate's campaign staff.

Electing the 501(h) Expenditure Test

Most 501(c)(3) public charities will benefit from "electing" the 501(h) lobbying expenditure test. The rules that govern lobbying under 501(h) are clearer than those that apply under the "insubstantial" standard.

Step 1 – Complete Form 5768

IRS Form 5768, *Election/Revocation of Election by an Eligible Section 501(c)(3) Organization To Make Expenditures To Influence Legislation*, is the first step in electing to be governed by the 501(h) expenditure test. An organization simply supplies its name, address, and the first tax year to which it wants the election to apply. The form needs to be signed by an authorized officer, usually the president or treasurer. The election applies retroactively to the first day of the fiscal year in which the form is filed and, generally, to all subsequent years. For example, a form filed in December 2006 will bring an organization under section 501(h) from January 1, 2006 forward (assuming the organization operates under the calendar year).

Step 2 – Make a Copy

Make a copy of Form 5768 before mailing it to the IRS because the agency will NOT send a confirmation letter.

Step 3 – Track Lobbying Expenditures

Under 501(h), your organization can spend up to 20% of its first $500,000 exempt purpose budget on direct lobbying. Direct lobbying is defined as any communication, with a legislator, expressing a view about specific legislation. Organizations with budget expenditures over $500,000 should apply the following formula:

20% of the first $500,000
\+ 15% of the next $500,000
\+ 10% of the next $500,000
\+ 5% of the remaining
= the overall lobbying limit

Grassroots lobbying is defined as any communication with the general public, expressing a view about specific legislation, with a call to action. A call to action refers to four different ways the organization asks the public to respond to its message: (1) asking the public to contact their legislators or staffers; (2) providing the address, phone number, website, or other contact information for the legislators; (3) providing a mechanism to contact legislators such as a tear off postcard, petition, letter, or email link to send a message directly to the legislators; or (4) listing the recipient's legislator, the names of legislators voting on a bill, or those undecided or opposed to organization's view on the legislation. An organization that has made the 501(h) election can never spend more than 25% of their overall lobbying limit on grassroots lobbying.

Therefore, a 501(c)(3), that has made the 501(h) election, with an annual budget of $500,000, would have an overall lobbying limit of $100,000 and a grassroots lobbying limit of $25,000.

All public charities, including 501(h) electing charities need to keep track of their lobbying expenditures for their 990 Form and in the event of an IRS audit.

Note: To revoke your organization's 501(h) election, follow steps 1 and 2, filling out the revocation portion of Form 5768 (question 2).

ALLIANCE FOR JUSTICE

11 Dupont Circle, N.W., 2nd Floor
Washington, D.C. 20036
Phone: 202-822-6070
Fax: 202-822-6068

www.allianceforjustice.org
advocacy@afj.org
866-NPLOBBY

519 17th Street, Suite 560
Oakland, CA 94612
Phone: 510-444-6070
Fax: 510-444-6078

Form **5768**

(Rev. December 2004)

Department of the Treasury
Internal Revenue Service

Election/Revocation of Election by an Eligible Section 501(c)(3) Organization To Make Expenditures To Influence Legislation

(Under Section 501(h) of the Internal Revenue Code)

For IRS Use Only ▶

Name of organization | **Employer identification number**

Number and street (or P.O. box no., if mail is not delivered to street address) | Room/suite

City, town or post office, and state | ZIP + 4

1 **Election**—As an eligible organization, we hereby elect to have the provisions of section 501(h) of the Code, relating to expenditures to influence legislation, apply to our tax year ending........................ (Month, day, and year) and all subsequent tax years until revoked.

Note: *This election must be signed and postmarked within the first taxable year to which it applies.*

2 **Revocation**—As an eligible organization, we hereby revoke our election to have the provisions of section 501(h) of the Code, relating to expenditures to influence legislation, apply to our tax year ending........................ (Month, day, and year)

Note: *This revocation must be signed and postmarked before the first day of the tax year to which it applies.*

Under penalties of perjury, I declare that I am authorized to make this (check applicable box) ▶ ☐ election ☐ revocation on behalf of the above named organization.

(Signature of officer or trustee) (Type or print name and title) (Date)

General Instructions

Section references are to the Internal Revenue Code.

Section 501(c)(3) states that an organization exempt under that section will lose its tax-exempt status and its qualification to receive deductible charitable contributions if a substantial part of its activities are carried on to influence legislation. Section 501(h), however, permits certain eligible 501(c)(3) organizations to elect to make limited expenditures to influence legislation. An organization making the election will, however, be subject to an excise tax under section 4911 if it spends more than the amounts permitted by that section. Also, the organization may lose its exempt status if its lobbying expenditures exceed the permitted amounts by more than 50% over a 4-year period. For any tax year in which an election under section 501(h) is in effect, an electing organization must report the actual and permitted amounts of its lobbying expenditures and grass roots expenditures (as defined in section 4911(c)) on its annual return required under section 6033. See Schedule A (Form 990 or Form 990-EZ). Each electing member of an affiliated group must report these amounts for both itself and the affiliated group as a whole.

To make or revoke the election, enter the ending date of the tax year to which the election or revocation applies in item **1** or **2,** as applicable, and sign and date the form in the spaces provided.

Eligible Organizations.—A section 501(c)(3) organization is permitted to make the election if it is not a disqualified organization (see below) and is described in:

1. Section 170(b)(1)(A)(ii) (relating to educational institutions),
2. Section 170(b)(1)(A)(iii) (relating to hospitals and medical research organizations),
3. Section 170(b)(1)(A)(iv) (relating to organizations supporting government schools),
4. Section 170(b)(1)(A)(vi) (relating to organizations publicly supported by charitable contributions),
5. Section 509(a)(2) (relating to organizations publicly supported by admissions, sales, etc.), or
6. Section 509(a)(3) (relating to organizations supporting certain types of public charities other than those section 509(a)(3) organizations that support section 501(c)(4), (5), or (6) organizations).

Disqualified Organizations.—The following types of organizations are not permitted to make the election:

a. Section 170(b)(1)(A)(i) organizations (relating to churches),

b. An integrated auxiliary of a church or of a convention or association of churches, or

c. A member of an affiliated group of organizations if one or more members of such group is described in **a** or **b** of this paragraph.

Affiliated Organizations.—Organizations are members of an affiliated group of organizations only if **(1)** the governing instrument of one such organization requires it to be bound by the decisions of the other organization on legislative issues, or **(2)** the governing board of one such organization includes persons (i) who are specifically designated representatives of another such organization or are members of the governing board, officers, or paid executive staff members of such other organization, and (ii) who, by aggregating their votes, have sufficient voting power to cause or prevent action on legislative issues by the first such organization.

For more details, see section 4911 and section 501(h).

Note: *A private foundation (including a private operating foundation) is not an eligible organization.*

Where To File.—Mail Form 5768 to the Internal Revenue Service Center, Ogden, UT 84201-0027.

Cat. No. 12125M Form **5768** (Rev. 12-2004)

Lobbying is defined under the federal tax code regulations under two different categories: direct and grassroots.

(In addition to federal tax issues, it is important when lobbying at the state and local level to be aware of the rules and regulations regarding reporting requirements that exist in your community.[21])

Direct Lobbying

Direct lobbying is a communication with a legislator expressing a view about specific legislation.[22] While the elements of the definition appear straightforward, the term *direct lobbying* and its components include some exceptions and require additional explanation.

For example, a *communication* can be more than a phone call or a conversation; it may include a symbol or physical items such as ribbons, bricks—or even cake. Several years ago the AARP, anxious to send a message about the need for a Medicare prescription drug plan in pending legislation, delivered 535 cakes to Congress. Each cake was missing a slice, symbolizing the missing Medicare prescription drug plan in proposed legislation. The cakes representing the Medicare bill received a lot of media attention and were an effective form of direct lobbying activity.

Similarly, a *legislator* can be a member of Congress, state legislator, city council member, or any other individual that participates in the formulation of legislation.[23] This includes governors and the president of the United States when they veto or sign a bill into law.[24] A legislator can also include other officials who have the ability to influence legislation.[25] Individuals who do not participate in the formulation of legislation, but who may set policy at a local level, are not considered legislators.[26] This category includes members of school boards or zoning/planning commissions.[27]

In addition to legislation that has already been introduced (e.g., legislation that already has a name or number attached to it), *specific* legislation also includes proposed legislation, or legislation that may not yet be fully developed. While the boundaries of specific legislation may appear broad, there are many things that seem like they would be considered legislation but that are not considered legislation for tax law purposes. For example, regulations, enforcement of existing law, executive orders, and litigation are not considered specific legislation.[28]

Particularly relevant for the social work community, at the federal level and for purposes of this chapter, communicating with agencies regarding *regulations* is not lobbying. So for example, communications with the U.S. Department of Human Services, the U.S. Dept of Homeland Security, or other such agencies regarding their regulations is not considered lobbying. Accordingly, communicating with legislators about the implementation of Social Security Administration (SSA) "No Match" Letters by the DHS, for example, would not be considered lobbying, as requirements regarding "No Match" letters involve regulations issued by an agency.

As reaffirmed by Congress in 1976 when it enacted new sections of the tax code addressing lobbying expenditures by public charities, 501(c)(3) public charities *can and should lobby* for policy change. In addition, some foundations make grants only to nonprofits that specifically state in their applications that they wish to conduct systems change, or advocacy. Because lobbying is one of the areas in which tax-exempt organizations and nonprofits are limited, it is important to understand the specifics regarding these limitations. Section 501(c)(3) organizations should be aware of their lobbying limits for each year in which they operate and be sure to track these activities and/or expenditures for reporting purposes.

Grassroots Lobbying

The other category of lobbying, *grassroots lobbying,* shares many of the same elements as direct lobbying but includes two key differences. Grassroots lobbying is a communication with *the general public* (e.g., through a Web site or billboard ad) expressing a view about specific legislation *with a call to action.*[29] Calls to action are very clearly set out in the tax code and regulations. There are only four distinct types of calls to action and a nonprofit must have one of these four on its communication for the communication to be counted as grassroots lobbying.[30]

1. Requesting your audience to call or contact their legislators
2. Listing the contact information for the legislators
3. Providing a mechanism by which the public can contact their legislators
4. Specifically identifying one or more legislators who will vote on the legislation as: opposing the organization's view with respect to the legislation; being undecided with respect to the legislation; being the recipient's representative in the legislature; or being a member of the legislative committee or subcommittee that will consider the legislation.[31]

Another important area where nonprofits can be active and effective is through ballot measures. Work on ballot initiatives, constitutional amendments, bond measures, and referenda is considered *direct* lobbying activity, and is permissible for public charities.[32] Although nonprofits communicating with the public to express a view about ballot measures may seem like grassroots lobbying, the *public* in the case of ballot measures are the *legislators*—the individuals voting the measures into law. Accordingly, communications with the general public about ballot measures should be tracked as direct lobbying.[33]

Private Foundations and Lobbying

As mentioned earlier, nonprofits, depending on their type, must follow special rules related to lobbying. Private foundations are no different although the rules that govern them are more stringent than those for public charities. Private foundations are subject to a significant tax on any lobbying expenditures and are *prohibited* from engaging in partisan election-related activity. Private foundations may engage in other types of advocacy—such as research, public education, supporting litigation, building capacity for public charities, or educating legislators—but they rarely engage in lobbying and never endorse candidates or parties for public office.

While most private foundations do not carry out lobbying campaigns themselves, it is common practice for private foundations to *fund* organizations that lobby. Private foundations may not *earmark* grants for lobbying; however, there are two "safe harbors" through which private foundations can fund lobbying: *general support grants* and *specific project grants*. (By safe harbor, we mean instances where a foundation can make a grant to a nonprofit organization to engage in lobbying activity without facing a taxable expenditure.)

A general support grant is one that grants a lump sum to a 501(c)(3) public charity for the general support of its programs and operations. This general support grant money may be used by the grantee for any purpose. Specific project grants are another method through which private foundations can fund lobbying activity of a 501(c)(3) public charity. A private foundation will review the grantee's budget for the project and then may fund up to the nonlobbying portion of that budget.[34]

CONCLUSION

This chapter provides the advocacy tools for effecting long-lasting and systematic policy change around immigrants' rights. Whether acting as individuals, groups, or hopefully through advocacy organizations, social workers must rise up on behalf of their clients and the communities they serve. This moment in American history will forever be remembered as another defining period in which the underrepresented needed a voice. Social workers cannot afford to be passive participants in this immigrants' rights movement; rather, they must be *active* advocates for change. The hope and challenge in writing this chapter and in teaching advocacy strategies is that social workers will be driven to move beyond micro advocacy efforts, and effect public policy at the *macro* level. In doing so, social workers can impact the lives, not just of individual clients, but of many immigrant communities for generations to come. Social workers can and should advocate for policy change.

CASE STUDIES

1. Lobbying or Advocacy?

Discuss the following scenarios. Would they be permissible for 501(c)(3)s? 501(c)(4)s? 501(c)(6)s?

- Deport Arnold Not Immigrants (DANI) is a nonprofit organization based in California. DANI wants to plan a voter registration campaign through which they will create a list for use in a GOTV drive later. The list will note not only the name of the individual being registered but which party he or she is registered with. DANI hopes to host GOTV trainings through which they encourage volunteers and staff members to call individuals who are registered Democrats and encourage them to get to the polls on Election Day.
- United We Stand (UWS), a Texas-based nonprofit, is hosting its annual conference in Austin, Texas. Ravi, the president of UWS, is extremely upset about the fact that the Comprehensive Immigration Reform Legislation did not pass in 2007. During a speech at the conference, he criticizes the president and the Texas congressmen and senators who failed to support the bill. Two of the congressmen mentioned are running for reelection in November. Before this speech, UWS had never publicly criticized any of the aforementioned legislators.
- We Hate Immigrants (WHI) is a religious nonprofit church/organization based in Oklahoma. The minister of WHI is well known

in the community. A month before the gubernatorial election, the minister invites Jim, a candidate for governor, to speak from the pulpit to the membership about his candidacy. No other candidates are invited by WHI. As he is introducing Jim, the minister states, "I know WHI is a nonprofit and I'm not telling you all how to vote on election day, but rest assured, I'll be voting for Jim, because he understands our message and will lead Oklahoma to greatness."

- Bobby is running for state senator in Illinois. He is pro–immigrants' rights and believes every immigrant deserves to be treated with dignity and respect. Many of Bobby's opponents, however, claim that immigrants take jobs from Americans, drive up crime rates, and do not pay taxes. Bobby approaches your organization, Welcome to America (WTA), a local nonprofit. Two years ago, WTA published several substantive reports on immigration issues, entitled *Jobs Americans Don't Want: Immigration Up, Crime Rates Down* and *Immigrants and Taxes: Myth vs. Fact.* Bobby asks if WTA can update the research in the reports so he can use them in an upcoming debate. WTA had no plans to update the reports, and would have to pull staff off of other projects to get the job done. But the debate will be broadcast on local television stations and could educate a wide audience, and get people interested in WTA.

2. Immigrant Advocacy Practice Scenarios: What Is Your Game Plan?

Discuss how you would develop an advocacy plan to react to each situation below. With whom would you work in coalition? Would you choose an administrative, legislative, or judicial avenue of change? Keep in mind timing issues, media, and local political climate. Would your analysis change if you were an advocate with a 501(c)(3) organization? A 501(c)(6)? What could you do as a student? Social work professional? Member of the community at large?

- You have recently become aware that there is a proposal to open a local Immigration and Customs Enforcement (ICE) office in your town. The chief of police has made it clear that he is not in favor of the proposal. The mayor is undecided and the community is split as well. You have two weeks before the city council votes on the proposal. What advocacy strategy would you develop to prevent the proposal from passing?

- Immigration reform legislation has failed to pass at the federal level. States across the country are enacting their own local and statewide ordinances and policies on immigrant issues. In your state, the state legislature has just enacted a law requiring employers to report staff without proper identification or citizenship status or face losing their business licenses. The law is just one of several harsh policies against the immigrant community in your state. The immigrant population is in a panic and immigrant advocacy organizations need to develop a strategy for action. Next year is an election year with the potential to vote in new state legislators. National legal services organizations like the ACLU, MALDEF, and others have offered to provide free assistance to any local nonprofits wishing to bring civil rights lawsuits on behalf of their members and affected constituents. Many of the local immigrant communities do not even understand the new policies and need assistance understanding their rights. What advocacy strategy or strategies would you incorporate to address these issues? Where would you focus your energy first?

IMMIGRANT ADVOCACY SUCCESS STORIES

The following are true stores of successful advocacy by nonprofit organizations.

Tennessee Immigrant and Refugee Rights Coalition

The Tennessee Immigrant and Refugee Rights Coalition (http://www.tnimmigrant.org/) is a statewide, immigrant, and refugee-led collaboration whose mission is to empower immigrants, and refugees throughout Tennessee to develop a unified voice, defend their rights, and create an atmosphere in which they are viewed as positive contributors to the state. Its achievements include:

- Helped pass legislation to increase immigrant access to driver's license. As a result, thousands of immigrant drivers learned the rules of the road and obtained auto insurance. They also helped organize a winning, immigrant-led campaign to obtain commitment from the Tennessee Department of Safety to translate the Tennessee driver's license test into additional languages (2004).

- Empowered immigrant day-laborers to successfully defeat a proposed ordinance in the Nashville city council that would have made it illegal to solicit work in public. This ordinance would have stifled free speech and would have prevented scores of Nashville nonprofits from raising the funds they need to serve the community (2005).
- Helped defeat "English-only" and "illegal renter" ordinances in the Nashville metro council. These bills would have divided the Nashville community, and would have made it much harder for Nashville immigrants and refugees to integrate into their new society (2006–2007).

The National Council of La Raza

The National Council of La Raza (http://www.nclr.org), a Latino civil rights and advocacy organization, achieved the following:

- Issued a report with the Urban Institute entitled *Paying the Price: The Impact of Immigration Raids on America's Children.* The report details the consequences of raids on the children's psychological, educational, economic, and social well-being.
- Is partnering with the National Association of Latino Elected and Appointed Officials (NALEO), Service Employees International Union (SEIU), and Univision for *Ya Es Hora ¡Ciudadanía!*—a national campaign to inform, educate, and motivate the over-eight-million legal permanent residents living in the United States who are eligible to apply for U.S. citizenship. Visit www.yaeshora.info for more details.

National Network for Arab American Communities

The National Network for Arab American Communities (http://www.nnaac.org) advocates on behalf of civil rights and civil liberties, immigration policy, increased funding and support for human services, and civic engagement. It has formulated a list of advocacy principles to which its constituents are dedicated:

- *Fixing our immigration system:* We need immigration reform that addresses backlogs, promotes family reunification, safeguards due process, offers a path to citizenship, and recognizes the contributions immigrants make to our country.

- *Protecting immigrant families from abuse:* We support initiatives that protect and restore the basic rights for all immigrants, and address both the surge in hate crimes and the continuing violations of civil liberties and rights.
- *Increasing access to human services for immigrants:* We believe human service programs promote dignity and independence among our already vulnerable immigrant communities. Access to education, health care, SSI, food assistance, and other essential human services will help immigrants improve their economic and social stability.
- *New programs for American citizenship for immigrants:* We want a naturalization program that is committed to the full integration of newcomers by providing them quality English instruction, promoting and preparing them for citizenship, and providing them with opportunities to improve their quality of life in the United States.

CASA of Maryland

CASA of Maryland (http://www.casademaryland.org) has a Community Organizing and Political Action (COPA) department that engages low-income community members in organizing campaigns. These campaigns encourage leadership development, seek to effect social change, and build power in the low-income Latino and immigrant community. COPA develops committees of women, workers, and tenants to advocate for community improvements such as increased repairs and safety in neglected rental housing, increased funding for adult education, access to public services, and immigration reform. Community members elect leadership structures within the committees, and receive key advocacy training in how to speak with the press, how to speak to elected officials, and how to engage others in collective actions. CASA also works in partnership with organizations such as the National Capital Immigrant Coalition and staffs a multiethnic and faith-based initiative called the Friends of New Marylanders to form strong coalitions that support institutional change.

NOTES

1. See also http://207.5.76.88/public/2718.cfm for a list of states that have passed legislation aimed at immigrants.

2. Private foundations granting money to non-501(c)(3) organizations must exercise *expenditure responsibility,* creating what can sometimes be an administratively burdensome process. For this reason many private foundations do not give grants to non-501(c)(3)s. 26 C.F.R. § 53.4945–5(a)(6)(ii)(b), 26 C.F.R. § 53.4945–5(b).
3. For more information on 501(c)(4) organizations and other types of 501(c) organizations please see Schadler, *The Connection: Strategies for Creating and Operating Affiliated 501(c)(3)s, (c)(4)s and Political Organizations,* under Suggested Readings.
4. 26 C.F.R. § 1.501(c)(4)-1(a)(2)(ii); Rev. Rul. 81–95; Rev. Rul. 2004–6.
5. Ibid.
6. 26 U.S.C. § 501(c)(3); 26 C.F.R. § 1.501(c)(3)-1(c)(3)(iii).
7. 26 C.F.R. § 1.501(c)(3)-1(c)(3)(iii).
8. Ibid.
9. Rev. Ruling 2007–41; Rev. Ruling 78–248.
10. 26 U.S.C. § 501(c)(3); 26 C.F.R. § 1.501(c)(3)-1(c)(3)(iii) stating: a 501(c)(3) may not "participate in, or intervene in (including the publishing or distributing of statements), any political campaign on behalf of (or in opposition to) any candidate for public office."
11. TAM 91–17–001 (Sept. 5, 1990); TAM 1999–07–021 (May 20, 1998); 11 C.F.R. § 100.22(a),(b).
12. Id.
13. Rev. Ruling 2007–41; Rev. Ruling 78–248.
14. Ibid.
15. Rev. Ruling 2007–41; Rev. Rul. 86–95; TAM 96–35–003 (April 19, 1996).
16. Ibid.
17. Rev. Rul. 80–282.
18. For more information about the *Ya Es Hora* GOTV Campaign see: http://www.nclr.org/content/programs/detail/47117/; and the *Yalla* Vote Campaign see: http://aai.3cdn.net/a6fc9f590130f95f6b_xzm6bnarv.pdf.
19. Rev. Ruling 2007–41.
20. For further information on election-related activity by nonprofits please see: Colvin & Finley, *Rules of the Game: An Election-year Legal Guide for Nonprofit Organizations,* under Additional Resources at the end of this chapter.
21. Alliance for Justice, a nonprofit advocacy organization based in Washington, D.C., has *state* resources, in addition to its federal guidance, available through its Web site, where individuals can access lobbying, campaign finance and ballot measures, and voter registration rules for all states. See www.afj.org for more information.
22. 26 C.F.R. § 56.4911–2(c)(1).
23. 26 C.F.R. § 56.4911–2(b)(1)(i)(A).
24. 26 C.F.R. § 56.4911–2(b)(1)(i)(B).
25. Ibid.
26. 26 C.F.R. § 56.4911–2(d)(4).
27. Ibid.
28. 26 C.F.R. § 56.4911–2(d)(1).
29. 26 C.F.R. § 56.4911–2(b)(2).
30. 26 C.F.R. § 56.4911–2(b)(2)(iii).
31. Ibid.
32. 26 C.F.R. § 56.4911–2(b)(1)(iii).

33. Ibid.
34. 26 C.F.R. § 53.4945–2(a)(6)(ii).

ADDITIONAL RESOURCES

Web Sites

American Civil Liberties Union (ACLU): www.aclu.org

American Friends Service Committee, immigrant's rights page: http://afsc.org/immigrants-rights/default.htm

Delete the Border, an online community of movements against borders: http://deletetheborder.org/node/1473

The Florence Project, a nonprofit legal service organization that provides free legal services to men, women, and children detained by the Immigration and Customs Enforcement (ICE): www.firrp.org

National Council of La Raza (NCLR): www.nclr.org

U.S. Committee for Refugees and Immigrants: www.refugees.org

Readings

Alliance for Justice. (n.d.). *Keeping track: Recordkeeping for 501(c)(3) public charities.* Washington, DC: Author.

Alliance for Justice. (2000). *Worry-free lobbying for nonprofits: Electing the 501(h) expenditure test.* Washington, DC: Author. (Available in Spanish [disponible en Español]).

Alliance for Justice. (2004). *Investing in change: A funder's guide to supporting advocacy.* Washington, DC: Author.

Alliance for Justice. (2005) *Build your advocacy grantmaking: An advocacy evaluation and capacity assessment tool.* Washington, DC: Alliance for Justice.

American Civil Liberties Union. (2000, September 8). *The rights of immigrants.* New York: Author. Available at http://www.aclu.org/immigrants/gen/11713pub20000908.html

American Immigration Law Foundation. (2007, March). *Resource lists: Employer sanctions and "know your rights."* Washington, DC: Author. Available at http://www.ailf.org/lac/sanctions.shtml

American Immigration Lawyers Association. (2007). *Being an advocate: Step-by-Step Guide to practicing grassroots advocacy.* Washington, DC: Author. Available at http://www.aila.org/content/default.aspx?docid=19886

Capps, R., Castenada, R. M., Chaudry, A., & Santos, R. (2007, October 31). *Paying the price: The impact of immigration raids on America's children.* Washington, DC: National Council de La Raza and Urban Institute. Available at http://www.urban.org/url.cfm?ID=411566

Capps, R., Fix, M., Passel, J., Ost, J., & Perez-Lopez, D. (2003, October 27). *A profile of the low-wage immigrant workforce.* Washington, DC: Urban Institute. Available at http://www.urban.org/url.cfm?ID=310880

Coalition for Comprehensive Immigration Reform. (n.d.). *Justice for immigrants: Learn the issues.* Washington, DC: Author. Available at http://www.cirnow.org/file/805.pdf

Coalition for Comprehensive Immigration Reform. (n.d.). *Know your rights: Can an employer fire an employee because the employee participated in an immigration rally?* Washington, DC: Author. Available at http://www.cirnow.org/file/456.pdf

Colvin, G. L., & Finley, L. (1996). *The rules of the game: An election year legal guide for nonprofit organizations.* Washington, DC: Alliance for Justice.

Esbenshade, J. (2007, Summer). *Division and dislocation: Regulating immigration through local housing ordinances.* Washington, DC: American Immigration Law Foundation. Available at http://www.aclu.org/immigrants/gen/11713pub20000908.html

Fair Immigration Reform Movement. (n.d.). *Fighting for immigrant justice at the local level: A guide to fighting anti-immigrant ordinances.* Center for Community Change. Washington, DC: Author. Available at http://www.fairimmigration.org/toolkit/

Federal Election Commission guidance at http://www.fec.gov/info/publications.html

Harmon, G., Ladd, J., & Evans, E. (1995). *Being a player: A guide to the IRS lobbying regulations for advocacy charities.* Washington, DC: Alliance for Justice.

Internal Revenue Service. (n.d.). *IRS revenue ruling 2004–6.* Author. Available at http://www.irs.gov/irb/2004–04_IRB/ar10html

Internal Revenue Service. (1997). *Lobbying issues.* Washington, DC: Author. Available at http://www.irs.gov/pub/irs-tege/topic-p.pdf

Internal Revenue Service. (2002). *Election year issues.* Washington, DC: Author. Available at http://www.irs.gov/pub/irstege/topic102.pdf

Internal Revenue Service. (2003). *Political campaign and lobbying activities of IRC 501(c)(4), (c)(5) and (c)(6) Organizations.* Washington, DC: Author. Available at http://www.irs.gov/pub/irs tege/eotopic103.pdf

National Association of Social Workers. *Immigration Policy Toolkit.* Includes policy statements, fact sheets, and other advocacy materials. Available at http://www.socialworkers.org/diversity/ImmigrationToolkit.pdf

National Council of La Raza. (2007). *Legislative advocacy for community-based organizations: An NCLR toolkit.* Washington, DC: Author. Available at http://www.nclr.org/content/publications/detail/49474/

National Immigration Forum. (2005). *Immigration basics 2005.* Washington, DC: Author. Available at http://www.immigrationforum.org/documents/Publications/ImmigrationBasics2005.pdf

Rumbaut, R. G., & Ewing, W. A. (2007, Spring). *The myth of immigrant criminality and the paradox of assimilation: Incarceration rates among native and foreign-born men.* Chicago: Immigration Policy Center. Available at http://www.ailf.org/ipc/special_report/sr_022107.pdf

Schadler, H. (2006). *The connection: Strategies for creating and operating affiliated 501(c)(3)s, 501(c)(4)s, and political organizations.* Washington, DC: Alliance for Justice.

REFERENCES

Gillam, C. (2007, November 1). U.S. states turning up the heat on illegal immigrants. *Reuters.* Available at http://www.reuters.com/article/domesticNews/idUSN0118499720071101?feedType=RS

Grant, H. M., & Crutchfield, L. (2007, October). *Forces for good: The six practices of high impact nonprofits.* San Francisco: Jossey-Bass.

Hoyt, J., & Tsao, F. (2006, June 29). *Today we march, tomorrow we vote: The untapped power of immigrant voters.* Chicago, IL: Illinois Coalition for Immigrant and Refugee Rights. Available at http://www.icirr.org/index_files/tomorrowwevote.pdf

Matos, K. (2007, August 8). *Local immigration ordinances: The result of federal inaction on comprehensive reform.* Speech to the Center for American Progress, New Haven, CT.

McKinley, J. (2007, November 14). ID cards for residents pass vote in California. *New York Times.* Available at http://www.nytimes.com/2007/11/15/us/15frisco.html

Medina, J. (2007, June 8). Arrests of 31 in U.S. sweep bring fear in New Haven. *New York Times.* Available at http://www.nytimes.com/2007/06/08/nyregion/08haven.html

Powell, M., & Garcia, M. (2006, August 22). Pa. city puts illegal immigrants on notice. "They must leave," mayor of Hazleton says after signing tough new law. *Washington Post,* A03. Available at http://www.washingtonpost.com/wpdyn/content/article/2006/08/21/AR2006082101484html

Schultz, J. (2003). *The democracy owners' manual: A practical guide to changing the world.* New Brunswick, NJ: Rutgers University Press.

Epilogue

ELAINE CONGRESS AND FERNANDO CHANG-MUY

Social Work With Immigrants and Refugees: Legal Issues, Clinical Skills and Advocacy concludes with this Epilogue, but the story of immigration in the United States continues. As this book went to press, the editors were cognizant of changing laws that will continue to have an impact on immigrants and refugees. This is part of the American legal system generally, and immigration law specifically; in fact, although the Immigration and Nationality Act was first enacted in 1952, Congress continues to amend it. This is particularly true in an election year; after November 2008 there may be still more changes in immigrant laws that will affect our clients. Because of this constantly shifting legal landscape, it is crucial that social workers keep up to date with current information about policies and laws that affect immigrants. This can be done through attention to newspaper and television media, as well as immigrant advocacy Web sites (many of which are included in the Additional Resources sections of each chapter).

One of the coeditors (Elaine Congress) has had the opportunity to serve on the NASW Presidential Diversity Initiative that specially looked at issues and advocacy around immigrant issues. The toolkit report from this initiative is available on the national NASW Web site (www.naswdc.org), which can be an ongoing resource for current information about immigration.

Here, we would like to muse on issues that have, and will continue to have, an impact on immigration to the United States.

GLOBALIZATION

Advances in transportation, communication, and information technologies have led to globalization; immigration will increase as products and people are moved from country to country (and often, from poorer to richer countries). The United States will continue to be the recipient of poorer immigrants from poor countries around the world.

While Mexican, Central American, and South American immigrants—especially those who are undocumented—have a difficult time crossing the border by land, increased airline transportation has made it possible for many immigrants to have a speedy, relatively painless method of immigration, as well as the ability to return home frequently for family emergencies and celebrations. (Though even here, airline travel is also difficult, given that airline carriers have to ensure that the passports and visas are valid, otherwise they risk sanctions.) This will lead to an increased number of transnationals—bicultural immigrants who live in two countries with frequent trips between the two.

While some migrants frequently travel back and forth, for others—usually political or religious refugees or undocumented people—migration is one-directional. It is interesting to note, however, that even when migrants "can't go home again," they often maintain a continued financial connection with those who have remained in their homelands. One has only to visit a crowded Western Union office on a Friday afternoon to see the continual financial link between immigrants and the families they have left behind. These individual remittances have done much to provide informal, personal foreign aid to developing countries, filling the gap where our own or other countries have failed to assist with larger steady grants or loans.

CLIMATE CHANGE

The consequences of climate change have been the subject of much recent doom and gloom media coverage. Rich countries create much of the gas emissions but those in poorer countries are most detrimentally affected by climate change. People who were once dependent on agriculture can no longer grow crops because of arid or flooded land conditions. The loss of their livelihood has led them to an increased immigration.

The United Nations, many national governments, and the nongovernmental organization (NGO) community have worked on numerous community and social development projects so that those from poor countries will not be forced to leave their homelands because of devastating poverty. Yet some community improvement projects—such as the building of dams and clearing of forests—ironically have had the opposite effect of depriving many of the world's poorest people of even a very meager livelihood and forcing them to leave their homelands to immigrate to the United States or other developed countries in order to survive.

Of all immigrant groups, indigenous peoples are often the most vulnerable. Indigenous peoples live in 70 countries around the world, often in very remote and inaccessible locations. Climate change and community development projects have often forced them to relocate. While immigration is stressful for all migrants, indigenous peoples who have had a special relationship with the land may find relocation particularly devastating. In the United States we have seen the immigration of many indigenous peoples from Mexico, Central America, and South America. In addition to forced dislocation from the lands that defined so much of their being, indigenous peoples often experience particular challenges as they may not speak a major language and may come from rural areas that are very different from the urban American cities to which they immigrate. This phenomenon should have an impact on our social service agencies, to ensure that we make our services accessible through provision of bilingual bicultural workers and written materials.

TECHNOLOGY

Technology has revolutionized the way in which people around the world communicate. Even people from very rural, isolated parts of the world are now connected through the Internet. What impact has increased communication had on migration? First, we think that it has led to an increase in migration as people who once were isolated and knew little of cities and countries beyond their own region now can very readily learn about the possibility of life in other parts of the world.

Second, through e-mail communication, those who have migrated can remain in continual contact with relatives and friends back home.

When communication occurred through written letters and with limited postal access in developing countries, once people migrated they often were forever removed from the families they left behind. When communication is a daily, instant occurrence, families across oceans and continents are able to maintain closer ties. This is particularly important in light of the fact that whole families do not usually immigrate together. Frequently men and/or women may come first to the United States in order to work and financially support their children who are left behind. Although children may still struggle with separation and loss issues, the possibility of frequent instant e-mail and telephone communication does serve to maintain family connections across countries. E-mail and telephone communication is also used to share information with extended families and friends from countries of origin about immigrants' experiences in the United States. Frequent communication can serve to encourage those left behind to think about emigrating themselves.

IMMIGRATION POLICY

Immigration is one of the most controversial areas in current political discourse. There is a wide diversity between those who see an open immigration policy as threatening to American-born workers and others who believe that America's well-being is dependent upon a continual source of cheap immigrant labor. We are particularly concerned about the many human rights violations against those who are apprehended and incarcerated after they tried to enter illegally or overstayed their visas. We also are troubled by the current antiterrorism focus that sees many immigrants (both legal and undocumented) as safety and security risks and results in denying them the basic civil and political rights enjoyed by others.

As discussed in chapter 1, U.S. policies have often changed in light of economic trends. When cheap labor is needed and we enjoy economic prosperity, we see a relaxation of immigration laws. When unemployment is high and we face national financial concerns, there is a tightening of laws and regulations to exclude newcomers. In addition to the current economic crisis, there is an ever-present concern about terrorism and national security that serves further to exclude any person that is perceived as different. In viewing our restrictive immigration policies, one also has to look through a racism lens. Throughout our history Americans have often been xenophobic—especially when immigrants have been of a darker color than they are. In the face of all these concerns, then, individual states and localities will often take a restrictive approach. For example, they attempt to enact English-only laws or laws that try to convert landlords, police, and state motor vehicle departments into agents of the federal Department of Homeland Security.

What is happening in the United States is not unique. Many countries all over the world are experiencing huge waves of immigration. While the United States has always been diverse, even countries that have traditionally been very homogenous are now becoming more diverse. With all countries becoming more diverse and bicultural, and in view of more frequent communication and travel between countries, one can predict a blurring of national boundaries or ultimately a world without borders. In the United States we are witnessing the beginning of this wave. Because social workers are educated to understand and work effectively with diverse immigrant populations, they are in the foreground of this expanding arena.

Immigration and Social Work Education

Teaching American students about immigrants is not new, although the way we discuss the cultural diversity of immigrants has changed. A generation ago in school we learned that the goal of immigrants who came to the United States should be assimilation. The term *melting pot* was frequently used. Today, students learn about "mosaics," the importance of immigrants remaining bicultural, and the desire for long-term natives (whose ancestors were once newcomers themselves) to embrace this diversity. Again, improvements in travel and communication have contributed to immigrants' ability to remain firmly rooted in two cultures—that of their home country and of the United States.

What do social work students, in particular, learn about immigrants and what will be the future direction of social work education in this regard? A major focus in social work education is preparing students to work with populations that are vulnerable and marginalized. In the most recent Educational Policy and Accreditation Standards (EPAS) of the Council on Social Work Education (CSWE), immigrant status is seen as a source of discrimination and bias, and the need to educate students about this population is required.

Social workers have always worked with immigrants, going back as far as Jane Addams's settlement houses in Chicago. Earlier attention to immigrants, however, was based more upon a deficit, problem-focus model while modern social work practice stresses the importance of the strengths perspective and client empowerment. These themes are particularly germane in the study of social work practice with immigrants. As part of their education, social workers must learn not to see their immigrant clients as helpless victims but recognize the many strengths that immigrants have brought with them to the United States and continue to use to survive in this complex environment.

While an earlier generation of students learned about immigrants primarily through generalizations about different national groups, current social work education stresses the diversity of immigrants. Social workers should be taught to individualize immigrant clients rather than view them as a monolithic population. There is now a current recognition that even immigrants from within the same country often demonstrate much diversity based on class, education, immigration experience, and personality characteristics. The importance of individualizing immigrants and their families is key to effective professional work with immigrants.

The focus of social work with immigrants has also shifted from a concern only with immigrants here in the United States, toward that of a binational approach. Students in the twenty-first century are no longer as fixed in location as many of their predecessors were. They see and understand that successful social work practice with immigrants can best be understood by learning not only about their clients' experience here in the United States, but also their ongoing connections with their home countries, as well as their premigration experiences. Thus, many students are involved in study trips to better understand where their clients have come from. For example, the New York City Social Work Education Consortium Immigrant Child Welfare Fellowship Project affords students a chance to make an annual study trip to Ghana to better understand the premigration experiences of their clients, many of whom come from western African countries. And increasingly, undergraduate and graduate social work schools offer their students internships abroad to expand their education so that they can be better informed professionals.

Modern social work students who are interested in global service do not always expect that immigrants will walk into the traditional office; rather they realize the importance of being out in the community, both locally and globally, to work more closely with their immigrant clients. They truly see social work without the traditional borders.

Preparation for work with immigrants begins with social work education. As mentioned earlier, some positive steps can be seen in CSWE's recent Educational Policy and Accreditation Standards (EPAS), which now requires social work educators to teach that immigration status might be a source of discrimination. Also increasingly, social work schools—especially those in urban areas—have incorporated policy and practice courses on immigrants into their curriculum.

There are several concerns though. For practice courses, there is a need to teach the most effective methods for working with immigrant clients. Traditional psychodynamic theories or even newer cognitive behavioral methods that are evidence-based with other populations may not be the best methods to use in working with immigrant families. Individual psychotherapy with a focus on deficits and family history may not be helpful for an immigrant client who is very connected with his or her family of origin and is struggling with current social economic problems. Even before using some of the newest evidence-based methods of working with clients who have been traumatized, social workers need to ascertain if these methods have been evaluated with immigrant populations. Focusing on relationship building, addressing the problems that clients present, and understanding the legal and policy context seem to be the most effective methods in working with immigrant clients.

While the increase in specialized elective courses on immigrants and refugees throughout the schools of social work is positive, there is a concern that only a selected number of students will choose these courses, leaving the vast majority of students without education on social work practice with immigrants and refugees. Yet there is an increasing possibility that many, if not all, social work students—whether in urban or rural areas—will eventually work with immigrants at some point in their professional careers. Immigrants are settling not only in urban areas, but everywhere throughout the United States.

In teaching students about work with immigrants—be it in required or elective practice courses—social work educators must be sure to teach students not only about direct practice skills, but also the need to use community resources and understand policies and laws that affect their clients. With immigrants perhaps more than any other population, students need to learn to see the link between what C. Wright Mills coined as "private troubles and public issues." Students who study direct practice with immigrants can also benefit by following coverage media and then becoming involved with advocacy efforts organized through NASW and immigrant advocacy groups to promote the rights of immigrant people.

A major component of social work education includes two years (minimum of 900 hours) in supervised field placements in a social service agencies. Thus these experiences provide major opportunities for students to learn about working with immigrants. In many field placements, field instructors can help students learn to adopt a policy/legal/social work practice perspective in working with immigrant and refugee families.

Social Work Practice With Immigrants

Social workers in every field and role of practice see immigrants and can incorporate knowledge and skills to help them better work with this population. Direct service with immigrants occurs in the mental health, health, child welfare, substance abuse, education, and social service fields. In fact, in most social service agencies across the United States, it would be almost impossible to not have a single immigrant client in one's caseload. Understanding the immigrant experience on a continuum that involves the client's country of origin, transit experience, and postimmigration living situation is important in effective work with immigrants. Furthermore, identifying social justice issues that continue to negatively impact the welfare of immigrant clients and their families is essential.

For direct practitioners, understanding the policy and legal context in which immigrants live is needed in order to provide counseling services. We hope that this book will provide needed content in this area. While knowing the policy content is needed, it is not sufficient for effective work with immigrants. Social workers need to advocate individually for their clients, but also learn to advocate on larger organization, community, and legislative levels for the rights of their clients. Social workers also need to be aware of available community resources that can help their clients and be able to make appropriate referrals.

Social Service Organizations and Immigrants

Needed social services are provided for immigrants at a variety of agencies, including those that provide mental health, health, child welfare, social service, substance abuse, education, and family services. There is much these organizations can do to make their services available and welcoming to all immigrant populations.

First, these agencies need to include professionally educated bilingual and bicultural staff. In order to provide effective services to immigrant clients, it is important to move away from delegating interpretation to an agency support person or—even worse—to the children of immigrant clients. Establishing a relationship and learning important content about a client may not happen when an unskilled interpreter is used, as this example illustrates: A social work student, using an agency secretary as an interpreter, reported that when she asked an immigrant client how she felt, the client spoke for about 10 minutes. The interpreter translated: "She said she feels fine." Something was certainly lost in that translation!

Using children who have developed bilingual skills is also to be avoided for several reasons. First, children may be exposed to family and personal issues that are not appropriate for them to hear; secondly, as part of their family system, children's interpretation may not always be that accurate; and last but not least, children may be kept out of school in order to help their families deal with social service and medical problems. An extreme example of the use of an inappropriate family interpreter occurred in this unfortunate, but unfortunately true, incident during which a teenage boy who had accompanied his mother to a medical clinic because of reoccurring gynecological problems was called upon to interpret his mother's ailments.

Social work administrators can look at diversity not just through the use of bilingual, bicultural staff members, but also by encouraging diversity in volunteers and board members as well.

In addition to increasing bilingual, bicultural staff, social work administrators have to look at the access to their agencies. The most helpful programs and staff will not be beneficial if immigrants cannot locate them or feel welcomed by them. I (Elaine Congress) recently made a presentation at a community agency that prided itself on servicing immigrants. The agency was on an urban city block with formidable concrete buildings. After circling the block twice I saw a small business card with the Anglicized name of the agency (which shall remain nameless) affixed about six feet from the ground next to a door with a small barred window. To gain entrance to this agency I opened the door (with some difficulty; at first I thought it was locked) and then went down a long corridor to a desk where a uniformed security guard was seated. Considering the difficulties I had in accessing the place, I am not sure how easily immigrant clients could have located this agency or whether they could have seen it as a place that could provide help to them and their families. Administrators can conduct an agency scan on everything from signage to Web sites to marketing and technology to ensure access for all.

Finally, social service administrators also need to reexamine their policies toward providing services to immigrant families. In view of shrinking benefits for immigrants—especially those that are undocumented—many social service agencies have placed restrictions on the types of clients that can be seen. All social workers, whether in direct service or administration, have an ethical responsibility to combat discrimination and work to provide services to clients regardless of their immigration status.

Even if government reimbursement is not forthcoming for undocumented immigrants in their agencies, social work administrators ethically need to be prepared to provide at least some pro bono services to this population, or arrange for some alternate services to be provided.

Administrative social work to promote the welfare of immigrants does not end, however, within the agency. Agency social work leaders should take a major role in advocating for more equable immigration laws and policies on the state and national level. In addition to ethical responsibilities, if the agency is the recipient of federal funds, it is obligated under the Civil Rights Act of 1964 to make its services available and not discriminate based on national origin.

We hope that this volume has given readers a greater awareness of the issues, strengths, and challenges that immigrant populations bring, as well as strategies to surmount obstacles and provide immigrant families with the tools they need to succeed. We are and will continue to be a nation of multiple ethnic identities—which should be cherished and supported, rather than denigrated.

Appendices

Appendix A
Sample Affidavit in Support of Application for Asylum

Editor's Note: The following is an actual application for political asylum. Names and other identifying details have been removed; notes by the preparer, regarding further information required within the document, have been retained and are in italics. Social workers often can help immigrant clients draft the biographical sections and lay out the narratives of these applications.

TABLE OF CONTENTS

Guinea: Report on Female Genital Mutilation (FGM) or Female Genital Cutting (FGC), June 2001, **U.S. Department of State** J

NONGOVERNMENTAL ORGANIZATION DOCUMENTS

Country Report on GUINEA, March 6, 2001, **International Women's Rights Action Watch** K

Jane Little, "Debate Rages over Women and Sharia," June 11, 2003, **BBC News** L

Emad Makay, "Female Genital Mutilation Continues, Says Report," February 7, 2004, **Inter Press Service** M

Michelle Rice, "Domestic Violence," **National Center for PTSD** N

U.S. Department of Homeland Security
Bureau of Citizenship and Immigration Services
Newark Asylum Office
1200 Wall Street West
Lyndhurst, NJ 07071

Affidavit in support of Application for Political Asylum of **[Applicant]:**

1 My name is [Applicant's name].
2 I am seeking asylum and withholding of removal because I am afraid I will face persecution in Guinea based on account of my membership in a particular social group, on account of my political opinion, and on account of my religious opinion. I am also afraid that my daughters will face persecution on account of their membership in a particular social group. I fear I will be socially and physically persecuted and subjected to a forced marriage as a woman with children out of wedlock. I fear that my daughters will be socially persecuted and subject to the physical torture of female genital mutilation.
3 My fear of returning to my country of origin is genuine and well-founded. I am a member of a strictly religious Muslim family, but I left my husband without the permission of my family in Guinea and subsequently had children out of wedlock with a man in the United States. I fear that return to Guinea will cause my family to beat me severely and regularly, to remove my children from my

care if I return to them, and to force me into another marriage. I fear that within another marriage I will face the same severe physical, emotional, and sexual abuse that is common in marriages in Guinea and which the police and authorities either condone or are powerless to prevent, and which I experienced in my previous marriage. I also fear that my daughters will be genitally mutilated so that they, too, can be married.

INFORMATION ABOUT ME

4 I am a citizen of the Republic of Guinea. I left my country to move here to escape my ex-husband. I am afraid to return because I have broken tradition in leaving and also by having two children out of wedlock. The penalties for defying one's family and culture can be very severe, including public beatings by senior family members and forced marriage to another man. There will be no help for me if I return because the government is unable or unwilling to help victims of domestic abuse and living in a different part of the country as a woman alone and rejected by her family would leave me vulnerable to social ostracism.

5 I was born on [date] in Conakry, the Republic of Guinea. I have two children. My oldest daughter, [daughter's name], was born in Pennsylvania on [date] and suffers from severe congenital heart disease, for which she has already undergone multiple operations. *[See exhibit C, medical records for (daughter)—need copies of med records.]* My youngest daughter, [daughter's name] was born on [date], also in Pennsylvania. They have the same father, a man to whom I am not married.

6 My ex-husband and I were married for many years and never had children. We were married in a religious ceremony in [year] in Guinea, when I was 13 years old. I was the second wife of my husband, [name], who is also related to me by blood, as he is my cousin. Before I was married I was genitally mutilated.

7 *[Details on applicant's experience with female genital mutilation]*

8 This was a marriage arranged by our family. My husband was... *[description of marriage].* I left the country because my husband was physically *[and sexually (she was very vague about the abuse, and clearly very traumatized—but the affidavit needs more detail)]* abusive toward me and no one would help me

end my marriage in Guinea. We are now divorced because in my family's religion, and its tradition of marriage, a husband and wife are divorced when they choose not to live together for three months; this is a legal divorce under Guinean religious law (Faula). I have heard that my ex-husband has taken other wives, but have no contact with him, nor with my father and mother since I left.

9 I came to the United States as a tourist a year before I left Guinea for good. It was during my three-month stay in New York with a girlfriend that I learned that there were places where women were not expected to be the slaves of their husbands. I saw that women were free to live their own lives and to not be beaten by their husbands nor to be their obedient servants.

10 Upon return to Guinea I realized that the conditions of my life there were intolerable and I decided I would have to leave since no one would help me. I had to wait nearly a year to get a new visa. *[What happened in this interim?]*

11 I arrived on [date] on a visitor's visa at *[which?]* airport in New York. I lived with friends in New York. I was very confused about how to make my life here in the United States. *[Need to know if applicant suffered from PTSD.]*

12 I met my children's father on [date]. I moved to Philadelphia on [date] to live with him. I earned money throughout this period by braiding hair, but it was very difficult to earn enough money to support myself.

13 After my oldest daughter was born on [date], I spent many months after taking care of her, taking her to doctors, and dealing with her special needs. She has had many surgeries *[dates and details]*. I was very busy and worried for my daughter. I was preoccupied with caring for my child's life, but in the back of my mind I also worried about the consequences of having a child out of wedlock, because it is very much against the traditions in which I was raised.

14 After my second daughter was born last [date], I began to worry even more about what would happen if I were sent back to Guinea with my children. I fear that my family will genitally mutilate my children and force them into marriages at a young age, just as they did with me.

15 I cannot go back to Guinea. There is no help for women who defy the traditions of their family, their culture, and their religion. In Africa, the family is allowed to decide what is best for their children and women even if it means that the child or woman suffers severe and regular beatings, that they experience the psychological and physical torture of female genital mutilation, that they cannot gain access to medical care, and that they are forced to be in marriages where they are abused. Returning to Guinea now, after having defied so many conventions, I fear for my life and safety and for the health and safety of my daughters.

16 The father of my children and his brother, [brother's name], have a sister who had a child out of wedlock in Guinea. [Brother] says that because she had sex outside of marriage, the entire family—father, mother, grandparents, aunts, and uncles—gathered to beat her. Everyone who wanted to could hit her and she was beaten very badly. Even though [brother] did not think that was right, he was not able to protect his sister, he was only able to abstain from beating her himself. The sister eventually had to flee out of Guinea and start a new life. *[Need (brother) to be willing to sign and notarize a statement.]*

17 My fear for my life if I go back: I believe that I will suffer physical abuse, emotional abuse, and social ostracism based on my membership in the particular social group of women in the Muslim Malinké community who have had children out of wedlock. I also fear persecution will be based on my political opinion and religious beliefs, which conflict with the conservative religious and cultural practices in my family and country.

18 My fear for my daughters' life and physical safety if I go back: I fear that my daughters will be taken from me and treated as orphans and that both of my daughters will be subjected to female genital mutilation as uncircumcised members of the conservative Muslim Malinké community.

Exceptional Circumstances for Missing the Timely File Deadline

19 [Applicant] has failed to file an application for asylum within one year of arriving in the United States; however, because she meets the requirements for exceptional circumstances and has filed within a "reasonable" period of time, her application should be considered. The applicant has experienced both changed circumstances, when she had children out of wedlock, and has faced extraordinary circumstances, since her first child suffers from congenital heart disease.

20 Noncitizens in the United States who are seeking asylum must file their applications for asylum within one year after their arrival in the United States. INA § 208(a)(2)(B), 8 USC § 1158(a)(2)(B) (2002). An application for asylum filed after the one-year deadline may only be considered if there are extraordinary circumstances related to the delay in filing the asylum application. INA § 208(a)(2)(D), 8 USC § 1158(a)(2)(D). The burden of proof is on the applicant to establish to the satisfaction of the asylum officer, the immigration judge, or the Board of Immigration Appeals that the circumstances were not intentionally created by the alien through his or her own action or inaction, that those circumstances were directly related to the alien's failure to file the application within the one-year period, and that the delay was reasonable under the circumstances. 8 C.F.R. § 208.4(a)(5).

21 8 C.F.R. § 208.4(a)(2)(i)(B) includes in "changed circumstances" changes in the personal circumstances, such as a conversion from one religion to another, abandonment of religion altogether, or recent political activism. Although [applicant] is still a Muslim, her nonconformity to the strict interpretation of Islamic doctrine that is practiced by her family, puts her at increased risk for suffering persecution if returned to Guinea. The applicant has taken a stand that clearly shows that she does not agree with the strict Islamic law that tightly controls the sexuality of women by making it a crime to have sex our of wedlock. Even though the applicant had already defied the traditions and wishes of her parents and family when she left the husband to whom she was married as a child, divorce is permissible in Muslim societies in general, and Guinea in particular. However, sex outside of marriage is a sin and a crime punishable by severe corporal punishments, and in some places even by death. Having a child by extramarital sex is a clear and unchangeable sign that the "sinful" activity has occurred, and the mother is therefore a criminal. The applicant, therefore, had changed circumstances upon the birth of her first child. However, there was a reasonable delay of a period of almost three years in the filing because [applicant] was experiencing difficult

and "extraordinary" circumstances due to the serious physical illness of her first child.

22 The BIA has held that an individualized case-by-case analysis should be employed to determine whether "extraordinary circumstances" delayed the filing of an asylum application. *Matter of Y-C-*, 32 I&N Dec. 286 (BIA 2002). The BIA cited the applicable regulation, 8 C.F.R. § 208.4(a)(5), as defining "extraordinary circumstances" to include factors directly related to the failure to meet the one-year deadline. 8 C.F.R. § 208.4(a)(5)(vi) includes the serious illness of an applicant's immediate family member as a grounds for extraordinary circumstances. The applicant's daughter, [daughter's name], was born on [date] with congenital heart disease. Since her birth she has undergone numerous operations and has required even more care than an ordinary newborn, infant, and toddler. [Applicant] has been responsible for the care of her daughter at home, as well as ensuring her care in the hospital. This burden has been the constant preoccupation of the applicant's life and she was unable to take on the additional burden of filing until she could be certain that her daughter was out of the most severe danger.

23 8 C.F.R. § 208.4(a)(5)(i) includes mental or physical disability, including any effects of persecution or violent harm suffered in the past, as extraordinary circumstances grounds for missing the one-year filing deadline. The symptoms of posttraumatic disorder (PTSD) are within the meaning of the statute (see Asylum Officer Basic Training Course, Lesson on One-Year Filing Deadline, March 15, 2001). PTSD is a syndrome that affects battered and abused women and makes it difficult for them to function, sometimes even at the most basic levels (*see*, exhibit N). *[Need more info to make an argument that client suffered from PTSD.]*

24 Having met the requirements for exception to the one-year filing deadline, [applicant] should be considered for asylum.

STANDARD OF ELIGIBLITY FOR ASYLUM

25 To receive a grant of asylum, an applicant must establish that he or she is a refugee under the law of the United States. See

INA §§ 208(a)(1), 208(b)(1). The INA defines a refugee as any person outside their country of origin who is "unable or unwilling to avail himself or herself of the protection of that country because of persecution or a well-founded fear of persecution on account of race, religion, nationality, membership in a particular social group, or political opinion." INA § 101(a)(42).

26 The applicant retains the burden of establishing eligibility as a refugee. 8 C.F.R. § 208.13. An applicant can sustain her burden of proof for asylum by establishing a well-founded fear of persecution if a pattern or practice of persecution exists in his/her country on account of race, religion, nationality, political opinion, or membership in a social group. The applicant must establish her inclusion in one such persecuted group. 8 C.F.R. § 208.13.

THERE IS A WELL-FOUNDED FEAR OF PERSECUTION

27 To establish a "well-founded fear of persecution" an applicant for asylum must demonstrate that a reasonable person in the same circumstances would fear persecution if returned to his or her native country. A well-founded fear includes both a subjective and an objective component. The subjective component requires a showing that the alien's fear is genuine. The objective component requires a showing, by credible, direct, and specific evidence in the records, of facts that would support a reasonable fear that the petitioner faces persecution. *Matter of Mogharrabi,* 19 I. & N. Dec. 439 (BIA 1987).

28 The Supreme Court has held that "one can certainly have a well-founded fear of an event happening when there is less than a 50% chance of the occurrence taking place." *Cardoza-Fonseca,* 480 U.S. 421, 431 (1987). An applicant's fear need not arise out of applicant's own personal experiences, but can instead arise out of experiences of other individuals similarly situated to applicant on account of race, religion, nationality, membership in a particular social group, or political opinion. 8 C.F.R. § 208.13(b)(2).

29 A reasonable person in the applicant's circumstances would be afraid to return to Guinea. The applicant has experienced severe abuse by members of her family and her husband before she left Guinea. *[NEED the DETAILS (see, no. 7 supra).]* While in the United States, the applicant has defied the customs and religion of her people by having children out of wedlock and the punishment for doing so can be very severe. The applicant fears that her family will physically assault her, force her to marry against her will, or turn her out of her community. She fears that stigma on her as a woman who defied her family and had children out of wedlock will cause her to be socially ostracized even outside of her immediate community. The story of [sister] shows that women are severely beaten for having a baby outside of marriage. Islamic law says that adultery is a great sin, and it is considered adultery for a woman to have a child with any man who is not her husband, even if she is not married. In many strict Muslim countries, such as Nigeria, Saudi Arabia, and Pakistan, women may be stoned to death, or given lashes of a whip, for having a baby out of wedlock (*see,* exhibit L). Guinea has a multiple legal system that includes Islamic law, which is highly discriminatory against women. Although the penalties may be somewhat less severe in Guinea, the beatings, emotional abuse, and social ostracism would make [applicant's] life very difficult. In Guinea, it is very common for parents to severely beat their children and for husbands to abuse their wives (*see,* exhibits H and K). Culturally, it is considered the right of parents and husbands. Although law forbids domestic violence, "the law is ineffective as police and enforcement systems are reluctant to intervene in domestic disputes and such interventions are rare." (*See,* exhibit K; *see, e.g.,* exhibit H).

30 The treatment that the applicant would likely receive if she moved to a different part of Conakry or Guinea would likely also be very harsh. Guinea is a small nation, somewhat smaller than the state of Oregon, and family and community are very important there. It seems likely that the applicant would face social ostracism if she were forced to live in a different community than her family's community and that no one in her family could offer her any support without risking censure similar to that faced by the applicant. [sister] chose to flee the country; the applicant would face the same choice if returned.

THE APPLICANT FACES PERSECUTION IF RETURNED

31 The Immigration and Nationality Act does not explicitly define the term *persecution,* but the UNHCR Handbook directs that "a threat to life or freedom on account of race, religion, nationality, political opinion or membership in a particular social group is always persecution." *Office of the United Nations High Commissioner for Refugees* (UNHCR), *Handbook on Procedures and Criteria for Determining Refugee Status under the 1951 Convention and the 1967 Protocol relating to the Status of Refugees,* ¶51 (hereinafter "Handbook"). The BIA has defined persecution as the infliction of harm or suffering by a government, or persons a government is unwilling or unable to control, based on a characteristic of that victim. *Matter of Acosta,* 19 I&N Dec. 211 (BIA 1985).

32 In addition to physical persecution, the Handbook instructs that while differential treatment of various social groups is not necessarily discrimination that amounts to persecution, when discrimination leads to consequences of a substantially prejudicial nature for the person concerned, e.g., serious restrictions on right to earn his or her livelihood, that discrimination will amount to persecution. *Handbook,* at ¶54. Whether or not such measures of discrimination amount to persecution must be determined in light of all the circumstances. *Handbook,* at ¶55. Courts have also held that social ostracism can rise to the level of persecution. *In re. Kasinga,* 21 I. & N. Dec. 357 (BIA 1996). Persecution does not require a "punitive" or "malignant" intent on the part of the persecuting actor. *Alla Konstantinova Pitcherskaia v. INS,* 118 F.3d 641 (9th Cir. 1997).

33 The persecution must take place at the hands of the government or persons a government is unwilling or unable to control. The UNHCR Handbook directs that "[w]here serious discriminatory or other offensive acts are committed by the local populace, they can be considered persecution if they are knowingly tolerated by the authorities, or if the authorities refuse, or prove unable, to offer effective protection." *Handbook,* at ¶65.

34 The treatment that the applicant would receive if returned to Guinea would rise to the level of persecution and the government would be unwilling and unable to control those who would harm her. The applicant would certainly be beaten and humiliated; she may have her children taken from her, and have her freedom taken away from her through forced marriage. Her treatment would be in violation of articles 1–7, 12, 16, 18, and 19 of the Universal Declaration of Human Rights and related provisions of the ICCPR and CEDAW (*see,* exhibits E, F, and

G). These practices also clearly constitute harm sufficient to meet the "threat to life and freedom" requirement defined in *Matter of Acosta.*

PERSECUTION WILL BE "ON ACCOUNT OF"

35 The UN *Handbook* defines membership in a social group as comprising "persons of similar backgrounds, habits or social status." *Handbook,* ¶77. "Persecution on account of membership in a particular social group" refers to persecution directed toward an individual who is a member of a group sharing a "common, immutable characteristic." *Matter of Acosta,* 19 I. & N. Dec. 211 (BIA 1985). The common characteristic must be one that the group members cannot change, or should not be required to change, because the shared characteristic is fundamental to their individual identities or consciences. *Id.* at 233. Membership in a particular tribe or family, being of a particular gender, and being a mother are immutable characteristics that the applicant is unable to change. The Third Circuit has said that a social group can be "Iranian women who refuse to conform to the government's gender specific laws and social norms." *Fatin v. INS,* 12 F.3d 1233, 1241 (3d Cir. 1993). [Applicant] is a member of the social group of women who refuse to conform to the traditions of her family, religion, and community by having a child outside of marriage. This social group satisfies the test delineated in *Matter of Acosta,* requiring the presence of an "immutable" characteristic shared by all members of the group because she is a member of the group "women" "of her community" "with children out of wedlock" and there is no way she can or should change her membership therein. The applicant fears she will be physically and emotionally harmed by her family and community because of these immutable characteristics.

36 The Universal Declaration of Human Rights, as cited in the *Handbook,* guarantees the right to change religion and to "manifest it in public." *Handbook,* ¶71, *UDHR* art. 18. Persecution will be on account of religious belief where "serious measures of discrimination [are] imposed on persons because they practice their religion." *Handbook,* ¶72. Persecution will be on account of religious beliefs where beliefs about a woman's proper role and behavior differ from that of her family's beliefs. *In re S—A—*, Interim Dec, 3433 (BIA 2000). *In re S—A—*, concerns a Moroccan woman who is severely and regularly beaten by her father because she does not conform to his beliefs of how a Muslim woman should act. The woman was unable to go to the police because Morocco is a Muslim country that upholds the rights of fathers over their children. The applicant faces persecution on similar grounds because she has refused to conform to the religious beliefs of her people, both by refusing to obey her family and by having children out of wedlock. Guinea is a predominantly Muslim country where the government fails to take action to prevent fathers and husbands from abusing their children. The Court in *In re S—A—*distinguished that case from others where asylum had been denied because of the strong religious element. Unlike in *Gomez v. INS*, 947 F.2d 660 (2d Cir. 1991), persecution of [applicant] would not be on account of gender alone, but on account of her less fundamentalist religious practices. The religious reasons for the beatings faced by the applicant also mean that the persecution would not be only on the account of domestic violence alone, which was the reason for denying asylum in *Matter of R—A—*, Interim Dec. 3403 (BIA 1999).

37 Persecution on account of political opinions is also a grounds for asylum. *Handbook*, ¶80. A belief that women should have the right to make decisions about how they live is a form of political opinion. The Third Circuit had "little doubt that feminism qualifies as a political opinion within the meaning of the relevant statutes." *Fatin v. INS*, at 1242. In *Fatin*, Ms. Fatin was not granted asylum because the court was not convinced that her beliefs required her to defy the antiwomen laws. Here the applicant has already violated many of the customs designed to control and oppress women. These acts of defiance make [applicant] a target for further violence in her community.

WELL-FOUNDED FEAR OF PERSECUTION OF MY DAUGHTERS ON ACCOUNT OF SOCIAL GROUP

38 Finally, the applicant's daughters fear female genital mutilation (FGM) if returned to Guinea. Female genital mutilation is a very common practice in Guinea, with 60–90% of women experiencing the psychologically and physically scarring operation. FGM is often fatal and causes life-long adverse consequences (*see,* exhibit H). The applicant herself underwent excision (*see,* ¶7 supra). The United States Department of State has condemned the practice as being very harmful to women and recognizes that it is still practiced in Guinea, and that although the authorities there have made the practice illegal, steps to prevent FGM are often ineffectual. The Department of State has also found that the Guinean NGO that deals with FGM has declared that there is a well-founded fear of FGM for young girls who had not been excised previously (*see,* exhibit J). The BIA has agreed that FGM is persecution. *In re Kasinga,* 21 I. & N. Dec. 357 (BIA 1996). Like the woman in Kasinga, the applicant's daughters are young uncircumcised women of a family group that practices FGM and forced marriages. Given the power of the applicant's family to perform the operation on the applicant, it seems very unlikely that she could prevent it from happening to her daughters. FGM is performed by all the ethnic and religious groups in all parts of Guinea. The State Department report confirms that, despite laws against the practice, there have been no prosecutions and the practice continues (*see,* exhibit J).

SUMMARY OF MY FEARS AND REQUESTS

39 If deported to Guinea, it is more likely than not that I will suffer persecution on account of my membership in the social group of women who have had children out of wedlock, my religious opinion, which does not conform to beliefs about role of women and their treatment, and my feminist political opinion and practice.

40 If deported to Guinea, it is more likely than not that I will suffer severely in my family and community because of my state of motherhood and my nonconformity and that the police and government will not help me.

41 If deported to Guinea, it is more likely than not that I will suffer discrimination and social ostracism in any area of Guinea that I would live in on account of my status as a woman who had a baby out of wedlock and who defied the wishes of her family.

I may not be able to find a job due to pervasive employment discrimination against women in a very difficult economy. In addition, I may face even more severe condemnation by the strict Muslim communities.

42 I respectfully ask for asylum in the United States so that I may be free from persecution in Guinea.

VERIFICATION

I verify that the statements made in this declaration are true and correct. I understand that false statements herein are made subject to the penalties of perjury.

____________________________ ________________

[Name] [Date]

Appendix B
Sample Affidavit in Support of Application for Asylum

Editor's Note: The following is an actual affidavit in support of application for political asylum. Names and other identifying details have been removed; notes by the preparer, regarding further information required within the document, have been retained and are in italics. Social workers often can help immigrant clients draft the biographical sections and lay out the narratives of these applications.

TABLE OF CONTENTS

NONGOVERNMENTAL ORGANIZATION DOCUMENTS

Jon Lee Anderson, "After the Warlords," **New Yorker,** March 27, 2006 H
Lydia Polgreen and Marc Lacey, "Nigeria Will End Asylum for Warlord," **New York Times,** March 26, 2006 I
Moses Wantu, "Startling Revelation!" **AllAfrica.com,** March 24, 2006 J
Warren Hoge, "Liberian Seeks Extradition of Predecessor for Atrocities Trial," **New York Times,** March 18, 2006 K
Katharine Houreld, "Liberia: Healing the Wounds of Civil War," **Institute for War and Peace Reporting,** March 12, 2006 L
"Liberia: Despite Elections, Collapse of Justice Poses Risks," **Human Rights Watch,** September 30, 2005 M
"Easy Prey: Child Soldiers in Liberia," **Human Rights Watch,** September 1994 N
Bill Berkeley, "Liberia: Between Repression and Slaughter," **The Atlantic Monthly,** December 1992 O

EXHIBIT B

UNITED STATES DEPARTMENT OF JUSTICE

EXECUTIVE OFFICE FOR IMMIGRATION REVIEW

UNITED STATES IMMIGRATION COURT

PHILADELPHIA, PENNSYLVANIA

In the matter of [Applicant's name]
File No. [number]
In removal proceedings under section 240 of the Immigration and Nationality Act

AFFIDAVIT IN SUPPORT OF I-589 APPLICATION FOR ASYLUM

INTRODUCTION

1 My name is [name]. I am the respondent in the above-captioned removal proceeding. I respectfully submit this declaration in support of my claims for asylum and withholding of removal under Section 241(b) (3) of the Immigration and Nationality Act of 1952, as amended (hereinafter "Act" or "INA").

2 I am seeking asylum and withholding of removal because I am afraid that I will face persecution in Liberia on account of my race and membership in a particular social group.
3 I am afraid to return to Liberia on account of my membership in the Mandingo ethnic group.

INFORMATION ABOUT ME

4 I am a citizen and national of Liberia. I was born on [date] in Monrovia, Liberia.
5 I am a member of the Mandingo ethnic group. I speak Mandingo and English.
6 From [date] to [date], I attended preschool and elementary school at G. W. Gibson School in Monrovia.
7 From [date] to [date], I attended Zion Mission high school in Monrovia.
8 My father's name is [name]. He was killed by rebel soldiers in Liberia in 1994.
9 My mother's name is [name]. She disappeared in Liberia in 1992.

[[Note: respondent states that he is unsure of the names of his sisters, who disappeared after he fled Monrovia at the age of eight. [Name], his stepmother, may know their names.]]

10 My stepmother's name is [name]. She and my two half-brothers, [name] and [name], live in [city, state] in the United States. Both [half-brother] and [half-brother] were granted asylum by the Newark Asylum Office in Lyndhurst, New Jersey.
11 Presently, I live at [address].

FEAR

12 In 1990, my parents and I, along with my two sisters *[Ask respondent about his sisters; they are not mentioned in the I-589]*, were living at a house on [street] in Monrovia. *[Ask respondent to describe the neighborhood, as he later refers to the destruction of the area.]* My father, [name], was a businessman. My

mother, [name], was a housewife. My half-brothers, [name] and [name], lived next door to us with their mother [name], my father's second wife, and my stepmother, whom I called "[stepmother's nickname]."

13 In July 1990, Charles Taylor and his fighters of the National Patriotic Front of Liberia (NPFL) invaded Monrovia. They were specifically looking for Mandingo people to kill. At the time, I was eight years old and did not understand why the Mandingo people were being targeted. *[Ask respondent to describe the chaotic situation on the ground at the time.]* I remember hearing my mother's voice ordering me to "Run, run, run!" I ran out of our house and joined a crowd of people heading toward a bridge. During this time, I became separated from my family. I never saw my father, mother, or sisters again.

14 Some of the people with whom I fled knew my father. I found shelter with these family acquaintances, whom I knew as "[male acquaintance's nickname]" and his wife "[female acquaintance's nickname]." *[Ask respondent where [acquaintances] lived. Was this also on [street] in Monrovia?]* They were also of the Mandingo ethnic group. I called [male acquaintance] my "uncle," but we were not related to each other.

15 In late 1991, it became apparent that Charles Taylor's forces were again hunting down all Mandingo people in the Monrovia area. [Male acquaintance] and [female acquaintance] decided that we had to leave Liberia. One night, we took all the food we had and fled in a jeep.

16 [Male acquaintance] drove us toward the Liberia-Guinea border. Before we could make it into Guinea, three rebels in a jeep stopped us. [Male acquaintance] whispered to me to not tell them that we were Mandingo.

17 The rebels ordered [male acquaintance] out of the vehicle. They questioned him and ripped apart his clothes. They then tied him and took him into the surrounding bushes. I heard gunshots. I never saw [male acquaintance] again.

18 When the rebels came back, one of them asked me, "How old are you?" I said, "Nine almost." This rebel ordered me to come out of the jeep. They forced me into their own jeep, leaving [female acquaintance] behind. [Female acquaintance] was crying. I never saw her again.

19 One of the rebels hit my head with the butt of his gun, kicked me, and told me to sit on the floor of their jeep. I still have a scar on my forehead from this incident.

20 I did not know where the rebels were taking me, but it was a long trip. We arrived at a place that I found out later was called "SR Camp of Prince Johnson." The rebels told me that this was my new home and that if I did not obey their orders, they would "skin me alive." Prince Johnson had been a member of Taylor's NPFL but broke away to form another rebel group, the Independent National Patriotic Front of Liberia (INPFL).

21 There were many boys at the rebel camp. I and the other boys suffered many abuses for not obeying the rebels' orders to fight as child soldiers. They beat me on my back with a cane on a daily basis. They once banged my head against the wall. They broke my right thumb. I was starved for several days at a time. In addition, I was forced to watch other children killed for refusing rebel orders. These children were usually older children who were executed by shooting or beating to set an example for the rest of us. *[Refer respondent to Liberty Center for Survivors of Torture for a physical and psychological evaluation by a physician to support the asylum application.]*

22 I was held in the rebel camp from late 1991 until the Octopus War broke out in October 1992, when Charles Taylor's forces launched an all-out offensive on Monrovia. During the ensuing chaos, the rebels ordered me to fight. I managed to run away with another boy named [name].

23 [Boy's name] and I ran to the neighboring town, Bobolu. When people saw bloodstains on our shirts, they ran from us. They thought we were rebels coming to harm or kill them.

24 *[Ask respondent how he got from Bobolu to Monrovia, and what happened to [boy's name].]* At this point, I had not seen my family since July 1990. I was excited to see them, and I went searching for them in Monrovia. The morning that I arrived in Monrovia, I did not see anyone I recognized, and everything looked very different. [Street name], where I had lived with my family, was unrecognizable. My house was destroyed and abandoned.

25 I lived on the streets of Monrovia in a box, eating food out of the trash. I eventually found [male neighbor] and his family, Mandingo people who had been neighbors of my family. There were six or seven children who lived with the family, some of whom were also children that [male neighbor] had rescued off the street. I stayed with the family for three years in their house on [street name].

26 War among the different rebel factions again broke out in Monrovia on April 6, 1996. The family and I had to run away because Charles Taylor's rebels were yet again targeting Mandingo people to kill. *[Ask respondent where he and the family ran away to, and how long they were there.]* We returned to Monrovia when the fighting stopped. *[Ask respondent what happened between 1996 and 2002, and how the respondent left the family.]*

27 In March 2002, I began to work for money by cleaning houses. I would live in people's homes temporarily and work as their cleaning boy.

28 One day *[Ask respondent when this happened],* one of my customers, [customer name], told me that he had known my father. [Customer] told me that my father had been brutally killed by rebels. *[Ask the respondent which rebels he is referring to: Charles Taylor's NPLF, Prince Johnson's INPLF, or another rebel group.]* I later found out from my stepmother, [name], that my father was killed by rebels in 1994.

29 [Customer] also told me that he knew my stepmother, [name], and that she was living in the United States with her sons, my half-brothers [name] and [name].

30 With the help of [customer], my stepmother got in touch with me. I told her that I had heard that my mother, [name], was somewhere in Guinea near the Guinea-Liberia border *[Ask the respondent from whom he heard this.]* I wanted to search for my mother, but I did not have the money I needed to travel there. My stepmother sent me money so that I could search for my mother in Guinea.

31 I then traveled to Guinea in search of my mother. I never found her. Some people I met said that she had died on her way to Guinea from Liberia.

32 I returned to Monrovia and contacted my stepmother. I told her that I did not find my mother in Guinea. I realized I had no family members left in Liberia or Guinea. My stepmother told me that she would make financial arrangements with [customer] for me to come to the United States.

33 In late [date], I met [customer] and stayed at his house for a few days. We traveled to Gambia by boat on [date]. We spent two weeks in Gambia, and I obtained a Gambian passport using money that was sent by my stepmother, [name]. I did this because I was not able to obtain a Liberian passport. *[Ask respondent why he could not get a Liberian passport. Also, reconcile this with the Liberian passport referenced in part A.I., questions 19 through 21, of the I-589.]* [Customer] and I then went to Dakar, Senegal by automobile, a six-hour trip. We then boarded a flight to New York.

34 I entered the United States through John F. Kennedy Airport in New York on [date]. Upon arriving in New York, [customer] dropped me off at Penn Station, took my Gambian passport, and instructed me to board a Greyhound bus to Philadelphia. My stepmother, [name], and my half-brothers [name] and [name], met me in Philadelphia.

35 Because of my persecution as a Mandingo at the hands of both Charles Taylor's NPLF and Prince Johnson's INPLF, I fear my life is in danger if I return to Liberia.

WELL-FOUNDED

36 Article 1 of the 1951 Refugee Convention defines a refugee as an individual who "owing to well-founded fear of being persecuted for reasons of race, religion, nationality, membership of a particular social group or political opinion, is outside the country of his nationality and is unable, or owing to such fear, is unwilling to avail himself of the protection of that country."

37 In my twenty-one years of life in Liberia, I was forced to flee for my life three times when armed forces were targeting people from my ethnic group, the Mandingo.

38 My father was killed by rebel forces *[clarify which rebel group]* on account of being a Mandingo.

39 In addition to fleeing from the NPFL, I was persecuted by the INPFL. According to "Liberia: events since 1990," a Citizenship and Immigration Services Country Report by the United States Department of Homeland Security, the INPFL is a "dangerous and unpredictable group of armed men . . . [that Prince] Johnson led . . . in a manner that was described by the U.S. Committee for Refugees as 'erratic, mentally unstable, and psychotic.'" For nearly one year, I was held by the INPFL and subjected to physical and psychological abuse as described above.

40 Though Charles Taylor is now in exile in Nigeria, he has many loyalists who are still in Liberia causing problems for the Mandingo people. According to Human Rights Watch's "World Report 2001": "former Taylor faction fighters were placed in the security and police forces without serious efforts to provide training or to meet pledges to incorporate members from the other factions.... Ethnic Krahn and Mandingo people...were particularly susceptible to harassment at the hands of the state security apparatus."

41 Even with the election of Ellen Johnson Sirleaf as president of Liberia, the United States Department of State's consular information sheet for Liberia states that "the ability of Liberia's security forces to maintain law and order in the countryside is uncertain." The government is unable to control rebel elements, and fighting among the different rebel factions continues. I am convinced that there will never be peace in Liberia.

PERSECUTION

42 The United Nations High Commissioner for Refugees "Handbook on Procedures and Criteria for Determining Refugee Status" (hereinafter referred to as "UNHCR Handbook") states that "a threat to life or freedom on account of race, religion, nationality, political opinion or membership in a particular social group is always persecution."

43 The three times in my life when I had to flee were due to my fear that I would be killed as a member of the Mandingo ethnic group at the hands of Charles Taylor's NPFL forces.

44 According to the Human Rights Watch report "Easy prey: child soldiers in Liberia": "Life for children caught up in the civil war in Liberia is filled with random violence and acts of sickening cruelty." The same report consistently documents the use of child soldiers by the INPFL, the NPFL, and other rebel groups in Liberia. Due to my refusal to serve as a child soldier for Prince Johnson's INPFL, I was punished in the matter described above.

GROUNDS

45 The *UNHCR Handbook* states that "[r]ace…has to be understood in its widest sense to include all kinds of ethnic groups that are referred to as 'races' in common usage." Furthermore, the *Handbook* states that "a 'particular social group' normally comprises persons of similar background, habits or social status. A claim to fear of persecution under this heading may frequently overlap with a claim to fear of persecution on other grounds, i.e. race…"

46 People from the Mandingo tribe can be identified by their looks, dress, and language. While English is the language of education in Liberia, in common conversation, people speak their tribal languages, such as Mandingo. According to "Liberia: Events since 1990": "the Mandingoes (Malinke), the only recognized ethnic group that is geographically dispersed, are also ironically one of the most culturally, linguistically, and religiously unified of the groups."

47 Charles Taylor's NPFL has repeatedly targeted the Mandingo ethnic group as it considered the Mandingo to be supportive of President Samuel Doe, against whose government the NPFL was fighting. According to "Liberia: Events since 1990," "the NPFL kill[ed] primarily Mandingoes (Malinke) and Krahn (groups seen as supporters of Doe)."

48 [male acquaintance], with whom I was fleeing to Guinea when we were captured by the INPFL, was killed by the INPFL rebels due to his membership in the Mandingo tribe. The INPFL, though it turned against the NPFL from which it arose, was also opposed to the Samuel Doe regime and targeted its perceived supporters, including the Mandingo ethnic group.

RELIEF

49 For the reasons stated above, I respectfully ask the Court to grant me asylum in the United States because of my well-founded fear of persecution in Liberia.

50 Alternatively, I respectfully ask the Court to grant me withholding of removal from the United States because of my well-founded fear of persecution in Liberia.

VERIFICATION

51 I verify that the statements made in this declaration are true and correct. I understand that false statements herein are made subject to the penalties of perjury.

____________________________ ________________

[applicant name] [Date]

I declare that this document was prepared by me at the request of the Affiant on the basis of the information given to me by him.

____________________________ ________________

[Attorney name] [Date]

EXHIBIT C

THE UNITED STATES DEPARTMENT OF JUSTICE

EXECUTIVE OFFICE OF IMMIGRATION REVIEW

OFFICE OF THE IMMIGRATION JUDGE

PHILADELPHIA, PENNSYLVANIA

	)	
In the matter of:	)	
	)	
[applicant]	)	**[file number]**
	)	
	)	
Respondent.	)	
	)	

RESPONDENT'S MEMORANDUM OF LAW AND FACTS IN SUPPORT OF HIS APPLICATION FOR ASYLUM

Respondent, by his attorneys, representing him *pro bono,* submit this Memorandum of Law and Facts in support of his application for asylum or, in the alternative, withholding of removal. As set forth below, the facts, as well as statutes, case law, agency studies, and expert testimony support a grant of asylum.

I. INTRODUCTION

Until 1990, Respondent lived a normal life in Monrovia, Liberia. He lived with his parents and two sisters, with his two half-brothers and stepmother residing next door. In 1990, everything changed when Respondent's family was driven from their home because of Charles Taylor and the National Patriotic Front of Liberia (NPFL). Respondent was persecuted because of his membership in the Mandingo tribe. He was separated from his family and forced into a rebel camp as a child soldier. He ran away from this camp after being beaten, starved, and forced to watch the deaths of other children. Respondent lived in the woods and in the streets of Monrovia for months before being taken in by a family where he lived and worked as a housecleaner to earn money. One of his housecleaning clients eventually helped Respondent to leave Liberia, travel through Gambia and Senegal, and arrive in America.

Respondent fears persecution because the former NPLF members still target people of the Mandingo tribe. Respondent has been violently abused by the NPLF. They beat and threatened him because of his membership in the Mandingo tribe. Respondent knows that forced return to Liberia would likely lead to severe persecution and possibly to death. Mandingos are easily recognized by their dress, manners, and tribal language, and NPLF members are still active in Liberia. Because of his membership in the social group of the Mandingo tribe, Respondent has a well-founded fear of persecution if forced to return to Liberia.

II. FACTS

A Personal History

Respondent was born on [date], in Monrovia, Liberia, to [father's name] and [mother's name]. Respondent Aff. ¶ 4, 8, 9. He is a member of the Mandingo ethnic group, and speaks both English and Mandingo. Respondent Aff. ¶ 5. Until 1990, respondent lived in Monrovia with his parents and his sisters, and he attended preschool and elementary school at G. W. Gibson School. Respondent Aff. ¶ 6. His stepmother, [name], lived next door with his two half-brothers, [name] and [name]. Respondent's mother was a housewife and his father was a businessman. The family lived on [street], in downtown Monrovia. Respondent Aff. ¶ 12.

B Liberian Country Conditions

The Mandingo ethnic group continues to face grave dangers in Liberia. Underlying these dangers are deep-seated ethnic tensions revealed and exacerbated by more than two decades of brutal civil war. Throughout the 1990s, the Mandingo tribe suffered vicious acts of brutality and repression under the regime of Charles Taylor. He targeted the Mandingo tribe because of their purported backing of his predecessor, former President Samuel Doe, who was a member of the Krahn tribe. During Taylor's violent regime, political parties vied for power and pitted numerous indigenous ethic groups against one another. The entire country was devastated. In today's fragile postwar environment, the government is finding it difficult to stabilize the country and reintegrate more than one hundred thousand disarmed ex-combatants into society. Additionally, former perpetrators of human rights abuses currently hold positions of power in the newly formed government. Former warlords Adolphus "Peanut Butter" Dolo and Prince Yormie Johnson are only two such examples.[1]

During the years in which Charles Taylor and his rebels rose to power, the Mandingoes were at great risk of abuse from his party, the National Patriotic Front of Liberia (NPFL). "[One of the groups at risk] is constituted by those Liberians that are members of ethnic groups that have come to be identified as 'supporters' of one of the factions. Thus far this has primarily meant that Krahns and Mandingoes (Malinke) have been targets of violence."[2] Members of the Mandingo tribe were perceived as supporters of Doe, thus Taylor and his forces engaged in the systematic brutalization of the Mandingoes, civilians and political elites alike. Taylor successfully seized power in 1990 and left a war-ravaged country whose capital, Monrovia, was nearly destroyed.[3] Drawing on ethnic tensions between groups became a trademark of the civil war. For example, "Taylor recruited heavily from Nimba County, playing on the deep hatred many Nimbans feel for Krahns and Mandingoes."[4]

Human Rights Watch (HRW) reported in 1990: "The conflict kept its ethnic dimension, with the Taylor government indiscriminately accusing ethnic Mandingo, Krahn, and Gbandi citizens of Liberia of supporting the rebel incursion. Members of these groups faced growing discrimination, arbitrary arrests, and violence at the hands of the government and its supporters, based solely on their ethnicity." HRW found that Taylor and his political party, The National Patriotic Front of

Liberia (NPFL), had "violated the Geneva Conventions by committing widespread killing and torture of noncombatants, particularly Krahn and Mandingos."[5]

Warlords involved as many as 6,000 child soldiers in their brutal war. In 1994, The Human Rights Watch Children's Rights Project published a report entitled "Easy Prey: Child Soldiers in Liberia," which identified the use of child soldiers in Liberia as a grave human rights problem. Warlords found child soldiers easy to manipulate, and children often had no choice but to join with the warlords, as it was their only means of survival after the death of or separation from their families. These young fighters played many roles, ranging from spies, to executioners, to "cannon fodder to draw the fire of their adversaries."[6] Child soldiers were regularly beaten and abused by their own rebel factions, and many were drugged with amphetamines in an attempt to make them feel "strong and brave." Rebels threatened the children with death if they refused to carry out brutal acts of violence. They suffered severe mental and emotional trauma, and many experience symptoms of posttraumatic stress disorder.[7] Today, the government struggles to reintegrate these former soldiers into society.

Despite recent elections, the Mandingo people have many reasons to remain fearful. These ethnic tensions and Taylor's followers have not disappeared. A recent article published on AllAfrica.com reports that Taylor's loyalists are "holding secret meetings in an apparent attempt to cause havoc in the city."[8] As recently as 2000, Human Rights Watch reported that severe dangers continued for the Mandingoes:

> Ethnic Krahn and Mandingo people, historically seen to be allied with the repression of the former Doe government and with anti-Taylor factions during the war, were particularly susceptible to harassment at the hands of the state security apparatus. Following the violence in Monrovia in 1998, Krahn were targeted for extrajudicial executions, harassment, and politically motivated criminal charges. In the aftermath of the Lofa County incursions in 1999, security forces killed, tortured, and mistreated civilians, particularly members of the Mandingo ethnic group. During the incursions and counter-attacks in Lofa County, hundreds were killed and thousands of citizens as well as Sierra Leonean refugees were forced to flee the area. Although some of the alleged abuses by the security forces were investigated by the government, in all cases security personnel were treated leniently or exonerated. Since the 1999 and 2000 rebel incursions in Lofa County, Mandingo residents remain afraid to return to their homes.[9]

A writer for *The Liberian Times* identifies the ethnic tensions that set the stage for the 2005 election, and the challenges that lie ahead for the new government:

> Ethnic groups encourage the emergence of ethno-nationalism in order to mobilize supporters. The quest for power among politicians has engendered the sprouting of nearly 40 political parties representing various ethnic groups for the ensuing October presidential elections in Liberia.
>
> The proliferation of ethnic factions (Krahn, Mandingo, Gio, Mano, Lorma, Sarpo, etc.) during the 14-year civil war, ethnic cleansing and mass brutal murders committed by warring ethnic factions against harmless and innocent ethnic groups, are cases in point of ethnic loyalty eating the fabric of once stable Liberia. How can post-war Liberia eradicate or minimize this cancer that is consuming the unity and nationalism of Liberia? In my opinion, eradicating ethnic loyalty is illogical. . . .
>
> Ethnic affiliation as an extended family is a great asset in nation building especially when acting as a moral retaining influence upon, and means of security for its members. Furthermore, family, clan, and ethnic group are still the essential structures of social relationship in Liberia.[10]

The newly elected government is not yet able to protect the Mandingo people. Even rebuilding its capital, Monrovia, and providing basic needs, such as running water and electricity, continues to prove difficult. Taylor fled to Nigeria in 2003 as a temporary measure in a deal brokered by the international community to restore some semblance of peace in Liberia. In 2005, Liberia held what has been hailed as a successful democratic election. The people elected Ellen Johnson Sirleaf as their president. She has the support of the United States and the international community. Recently, however, she too, admitted that maintaining peace in Liberia and thus protecting its citizens remains an uphill battle. She said at a news conference: "Liberia's peace is fragile. There are many loyalists in our country to Mr. Taylor, there are many business interests he has. Whatever decision is taken by the African leadership must ensure that the safety of the Liberian people and the stability of our nation is not undermined."[11]

Further threatening peace and presenting a continuing danger to the Mandingo people is the fact that many of Charles Taylor's supporters remain inside Liberia, and some may aim to destabilize the political situation.[12] The *New York Times* reports that "even from exile, [Taylor] has maintained influence in Liberia, with thousands of young combatants still loyal to him, Ms. Johnson Sirleaf said, making her plea [that Nigeria hand over Taylor] 'courageous but risky.'"[13] Both former members of Taylor's government and former warlords have been elected to powerful positions within Johnson Sirleaf's government. For example, Edwin Snowe, a prominent member of Taylor's government, has been elected speaker of the house, and thus holds the third most powerful political position in Liberia. Prince Johnson, former head of the Independent National Patriotic Front of Liberia (INPFL), is now a senior senator from Nimba County. Johnson was notorious for two things: his use of child soldiers and his brutal torture and murder of former president Samuel Doe, an event which was captured on videotape and is still today circulated throughout Monrovia by street vendors.[14] The democratically elected Liberian leadership has not demonstrated an ability to protect its citizens—no matter their ethnicity—from the brutality of warlords like Charles Taylor and Prince Johnson.

Much work remains to be done before Liberia is safe for Mandingoes. Alan Doss, the head of the United Nations Mission in Liberia (UNMIL), has warned of the need for the continued presence of peacekeeping forces, which he sees as vital to bringing stability to Liberia during the coming years. The United Nations reports: "Mr. Doss stressed that UNMIL is crucial to help maintain security in the 'fragile' State until the national security structure is complete, to help extend State authority to the countryside, to facilitate the reintegration of ex-soldiers and displaced persons, and to assist reconciliation efforts. [...] 'I have personally visited all 15 counties of Liberia and witnessed at first hand the human and physical consequences of economic and social collapse," [Mr. Doss] said. "A massive effort will therefore be required to ensure that there is some tangible progress in the months ahead."[15]

Voluntary repatriation of Liberian refugees from neighboring countries has previously occurred. Each time, however, "while many thousands of Liberian refugees were able to return to Liberia without fear of political persecution, some members of the Mandingo and Krahn communities continued to have valid fears."[16] This situation remains true to this day, particularly in areas where anti-Mandingo sentiments and support of Taylor are rampant, like in Nimba County. As stated in the "Consular Information Sheet: Liberia," published by the United States Department of State on December 7, 2005: "Expectations are high for the future, but by most measures Liberia is still one of the poorest countries in the world and noticeable change will take time [...]. [t]he ability of Liberia's security forces to maintain law and order in the countryside is uncertain."[17]

C Evidence of Persecution and a Well-Founded Fear

In July 1990, Charles Taylor and his National Patriotic Front of Liberia (NPFL) invaded Monrovia.[18] Because Taylor perceived the Mandingo ethnic group as supporters of the existing Doe government, Taylor's forces sought to kill members of the Mandingo people.[19] At eight years old, Respondent was too young to understand why the Mandingo people were being targeted, but he remembers his mother's voice ordering him to "Run, run, run!" Frightened, he did as he was told, and followed a crowd of people heading towards a bridge. He became separated from his family and never saw his mother, father, or sisters again. Respondent Aff. ¶ 13. Some of the people with whom Respondent fled knew his family. Respondent found shelter with family acquaintances whom he knew as "[male acquaintance's nickname]" and his wife "[female acquaintance's nickname]." They were also members of the Mandingo ethnic group. Respondent Aff. ¶ 14.

In late 1991, Monrovia had become too dangerous for members of the Mandingo ethnic group. Respondent Aff. ¶ 15. One night, Respondent, [male acquaintance], and [female acquaintance] fled in a jeep. This was the Respondent's second experience fleeing in fear from the NPFL because he was a member of the Mandingo ethnic group. As they drove toward the Liberia-Guinea border, three rebels stopped them. Respondent was told by [male acquaintance] not to tell the rebels that they were Mandingo. Respondent Aff. ¶ 16. The rebels ordered [male acquaintance] out of the jeep. Respondent watched them question him and tear apart his clothes. He saw them tie [male acquaintance] and take him into the surrounding bushes. Respondent then heard gunshots, and never saw [male acquaintance] again. Respondent Aff. ¶ 17.

Respondent was then kidnapped by the rebels. As he waited alone in the jeep with [female acquaintance], who was crying, Respondent was approached by one of the rebels. They asked him how old he was. "Nine almost," he replied. The rebel ordered Respondent out of the jeep, and forced him into their jeep. Respondent never saw [female acquaintance] again. Respondent Aff. ¶ 18. Once in the rebel's jeep, Respondent was struck in the head by one of the rebels, using the butt of a gun. He was kicked, and told to sit on the floor of the jeep. Respondent still has a scar on his forehead from this beating. Respondent Aff. ¶ 19.

Respondent was not told where the rebels were taking him, but after a long journey, Respondent arrived at a place he later learned was called "SR Camp of Prince Johnson." Respondent Aff. ¶ 20. Prince Johnson was formerly second-in-command under Charles Taylor's NPFL, but broke away to form another rebel group, the Independent National Patriotic Front of Liberia (INPFL).[20] The rebels told the Respondent that this was his new home, and that if he did not obey their orders, they would "skin [him] alive." Respondent Aff. ¶ 20. Respondent lived at the rebel camp with many other boys who were expected to fight as child soldiers. Respondent suffered severe abuses for refusing rebels' orders to fight as a child soldier for the INPFL. On a daily basis, the rebels beat Respondent on his back with a cane. They banged his head against a wall, and broke his right thumb. He was starved for several days at a time. The rebels forced Respondent to watch them kill (by shooting or beating) other children for refusing rebel orders. The INPFL rebels intended to set an example for and instill fear in Respondent, and other captive children. Respondent Aff. ¶ 21.

Respondent was held in the INPFL rebel camp from late 1991 until October 1992, when the Octopus Operation broke out in Monrovia.[21] During the ensuing chaos, the rebels ordered Respondent to fight. He refused, and managed to run away with another boy, named [name]. Respondent Aff. ¶ 22. With [name], Respondent ran into the neighboring town. When people saw the boys' blood-stained clothing, they ran from them, thinking they were rebels coming to harm or kill them. Respondent Aff. ¶ 23.

Respondent made his way to Monrovia *[what is proximity between this town—"Bobolu" and Monrovia?]* where he was determined to find his family again. By this point, war-torn Monrovia looked completely different, and Respondent could not find anyone he knew or recognized. His family's street, [street name], was unrecognizable. His house was destroyed and abandoned. To survive, Respondent lived on the streets, in a box, eating food out of the trash. Respondent Aff. ¶ 24–25. Eventually, Respondent found [male neighbor] and his family, Mandingo people who had been neighbors on [street]. Respondent lived with the family for three years, along with six or seven children, some of whom had also been rescued off the street.

War broke out between rebel factions in Monrovia on April 6, 1996,[22] forcing Respondent to flee for his life, for a third time. Some of the rebel factions again targeted the Mandingo ethnic group and sought to kill Mandingoes. Respondent was frightened and fled with the family. Respondent Aff. ¶ 26.

In March 2002, Respondent learned that his father had been killed by rebels because he was Mandingo. Respondent had been working for money cleaning people's houses, while living in their homes. Respondent Aff. ¶ 27. One of Respondent's customers, [name], told Respondent that he had known Respondent's father. He reported that Respondent's father had been brutally killed by rebels because he was Mandingo. *[Not clear whether these rebels were part of NPFL, INPFL, or another faction.]* Respondent Aff. ¶ 38. Respondent later confirmed this with his stepmother, who told Respondent his father had been killed by rebels in 1994. Respondent Aff. ¶ 28. [Customer] put Respondent in touch with his stepmother, who was living in the United States with Respondent's half-brothers. Respondent's stepmother helped him by sending him money so he could try to search for his mother, who Respondent had heard was in Guinea near the Guinea-Liberia border. Respondent Aff. ¶ 30. Respondent, however, never found his mother. He traveled to Guinea, where he learned that his mother had died on her way there from Liberia. Respondent Aff. ¶ 31. Realizing that he had no family members left in Guinea or Liberia, Respondent again contacted his stepmother and began to make arrangements to travel to the United States, where his only known relatives resided. Respondent Aff. ¶ 32.

III. ARGUMENT

This Court should grant Respondent's application for asylum or, in the alternative, withholding of removal. To receive a grant of asylum, an applicant must demonstrate (1) that he or she is statutorily eligible for asylum and (2) that discretion should be exercised in his or her favor. 8 U.S.C.A. § 1158(b) (1999); *INS v. Cardoza-Fonseca,* 480 U.S. 421, 443 (1987). The Respondent is eligible under the statute because he was persecuted in the past by the NPLF on account of his social group membership and he has a well-founded fear of future persecution if forced to return. Further, in light of the lasting effects of the psychological and physical abuse of the Respondent, a favorable exercise of discretion is warranted. Because the Respondent can satisfy both prongs of the statute, this Court should exercise its discretion and grant his application for asylum.

A Respondent Is Eligible for a Grant of Asylum Because He Has Suffered Past Persecution in His Homeland and Has a Well-Founded Fear of Future Persecution if Forced to Return.

The Respondent is eligible for asylum under Section 208 of the Immigration and Nationality Act (the "Act"), which authorizes the Attorney

General to grant asylum to any alien determined to be a refugee. 8 U.S.C.A. § 1158(b) (1999). A "refugee" is a person who is "unable or unwilling to return to, and is unable or unwilling to avail...himself of the protection of, [his home] country because of persecution ***or*** a well-founded fear of persecution on account of race, religion, nationality, membership in a particular ***social group,*** or political opinion." 8 U.S.C.A. § 1101(a)(42)(A) (1999) (emphasis added). Respondent clearly meets the statutory definition of a refugee because his credible sworn affidavit and anticipated testimony at the hearing of this matter demonstrate that he was persecuted in the past by the NPLF on account of his social group. *Vente v. Gonzales,* 415 F.3d 296, 300 (3d Cir. 2005) (noting that "[t]o establish eligibility for asylum, an applicant must demonstrate past persecution by substantial evidence"). *Chen v. Gonzales,* 434 F. 3d 212, 217 (3d Cir. 2005) (stating that "relief may be granted solely on the credible testimony of the applicant). The Respondent also meets the statutory definition of a refugee because he has a well-founded fear of future persecution on account of his social group should he be forced to return to Liberia. *Vente v. Gonzales,* 415 F.3d at 300. Accordingly, this Court should favorably exercise its discretion and grant asylum to the Respondent.

1 Respondent Has Suffered Past Persecution on Account of His Social Group

a The Liberian Armed Rebels' Treatment of Respondent Constitutes Persecution.

Neither the INA nor accompanying regulations define persecution. However, the Third Circuit has described it as "threats to life, confinement, torture, and economic restrictions so severe that they constitute a threat to life or freedom." *Fatin v. INS,* 12 F.3d 1233, 1240 (3d Cir. 1993). Persecution encompasses "severe" conduct, but not "all treatment our society regards as unfair, unjust or even unlawful or unconstitutional." *Id.* Persecution also includes non–life threatening violence and physical abuse. *Voci v. Gonzales,* 409 F.3d 607, 615 (3d Cir. 2005) ("[M]ultiple beatings inflicted on the same respondent on multiple occasions are more likely to give rise to a finding of persecution"). Also, the persecution must be committed either by the government or a group that the government cannot or will not control. *Gao v. Ashcroft,* 299 F.3d 266, 272 (3d Cir. 2002).

Respondent was persecuted by the NPLF, a clandestine force under the command of Charles Taylor. He was separated from his family, beaten, starved, and threatened with death over the course of many of his adolescent and childhood years. During Respondent's imprisonment in the rebel camp, he was beaten, starved, detained in deplorable conditions, and witnessed various murders. He lived on the streets of Monrovia for many months after running away from the rebel camp. Respondent lived in constant fear of further Mandingo killings. Respondent was only able to escape because one of his housecleaning clients provided him with a means to escape. These acts unquestionably constitute persecution.

b The Persecution Respondent Suffered Was on Account of His Membership in a Social Group.

According to *Matter of Acosta,* a social group may be based on a common, immutable characteristic. 19 I&N Dec. 211, 232 (BIA 1985). A social group comprised of members of a tribe which has been targeted by militant, rebel forces fits within a reasonable interpretation of this phrase. First, Mandingos have the "immutable characteristic[s]" of looks and language. In the context of Liberia, each member of the social group is a target of Charles Taylor and the NPLF, a reality that Respondent is powerless to change. *Matter of Kasinga,* 21 I&N Dec. 357, 366 (BIA 1996). ("The characteristics of being a 'young woman' and a 'member of the Tchamba-Kunsuntu Tribe' cannot be changed."); *Fatin v. INS,* 12 F.3d 1233, 1239–1240 (3rd Cir. 1993).

Respondent's status as a Mandingo also meets the social group standard set forth by the *UNHCR Handbook on Refugees:*

> Membership in a social group may be at the root of persecution because there is no confidence in the group's loyalty to the Government or because the political outlook, antecedents, or economic activity of its members, or the very existence of the social group as such is held to be an obstacle to Government policies.

UNHCR Handbook at 78.

2 The Respondent Also Has a Well-Founded Fear of Future Persecution on Account of His Membership in a Social Group

Notwithstanding that his past persecution independently supports a grant of asylum, the Respondent's case is even more compelling because he also has a well-founded fear of future persecution on account of his membership in a social group.[23] An applicant who establishes past persecution ***is presumed to*** have a well-founded fear of future persecution. 8 C.F.R. § 208.13(b)(l) (2002) (emphasis added); *Matter of Chen,* 20 I. & N. Dec. at 18 ("[A]n alien who has been persecuted in the past by his country's government has reason to fear similar persecution in the future"). Once an applicant establishes past persecution, the burden of proof shifts to the government to rebut the presumption. This presumption may be rebutted ***only*** if the government demonstrates by ***a preponderance*** of the evidence that since the applicant's persecution occurred, there has been a "fundamental change" in conditions such that the applicant (a) no longer has a well-founded fear of persecution in his home country or (b) could avoid future persecution by relocating in his home country and that relocating would be reasonable. 8 C.F.R. § 208.13(b)(l)(i)-(ii) (emphasis added).

This presumption notwithstanding, through his credible sworn affidavit and his anticipated testimony at the hearing on this matter, Respondent has demonstrated a well-founded fear of future persecution by Liberian rebels on account of his membership in a social group. To establish a well-founded fear of future persecution, Respondent need only show that persecution is a "reasonable possibility" in light of objective, credible evidence. *Cardoza-Fonseca,* 480 U.S. at 440.

The INS regulations (as adopted under the Bureau of Citizenship and Immigration Services ("BCIS") under the Department of Homeland Security) establish a three-part test (the "BCIS Test") to determine if an applicant has a well-founded fear of persecution. Respondent meets this test if (a) he subjectively fears persecution in Liberia on account of one or more recognized bases for asylum, (b) there is a "reasonable possibility" that he will suffer persecution if he returns to Liberia, and (c) he is "unable or unwilling to return to, or avail... [himself] of the protection of [Liberia] because of such fear." 8 C.F.R. § 208.13(b)(2)(A)-(C). Respondent meets all three parts of this test.

a Respondent Subjectively Fears Future Persecution if Forced to Return to Liberia, and His Fear Is Genuine.

Respondent strongly believes that if he is forced to return to Liberia, he will be persecuted by Liberian rebels on account of his membership in a social group. Therefore, Respondent satisfies the first part of the BCIS test. 8 C.F.R. § 208.13(b)(2)(A).

b Respondent's Fear of Persecution Is Objectively Reasonable.

Respondent also meets the second part of the BCIS test because there is a "reasonable possibility" that Respondent will be persecuted if forced to return to Liberia. 8 C.F.R. § 208.13(b)(2)(A). Respondent's fear is reasonable in light of the persecution he has already suffered at the hands of the Liberian rebels. *In re N-M-A-*, 22 I. & N. Dec. 312 (BIA 1998) (recognizing "past [persecution] serves as an evidentiary proxy for the future").

Further, Respondent's fear is reasonable because it is clear that the Liberian rebel forces are still present in the country and have not been brought to justice. Additionally, country conditions in Liberia have not fundamentally changed. An election in late 2005 did little to diminish the power of the armed rebel forces in the country; United Nations military forces are still present in the country and their continued presence is crucial to the maintenance of stability in the nation. As such, it is reasonably possible, indeed, reasonably probable, that Respondent will be persecuted if he returns to Liberia. Respondent therefore satisfies the second prong of the BCIS Test.

c Respondent's Fear of Persecution Is the Primary Reason He Is Unable and Unwilling to Return to Liberia.

The third and final part of the BCIS Test requires Respondent to demonstrate that his fear of persecution is the primary reason he is unable or unwilling to return to Liberia. 8 C.F.R. § 208.13(b)(2)(C). Respondent meets this requirement. As he will credibly testify at the hearing and as he stated in his sworn affidavit, he cannot return to Liberia because he fears persecution, kidnapping, and torture because of his membership in a social group. He is afraid that he will be tortured and ultimately executed by the rebel forces with no regard for his rights. Respondent continues to fear for his safety and his life if he is forced to return to Liberia.

Accordingly, Respondent has demonstrated a well-founded fear of future persecution because he satisfies all three parts of the BCIS test. Therefore, in addition to being eligible for asylum based on his past persecution, he is also statutorily eligible for asylum because he has demonstrated a well-founded fear of future persecution on account of his social group. This Court therefore should favorably exercise its discretion and grant Respondent asylum.

B The Government Cannot Meet Its Burden of Proving That Respondent No Longer Has a Well-Founded Fear of Persecution or That He Could Avoid Persecution by Relocating Within Liberia and That It Would Be Reasonable for Him to Do So.

Despite the recent election in Liberia, human rights abuses and impunity persist. The supporters of Charles Taylor, as well as other warlords, are largely being recycled into the new government. A Human Rights Watch Report of late 2005 clearly states that in order to consolidate peace in Liberia "the individuals responsible for war crimes and crimes against humanity committed during Liberia's armed conflicts must be kept out of the civil service, police and army and be held accountable for their crimes,"[24] which is not being heeded. Moreover, the rise of the clandestine groups has further deteriorated the human rights conditions. Were Respondent to return to Liberia, he would be in danger for any number of these reasons.

The government cannot show that, since the time of Respondent's persecution and flight from Liberia, there have been fundamental changes that would eliminate the basis for his well-founded fear of persecution. There is no evidence that the new regime of President Johnson Sirleaf has made any progress in bringing armed rebel groups to justice.

Finally, relocation in Liberia is not a possibility as ethnic tensions between groups became a trademark of the civil war. For example, Taylor was known to recruit from certain regions in Liberia that used a deep "hatred many Nimbans feel for Krahns and Mandingoes, and Nimba has since been routinely identified as Taylor's strongest area of support" (see Exhibit G); thus it is likely that Respondent will be in danger in many other areas of the nation as they were anti-Mandingo and supported the massacres of the tribe during the presidency of Taylor.

C Date Discrepancies on Forged Documents Are Insignificant and Easily Explained [explain why documents are forged].

D This Court Should Exercise Its Discretion and Grant Respondent's Application for Asylum.

In exercising its discretion to grant an application for asylum, this Court should consider the totality of the circumstances and Respondent's actions in his flight from Liberia, as well as the regulations and case law. *In re H*____, 21 I. & N. Dec. 337, 347 (BIA 1996). The BIA has advised that "[c]entral to a discretionary finding in past persecution cases should be careful attention to compelling, humanitarian considerations that would be involved if the refugee were to be forced to return to a country where he or she was persecuted in the past." *Id.* In addition, "the danger of persecution should generally outweigh all but the most egregious of adverse factors." *Id.* at 348 (*quoting Matter of Pula,* 19 I. & N. Dec. 467, 474 (BIA 1987)) (superseded by regulation on other grounds).

Respondent is still traumatized by his kidnapping, beatings, imprisonment, and the child soldier camp that he knew in Liberia. See Waggeh Aff. Respondent fears for his safety in Liberia. Forcing him to return would put his life in serious danger. Further, it would aggravate the psychological and physical recovery efforts that he has made. As such, it would be inhumane to force Respondent to return to Liberia. Therefore, this Court should grant Respondent's application for asylum.

E If This Court Does Not Grant Respondent Asylum, He Is Entitled to Withholding of Removal.

a Respondent Is Entitled to Withholding of Removal Because It Is More Likely Than Not That He Will Face Persecution if Forced to Return to Liberia.

If this Court denies Respondent's application for asylum, Respondent is entitled to withholding of removal pursuant to Section 241 of the Act, which prohibits the Attorney General from removing an alien to a country if the alien's "life or freedom would be threatened in that country" on account of race, religion, nationality, membership in a particular social group or political opinion. 8 U.S.C.A. § 123l(b)(3)(A) (1999). The United States Supreme Court has interpreted the phrase "would be threatened" to require a showing that it is "more likely than not" that the applicant will be subject to persecution upon deportation. *Cardoza-Fonseca,* 480 U.S. at 430. Once an applicant makes this showing, withholding of removal is mandatory. *Id.* at 443–444.

As with asylum, if the applicant has shown past persecution, he is entitled to a presumption that his life or freedom would be threatened on return to that same country. 8 C.F.R. § 208.16(b)(l)(i) (2003). This presumption may be rebutted only by a preponderance of evidence establishing that conditions in that country have changed to such an extent that it is no longer probable that he would be persecuted or that he could avoid persecution by relocating within the country and that it would be reasonable for him to do so. *Id.*

Respondent is entitled to withholding of removal because the government cannot prove that it is no longer more likely than not that Respondent would be persecuted if forced to return to Liberia or that relocation is a viable, reasonable alternative. Respondent has established that the armed rebels persecuted him on account of his membership in a social group. Respondent has suffered physically and psychologically because of this persecution. Respondent's testimony, as well as other objective evidence, demonstrates that not only is it "more likely than not" that he would suffer continued persecution if forced to return to Liberia, but he would probably be kidnapped, tortured, and put to death.

b The One Year Bar Does Not Apply to Respondent, Because He Filed Within One Year of His Arrival.

Respondent entered the United States on [date]. He filed his initial application for asylum within one year, but was denied because he did not produce his I-94 card at his interview with an asylum officer. However, he is now able to produce this required document. See attachments to I-589.

IV. CONCLUSION

For all of the reasons set forth above, [applicant], by his attorneys, respectfully requests that this Court grant his request for asylum or, in the alternative, withholding of removal.

EXHIBIT D

Country Conditions: Liberian Politics and Dangers to the Mandingo Ethnic Group

For more than a decade, the Mandingo tribe suffered vicious acts of brutality and repression under the regime of Charles Taylor. He targeted the Mandingo tribe because of their purported backing of his predecessor, former President Samuel Doe, who was a member of the Krahn tribe. The bloody civil war that took place in Liberia over the past two decades pitted indigenous ethic groups against one another, while numerous political parties vied for power and devastated the country.

The war revealed and exacerbated deep-seated ethnic tensions, which remain high in today's fragile postwar environment as the government is finding it difficult to reintegrate more than one hundred thousand disarmed ex-combatants into society. These obstacles continue to pose a threat to the Mandingo people as even former perpetrators of human rights abuses currently hold positions of power in the newly formed government. Former warlords Adolphus "Peanut Butter" Dolo and Prince Yormie Johnson, notorious for supervising the torture and killing of the former president Samuel Doe in 1990, are only two such examples.[25]

During the years in which Charles Taylor and his rebels rose to power, several groups were prone to abuse from his party, the National Patriotic Front of Liberia (NPFL). One such "[. . .] group is constituted by those Liberians that are members of ethnic groups that have come to be identified as 'supporters' of one of the factions. Thus far this has primarily meant that Krahns and Mandingoes (Malinke) have been targets of violence."[26] Members of the Mandingo tribe were perceived as supporters of Doe, thus Taylor and his forces engaged in the systematic brutalization of the Mandingoes, civilians and political elites alike. Taylor successfully seized power in 1990, and left a war-ravaged country whose capital, Monrovia, was nearly destroyed.[27] Drawing on ethnic tensions between groups became a trademark of the civil war. For example, "Taylor recruited heavily from Nimba County, playing on the deep hatred many Nimbans feel for Krahns and Mandingoes, and Nimba has since been routinely identified as Taylor's strongest area of support."[28]

A 1990 article in *The Nation* magazine stated:

> The war in Liberia, in which rival rebel forces led by Charles Taylor and Prince Johnson have been trying to destroy each other and overthrow the regime of President Samuel Kanyon Doe, has turned into a nightmare for that small West African nation's civilian population. Much of the country has been laid to waste. Hundreds of thousands have had to flee their homes and thousands of noncombatants have been murdered, including many women and children who had taken shelter in churches and in settlements under the protection of the International Committee of the Red Cross. Members of the Gio and Mano tribes have been massacred by government troops because they are considered supporters of the forces attempting to topple Doe; in turn, rebel troops have attacked members of Doe's Krahn tribe and of the Mandingos, a mercantile tribe considered too accommodating to Doe.[29]

Human Rights Watch (HRW) reported in 1990: "The conflict kept its ethnic dimension, with the Taylor government indiscriminately accusing ethnic Mandingo, Krahn, and Gbandi citizens of Liberia of supporting the rebel incursion. Members of these groups faced growing discrimination, arbitrary arrests, and violence at the hands of the government and its supporters, based solely on their ethnicity." HRW found that Taylor and his political party, The National Patriotic Front of Liberia (NPFL), had "violated the Geneva Conventions by committing widespread killing and torture of noncombatants, particularly Krahn and Mandingos."[30] Despite recent elections, these ethnic tensions and Taylor's followers have not disappeared. A recent article published on AllAfrica.com reports that Taylor's loyalists are "holding secret meetings in an apparent attempt to cause havoc in the city."[31]

Warlords involved as many as 6,000 child soldiers in their brutal war. In 1994, The Human Rights Watch Children's Rights Project published a report entitled "Easy Prey: Child Soldiers in Liberia," which identified the use of child soldiers in Liberia as a grave human rights problem. Warlords found child soldiers easy to manipulate, and children often had no choice but to join with the warlords, as it was their only means of survival after the death of or separation from their families. These young fighters played many roles, ranging from spies, to executioners, to "cannon fodder to draw the fire of their adversaries."[32] Child soldiers were regularly beaten and abused by their own rebel factions, and many were drugged with amphetamines in an attempt to make them feel "strong and brave." Rebels threatened the children with death if they refused to carry out brutal acts of violence. They suffered severe mental and emotional trauma, and many experience symptoms of posttraumatic stress disorder.[33] Today, the government struggles to reintegrate these former soldiers into society.

As recently as 2000, Human Rights Watch reported that severe dangers continued for the Mandingo people:

> Ethnic Krahn and Mandingo people, historically seen to be allied with the repression of the former Doe government and with anti-Taylor factions during the war, were particularly susceptible to harassment at the hands of the state security apparatus. Following the violence in Monrovia in 1998, Krahn were targeted for extrajudicial executions, harassment, and politically motivated criminal charges. In the aftermath of the Lofa County incursions in 1999, security forces killed, tortured, and mistreated civilians, particularly members of the Mandingo ethnic group. During the

incursions and counter-attacks in Lofa County, hundreds were killed and thousands of citizens as well as Sierra Leonean refugees were forced to flee the area. Although some of the alleged abuses by the security forces were investigated by the government, in all cases security personnel were treated leniently or exonerated. Since the 1999 and 2000 rebel incursions in Lofa County, Mandingo residents remain afraid to return to their homes.[34]

Despite recent elections, the Mandingo people have many reasons to remain fearful. These ethnic tensions and Taylor's followers have not disappeared. A recent article published on AllAfrica.com reports that Taylor's loyalists are "holding secret meetings in an apparent attempt to cause havoc in the city."[35] A writer for *The Liberian Times* identifies the ethnic tensions that set the stage for the 2005 election, and the challenges that lie ahead for the new government:

> Ethnic groups encourage the emergence of ethno-nationalism in order to mobilize supporters. The quest for power among politicians has engendered the sprouting of nearly 40 political parties representing various ethnic groups for the ensuing October presidential elections in Liberia.
>
> The proliferation of ethnic factions (Krahn, Mandingo, Gio, Mano, Lorma, Sarpo, etc.) during the 14-year civil war, ethnic cleansing and mass brutal murders committed by warring ethnic factions against harmless and innocent ethnic groups, are cases in point of ethnic loyalty eating the fabric of once stable Liberia. How can post-war Liberia eradicate or minimize this cancer that is consuming the unity and nationalism of Liberia? In my opinion, eradicating ethnic loyalty is illogical. . . .
>
> Ethnic affiliation as an extended family is a great asset in nation building especially when acting as a moral retaining influence upon, and means of security for its members. Furthermore, family, clan, and ethnic group are still the essential structures of social relationship in Liberia.[36]

The tensions and dangers continue in the war-ravaged country. Even rebuilding its capital, Monrovia, and providing basic needs such as running water and electricity, continues to prove difficult. Taylor fled to Nigeria in 2003 as a temporary measure in a deal brokered by the international community to restore some semblance of peace in Liberia. In 2005, Liberia held what has been hailed as a successful democratic election. The people elected Ellen Johnson Sirleaf as their president. She has the support of the United States and the international community. Recently, however, she too, admitted that maintaining peace in Liberia and thus protecting its citizens remains an uphill battle. She said at a news conference: "Liberia's peace

> is fragile. There are many loyalists in our country to Mr. Taylor, there are many business interests he has. Whatever decision is taken by the African leadership must ensure that the safety of the Liberian people and the stability of our nation is not undermined."[37]

Johnson Sirleaf continued, describing the volatile political climate: "We inherited a problem, we are faced with serious pressure, we are a small country, we have no powers that others have, we have no security forces to protect our people and the safety of our nation, so we are caught in a situation that we have to take a major decision that should have been taken long before, giving us an opportunity to pursue our development agenda."[38]

Further threatening peace and presenting a continuing danger to the Mandingo people is the fact that many of Charles Taylor's supporters remain inside Liberia. The *New York Times* reports that "even from exile, [Taylor] has maintained influence in Liberia, with thousands of young combatants still loyal to him, Ms. Johnson Sirleaf said, making her plea 'courageous but risky.'"[39] Former members of Taylor's government and former warlords have been elected to powerful positions within Johnson Sirleaf's government. For example, Edwin Snowe, a prominent member of Taylor's government, has been elected speaker of the house, and thus holds the third most powerful political position in Liberia. Prince Johnson, former head of the Independent National Patriotic Front of Liberia (INPFL), is now a senior senator from Nimba County. Johnson was notorious for two things: his use of child soldiers and his brutal torture and murder of former president Samuel Doe, an event which was captured on videotape and is still today circulated throughout Monrovia by street vendors.[40]

In September 2005, Human Rights Watch published a report entitled "Liberia at the Crossroads: Human Rights Challenged for the New Government." It warned:

> Candidates in the upcoming elections include at least three former leaders of armed factions, five individuals subject to United Nations sanctions for activities aimed at undermining peace in Liberia and the sub-region, and several former high-level military commanders accused of war crimes. These individuals, who have in the past shown complete disregard for the rule of law and due process, could resort to force and other extra-legal measures to circumvent and subvert Liberia's political process and the legal system if elected to office.

The report noted the urgent need to rebuild the judicial system, restructure the police forces and army, and bring past violators of human rights to justice.[41]

Much work remains to be done before Liberia is safe for Mandingoes. Alan Doss, the head of the United Nations Mission in Liberia (UNMIL) has warned of the need for the continued presence of peacekeeping forces, which he sees as vital to bringing stability to Liberia during the coming years. The United Nations reports: "Mr. Doss stressed that UNMIL is crucial to help maintain security in the 'fragile' State until the national security structure is complete, to help extend State authority to the countryside, to facilitate the reintegration of ex-soldiers and displaced persons, and to assist reconciliation efforts. [...] 'I have personally visited all 15 counties of Liberia and witnessed at first hand the human and physical consequences of economic and social collapse," [Mr. Doss] said. "A massive effort will therefore be required to ensure that there is some tangible progress in the months ahead."[42]

The Mandingo people of Liberia continue to face grave dangers. Decades of civil war fueled by conflict between indigenous groups, and preceded by more than a century of oppressive rule under the minority, elite Americo-Liberians, have left members of various ethnic groups at odds with one another. Charles Taylor and his forces systematically tortured and brutalized the Mandingo tribe and many of his loyal supporters are still in Liberia plotting to destabilize the situation.[43] The democratically elected Liberian leadership has not demonstrated an ability to protect its citizens—no matter their ethnicity—from the brutality of warlords like Taylor. It is not yet safe for members of the Mandingo tribe to return to Liberia.

Voluntary repatriation of Liberian refugees from neighboring countries has previously occurred. Each time, however, "while many thousands of Liberian refugees were able to return to Liberia without fear of political persecution, some members of the Mandingo and Krahn communities continued to have valid fears."[44] This situation remains true to this day, particularly in areas where anti-Mandingo sentiments and support of Taylor were rampant, like in Nimba County. As stated in the "Consular Information Sheet: Liberia," published by the United States Department of State on December 7, 2005: "Expectations are high for the future, but by most measures Liberia is still one of the poorest countries in the world and noticeable change will take time [...]. The ability of Liberia's security forces to maintain law and order in the countryside is uncertain."[45]

EXHIBIT E

Liberian Political Timeline

July 26, 1847:	Liberia becomes independent. The Liberian Declaration of Independence is adopted and signed.
October 5, 1847:	Governor Joseph Jenkins Roberts is elected the first Liberian president.
January 3, 1848:	Joseph Jenkins Roberts is inaugurated into office. He will be reelected and serve a total of eight years. During Roberts's presidency, the country's first university is established, and the smuggling of slaves, which had continued to occur on the coast, is suppressed.
1860:	Liberia's territorial boundaries are expanded, with assistance from the United States. Following various treaties, purchases, and battles with indigenous chiefs, by 1860 Liberia's boundaries are extended to include a 600-mile coastline.
June 3, 1862:	The United States formally recognizes Liberia's independence. The United States establishes formal diplomatic relations and signs a treaty of commerce and navigation with Liberia.
1871:	The Liberian government takes out the first of several major foreign loans. The loans come primarily from Britain.
December 7, 1874:	Indigenous chiefs meet in the National Legislature for the first time.
1903:	The British and Liberian governments come to an agreement about the borders between Sierra Leone and Liberia.
1904:	The Liberian government institutes an administrative system that brings

indigenous peoples into an indirect political relationship with the central government through their own paid officials.

May 7, 1907: The constitution is amended, changing the presidential term from two years to four.

July 10, 1914: Liberia declares neutrality at the outset of World War I. At the time that war breaks out in Europe, Germany is Liberia's strongest trading partner, and Liberia is reluctant to declare war against a nation to which its economy is so closely tied.

May 8, 1917: Pressured by Great Britain and the United States, Liberia withdraws neutrality and declares war on Germany. Within the year, Germany will retaliate against Liberia's declaration of war by shelling the capital, Monrovia. The Liberian economy is subsequently crippled when the country loses its great economic ally.

1919– Liberia was one of the nations to sign the League of Nations covenant after World War I.

1926: Firestone Tire and Rubber Company opens a rubber plantation on land granted by the Liberian government. The agreement grants Firestone the right to lease one million acres of land for 99 years and to exploit any gold, diamonds, and other minerals found on that land.

1929: An International Commission investigates charges of slavery and forced labor in Liberia. A year later, the committee cannot substantiate such charges according to international law. They do find, however, that Liberian officials, including the republic's vice president,

	profited from indigenous peoples' forced labor.
April 28, 1929:	Booker T. Washington Institute is founded by a group of American missionary and philanthropic groups, including the American Colonization Society. Modeled after Washington's Tuskegee Institute in Tuskegee, Alabama, BWI is the first formal vocational institution established in Liberia. Like its American counterpart, it emphasized vocational training in such areas as agriculture, auto mechanics, carpentry, and masonry.
March–December 1930:	A League of Nations report exposing forced-labor practices in Liberia leads to the president's resignation. The Liberian government comes under international censure for allowing a system of forced labor "hardly distinguishable from slavery." Implicated in the scandal, President Charles D. B. King resigns on December 3 after pressure from the Liberian legislature.
1936:	Forced-labor practices are abolished.
1943:	U.S. president Franklin D. Roosevelt stops in Liberia on his North African tour to visit U.S. troops. Liberia views Roosevelt's visit as a symbol of its strong relationship with the United States, and as confirmation that the United States will be a source of support and aid to Liberia.
January 3, 1944:	William V. S. Tubman is inaugurated as president. President Tubman pursues a policy of national unification to draw the indigenous people into the state and society, formally establishing laws to rid Liberia of practices that favor those of settler descent. He encourages economic

	development through foreign investment, deepens political and economic relations with the United States, and begins to transform Liberia into a modern African state. Under him, Liberia becomes a founding member of the Organization of African Unity and the United Nations.
January 27, 1944:	Liberia enters World War II, declaring war against Germany and Japan in support of the Allies.
1946:	The right to vote and participate in elections is extended to Liberia's indigenous peoples.
May 1951:	Women and indigenous property owners vote in the presidential election for the first time.
1951:	Liberia and the United States sign a Mutual Defense Assistance agreement.
June 27, 1955:	Tubman crony-turned-political opponent S. David Coleman and his son John are hunted down and killed by Liberian soldiers for allegedly plotting to overthrow Tubman. The Coleman funeral is meagerly attended, as people are afraid of being considered Coleman sympathizers.
1955:	The constitution is amended to allow President Tubman to remain in office well beyond the two-term limit.
August 1957:	The United States erects a Voice of America relay facility, one of several U.S. communications facilities to be placed on Liberian soil during the Cold War.
1958:	Racial discrimination is outlawed. Liberian representatives attended the first conference of independent African nations.

1962:	The U.S. Peace Corps program begins in Liberia. The U.S. government agency's program will run for nearly 30 years in Liberia, until 1990 and the outbreak of civil war. Peace Corps service to Liberia has not yet resumed.
1967:	Liberian officials served on the Organization of African Unity's Consultation Committee on Nigeria's civil war.
1971:	Tubman dies and is succeeded by William Tolber, Jr.
1972:	William R. Tolbert, Jr., is elected to Liberia's presidency after finishing Tubman's unexpired term.
1974:	Government accepts aid from the Soviet Union for the first time.
1978:	Liberia signs trade agreement with the European Economic Community.
April 14, 1979:	More than 40 people are killed in riots following a proposed increase in the price of rice.
1980:	A military coup led by Samuel K. Doe, a Liberian of non-American descent, assassinates President Tolbert and overthrows the government that had held sway over Liberia since 1847. A People's Redemption Council headed by Doe suspends constitution and assumes full powers. This ended Liberia's first republic.
1984:	Doe's regime allows return of political parties following pressure from the United States and other creditors.
1985:	Doe wins presidential election.
1986:	A new constitution establishes the second republic of Liberia. Doe retains power as head of state.

1989:	National Patriotic Front of Liberia (NPFL), led by Charles Taylor, begins an uprising against the government and topples the Doe-led government. This action helps precipitate a civil war. Various ethnic factions fight for control of the nation.
1990:	Economic Community of West African States (Ecowas) sends peacekeeping force. Doe is executed by a splinter group of the NPFL.
1991:	Ecowas and the NPFL agree to disarm and set up an Interim Government of National Unity.
1992:	The NPFL launches an all-out assault on West African peacekeepers in Monrovia. The latter respond by bombing NPFL positions outside the capital and pushing the NPFL back into the countryside.
1993:	Warring factions devise a plan for a National Transitional Government and a cease fire, but this fails to materialize and fighting resumes.
1994:	Warring factions agree on a timetable for disarmament and the setting up of a joint Council of State.
1995:	The 16-member Economic Community of West African States (ECOWAS) brokers a peace treaty between Liberia's warring factions. An interim State Council establishes a tentative timetable for elections.
April 1996:	Factional fighting resumes and spreads to Monrovia.
August 1996:	West African peacekeepers begin a disarmament program, clear land mines, and reopen roads, allowing refugees to return.

July 1997:	Presidential and legislative elections are held. Charles Taylor is elected president of the third republic of Liberia and his National Patriotic Party wins a majority in the National Assembly. International observers declare the elections free and fair.
January 1999:	Ghana and Nigeria accuse Liberia of supporting Revolutionary United Front rebels in Sierra Leone. Britain and the United States threaten to suspend aid to Liberia.
April 1999:	Rebel forces thought to have come from Guinea attack the town of Voinjama. Fighting displaces more than 25,000 people.
September 1999:	Guinea accuses Liberian forces of entering its territory and attacking border villages.
September 2000:	Liberian forces launch a massive offensive against rebels in the north. Liberia accuses Guinean troops of shelling border villages.
February 2001:	Liberian government says Sierra Leonean rebel leader Sam Bockarie, also known as Mosquito, has left the country.
May 2001:	UN Security Council imposes arms embargo to punish Taylor for trading weapons for diamonds from rebels in Sierra Leone.
January 2002:	More than 50,000 Liberians and Sierra Leonean refugees flee fighting. In February Taylor declares a state of emergency.
March 2003:	Rebels advance to within 10 kilometers of Monrovia.
June 2003:	Talks in Ghana aimed at ending rebellion are overshadowed by indictment accusing

	President Taylor of war crimes over his alleged backing of rebels in Sierra Leone.
June 4, 2003:	President Obasanjo, alongside other African leaders, attends the opening of an ECOWAS-brokered Peace and Reconciliation Conference for Liberia under the leadership of General Abdulsalami Abubakar in Akosombo, Ghana.
June 11, 2003:	The forum secures a ceasefire agreement from the government and rebel factions.
June 15, 2003:	The National Emergency Relief Agency (NEMA) begins evacuating Nigerians and Liberians from Monrovia to Lagos as fighting between government and rebel forces escalates.
July 6, 2003:	President Obasanjo in an unscheduled visit offers Taylor temporary asylum in Nigeria, after consulting with other African leaders. Taylor accepts.
July 9, 2003:	President Obasanjo requests approval from the Senate to deploy two battalions of Nigerian troops to keep the peace in Liberia in accordance with an ECOWAS mandate. He also informs the Senate of a proposal to shelter Taylor in Nigeria on a temporary asylum.
July 16, 2003:	A surveillance squad dispatched by the Nigerian Army and led by Colonel Emeka Onwuamaegbu is mobbed by grateful Monrovians as the colonel is carried shoulder-high by Liberians longing for the presence of Nigerian peacekeepers.
July 18, 2003:	West African mediators, led by General Abdulsalami Abubakar, secure a draft comprehensive peace agreement through

	which the warring factions in Liberia agreed to halt fighting, share power, and establish a transition timetable.
July 21, 2003:	President Obasanjo criticizes renewed fighting instigated by rebels of the Liberians United for Reconciliation and Democracy (LURDS) and threatens to withhold deployment of Nigerian peacekeepers unless they obey the cease-fire agreement.
July 28, 2003:	UN Secretary General, Kofi Annan, warns of the volatile situation in Liberia as posing a threat to the peace of West African countries and pledges to assist in transporting Nigerian troops serving with the UN Mission in Sierra Leone to Monrovia.
July 29, 2003:	At a forum in London with the British prime minister and the World Bank president, President Obasanjo promises to deploy two battalions of battle-ready contingents to halt the slide to anarchy in Liberia as rebels threaten to encircle Charles Taylor.
July 2003:	Fighting intensifies; rebels battle for control of Monrovia. Several hundred people are killed. West African regional group Ecowas agrees to provide peacekeepers.
August 2003:	Nigerian peacekeepers arrive. Charles Taylor leaves Liberia after handing power to his deputy Moses Blah. U.S. troops arrive. Interim government and rebels sign peace accord in Ghana. Gyude Bryant is chosen to head the interim administration.
August 4, 2003:	Tremendous relief as first batch of 30 Nigerian soldiers arrives in Monrovia.

	The troops, taken from a UN-decorated peacekeeping battalion in Sierra Leone, quickly move to secure the international airport and the seaport.
August 11, 2003:	Prominent African presidents lead Charles Taylor out of the presidential mansion in Monrovia to begin temporary asylum in Nigeria. AU Chairman, President Joachim Chissano of Mozambique, ECOWAS Chairman, President John Kuffour of Ghana, and South African President Thabo Mbeki all escort Taylor to Nigeria.
August 12, 2003:	The Nigerian Senate passes a motion congratulating President Obasanjo's role in resolving the Liberian and Sao Tome impasse.
August 14, 2003:	President Obasanjo visits troops departing for Liberian peacekeeping duties at the Murtala Mohammed Airport, Lagos, where he inspects 68 armored tanks marshaled by the Nigerian Army for the operations.
August 17, 2003:	President Obasanjo orders additional 700 Nigerian troops deployed in Liberia for peacekeeping as part of the 1,500-strong contingent.
August 18, 2003:	Under the auspices of General Abdulsalami Abubakar, former Nigerian Head of State, the Government of Liberia and warring factions sign a historic peace agreement in Akosombo Ghana, setting the stage for the easing out of office of Charles Taylor, the constitution of an interim government and the conduct of elections in 2005.
August 25, 2003:	President Obasanjo orders dispatch of the second batch of relief materials and

	humanitarian aid to Liberia. The items include rice, beans, blankets, soaps, and medicines.
August 26, 2003:	President Obasanjo strongly condemns reports of massacre of civilians in Monrovia and warns warring factions to appreciate the enormous efforts made by Nigeria, ECOWAS, and the UN to return peace to Liberia.
September 15, 2003:	President Obasanjo receives the chairman of Liberia's Transitional Government, Gyude Bryant, at the State House. Abuja pledges more assistance to Liberia.
September 29, 2003:	President Obasanjo waves aside criticism of the asylum granted to Taylor by Nigeria as a decision taken in the interest of Liberia.
September/October 2003:	U.S. forces pull out. UN launches major peacekeeping mission, deploying thousands of troops.
February 2004:	International donors pledge more than $500 million in reconstruction aid.
July 15, 2004:	The African Union, at its Fifth Ordinary Session of the Council in Addis Ababa, congratulates Nigeria for granting asylum to Charles Taylor "in accordance with the wishes of the AU and ECOWAS and the understanding of the International Community."
October 2004:	Riots in Monrovia leave 16 people dead; the UN says former combatants were behind the violence.
November 14, 2004:	African leaders meeting in Abuja commend Liberians for their peaceful, free and fair elections of November 8, 2004, and remind them of the huge

	sacrifices made by ECOWAS, the AU, the UN, and the international community toward peace and reconciliation in their country.
January 27, 2005:	At the 28th Summit of ECOWAS heads of state and government in Accra, AU Chairman President Obasanjo commends the efforts of the body in restoring peace to the region, especially Liberia.
May 7, 2005:	At a dinner in honor of General Colin Powell in Washington, DC, United States, President Obasanjo explains that granting asylum to Taylor was a response to international request and a prerequisite for peace in Liberia.
June 2005:	UN extends a ban on Liberian diamond exports—a source of funding for the civil war—and urges Liberia to freeze Charles Taylor's assets.
September 2005:	Liberia signs an agreement under which the international community will supervise the state's finances in an effort to counter corruption.
September 14, 2005:	In his capacity as AU Chairman, President Obasanjo tells the United Nations General Assembly of efforts by ECOWAS and the AU to resolve Africa's many conflicts, including Liberia's.
September 16, 2005:	Some 300 Liberian police officers graduate from a six-week training course at the Nigerian Mobile Police Training School in preparation for their country's general elections
October 8, 2005:	President Obasanjo arrives in Liberia to reconcile the 22 candidates in Liberia's presidential elections scheduled for

	October 11, as two of them threatened a boycott in response to their names not appearing on the ballot.
November 15, 2005:	President Obasanjo is awarded the Coventry International Prize for Peace and Reconciliation in the United Kingdom for his "outstanding and sustained contributions towards peace and reconciliation in Africa."
November 23, 2005:	Ellen Johnson-Sirleaf wins presidential elections, becoming the first woman to be elected as an African head of state.
November 30, 2005:	President Obasanjo receives and congratulates Ellen Johnson-Sirleaf, who pays him a courtesy visit at the State House, Abuja.
December 27, 2005:	President Obasanjo receives George Weah, soccer superstar and defeated presidential candidate in Liberia's election, whom he congratulates for choosing the path of peace and accepting the outcome of the elections.
January 12, 2006:	At the 29th ECOWAS Session, President Obasanjo congratulates ECOWAS over the success of the Liberian elections and transition to democratic rule.
January 16, 2006:	President Obasanjo graces the inauguration of Johnson-Sirleaf as president of Liberia, at which he is given a standing ovation.
February 2006:	Truth and Reconciliation Commission set up to investigate human rights abuses between 1979 and 2003.

Compiled from information at the following Web sites:
http://www.nigeriafirst.org/printer_5340.shtml

http://memory.loc.gov/ammem/gmdhtml/libhtml/liberia.html#onmp
http://news.bbc.co.uk/1/hi/world/africa/country_profiles/1043567.stm
http://www.pbs.org/wgbh/globalconnections/liberia/timeline/

NOTES

1. Katharine Houreld, *Liberia: Healing the Wounds of Civil War,* Institute for War and Peace Reporting, March 12, 2006, available at http://www.iwpr.net/?p=acr&s=f&o=260310&apc_state=henh.
2. *Liberia: Events Since 1990,* Citizenship and Immigration Services Country Reports, United States Department of Homeland Security, November 1, 1993.
3. John Balzar, "Hope of Peace Seems Faint in War-Exhausted Liberia," *Dallas Morning News,* February 19, 1995.
4. *Liberia: Events Since 1990,* Human Rights Watch, available at http://www.unhcr.org/cgi-bin/texis/vtx/home/opendoc.htm?tbl=RSDCOI&page=research&id=3ae6a6088.
5. *Liberia: A Human Rights Disaster,* Human Rights Watch, available at http://www.hrw.org/reports/1990/liberia/.
6. *Easy Prey: Child Soldiers in Liberia,* Human Rights Watch, September 8, 1994, available at http://www.hrw.org/reports/1994/liberia2/.
7. *Id.*
8. Moses Wantu, *Startling Revelation!* AllAfrica.com, March 24, 2006, available at http://allafrica.com/stories/200603240379.html.
9. *World Report 2001: Liberia,* Human Rights Watch, available at http://www.hrw.org/wr2k1/africa/liberia.html.
10. Joseph Sherman, "Liberia: The Challenge of Ethnicity and Conflicts in Post-War Liberia," *Liberian Times,* March 17, 2005, available at http://www.theliberiantimes.com/article_2006_03_16_0142.html.
11. Warren Hoge, "Liberian Seeks Extradition of Predecessor for Atrocities Trial," *New York Times,* March 18, 2006.
12. Moses Wantu, *Startling Revelation!* AllAfrica.com, March 24, 2006, available at http://allafrica.com/stories/200603240379.html.
13. *Id.*
14. Jon Lee Anderson, "After the Warlords," *New Yorker,* March 27, 2006, at p. 58.
15. *Head of UN Mission in Liberia Appeals for Assistance in Cementing Peace There,* U.N. News Centre, March 24, 2006, available at http://www.un.org/apps/news/story.asp?NewsID=17929&Cr=liberia&Cr1.
16. *Liberia: Human Rights Developments,* World Report 2001, Human Rights Watch, available at http://www.hrw.org/wr2k1/africa/liberia.html.
17. *Consular Information Sheet: Liberia,* United States Department of State, December 7, 2005, available at http://travel.state.gov/travel/cis_pa_tw/cis/cis_950.html.
18. Taylor's uprising against then-President Samuel Kanyon Doe's regime commenced in 1989, but fighting broke out in Monrovia in 1990. *Liberia: A Chronology of 25 Years of Conflict and Turmoil,* IRINNews.org, UN Office for the Coordination of Humanitarian Affairs, January 17, 2006, available at http://www.irinnews.org/S_report.asp?ReportID=51167&SelectRegion=West_Africa; Doe was captured and

killed in Monrovia in September 1990, by Brigadier General Prince Johnson, who led a competing faction of rebels and is today a senior senator in Liberia's newly elected democratic government. *See* Bill Berkeley, "Liberia: Between Repression and Slaughter," *Atlantic Monthly,* December 1992; Jon Lee Anderson, "After the Warlords," *New Yorker,* March 27, 2006.

19. "Watching Rights; Human Rights in Liberia, Soviet Union, Eastern Europe, South Africa," *Nation,* September 17, 1990.
20. *Liberia: Events Since 1990,* Citizenship and Immigration Services Country Reports, United States Department of Homeland Security, November 1, 1993, available at http://www.unhcr.org/cgi-bin/texis/vtx/home/opendoc.htm?tbl=RSDCOI&page=research&id=3ae6a6088.
21. *See Easy Prey: Child Soldiers in Liberia,* Human Rights Watch, September 8, 1994, available at http://www.hrw.org/reports/1994/liberia2/ (Reporting "during the Octopus Operation in 1992, children were used by NPFL as cannon fodder. They were in the first wave of troops, and the older fighters were behind them. At first the ECOMOG troops [a peacekeeping force under the auspices of the Economic Community of West African States] didn't want to shoot at the kids; some told us they were shocked to see such small kids fighting. But when the kids began shooting at them they had no alternative, so they began shooting and killing kids.")
22. *See Liberia: A Chronology of 25 years of Conflict and Turmoil,* IRINNews.org, UN Office for the Coordination of Humanitarian Affairs, Jan. 17, 2006, available at http://www.irinnews.org/S_report.asp?ReportID=51167&SelectRegion=West_Africa (stating "gun battles erupt[ed] in Monrovia between allied forces of Charles Taylor and Alhaji Kromah against forces of dead warlord Roosevelt Johnson who had led a splinter group from Kromah's ULIMO. Some 1,000 civilians were killed in the violence and private homes and UN facilities looted").
23. Past persecution is an independent basis for asylum. 8 C.F.R. § 208.13(b) (2003) ("The applicant may qualify as a refugee *either* because he or she has suffered past persecution *or* because he or she has a well-founded fear of future persecution.") (emphasis added); *Berroteran-Melendez v. INS,* 955 F.2d 1251, 1256 n.3 (Ninth Cir. 1992) ("Past persecution alone, independent of establishing a well-founded fear of future persecution, can suffice to establish an asylum claim."); *Desir v. Ilchert,* 840 F.2d 723, 729 (Ninth Cir. 1988) ("[P]ast persecution, without more, satisfies the [definition of 'refugee']."); *Singh v. Ilchert,* 801 F.Supp. 313, 321 (N.D. Cal. 1992) ("[U]nder the plain language of [the statute], a showing of past persecution is sufficient in and of itself for asylum eligibility. There is no need to show a threat of future persecution."); *In re B—,* 21 I. & N. Dec. 66, 69 (BIA 1995) ("An applicant for asylum under…the Act may establish his claim by presenting evidence of past persecution in lieu of evidence of a well-founded fear of persecution."); *Matter of Chen,* 20 I. & N. Dec. 16, 18 (BIA 1989) ("If an alien establishes that he has been persecuted in the past…, he is eligible for a grant of asylum.").
24. http://hrw.org/backgrounder/africa/liberia0905/4.htm#_Toc115614226
25. Katharine Houreld, *Liberia: Healing the Wounds of Civil War,* Institute for War and Peace Reporting, March 12, 2006, available at http://www.iwpr.net/?p=acr&s=f&o=260310&apc_state=henh.
26. *Liberia: Events Since 1990,* Citizenship and Immigration Services Country Reports, U.S. Department of Homeland Security, November 1, 1993.

27. John Balzar, "Hope of Peace Seems Faint in War-Exhausted Liberia," *Dallas Morning News,* February 19, 1995.
28. *Liberia: Events Since 1990,* Citizenship and Immigration Services Country Reports, U.S. Department of Homeland Security, November 1, 1993.
29. Aryeh Neier, "Watching Rights: Human Rights in Liberia, Soviet Union, Eastern Europe, South Africa," *The Nation,* September 17, 1990.
30. *Liberia: A Human Rights Disaster,* Human Rights Watch, available at http://www.hrw.org/reports/1990/liberia/.
31. Moses Wantu, *Startling Revelation!* AllAfrica.com, March 24, 2006, available at http://allafrica.com/stories/200603240379.html.
32. *Easy Prey: Child Soldiers in Liberia,* Human Rights Watch, September 8, 1994, available at http://www.hrw.org/reports/1994/liberia2/.
33. *Id.*
34. *World Report 2001: Liberia,* Human Rights Watch, available at http://www.hrw.org/wr2k1/africa/liberia.html.
35. Moses Wantu, *Startling Revelation!* AllAfrica.com, March 24, 2006, available at http://allafrica.com/stories/200603240379.html.
36. Joseph Sherman, "Liberia: The Challenge of Ethnicity and Conflicts in Post-War Liberia," *Liberian Times,* March 17, 2005, available at http://www.theliberiantimes.com/article_2006_03_16_0142.html.
37. Warren Hoge, "Liberian Seeks Extradition of Predecessor for Atrocities Trial," *New York Times,* March 18, 2006.
38. *Id.*
39. *Id.*
40. Jon Lee Anderson, "After the Warlords," *New Yorker,* March 27, 2006, at p. 58.
41. *Liberia: Despite Elections, Collapse of Justice Poses Risks,* Human Rights Watch, September 30, 2005, available at http://hrw.org/english/docs/2005/09/27/liberi11794.htm.
42. *Head of UN Mission in Liberia Appeals for Assistance in Cementing Peace There,* U.N. News Centre, March 24, 2006, available at http://www.un.org/apps/news/story.asp?NewsID=17929&Cr=liberia&Cr1.
43. Moses Wantu, *Startling Revelation!* AllAfrica.com, March 24, 2006, available at http://allafrica.com/stories/200603240379.html.
44. "Liberia: Human Rights Developments," World Report 2001, Human Rights Watch, available at http://www.hrw.org/wr2k1/africa/liberia.html.
45. "Consular Information Sheet: Liberia," United States Department of State, December 7, 2005, available at http://travel.state.gov/travel/cis_pa_tw/cis/cis_950.html.

Appendix C
Sample Affidavit in Support of Application for Asylum

Editor's Note: The following is an actual affidavit in support of application for asylum. Names and other identifying details have been removed. Social workers often can help immigrant clients draft the biographical sections and lay out the narratives of these applications.

UNITED STATES DEPARTMENT OF JUSTICE EXECUTIVE OFFICE FOR IMMIGRATION REVIEW, UNITED STATES IMMIGRATION COURT, YORK, PENNSYLVANIA

In the Matter of:	)	
	)	File No.: [number]
[Name]	)	
	)	
In removal proceedings	)	

RESPONDENT'S AFFIDAVIT IN SUPPORT OF APPLICATION FOR ASYLUM

HERE COMES [name] (aka [name])(hereinafter "respondent") and declares as follows:

1 My name is [name]. I am the respondent in the above-captioned removal proceeding. I respectfully submit this declaration in support of my claims for Asylum and Withholding of Removal under Section 241(b)(3) of the Immigration and Nationality Act of 1952, as amended (hereinafter "Act" or "INA") and for Relief under Article 3 of the United Nations Convention Against Torture or Other Cruel, Inhuman or Degrading Treatment or Punishment (hereinafter "Convention Against Torture" or "CAT").

2 I am seeking asylum, withholding and/or deferral of removal because I am afraid that I will face horrible acts of persecution,

rape, torture, and/or death in my home country, the Democratic Republic of the Congo, formerly Zaire (hereinafter the Congo).

3 I am afraid to return to the Congo because of human rights abuses committed by soldiers against my family. Soldiers near our home raped my mother and my father attempted to report the rape to the human rights office. In retaliation, the soldiers attacked my family, killing my father, brother and uncle. They kidnapped me and held me for several weeks in a camp with several hundred women where they attempted to rape and sexually abuse me.

INFORMATION ABOUT ME

4 I am currently detained in the custody of the U.S. Immigration and Naturalization Service at the York County Prison in York, Pennsylvania.

5 I was held in INS custody in [date], when I arrived at John F. Kennedy International Airport in New York without the proper documents.

6 I was born on [date] in the Congo. I am 26 years old. I grew up in the village Baraka, which is in the southern part of the Kivu province. My ethnic tribe is Bembe.

7 I lived with my father, mother, two brothers, and sister in Baraka until February 1999. At that time I was married. It is our tradition for a woman to marry her husband in his home, but because of the civil war and military occupation of Fizi, my husband's village, and Baraka, my village, we were married in Dar-Es-Salaam, Tanzania. After our marriage, I lived with my husband's family in Fizi, which is near Baraka, for one year and six months.

8 My husband's name is [name]. Soon after we were married, my husband came to the United States. He is a legal permanent resident of the United States. He currently lives in Minneapolis, Minnesota. I am unsure of his occupation. We have no children.

9 My mother's name is [name]. I do not know where she or my sister currently are. I do not know if they survived the soldiers' attack on our home.

10 My father's name is [name]. My father, brothers, [name] and [name], and my uncle were all murdered by the soldiers in November 2000.

FEAR

11 I am afraid to return to the Congo because of acts committed against my family and me in November 2000.

12 In November 2000 my mother went into the forest near our home to gather firewood. In the forest, soldiers attacked and raped her. After the rape, my mother became very ill and was bed-ridden. It was at this time that I moved back to my parent's house from my in-law's house in Fizi. I moved home to help take care of my mother.

13 After my mother was raped, my father repeatedly declared he would to go to the human rights office to report what the soldiers had done to my mother. One afternoon, a neighbor came to visit my mother and overheard my father discussing his plans to go report the soldiers' abuses. Two days later, the night before my father was to make the trip to the human rights office, a group of soldiers arrived at our house. My father was never able to file a report against the soldiers that raped my mother.

14 There were about ten soldiers. I opened the door when they knocked. They grabbed my throat and yelled for me to sit down. My father told the soldiers not to hurt me. They tore my clothes down the front with a knife. I was very scared. I cried.

15 The soldiers asked my father why he would report them to the human rights office. My father just kept telling them not to hurt me. The soldiers tied my father's legs and arms together. They did the same to my uncle and brothers, [name] and [name]. I saw the soldiers cut all of their throats.

16 The soldiers abducted me. They took me and one of my neighbors, also a woman, to a house in the forest. Then we were put on a truck. We traveled for about eight hours. They took me to a camp in the forest where approximately 300 other captured women were already imprisoned.

17 There were only women at the camp. There were women of different ethnic tribes. The women were both old and young. Some of the young ones were only 15 years old. While I was at the camp, I saw that the soldiers had also captured a Red Cross worker.

18 I arrived at the camp still wearing my ripped clothes. There were no clothes at the camp. There was no food. An older woman gave me a long cloth to wrap around my body. She told me she had been at the camp for 6 months. She told me she was

raped. The soldiers did not tell any of us why we were captured and why we were being held.

19 The women at the camp were forced to cook for the soldiers. The soldiers also forced many of the women to have sex with them. They made the rest of us watch as they raped the women.

20 The soldiers would rape the women and they would force tree branches into the genitals of the women. One morning, I heard the screams of a woman. The soldiers were sticking a large branch into her vagina. They were doing this in front of the other women. The woman fainted from the pain. Several other women had scars on the insides of their legs and had damaged genitals because of the soldiers' brutal acts.

21 I knew they would attempt to do the same to me. I knew I had to escape. Many women held at the camp tried to escape but were often caught and brought back by the soldiers. I escaped with three other women, including the older woman who gave me clothes when I arrived at the camp.

22 We escaped at night. I ran away when I went to the toilet and no one was watching. I ran with the other women to a village nearby. The others I escaped with knew the area well. We traveled by boat across the lake to Tanzania.

23 In Tanzania, we arrived at the African Pentecostal Church and stayed there for about one week. The women at the church helped me. They gave me clothes and food.

24 The women at the church advised me to leave the Congo right away for my own safety. I could not safely stay in Tanzania because I did not have the proper documents. I could not return to Fizi to live with my in-laws because the village was by then occupied. I believe my husband's family was already living at a refugee camp.

25 A Kenyan woman who worked at the church named [name] gave me her passport and $20. She took me to the train station. We traveled for three days by train to Dar-Es-Salaam. We arrived at the airport where [name] paid for my plane ticket to New York.

26 I am afraid to be deported to the Congo because of the current civil war between the rebels and the government. Country condition reports support the claim that the rebels in the Congo engage in summary execution and that systematic violence and sexual persecution against women is widespread.

27 Right now, I have nightmares and can't sleep. I remember every day what has happened to me and what happened to my family. I feel like I have lost everything in my life.

28 All of my relatives and family members in the Congo are either killed or disappeared. I no longer know anyone or maintain any connection with the Congo.

29 I fear that if deported to the Congo I will be separated from the only family connection I now have, namely, my husband in Minnesota.

WELL-FOUNDED

30 Article 1 of the 1967 Refugee Protocol defines a refugee as an individual who "owing to well-founded fear of being persecuted for reasons of race, religion, nationality, membership of a particular social group or political opinion, is outside the country of his nationality and is unable or, owing to such fear, is unwilling to avail himself of the protection of that country." I am such an individual.

31 The United Nations High Commissioner of Refugees Handbook on Procedures and Criteria for the Determination of Refugee Status (hereinafter *UNHCR Handbook*) states that, "the applicant's fear should be considered well-founded if he can establish, to a reasonable degree, that his continued stay in his country of origin has become intolerable to him for the reasons stated in the [refugee] definition, or would for the same reasons be intolerable if he returned there" (par. 42).

32 I cannot return to the Congo because the civil war and the military occupation of my village threaten my life. I believe the soldiers in my village will recognize me, abduct me, and kill me because I escaped before, because I know how they torture women, and because I have been threatened with rape and torture.

33 I am afraid that the soldiers will target me because I am a woman. I am afraid I will be raped and sexually abused like the other women at the camp. Country condition reports indicate that even in Kinshasa, women face sexual persecution by military forces.

34 Paragraph 43 of the *UNHCR Handbook* states that the considerations for a well-founded fear do not have to be based solely on the applicant's experience, but that the experience of "his friends and relatives and other members of the same racial or social group may well show that his fear that sooner or later he also will become a victim of persecution is well-founded."

35 If deported to the Congo, I will face persecution because I am a recognizable member of a family with the political belief that the soldiers are violating human rights in the Congo. My family is known to have attempted to speak out against the soldiers. I fear that I will be killed, just like my father, for my opinions of the soldiers and their violations of human rights in the Congo. I am also in danger because I personally witnessed the torture and murder of my family members.

PERSECUTION

36 The Convention Against Torture defines torture as "any act by which severe pain or suffering, whether physical or mental, is intentionally inflicted on a person for such purposes as obtaining from him or a third person information or a confession, punishing him for an act he or a third person has committed or is suspected of having committed, or intimidating or coercing him or a third person, or for any reason based on discrimination of any kind" (Article 1).

37 Soldiers on both sides (rebel, government) have committed human rights abuses and have engaged in acts constituting torture against the people of the Congo. Both sides are also responsible for gender-specific violence against women.

38 Article 51 of the1977 Geneva Convention on the Protection of Civilians in Armed Conflict states that, "The civilian population and individual civilians shall enjoy general protection against dangers arising from military operations." The Congo is unable to provide such protections for its people.

39 Country condition reports indicate that the political situation has not improved since my departure from the Congo. South Kivu (eastern Congo) is currently occupied by rebel forces and is in the heart of an ongoing and very violent conflict. (See Map 1.) Rebel forces occupy both Baraka and Fizi and the populations of both villages have experienced massive displacements. The situation has been described by international observers as "close to chaos" with villagers unable to identify military or political affiliation of armed forces.

40 The *UNHCR Handbook* states that "being unable to avail" oneself of the protection of one's country "implies circumstances that are beyond the will of the person concerned. There may, for example, be a state of war, civil war, or other grave disturbance, which prevents the country of nationality from extending protection or makes such protection ineffective.... Such denial of protection... may indeed be an element of persecution" (par. 98).

GROUNDS

41 My fear of persecution is based on my actual and imputed political opinion and the social group of my family and my gender.

42 The *UNHCR Handbook* states, "a threat to life or freedom on account of race, religion, nationality, political opinion, or membership of a particular social group is always persecution" (par. 51). Paragraph 82 further states that persecution based on political opinion "implies that an applicant holds an opinion that either has been expressed or has come to the attention of the authorities."

43 The Board of Immigration Appeals has interpreted persecution to include threats to life, confinement, torture, and economic restrictions so severe that they constitute a threat to life or freedom. Matter of Acosta, 19 I&N Dec. 211, 222 (BIA 1985).

44 My family was targeted for persecution because of my father's political views about the soldier's human rights abuses, which he intended to make public. In retaliation for my father's intentions to report them to the human rights office, the soldiers killed him and the other men in my family and abducted me. Because of my family ties and my personal experiences of abduction, attempted rape, and torture, I will be in certain danger if returned to the Congo.

45 Several circuit courts have defined family membership as a "social group" for asylum purposes. The Ninth Circuit explained "particular social group" as consisting of "the immediate members of a certain family, the family being a focus of fundamental affiliational concerns and common interests for most people."

Sanchez-Trujillo v. INS, 801 F.2d 1571, 1576 (1986). Sister circuits have adopted this conclusion as well. Gebremichael v. INS, 10 F.3d 28 (First Cir. 1993); Iliev v. INS, 127 F.3d 638 (Seventh Cir. 1997).

46 The United Nations General Assembly Declaration on the Elimination of Violence Against Women (1994) states that violence against women means "an act of gender-based violence that results in or is likely to result in physical, sexual or psychological harm or suffering to women, including threats of such acts, coercion or arbitrary deprivation of liberty" (Article 1). Violence actually perpetrated or threatened includes "violence occurring within the general community, including rape, sexual abuse, sexual harassment" (Article 2).

47 Rape and other forms of severe sexual violence constitute persecution. Lazo-Majano v. INS, 813 F.2d 1432, 1434 (Ninth Cir. 1987) (Salvadoran woman raped and brutalized by an army sergeant had been "persecuted" within the terms of the Immigration and Nationality Act).

48 The Third Circuit concluded in Fatin v. INS, 12 F.3d 1233 (1993) that gender can define "social group" under the INA for asylum purposes.

49 For the reasons stated above, I respectfully ask this Court to grant me asylum in the United States so that I may be free from persecution and torture in the Congo.

50 Alternatively, I respectfully ask this Court to grant me withholding and/or deferral of removal from the Congo because of my well-founded fear of persecution and torture in the Congo.

VERIFICATION

I verify that the statements made in this declaration are true and correct. I understand that any false statements herein are made subject to the penalties of perjury.

____

[name]

Dated: [date]

[location]

Index